Social theory and the family

International Library of Sociology

Founded by Karl Mannheim

Editor: John Rex, University of Warwick

Arbor Scientiae
Arbor Vitae

A catalogue of the books available in the **International Library of Sociology** and other series of Social Science books published by Routledge & Kegan Paul will be found at the end of this volume.

Social theory and the family

D. H. J. Morgan
Department of Sociology
University of Manchester

Routledge & Kegan Paul
London & Boston

First published in 1975
by Routledge & Kegan Paul Ltd
Broadway House, 68–74 Carter Lane,
London EC4V 5EL and
9 Park Street
Boston, Mass. 02108, U.S.A.
Set in Monotype Times New Roman
and printed in Great Britain by
Western Printing Services Ltd, Bristol

ISBN 0 7100 8179 0 (c)
ISBN 0 7100 8180 4 (p)

Contents

Acknowledgments

The first debt I must acknowledge is to my students in various classes in the Sociology of the Family, both here and in Canada. Their critical comments and their contributions to discussions first suggested the idea of this book to me and I have gained from discussion with different groups of students ever since that time. Unfortunately these students are too numerous for me to name each one individually. It is difficult, also, to acknowledge by name all the various influences that have stimulated me and shaped my thinking at or around Manchester. There are, of course, many differences and disagreements between the broad, critical perspective provided by Professor Peter Worsley and the critiques of analytical sociology provided by the newer ethnomethodologists but I have gained immensely from both emphases and both, I think, are reflected in the following pages. I have presented some of my ideas formally and informally at Manchester and have benefited from a variety of critical comments from, among many others, Ian Craib, Isabel Griffiths, Bruce Kapferer, Ken Smith and Daphne Taylorson. Those whose names I have included here should not feel that they have to take the blame for what I have written; those whose names are excluded should not feel that they have not contributed, directly or indirectly, to my thinking about sociological theory and the family.

I should also mention Professors J. Clyde Mitchell and John Rex, both of whom gave encouragement to me in the early stages of this book, and to the members of the British Sociological Association's 'Family and Kinship Group' who, among other things, listened to and commented upon an early version of the concluding chapter. Outside Manchester I have gained particular benefit from conversations with Colin Creighton of the University of Hull and Marijean Suezle at a Summer School at the University of Alberta, Edmonton. Thanks also to Michael Shaw of Shaw-Maclean for frequent friendly encouragement and to Kay Millar and Mrs D. B. Riley for typing various sections of the manuscript.

This book is dedicated to Rosemary, Jacqueline and Julian; members of my nuclear family of procreation.

Introduction

Origins of this book

Conservative and radical critics of sociology alike would probably agree with the paradoxical statement that this discipline, the study of man interacting in society, so readily becomes divorced from its human subject matter. The conservative critic may argue that sociology does not connect with man as he is, with his uniqueness, his individuality, his soul. The radical critic may argue that sociology does not relate to man as he may become, that the subject does not direct itself to raising the consciousness of the agents of social change within society. Both groups of critics may point to the increasing use of mathematical models, and to reifications brought about by theory to the distancing effect of the specialized language of structural-functionalism or ethnomethodology.

I suspect that my experience of feeling this distancing effect in the process of attempting to teach sociology—particularly the sociology of the family—may not be a unique one. The family we discuss in lectures and tutorials—the family with its functions, its roles, its kinship and networks—often appears to be remote from the family we experience outside the lecture room or even the family we experience through the novel, through drama and through the cinema. We know that there are often very sound reasons for this distancing. There is the need for objectivity, particularly on a subject close to everybody's experience as the family. There is the need to be able to make general statements with a wide range of applicability. Yet, many teachers are aware that unless it is possible to make some links between the subject taught and the experience of those in the teaching situation the subject will, in its deepest sense, be untrue. On the one hand there is the subject matter of the text-book and the lectures, the subject matter which is shaped and discussed and organized into examination answers or dissertations; on the other hand there is the real world of sex, marriage and the family. Very often the living dialectic between the two appears to be lacking.

This sense of a gap between what was being taught and the experience of those actually involved in the course (including myself) was made particularly acute for me while I was teaching in a Summer School class in Edmonton, Alberta. I had just read Laing's *Politics of the Family*, the published version of his Massey Lectures for the Canadian Broadcasting Corporation in 1968, and was attempting to present some of his ideas in the class.[1] I attempted to present a sympathetic account of these ideas in contrast to the more widely taught theories of Parsons and the broadly functionalist school as represented in most of the texts. In spite of this, at least one student maintained that I was being unsympathetic to Laing and went on to ask why it was that there had been so much concentration on Parsons. It was clear that some of the students were responding to *The Politics of the Family* much more readily than to *Family, Socialization and Interaction Process*. And the reason for this was not that Laing was 'easier' than Parsons (both are difficult in different ways) but that Laing appeared to be talking about the family in a way which was closer to their experience and in particular that here was a discussion about families in terms stressing conflict, exploitation and contradictions.

It would be wrong to maintain that this problem is peculiar to the sociology of the family. I suspect that all the specialized areas—perhaps because they are specialized areas—face problems something akin to the one that I have described. But there are some reasons which would lead one to suspect that the problem may perhaps be greater in the sociology of the family than in some of these other areas. As I shall explore some of these reasons at greater length later in this book I shall merely note them at this point. The first reason is, paradoxically, the relative absence of a strong theoretical base in the subject. This lack is one which has been periodically noted by sociologists working within the field. Goode, for example, writes:[2]

> In the field of the family, theory has generally been neglected. Although more investigations are reported in this than in almost any other substantive field . . . few of those that are reported seek to advance the theory of the family.

And this is echoed by Mogey:[3]

> Over much of the world, family research is still highly descriptive. Much is still cast in the older mould of institutional analysis, heavily normative, moralistic and mingled with social policy and the social objectives of various action groups. Some is frankly archaic in its intellectual equipment.

Other sociologists have demonstrated their concern to me in this respect in informal conversation.

This reason has its paradoxical side in that theory may, of course, be as much a source of mystification as of illumination. However, it is also true that a strong tradition of theoretical argument can enable the practitioners within a particular area to make imaginative and illuminating connections with other, seemingly distant, areas. The sociology of religion (which has on the whole been better served by its theoreticians) may, for example, gain insights from Weber's discussion of authority, Durkheim's approach to integration or Marx's theory of alienation. It is worth noting, in passing, that none of these three founding fathers directly concerned themselves with the study and analysis of the family although they may be found to contribute more indirect insights. While there exist plenty of theories about particular parts of the sociology of the family—the incest taboo or fertility for example—there does not appear to be the same tradition of theoretical argument and discussion that we find in the sociology of religion or the study of organizations.[4] One of the consequences of this absence of a strong theoretical tradition has been the somewhat fragmented nature of the subject, ranging from sexual behaviour to kinship in modern urban society, from social factors affecting fertility to the changing roles of the sexes. Families in their entirety often appear to be missing in this process of fragmentation.

This noting of the relative absence of a strong tradition of theory in the sociology of the family leads us to a second possible reason for the apparent divorce between discipline and subject matter. This is the relative absence of a strong *critical* tradition, at least as reflected in the mainstream texts and studies. In one of the few critically provocative essays in this field, Barrington Moore notes:[5]

> Among social scientists today it is almost axiomatic that the family is a universally necessary social institution and will remain such through any foreseeable future. . . . I have the uncomfortable feeling that the authors, despite all their elaborate theories and technical research devices, are doing little more than projecting certain middle-class hopes and ideals onto a refractory reality.

Even one of the most recent, and certainly one of the most stimulating, theoretical analyses of the family remains largely within the mainstream of interactionism and role theory.[6] Yet a strong critical tradition, challenging assumptions, making new connections and redefining boundaries, is an essential component in the development of a theoretical perspective. It is one of the main aims of this book to show that there does exist a critical tradition in this field although it has existed largely at the periphery of sociology itself and that this tradition can make an essential contribution to the study of the family.[7]

As Barrington Moore suggests, if there be a major theoretical perspective in the sociology of the family, it is generally some variation on a functionalist theme. I deal with this approach in more detail in Chapter 1. In the course of the book as a whole it is to be hoped that the main themes involved in a critical perspective will emerge. This will entail stressing dysfunction rather than function, conflict rather than consensus, change rather than stability. This emphasis is prompted, not so much by a belief that these are the correct or the only theoretical perspectives—I shall have occasion to add some critical comments on *these* theories as well—but in the belief that the sociology of the family can only really begin to develop if these critical perspectives are brought into the main arena of discussion. Such an emphasis may also touch more directly on people's experience of the family than some of the functionalist perspectives; after all, a long tradition of folk stories and folk songs deal not with happy families but with unrequited love, with incest, with infanticide, fratricide, matricide and patricide.

The final reason for the problem in the teaching of the sociology of the family lies in the fact that the subject matter is perhaps too close to our everyday lives. We may never enter a factory or be a member of a religious sect but nearly all of us have been or will become part of a family. Full-time education may last from the ages of five to sixteen or from five to twenty-five; family living tends to last a lifetime. A need for 'objectivity' is stressed; we are not talking about 'your divorce' but divorce rates, not about 'my children' but about socialization. Perhaps it is also felt that some people are over-involved in their own families and there may be a desire—probably laudable—to distinguish sociology classes from encounter groups or therapy sessions. Furthermore, this closeness of and high degree of involvement in the family may sometimes inhibit research and this may be exacerbated by the fact that much family life in modern society is outside the public arena. Henry expresses this privatization in a characteristically arresting phrase: 'In our culture babies are a private enterprise—everybody is in the baby business as soon as he gets married.'[8] Almost, it would seem, by definition the family is a private area. Consequently the techniques of participant observation and other forms of qualitative methodology are often difficult if not impossible. So much family living depends on shorthand verbal or non-verbal communication, behaviour which can only be understood through long acquaintance with the context. Socialization, for example, may be affected as much through non- (or at least non-verbal) communication as through the issuing of explicit orders or the use of tangible rewards and punishments. Few of these subtle interactional cues can be picked up through the use of the questionnaire or even the non-directed interview. In spite of these difficulties we have several perceptive and provocative studies of the family in modern society—Seeley *et al.* on middle-class families, Komarovsky on blue-collar families, Laing and Esterson on the families of schizophrenics and so on[9]—and these studies, and others, will be used at several points in the following discussions.

These, then, are three problems facing the study and teaching of the sociology of the family: the relative weakness of its theoretical tradition, the relative absence of a critical tradition and the practical, and moral, problems involved in research into the family. In part, many of the criticisms which may be levelled at the sociology of the family are criticisms which may be levelled at dominant trends within the whole field of sociology. I have in mind the general criticisms presented by Mills, Gouldner, Atkinson, Blackburn and others.[10] It is not my purpose here to enter into this wider debate: it is hoped that this book represents an application of some of these wider critical approaches.[11]

By use of the word 'critical' here I hope to convey two themes. The first is an emphasis on a sociology that stresses action and potentiality rather than one which stresses constraint and order.[12] This is not to say that constraint and order are unimportant problems for the sociologists; I would suggest, however, that in the sociology of the family undue emphasis has been given to these problems at the expense of the other concerns. Further, I do not intend to make arbitrary divisions between sociological 'goodies' and 'baddies' nor do I argue that the discipline of sociology is inherently or necessarily conservative in its history or its practice. As I hope to show, some of the apparently 'radical' approaches to sociology often imply conservative images of man[13] and there are critical implications (in the concept of latent function, dysfunction and role-conflict for example) at the heart of much orthodox sociology. A critical sociology should perhaps begin with an appreciation of the deep-rooted ambiguities within the discipline itself.

A second implication of the use of the word 'critical' in this book is that sociology should be reflexive.[14] Again it should be noted that such reflexivity is not a new discovery but is at the heart of the subject, appearing at several points and in the context of several discussions. It is implied at least in the discussion of 'ideal types' and their construction which shows the sociologist as actively and consciously intervening between the 'real world' and his audience—in a sense creating that 'real world'—in the development of the sociology of knowledge showing the way in which sociology is ideologically situated and in the debates over participant observation again pointing to a dialectical relationship between the worlds of the observer and the observed. More recently, the question has been given sharper definition not merely in the extended critiques of Gouldner and Atkinson but also in critical examinations of sociological praxis developed by ethnomethodologists. All of these arguments, in their different forms, remind us that sociological work is not a once and for all achievement, a simple lineal process of work culminating in a finished study or a theory, but rather an ongoing dialectic in which the sociologist is situated in and creates the world he is studying and that sociological work must include, as part of that work, a reflexive awareness of its own practices.

Thus a critical sociology is one which stresses action and potentiality and one which is reflexively aware of itself. The reflexivity is essential if the term 'critical sociology' is not to degenerate into a comforting rhetoric. Perhaps the best account of what a critical sociology might achieve has been provided by O'Neill:[15]

> The voice of such criticism is neither fanatical nor cynical, although it is in no way a simple affirmation of the claims of the community and tradition in which it belongs. What I have in mind is a conception of criticism which does not exploit the differences between the way things are and how they might be but rather leaves itself open to the experience of their reversal, to the care for what is sublime as well as of what is desperate in the human condition and the times through which it passes.

Aims of the book

It should be clear at this point that the aim of the present book is more concerned with sociology *and* the family than with the sociology *of* the family. In other words it is not my aim to write another text-book dealing with sociology of the family. There are already several of these. Rather, I am attempting to examine some of the theoretical assumptions which underlie many of these text-books and, indeed, much of the material written in this field.

I am, therefore, more concerned with theories about the family than with the substantive body of empirical findings within the sociology of the family. In a sense, also, it may be said that I am concerned with *social* theory rather than with sociological theory. This is because I shall be looking at the work of several writers—Laing, Marcuse, authors on Women's Liberation, etc.—who may not conventionally be described as sociologists and who might, indeed, quite explicitly reject the label. The aim is to use these, and other, writers to examine some of the current assumptions in the sociology of the family and thereby, hopefully, to make a contribution to the theoretical development of the field.

It should also be noted that there are two further possible aims which are not, in fact, part of my intention. In the first place, while I am clearly concerned with theoretical issues in this field, it is not my intention to provide a (or the) theory of the family. At present I am not sure if such an enterprise would be a worthwhile one; for one thing it is by no means certain that theoretical boundaries in sociology necessarily or usefully coincide with conventional institutional boundaries such as 'the family', 'religion', 'industry' and so on. I am certainly not sure what a 'theory of the family' would look like even if it were to be developed. In the final chapter I shall attempt to outline some major theoretical issues in the study of the family which arise out of my analysis of specific problem areas. Major contributions have already been made to the subject by functional and interactionist theories; I am making a plea here for the incorporation of a largely Marxian and existential perspective into our understanding of the family.

In the second place this is not a book about the 'future of the family' nor is it a plea for the abolition of the family. Again, there is a growing body of literature in this field.[16] Therefore I spend little time in examining certain well publicized and much debated alternatives to the nuclear family such as kibbutzim or modern 'hippie' communes. Nor shall I spend much time in examining aspects of the 'sexual revolution' such as wife-swapping, abortion, consensual unions, etc. There is plenty of material here for at least two more books but the present task is less ambitious.

Yet clearly an examination of some basic theoretical issues in the study of the family can make a contribution to the debate about the future of the family. The discussion about the future of the family cannot proceed merely by passively extrapolating certain current statistical trends (relating to demographic variables or indices such as divorce rates) into some defined date in the future. Such an approach implicitly denies the possibility of human freedom to change and control society's future institutions. Rather we should consider what kind of family system we might desire and analyse the way in which these desired ends might be achieved as well as some of the likely obstacles to their realization. A theoretical approach which does not take the functions of the family for granted and which examines some of the defects in the present family system is an essential part of this undertaking.

I do not intend to offer a definition of the 'family' at this point. It will, I hope, become clear that it is difficult to talk about 'the' family at all. The family, of course, differs considerably between classes, different parts of the world, different ethnic and religious groups and so on. Furthermore, each individual 'family' is constantly changing over time as its members die, get married and have children. And yet, in another sense, it is very easy to talk about the family. I know who is 'in' my family and the families of others appear to me to be recognizable entities. I can talk about 'the Jones's' next door and 'the Smiths' down the road. Similarly, the Jones's and the Smiths have some idea of the 'Morgan family'. It is true that these perspectives do not overlap completely. Some of the Jones's or the Smiths are invisible to me as an outsider because they live in Australia or perhaps even because they are dead. Yet these others, invisible to me, may be important elements in the Jones's and the Smiths' notions of their own families. Similarly I may mistakenly include individuals in the membership of these other families. Aunt Jane may 'not be an Aunt really' or others with formal claims in terms of kinship may not, in practice, be recognized. Children, in particular, are apt to make 'mistakes' in the assignment of kinship terminology to other adults. The point is that, within any 'family' defined according to some formal terms of marriage and kinship, there are a multiplicity of overlapping perspectives on the part of the actors within each family system. Our definition and understanding of the 'family' must in some way take account of this multiplicity of perspectives. This point will be developed at greater length in the concluding chapters of this book.

There are, therefore, a variety of definitions of the family available for different purposes. There are legal and administrative definitions, there are statistical and demographic models and there are ideal typical definitions of, for example, the 'nuclear family' or the 'extended family'. There are actors' definitions of their own and other families and summations of typifications of these definitions. There are also ideal models of what the family *ought* to be like, evaluations of the importance and meaning of family life in the context of society as a whole. Such evaluations may be considered under the general heading of 'familism', defined by Bell as 'investment in the familial system of the society'.[17] Important here is the varying degree of commitment to the idea of the family, the centrality or otherwise of the family in the lives of social actors, the ideal structures, scope and forms of the family which are held by members of a society. Familism may, for example, be evaluated according to the degree of assent given to statements such as 'blood is thicker than water' or 'you know where you are with kin'. Thus in our definitions of the family we must also take note of these ideal expectations and the extent and way in which they relate to actually existing family forms. The relations between 'familism' and the family are considered at greater length in the concluding chapter.

In practice I shall be dealing with what is generally understood to be the nuclear family of two adults of opposite sexes, living together in some socially recognized form of relationship and the children who are biologically or socially related to these adults. Even this very general definition may not be inclusive enough for it fails to recognize the possibility (realized in many parts of the world) of there being the mother–child dyad, with the biological father playing little, if any, part in the running of the household or the socialization of the child.[18] While I recognize the importance of this modification, the theoretical themes that I shall be considering usually relate to the more conventionally defined nuclear family which is, of course, linked to two other nuclear families, the families of origin of the parents.

In essence, therefore, the family that I am concerned with contains the following two essential elements:

1 Relationships between the sexes, usually but not always between husbands and wives. (Also male siblings and female siblings.)
2 Relationships between generations, between parents and children, between grandparents and parents and between grandparents and children.

The dyadic and triadic structures that arise in a simple nuclear family system are examined in Chapter 4.

Outline of the book

In Part One I shall examine briefly and selectively some of the current themes in the sociology of the family.[19] I suggest that a dominant theoretical theme in much of the writing is either explicitly or implicitly of a 'functionalist' nature. I shall point out, in fact, that there does not appear to be any clear consensus as to what is meant by 'functionalism' in relation to the family and I shall critically examine the variety of theories that have been developed and applied in this area. A second major concern in much of the current writing on the family deals with the nature and importance of kinship in modern society. In brief, the debate has been about the alleged decline in the importance of kinship in modern urban, industrial society. A large part of current research and writing deals with this theme.

Some of the assumptions made by the various protagonists in this debate will be examined and it will be asked whether this research, much of it of high quality, does not divert our attention from some more fundamental issues. Another current theme, linked to this last discussion, is the debate over the alleged 'decline of the family' in modern society. In so far as this last theme also asks the question 'has the family lost, or has it changed, its functions?' it is linked to the first theme, that is the dominant functional approach to the family.

In Part Two of the book I shall set against these current concerns some of the themes which can be and have been developed in critical writings on the family. I shall place the debate in the context of the often discussed division within sociology between the 'consensus' approach and the 'conflict' approach, suggesting that, in the sociology of the family, the 'consensus' approach has received too much emphasis. These critical writings, deriving largely from the Marxist and existential traditions, will be focused on three main problem areas: the position of women in society, sex and society and what might be called the 'dysfunctions of the family'.

The concluding chapter will attempt to summarize these two opposed traditions. As I have stated, it is not the intention of this book to provide a 'theory of the family'. It is believed, however, that it should be possible in the light of this debate, to sketch out some of the major problem areas within the sociology of the family. These will include the question of the 'boundaries of the family', the relations of the family to the outside world, the family and social-historical change. While there is not space in a book of this size to discuss alternatives to the nuclear family, some of the practical implications will be mentioned.

Some limitations

Some limitations of this book will be obvious to the reader, some will be unintended. I shall note here some of the limitations that I recognize and which I have not gone out of my way to avoid. This is not, of course, to say that all these limitations are justified.

The first point to note is that while, I hope, the book will be argumentative in tone, it is not intended to be a polemic. While I adopt the force of many of the radical critiques of sociology I do not find myself holding a perspective which makes a stark distinction between radical (or revolutionary) sociology and bourgeois sociology. This debate can too often become sterile simply because it so often ceases to be a debate. Nor do I hold a clearly defined position in the other major area of dispute in sociology, that between the proponents of a 'scientific' model of sociology, concerned with the rigorous development and testing of hypotheses and the increasing use of sophisticated mathematical causal models on the one hand, and the critique of this position developed by the also growing school of symbolic interactionism or ethnomethodology on the other hand. This too can easily degenerate into a sterile holding of positions. On the whole, I find myself in sympathy with the well-known position outlined by C. Wright Mills at the beginning of his *Sociological Imagination*: 'The sociological imagination enables us to grasp history and biography and the relations between the two within society. That is its task and its promise.'[20] Whether this book succeeds in approaching the exacting demands laid down by Mills or whether it appears as an exercise in sitting on a multitude of fences will, of course, be determined by the reader.

It will also be clear, secondly, that the emphasis in this book is largely theoretical. Empirical studies will be used and referred to as illustrations of the issues raised here but I shall not attempt a complete survey of the literature. Several good surveys are already available.[21] In so far as I shall use empirical material I shall largely use material relating to modern industrial society. There will be few references to comparative or specifically historical materials. The controversies that I shall be dealing with have all developed, to various extents, in relation to a concern about the position of the family in modern society. In some cases, industrialization is seen as the major causal factor influencing the changing forms and functions of the family. The debates have taken their sharpest outlines in the context of an industrial or perhaps even a 'post-industrial' society. Undoubtedly sociology has suffered in the past and is still suffering from ethnocentric bias, a bias which implicitly does not acknowledge the existence of the communist or the third world or, where these areas are acknowledged, they are not incorporated into the particular theories and analyses. Clearly, were I to have written the book with these areas in mind the outcome might have been very different. Yet, while I do not suppose that the theories and themes that I have outlined here may have direct applicability to, say, Communist China or Latin America, I do not believe that this debate, while originating in the context of Western capitalist society, is totally irrelevant to the other major areas of the world. The problems of the relationship between the family and other institutions in society, of the roles of the sexes and the relationships between generations are clearly, in different ways, of concern to all societies, capitalist or communist, developed or developing, urban or rural. My hope is that, if we can begin to state these, and other, problems, in as clear terms as possible we may begin to develop an understanding of them in a context which is much wider than the one in which these problems were originally raised.

Another omission will also be apparent to the reader. There are few references to such traditional topics as the incest taboo or the relationship between biology and culture. To some extent, of course, reference to some of these questions is inevitable. There is, I suppose, little point in discussing the *roles* of the sexes if one believes that 'biology is destiny'. There is little point in discussing the future of the family if one considers the family to be some kind of socio-biological imperative. It will be clear that, in common with the majority of sociologists, I do not hold these views. There is sufficient variation in the patterns of socialization, in the allocation of roles according to sex and age and in the structure of the 'family' to justify the assumption that, while biology or physical necessity impose certain limits on human choices (men cannot bear children, and children cannot survive on their own in the earliest years) these must be seen as limitations rather than determinants. There is clearly scope for a much more sophisticated analysis of the interactions between biology and culture but, again, this is not the main concern of this book.

If, as I believe, it is possible for me in a book of this nature to avoid a lengthy consideration of biological or demographic factors, the same is not true for psychological factors. A considerable section of the book will be devoted to what has been called the 'psycho-social interior of the family'.[22] In particular I devote several pages to a discussion of the theories of R. D. Laing, an existential psychologist. Such a venture outside the boundaries of sociology is, I believe, inevitable and essential. Indeed, when considering the institution of the family it is difficult to know where to draw the line between the sociological, the social psychological and the psychological. The widely used concept of 'role', for example, clearly deals with an area of intersection between individual experiences, perceptions and behaviour on the one hand and social and cultural institutions on the other. While I shall have occasion to be critical of the theories of Parsons in relation to the family at several points of this book, I fully recognize the importance of his attempt to analyse and systematize the intimate interactions between the individual personality system, the cultural system and the social system.

In general I shall attempt to follow the subtle advice of Lord Coleridge:[23]

> The Attorney-General has asked us where we are to draw the line. The answer is that it is not necessary to draw it at any precise point. It is enough for us to say that the present case is on the right side of any reasonable line that could be drawn.

Thus I do not consider it necessary to enter into a debate about the nature and aetiology of schizophrenia although I do consider Laing's discussion of the family, derived in a large part from his studies of the families of persons described as schizophrenics. Again, I shall leave it to the reader to determine where I have improperly overstepped the limits of my training within the field of sociology.

Similar observations may be made about my use of material which might be defined as 'philosophical'. Again this is true in the case of R. D. Laing who derives his inspiration as much from Sartre as from Freud or Sullivan. This will also be true in my examination of writers such as Marcuse and, indeed, of Marx. My justification here is similar. These writers are clearly dealing with issues which are of considerable relevance to and importance for sociologists. Where necessary, I shall deal with these authors and their themes, recognizing that a treatment of the same authors by a philosopher and a psychologist would almost certainly be different. In the case of 'philosophy', however, there is a further justification. Too often, it appears that the label 'philosophy' is used as a kind of waste bin in which we place areas of social understanding or analysis which do not seem to fit too readily. Thus to take an example from another area we may use Blauner or Seeman's dimensions of 'alienation' while placing the main thrust of Marx's argument into a bin marked 'philosophical', usually taken to mean unexaminable or immeasurable. Doubtless similar processes take place in departments of philosophy and, while it would be wrong to deny that each discipline develops its own field of competence and style of enquiry, it would also seem that these boundaries often have as much to do with university politics as with the major concerns of scholarship.

Finally, a word about my own position. Until fairly recently my main areas of interest were in the fields of the sociology of religion and industrial sociology. I developed an interest in the family, indirectly, through studying a factory which employed a high percentage of women. As yet, however, I have not undertaken any research specifically in this area.[24] As I noted at the beginning of this chapter, this book was written in response to some difficulties which I felt in teaching the sociology of the family.

I am married with two children and live what might be viewed as, I suppose, a reasonably conventional married and academic life. Possibly some readers will feel that this fact alone may disqualify me from writing a book of this kind.[25] That, as well as the question as to whether I have succeeded in developing the possibility of a critical sociological approach to the family, must be left to the reader to decide.

part one

1 Varieties of functionalism

Introduction

The functionalist perspective has had a long and controversial part to play in the development of sociological theory. For various reasons it appears to have been more deeply entrenched in the field of the sociology of the family than in some other sub-disciplines. Few text-books of the family (or general text-books which almost invariably include a chapter on the family) fail to include a discussion of the functions of the family or a reference to the change in or loss of these functions. Thus, for example, the recent material developed for the Open University foundation course in the Social Sciences includes a comprehensive list of the functions of the family, although a footnote indicates some of the difficulties involved in a functional approach.[1] A widely adopted text-book, also used in conjunction with this Open University material, contains a similar account of the functions of the family.[2] The juxtaposition of the words 'family' and 'function' appears almost inevitably irrespective of the degree of commitment or otherwise to an overall functionalist theory of Society.[3]

My intention in this chapter is to consider the various functional approaches in so far as they have a bearing on the development of the sociology of the family, and I do not intend to consider at any length the wider controversies. I shall confine a general discussion to the provision of a few introductory distinctions.

In the first place, a distinction can be made between two major contexts in which the functional approach has been developed. The first, identified largely with Durkheim and Parsons, is that of a general macro-theory of society. The concern is with developing some model of a society or a social system and the examination of the way in which the various parts or levels are linked together. Here we are interested in the relationships between the individual and society, between the various parts or institutions that go to make up a society, between the personality system, the cultural system and the social system. The problem is the 'problem of order',[4] seen largely from a perspective which emphasizes consensus and integration. At a very general level it may be said that functionalism, in this context, is concerned with the relationships between 'parts' and 'wholes'.

The second context in which functionalism has developed is as a mode of enquiry. Functionalism here provides a set of orientations which guide the sociologist in the investigation of particular problems and which direct him to ask particular questions. The emphasis here is on particular problems or institutions, the theoretical level is roughly that of the 'middle range'. Merton's reformulation and development of the functionalist perspective may be seen as providing a set of analytical tools within this kind of context.[5] The test of the value of functionalism here tends to be a pragmatic one: does it direct us to asking questions which are illuminating or helpful?

These two contexts are, of course, interdependent. A functionalist approach to a particular problem derives, directly or indirectly, from a wider theory. But a functional approach or orientation can also, to some extent, exist independently of an assent to an overall functionalist theory. Thus we may ask, as a research strategy, what are the functions and dysfunctions of, say, organized crime, without necessarily committing ourselves to a functionalist model of society as a whole or to an assumption that 'everything must have a function'. It follows, therefore, that the criticisms we may direct at functionalism as a theory need not necessarily apply to functionalism as a research strategy.

A second distinction that we may make is between 'hard' and 'soft' functionalism or between 'explicit' and 'implicit' functionalism. 'Hard' or 'explicit' functionalism implies either a definite commitment to a functionalist theory or a clearly articulated set of propositions couched in functionalist terms, or both. 'Soft' or 'implicit' functionalism implies an unarticulated or unexamined functionalist perspective which is latent in the work concerned. The presence of a 'soft' version of functionalism may often be discerned through the use of phrases such as 'serves to', 'has the role of', or sometimes 'has the consequence', where this is not a specifically historical statement.

Functionalism and the family

It is my impression that functional statements are more likely to be presented as self-evident propositions in the study of the family than in any other area of sociology. What is objectionable about many statements about 'the functions of the family' is not merely the actual list of functions presented but the lack of critical awareness as to what kind of question is being asked and whether it is a meaningful question at all.

There are some possible reasons for the continued presence of often unexamined functionalist statements in the study of the family. One is the apparent universality of the family. Another is the apparent connection between the institution of the family and certain biological imperatives. Such imperatives would include the fact that sexual reproduction requires a male and a female, that women bear children, that while the identity of the biological mother is never in doubt, that of the biological father may be, and the fact that human infants require a long period of care and protection by more senior members of the human species.

Thus the simplest statement about the functions of the family will be roughly that the family is a universal institution and must therefore perform some universal functions. This appears to be the position of Murdock, and will be examined in more detail in the next section. A slightly more sophisticated—and reversed—version of this assumption is that there are certain basic functional prerequisites that must be met if society is to survive and the institution of the family is uniquely or best able to meet these functions. This version does imply, however, that it might be possible for other institutions to fulfil some or all of these functions at least at some stage in the future.

These rather simplistic perspectives are, however, opposed by another functionalist orientation which recognizes that the family can lose some of its functions or that the functions can change. Thus the institution of the family is not inextricably bound up with some universal and necessary functions. This approach, most clearly represented by Parsons, is linked to an evolutionary perspective. Briefly, this states that societies evolve through a process of structural differentiation whereby social institutions become differentiated from each other and develop some measure of autonomy in relation to society as a whole. Thus, for example, work becomes separate from the home in modern society. This implies that the functions of the family can change as the relationship between the family and society as a whole changes. The implication of this perspective is that statements about the universality of the institution of the family are, in principle at least, separable from statements about its changing functions.

Enough should have been said in this brief introduction to indicate that the label 'functionalist' as applied to the study of the family can encompass a wide variety of perspectives between which there is not necessarily any high degree of agreement. This chapter is concerned with the variety of functional approaches that have been developed and the general criticisms that can be applied to them all. I shall not attempt a complete survey of the literature but, rather, I shall attempt to pick some of the most influential and representative figures: Murdock, Coser, Parsons (together with Bell and Vogel) and Goode. Finally I shall provide an example of a functional approach to a specific problem, that of the emotionally disturbed child as a scapegoat. I shall also look at a recent version of role theory as it is applied to the study of the family. On the basis of these accounts I shall present some general critical comments.

Murdock

Murdock's list of the four functions of the nuclear family, or some close variation on this theme, has been widely reprinted since it was first presented. A statement which begins 'the functions of the family are . . .' has a deceptively simple ring about it, indicating that we are in the presence of a universal empirical generalization. When in a contribution to a collectively written text-book, I listed Murdock's functions largely in order to present a critical evaluation of them, I did not intend that many of my students would reproduce this list of functions without mentioning the criticisms.[6] Yet any statement listing the functions of the family is a theoretical and ideological statement rather than a simple empirical statement.

In spite of the influential nature of Murdock's list, he cannot be described as a 'hard' functionalist. Indeed, at several points in his *Social Structure* he is critical of the functionalist school of anthropology; he argues, for example, that the functionalist school makes no provision for the analysis of social change.[7] Murdock, therefore, holds no overall functional theory of society as a whole and he does not list the functions of the family in terms of any such theory. Rather his study is based upon the cross-cultural analysis of data from '250 representative human societies' and his statement about the functions of the nuclear family is presented as if it derives from this empirical study.

Murdock defines the family, in general, in these terms:[8]

> The family is a social group characterised by common residence, economic co-operation, and reproduction. It includes adults of both sexes, at least two of whom maintain a socially approved sexual relationship, and one or more children, own or adopted, of the sexually cohabiting adults.

More specifically, the nuclear family is defined as being, typically: 'a married man and woman with their offspring, although in individual cases one or more additional persons may reside with them.'[9]

On the basis of his cross cultural material, Murdock concludes that the nuclear family as defined is a 'universal human grouping'.[10] This universality is bound up with the basic functions which the family is said to perform:[11]

> In the nuclear family or its constituent relationships we thus see assembled four functions fundamental to human social life—the sexual, the economic, the reproductive, and the educational. Without provision for the first and third, society would become extinct; for the second, life itself would cease; for the fourth, culture would come to an end. The immense social utility of the nuclear family and the basic reason for its universality thus begin to emerge in strong relief.

It is, of course, no difficult task to take these functions one by one and to demonstrate that in very few, if any, cultures does the institution of the nuclear family have exclusive command over these functions. Thus, for example, in very few societies is sex, either ideally or in practice, exclusively and legitimately carried out only between married partners. However, it might be argued that this line of attack is a little unfair in that it picks on the functions singly and fails to see that the unique importance of the family lies in the fact that it is the only institution which fulfils *all* these functions together. As Murdock argues, other institutions may take over some aspects of some of the functions but no institution has yet been devised to replace all these functions. Furthermore, Murdock would argue that all these functions reinforce each other. Fulfilment of the sexual function leads to achievement of the reproductive function (and hence also the socialization function) and children may later become economic assets for the family. We are still, however, faced with the problem that a set of essential functions (sexual, reproductive and educational) are linked to a particular institution (the family) in a way that appears to be inevitable and unchangeable. In sum, what this list is saying is that any society must make provisions for its present survival and for its biological and social continuity, features which might almost be seen as an essential part of any definition of a 'society'. The central and unanswered question here is to what extent these basic functions are inevitably linked with the institution of the nuclear family.

Ignoring here the methodological difficulties involved in the use of the cross-cultural comparative method which in this case appears to give equal weighting to China and the Cheyenne,[12] there are one or two more general criticisms that may be made against Murdock's argument. In the first place he is not so much writing about functions as 'eufunctions', that is *successful* adaptations to the needs and survival of society.[13] Murdock's nuclear family is a remarkably harmonious institution. Husband and wife have an integrated division of labour and have a good time in bed. The resultant children contribute to this overall domestic harmony: 'Any factor which strengthens the tie between one member and a second also operates indirectly to bind the former to a third member with whom the second maintains a close relationship.'[14] Even if we accept that these functions are closely integrated and connected with each other, does this also not imply the possibility of a vicious circle as well as a virtuous circle? Quarrels break out between husband and wife over who should do what in the fields. They refuse to sleep with each other and use the children as a weapon in their marital battles. Thus integration of function does not necessarily lead to harmony of relationships.

Further, we cannot necessarily assume—as Murdock appears to assume—that what is functional for society is also functional for the individual and vice versa. 'Society' may need new members to survive but an additional pregnancy may be an almost intolerable burden on a particular mother or family. Or an additional child may be proof of my virility but society as a whole may be overpopulated. Murdock assumes an almost automatic coincidence between what is 'good' for the individual or the individual nuclear family and what is good for society as a whole.

Many of the criticisms that can be levelled at Murdock's list of functions of the family can also be levelled at similar lists.[15] In so far as they direct us in a general way to consider problems of the relationships between the institution of the family and other institutions in society there is little harm in these lists. Furthermore, again in a general way, few people would dissent from the argument that in most societies there is an overlap, in many cases a close overlap, between the institutions of the family and the activities of sexual intercourse, reproduction and primary socialization. But it would appear that statements listing the functions of the family appear to carry greater theoretical weight than they should in fact bear, and that there is an almost inevitable slide into apparent statements of universality, necessity and inevitability.

Coser

Coser uses an explicit functionalist framework in presenting her collection of readings.[16] Up to a point it is unfair to criticize something which has the relatively modest aim of introducing a useful set of articles and which is not developed at any great length. However, Coser's collection is probably a widely used text (it has been reprinted in paperback form) and the argument, brief as it is, does have the virtue of illustrating further some of the varieties, and ambiguities, of functionalist argument as it is applied to the family.

Coser appears to accept that the family is a universal institution but argues that this universality 'cannot be explained simply by its manifest functions—such as reproduction, economic activities, socialisation of the young—all of which could conceivably be fulfilled outside the institutionalised family'.[17] However, by the end of the introduction she reaches a conclusion which looks very much like a list of functions:[18]

> a brief review of the main functions of the family—the institutionalisation of social fatherhood, the establishment through marriage of alliances outside of blood relations, the imposition of social norms on the biological organism, and the bestowing of social identity on its members—leads one to the conclusion that in all these tasks the family ensures the victory of the social over the biological.

Within this list of the 'main functions of the family' there is an important distinction between the first two, which are given special attention, and the last two. The third function—'the imposition of social norms on the biological organism'—appears to be indistinguishable from the earlier 'socialisation' function and could, in Coser's words, 'conceivably be fulfilled outside the institutionalised family'. This is true of the fourth function—'the bestowing of social identity on its members'. Similarly, the statement that 'the family ensures the victory of the social over the biological' is almost a tautology since the family is defined as a social institution in the first place. Furthermore, it is arguable that other institutions—such as a 'full-blown' commune for example—would in some senses represent an ever greater victory in so far as they might abolish the relevance of all biological facts such as differences between the sexes and biological parenthood.

The first two functions are, however, given special emphasis as features which 'stand out universally'.[19] The first function is based on Malinowski's 'principle of legitimacy', while the second is based on Lévi-Strauss's 'principle of reciprocity'. The former: 'holds that every child shall have a father, and one father only'.[20] The latter principle revolves around one commonly argued theory of the 'incest taboo' namely that it ensures 'a patterned exchange of sexual partners' and thereby 'makes social life possible'.[21]

The first principle rests on the assumption that there is a 'universal insistence on fatherhood', that is social fatherhood.[22] There is nothing biologically necessary about this; theoretically a female could be impregnated by any male and there need be no further ties between that particular male and the resultant child. In practice, however, the notion of fatherhood appears to be necessary to give the child identity, to place that child in society and to provide a socially recognized and orderly transfer of rights, duties and identities from one generation to another. Coser argues that the mother–child dyad is sociologically incomplete.[23]

There are a variety of objections that may be made to this argument. Empirically it does not seem to be the case that the mother–child dyad is 'always considered incomplete sociologically'. Indeed, on the basis of the commonness of this very dyad in Caribbean and Latin American countries, Adams argues that we should consider it, rather than the triadic nuclear family, as the basic domestic unit.[24] Goode also considers the same 'deviant' material but comes to a slightly different conclusion that the 'principle of legitimacy' varies in its importance according to one's position in the social structure.[25] Because there is more at stake in the way of property and prestige, the higher status groups in society are likely to demand greater conformity to the principle of legitimacy than are lower status groups. It is not far from this modification (whereby the 'law-like' statement is demoted to the status of a variable social rule) to the argument that with the increase in corporate property as against private property and with the development of bases of identity outside the family (work, the community, leisure, etc.) the importance of legitimacy is likely to be undermined in modern society.

The stress on the principle of legitimacy also raises a further question, namely why it is thought necessary for the *father* to provide social identity? The answer would appear to lie in the unequal distribution of power, status and authority between the sexes and the basis of this inequality. As this theme is considered at greater length in Chapter 5 I shall not develop it here. All that needs to be noted is that there is no logical reason why social identity should derive from the notion of fatherhood, although it is recognized that, in fact, the two have been closely although not universally connected.

The circularity of this section of the argument, and many similar arguments about the functions of the family, must be recognized. The definition of the family includes within it a definition of marriage which links the adult members. Marriage establishes the 'institution of social fatherhood'. Yet it can scarcely be maintained that the family exists to fulfil the legitimacy of the offspring as a function, for this legitimacy of the offspring depends upon the definition of social fatherhood which is, in turn, part of the definition of marriage. As Rivière points out, the marital institution and its function are used to define each other.[26]

Similar questions may be raised in relation to the second principle, the 'principle of reciprocity'. I shall avoid a lengthy debate that has arisen around the incest taboo,[27] except to point out that the explanation presented in Coser is only one of several functional explanations and that the incest taboo usually refers to sexual relationships between prohibited persons, whereas the 'principle of reciprocity' is referring largely to marital alliances. Again it is not clear in what way 'the establishment through marriage of alliances outside of blood relations' can be said to represent a main function of the family since the two are closely associated, almost by definition.

Further, in modern society it is only by stretching the concept of 'social exchange' that it can be said that the principle of reciprocity operates in relation to marital alliances. Lévi-Strauss appears to extend the concept of exchange to the point that it includes *all* possible social relationships:[28]

> But no matter what form it takes, whether direct or indirect, general or special, immediate or deferred, explicit or implicit, closed or open, concrete or symbolic, it is exchange, always exchange, that emerges as the fundamental and common basis of all modalities of the institution of the marriage.

In contemporary societies people enter into wide ranges of social relationships through all kinds of channels and not merely through the institution of marriage operating on the basis of the principle of reciprocity. Again there is probably variation between social classes and status groups; generally it might be proposed that the higher the status of one or both of the partners the more relevant the concept of marriage as an alliance.

Alongside this functional framework there exists a general recognition of the changing relationship between family and society, broadly similar to the Parsonian structural differentiation model. It is here that a second, weaker functionalism makes its appearance as, for example, where she writes about the family being 'adapted to the structural arrangements of the society' or states that: 'relationships within the family and its pattern of life must be to some extent congruent with the demands that the community makes upon its members'.[29] There is an explicit and implicit recognition that the functioning and structure of the family may change as society changes. It is perhaps curious, therefore, that this analysis of change is not extended to the notions of legitimacy and reciprocity.

Parsons

It would not be too much of an exaggeration to state that Parsons represents *the* modern theorist on the family. His explicit 'hard' functionalist approach is an attempt to organize and analyse a wide range of topics—relationships between spouses, the family and industrial society, the socialization process, the incest taboo—within a single theoretical perspective. It is an attempt to bring together, for example, Freud's developmental approach to personality and Durkheim's account of the social basis of morality. His influence and importance in the study of the family is unquestioned; he has not only provided a framework to argue within or against but he has, to a large extent, defined the rules within which people argue. To stretch Kuhn's analysis of scientific discovery to include sociology (possibly a questionable extension) we may say that, in this particular field, Parsons has provided the major 'paradigm' within which 'normal' sociology is carried out.[30] Leslie, for example, has thirteen references to Parsons in his index and includes a brief critical account of Parsons's main theories.[31] Williamson refers to Parsons's discussion of the functions of the family, socialization, adolescence, compulsive masculinity, courtship and love in the second edition of his book.[32] Extracts from Parsons appear in Anderson's reader[33] and Turner has several, largely uncritical, references to Parsons in his interactionist study.[34]

It is worth stressing the importance of Parsons because in other areas of sociology his position would appear to be much less secure. His total system has been subjected to a variety of attacks, from C. Wright Mills to, more recently, Atkinson and Gouldner.[35] The dominant position of Parsons (and functionalism in general) is now no longer assured in the light of attacks from radical sociology, symbolic interactionism and ethnomethodology. In the field of the family, however, Parsons, if he does not reign supreme, still dominates the field. Although I shall be critical of the central arguments that Parsons puts forward I shall attempt to demonstrate that, in this field at least, he still deserves serious consideration if only for the boldness of his attempt and the sharpness of his individual insights.

In the following pages I shall attempt to draw out some of the major theoretical themes in Parsons's approach to the family. To some extent it is difficult to separate these various themes as they are all highly interconnected and form part of an overall functional approach to the social system as a whole. Having outlined these major themes and shown how they are interrelated I shall present some specifically critical points at the end of this section.

The functions of the modern American family

On the whole, Parsons shows little interest in cross-cultural analysis or comparison and implicitly, and often explicitly, he is dealing with the modern American family. Here, Parsons counters those critics who argue that the family is facing dissolution and a loss of function by arguing that we are witnessing a process of change rather than one of dissolution. A key concept here is that of 'differentiation'.[36] As modern industrial society has evolved so particular institutions which in the past have performed two or more functions become more differentiated and specialize in fewer functions, while other institutions develop to carry out the functions no longer performed by this institution. Thus the family was once an economic unit of production and consumption as well as a residential unit; with the Industrial Revolution the production function was taken out of the home into a specialized factory. The functions that the family now performs on behalf of society are more indirect. To understand the functions of the family we must look specifically at the ways in which it functions on behalf of the individual as a member of society.

The modern American family is not, therefore, facing dissolution but has become stripped down to two essential functions. Its most important function is that of the socialization of the child. This is functional both for the individual personalities of the children (and indeed the parents) and for society as a whole. But second, the modern family also performs the function of 'stabilization of the adult personalities of the population of the society'.[37] This is related to the central importance of marriage in our society and the way in which it is increasingly perceived in 'human relations' terms. Thus higher divorce rates do not necessarily indicate a flight from the institution of marriage but may, paradoxically, reflect the high expectations that individuals have of marital relations. Further, a greater proportion of the population than ever before is getting married at an earlier age and a high proportion of divorcees will remarry another partner.

The relative isolation of the nuclear family

It is in the context of this discussion of the process of structural differentiation in modern industrial society and the associated increasing specialization of the functions of the nuclear family that we can consider what is probably the most widely discussed of Parsons's arguments, namely that relating to the relative isolation of the modern nuclear family. The American kinship system is, in his words, an 'open, multilineal, conjugal system'.[38] It is open because there are no bounded kinship based units such as lineage groups or clans, it is multilineal because there are no clearly marked out rules of descent and it is conjugal in that the key point of reference is the marital relationship between a husband and wife. The main terms used are 'family' (meaning either the nuclear family of origin or the nuclear family of procreation) and an undifferentiated and unbounded category of 'relatives'. The preferred residential pattern is neolocality, the setting up of an independent unit by the couple on marriage. The chief obligation of the spouses is to each other and to their children as opposed to their own families of origin.

A full discussion of the implications and controversy surrounding Parsons's argument will be deferred until the next chapter. It is worth stressing at this point, however, that Parsons is constantly referring to the '*relative*' isolation of the nuclear family. There is never, nor can there be it would seem, a complete break with the family of origin on marriage. There is, however, a normative expectation that the spouses should 'stand on their own feet' and not rely on the continued support of kin and the chief focus of attention is upon the marital relationship.

The way in which the modern nuclear family functions indirectly for the system as a whole can be seen in this analysis. This relatively isolated nuclear family system is particularly well suited to the normative requirements of a modern industrial system. Generally speaking, industrial society with its emphasis on universalism and individual achievement as a basis for filling key roles in the economic system presents a sharp antithesis to the 'ascriptive solidarity' of kinship groups.[39] Extensive obligations to kin and membership in a kinship group as a basis for role allocation is dysfunctional for the demands of an industrial system with its stress on social and geographical mobility and individual achievement as a major culturally derived motivation. The 'kinship system' of the modern USA is the one which interferes least with the demands of the occupation as a key unit of industrial society. Rodman makes the point sharply when he argues that the stress on 'free' choice in the selection of marriage partners and the relative independence of the nuclear family reflects the 'basic American value of "instrumental activism" '.[40] The values of 'achievement, mastery, efficiency and rationality' are worked out in the context of the independent, relatively isolated, nuclear family.[41] This family unit assumes, as we have seen, the prime responsibility for the emotional stabilization and growth of adult personalities.

The structure of the nuclear family

As a prelude to Parsons's analysis of the main functions of the nuclear family it is necessary to look at his account of the basic four-fold structure of this family unit. Here Parsons derives his analysis from Bales's studies of small groups in experimental settings. The tendency to role differentiation and specialization within the nuclear family reflects basic problems and their solutions faced and undertaken by all small groups. In all small groups there is a tendency for some person or persons to take on leadership roles and for others to take on more subordinate roles. In other words, small groups become differentiated on an hierarchical basis. 'Leadership', however, is an imprecise term; in particular there is also a tendency for differentiation to develop between the 'ideas' man and the man who is the 'custodian of the common task culture'.[42] The basic orientation of the 'ideas' man is towards problem solving, that is towards the attainment of tasks placed on the group by some part of its environment, that is he has an 'external' orientation. The 'custodian of the common task culture', on the other hand, is concerned with the internal integration of the group. He will, for example, attempt to resolve internal tensions and conflicts within the group (tensions which develop as it attempts to solve the externally set tasks) by such well-known mechanisms as joking, interpreting different views and so on.

In more formal terms, therefore, groups come to be differentiated along two intersecting axes: a vertical axis based on differentiation of power and an horizontal axis based on the distinction between instrumental and expressive roles. Instrumental activity is defined formally as 'the goal attainment and adaptation aspects of the coordinate system'; and expressive as 'the integrative and tension aspects of the coordinate system'.[43] Put simply, instrumental activity corresponds to our externally orientated 'ideas' man, while expressive activity is the activity associated with the 'internally' orientated 'custodian'.

The nuclear family, therefore, can be seen as a special case of this tendency of small groups to differentiate according to a four-fold role pattern. The main axes of sex and generation can be superimposed on the analytical axes of leader-follower and instrumental-expressive, as in Figure 1. The analysis of the nuclear family in terms of this four-fold role structure is a fundamental basis of Parsons's account of the socialization process and sex-role differentiation.

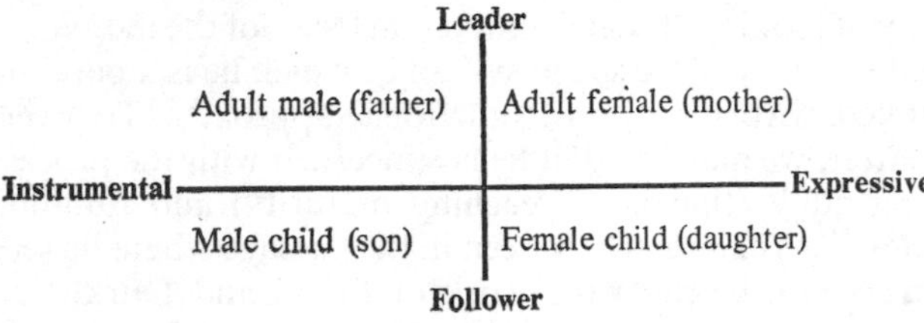

Figure 1

This is not, of course, to say that nuclear families are like small groups in experimental settings in every respect. Bales's groups were single sex and had little differentiation in terms of age. Differentiation in terms of sex and generation, on the other hand, are crucial elements in the structure of the family. Furthermore, Bales's groups were transitory, set up for the limited purposes of the experiment; families last for a long time and have change built into them. Yet Parsons argues that the insights derived from the experimental analysis of small groups can, in conjunction with other analytical tools, provide us with a key to understanding the socialization process and role specialization within the nuclear family.

The socialization process

Parsons's account of the socialization process is the most detailed and the most complex part of his overall functional analysis of the family.

It is not necessary to go into all the details of his analysis here; readers who wish to do so should consult his *Family: Socialization and Interaction Process*. The object here is to present the main points of his analysis and show how they fit into his overall functional framework.

There are several general introductory points that may be made before proceeding to an account of Parsons's analysis of the socialization process. The first is to note that socialization has two related meanings in Parsons's work. In the first place socialization refers to the internalization of a given culture as it is mediated through the nuclear family. In the second place socialization is seen from the point of the individual being socialized, as a process whereby the individual personality becomes prepared to take on an autonomous role in society. This 'two sides of the same coin' approach is a central theme in Parsons's writings on socialization; he is constantly looking in the direction of the culture and the individual personality at the same time. It should be noted that Parsons's main concern is with what is usually referred to as 'primary socialization', that is, the first, most general and most basic period of socialization that typically takes place within the nuclear family. Secondary socialization—in school and peer group for example—also receives some attention.

This dual way of looking at socialization—in terms of the individual personality and in terms of the social system of which he is a part—is very much linked with his overall functional approach. To oversimplify the matter, we may say that he is concerned with the process of becoming an adult (that is of reaching maturity) and fulfilling adult social *roles*. This can clearly be seen in the passage where he sees a fruitful convergence between the work of Freud and Durkheim. Freud's superego, he argues, can be understood in terms of a relationship between the personality and the total common culture. Freud paid little attention to the *interaction* of persons as and in a system. Durkheim, on the other hand, paid little attention to the psychological process whereby the culture is internalized by actors in a social system. We can most fruitfully apply the insights of these two theorists if we see them in terms of an interactive system (such as that between parent and child) involving cognitive, cathectic and evaluative elements, this interaction being mediated through a common culture and a common language.[44]

Thus the socialization function of the modern nuclear family operates on behalf of both the social system and the personality system. In a sense the personality system is a kind of mirror image of the experienced social system and this is amply demonstrated in Parsons's apparent fascination (some would say intoxication) with four-fold boxes within boxes, each one a sub-system of some wider system which in its turn may often be a sub-system of yet a wider system. Thus we may consider the personality as a system or as a sub-system in the family system which in its turn is a sub-system of the wider social system. It is for this reason that, in his analysis of the socialization process, Parsons does not confine himself to the cultural or social aspects of socialization (internalization of class values for example) but also devotes much space to a more or less Freudian account of psycho-sexual development.

Second, this socialization function is the prime responsibility of the nuclear family. This would be true in all cultures but, argues Parsons, the modern nuclear family is heavily specialized in this direction.

Third, Parsons sees importance in the fact that the nuclear family is typically a *small* group and suggests that a large family might represent a different kind of family system.[45] The smallness is important in that it contributes to the frequency and intensity of the interaction within the family system. He also sees importance in the 'fact' that it is differentiated in the four-fold way characteristic of all small groups as outlined in the previous sub-section. The instrumental-expressive axis will be the subject of a more detailed comment in the next section. The power dimension is of crucial importance in our analysis of the family for the children are placed in a system where 'more powerful and responsible persons are themselves integrated in the cultural value system in question'.[46] From the point of view of the child this is a very sharp difference in terms of power. Elsewhere, Parsons notes the plasticity, sensitivity and dependence of the child and sees these in combination as a 'fulcrum for applying the lever of socialization'.[47]

Fourth, this family, however, is not and never can be an isolated unit of a total system however it might seem to the child. If it were a little cultural 'island' the question of socialization—in terms of the wider system—would be much more problematic. However, in the first place, the family is linked to the wider system largely through the father's role in the occupational sphere. In the second place, families are not static entities but change over time. In particular (through the operation of the incest taboo) children grow up, become adults and form new nuclear families of their own. Thus Parsons is not concerned just to analyse the family as a system but also to see it in relation to the wider society.

We are now in a position to examine some of the main elements in Parsons's analysis of the socialization process. In the first place it is most clearly a *process*. That is to say there is an orderly and cumulative sequence of events which are followed by all persons undergoing socialization. Parsons argues that the socialization process is somewhat akin to the process of therapy. A patient enters into a relationship with the therapist. This relationship passes through several stages, permissiveness, support, denial of reciprocity and the manipulation of rewards. In very general terms it is essential for the patient to enter into a relationship with the therapist and yet, if he is to benefit from the therapy, to pass through these stages and sever his relationship with the therapist at the end.[48] Using a more homely metaphor, Parsons argues that the socialization process is like a man climbing a ladder, where he always keeps one foot on a lower rung before raising himself up to the next. However socialization is illustrated, the processual element in it should be clear and the fact that this is very definitely seen as a set of stages.

At one level Parsons can be seen as using and extending the theories of G. H. Mead. Socialization is an interactive process between the mother and the child whereby the child learns to identify with the mother and to internalize her values. Such an interaction, as we have seen, consists of cognitive, cathectic and evaluative elements. The process of socialization is a process of generalization from 'do this because mother says so' to 'do this because it is right'. Such an approach is scarcely new, and is, with some variations, shared by Mead, Piaget and, more recently, Berger and Luckmann.

What does give Parsons's approach some element of novelty is the way in which this process is formally analysed in terms of binary fission. This element appears to come from the fusion of the Meadian approach to socialization with the small group studies of Bales and his associates. Socialization is seen as a process of differentiation and 'opening out' of one's personal horizons within and ultimately beyond the four-fold structure of the nuclear family. Thus initially the child does not participate in the full family system but in the mother-child dyad, an 'authentic social system'.[49] But the mother herself is part of the wider family social system and, while initially the child identifies with the mother, the child ultimately comes to learn to make distinctions between the mother-child sub-system and the whole family system. Later, in the 'normal' process of socialization, further distinctions are made. The child comes to understand the meanings of the family 'we', the identities of 'we' siblings and sex-role differentiation and identification. The family 'we' implies a distinction between this and an external 'non-we'. Later, as the child participates more in the wider system outside the family (through peer groups and school) further binary distinctions within this outside system are made.

This process of binary fission is examined in great detail and complexity by Parsons with his familiar 'pattern variables' and two by two or four by four tables. It is not necessary to go into these details here. The important point, and here we can see the significance of Parsons's ladder metaphor, is that, in the first place, the mother is part of a wider family system and second, and later, the father is part of a wider social system external to the family. By learning to identify with and differentiate between these parents the child is being socialized not only into a family system but into a wider social system as well. This is why Parsons stresses that the family can never be a completely closed and self-sufficient social system. Essentially, Parsons is attempting to explain an apparent paradox: given the relative autonomy of the family unit as a result of the process of structural differentiation how is it possible for a child to be socialized into a social system which is wider than this family into which he is born? The main answer lies in the fact that the father, through the role of the occupation, participates in the wider social system. This is the basis of the instrumental-expressive distinction which will be examined in more detail in the next section.

The way in which Parsons incorporates Freud in his analysis of the discontinuities in the socialization process can be seen in the way in which he discusses the role of eroticism. Eroticism plays an important role in the socialization of the child. Yet the importance of eroticism creates further problems; in Parsons's terms it represents the creation of a 'pact with the devil'.[50] Eroticism is different from a 'sex interest' or a reproductive instinct. Erotic gratification for the child provides a sensitive source of conditioning. Through eroticism the child builds up a diffuse attachment to the socializing object, a 'generalization of cathexis'.[51] The socializing agent should be in a position ultimately to frustrate the child in this respect without losing control over him; this, in essence, is the Oedipal crisis.

It might appear that Parsons treats the socialization process as being a one-way one whereby the child—the socialisee—is acted upon and moulded by the adult socializing agents. While it may be a legitimate criticism of Parsons that he does in fact overstress this aspect of the socialization process, it is not true to say that he entirely ignores the importance of socialization for the parents. For one thing the children have an importance for the parents in that they enable the parents to act out the 'childish' elements in their own personality in a socially legitimate setting. Most obvious here are the important 'play' elements in socialization which are clearly a source of delight and gratification to the parents as well as to the children. Socialization is not a matter of grim and conscious duty; indeed the fact that it is pleasurable to both parties gives the process its apparent 'unplanned', inevitable quality.

Furthermore, in a passage which deserves to be read more widely, Parsons suggests some ways in which the child has meaning for the parents. The 'neonate' (the young, and as yet not fully socialized, infant) is initially a 'possession' of the family and 'specifically of the mother'.[52] It is an object of pride and is displayed and shown off. Later the child comes to be seen in terms of its future—that is the future desired by the parents—and not just in terms of its present. It is true that these accounts do not present a fully *inter*active account of the socialization process. They do, however, remind us that socialization can fulfil important functions for the parents as well as for the child and that the adults' functions as parents may reinforce their functions as spouses.

Parsons's account of the socialization process refers of course to an ideal family situation. No actual socialization process will ever conform completely to this model. Parsons does note some major sources of deviation from this model. In the first place there will be variations in the actual structure of the nuclear family as a result of differences in family size and sex composition, absence of one or both of the spouses through death, divorce and separation and possibly the close presence of other kin. How far this source of variation represents a fundamental challenge to Parsons's theory will be examined later.

Second, there may be 'deviant behaviour on the part of the socializing agents'.[53] The parents, through being too permissive or too demanding, may retard the child's maturation and successful passage through these discontinuous stages outlined above. For example, while it is true that socialization fulfils functions for the parents as well as for the children, it is possible that the former functions may be fulfilled at the expense of the latter. There may be an over-concentration on the acting out of fantasies through the child to an extent that may retard the child's personality development.

The extreme case of deviant behaviour on the part of the 'socializing' agent is of course that of incest and Parsons adds his own contribution to the long debate over the incest taboo. This is related to the problem of handling eroticism within the family, discussed earlier. At its simplest, the incest taboo prevents this erotic component from 'getting out of hand'.[54] Eroticism is permitted but controlled. The incest taboo serves the function of 'propelling' the individual from the nuclear family in two senses. In the first place the individual leaves the nuclear family to form a new one through marriage. The erotic element is positively transferred to an object outside the family of orientation. In the second place, and this is especially true for the male, it directs the individual into non-familial roles. This is through the renouncing of the erotic attachment to the mother and the transference of identification to the father who is, as we have seen, involved in the extra-familial social system. Again, therefore, we can see how the incest taboo is functional both for the individual personality and for society as a whole. It is a basic key to understanding the link between the family and the wider social world.

We have outlined the main features of Parsons's central concern with the socialization process. One important question remains: how far is this socialization process necessarily connected to the institution of the nuclear family? Parsons, while entertaining a degree of agnosticism on this point, appears to be fairly convinced that the two are almost inseparable. At one point he states that even if the family as we know it were to cease to exist we would still need a small group generically the same as the family structure to carry out this function.[55] This would be in terms of the four-fold role structure which in a structurally differentiated society enables the sub-systems to be articulated with the wider system. It would appear that modern society cannot be other than structurally differentiated in this way and that therefore there is always a problem involved in bringing new members into this wider system. Whatever may replace the nuclear family will still be faced with the same kind of problem and will still have to resolve it by developing a structure that is differentiated along the instrumental-expressive and the power axes. And in *The Social System* Parsons notes the real limits that appear to confront society in this respect:[56]

> The important point is the near universality of the limitation of variability to such narrow limits both with respect to function and to structural type. Why is not initial status-ascription made on the basis of an assessment of individual organic and personality traits? Why is not all child care and responsibility sometimes placed in the hand of specialised organs just as formal education is? Why is not the regulation of sexual relations divorced from responsibility for child care and status-ascription? Why are kinship units not patterned like industrial organisations? It is, of course, by no means excluded that fundamental changes in any or all of these respects may sometimes come about. But the fact that they have not yet done so in spite of the very wide variability of known social systems in other respects is none the less a fact of considerable importance.

Thus Parsons's answer to the question as to whether the socialization function is necessarily associated with the institution of the nuclear family would appear to be a qualified 'yes'.

Sex roles

The second most important feature of Parsons's functional analysis of the family is his discussion of the allocation of roles according to sex within the family. This has a crucial link with the discussion of socialization and with the second main function of the modern nuclear family, to provide a source of emotional support and growth for adult members of society. The fundamental key to this problem is the differentiation of leadership roles along the expressive-instrumental dimension. In Zelditch's words:[57] 'the integrative-expressive "leader" can't be off on adaptive-instrumental errands all the time'. Society needs some clear definition as to who is to play these roles.

The next inevitable question is why it is that the man should play the instrumental role and the woman the expressive role. Parsons's answer would appear to be largely in terms of biology in that the bearing and rearing of children establishes a prior close relationship between the mother and the child. Once this has happened, and given the apparent necessity for clear differentiation of roles along this axis, the rest would appear to follow.

It will have been apparent, from the discussion of the socialization process, that sex-role identification and differentiation plays a vital role in the functioning of the family. The mother role is anchored between the mother–child dyadic sub-system and the family system while the father role stands between the family system and the wider extra-familial social system. The instrumental role of the father is essential if, in Zelditch's term, the child is to be 'pried loose' from the mother–child dyad.[58] This refers to the male child for whom there is the double problem of 'emancipation'. He has to free himself both from the mother–child dyadic system and from the family system as a whole. Thus the male child in our society is subject to greater strain in the process of growing up. This, Parsons suggests, may help us understand why there is greater male participation in 'deviant' adolescent groups.

While Parsons is, as we have seen, chiefly concerned with the modern American family, he sees some support for the argument that the instrumental-expressive distinction as mapped on to the male-female roles is near universal. In this he refers to Zelditch's contribution to *Family: Socialization and Interaction Process.*[59] Zelditch himself leans heavily on the cross-cultural research carried out by Murdock. Having prepared an operational definition of 'instrumental' and 'expressive', Zelditch finds that 46 societies out of a sample of 56 are differentiated on this basis. Women play the expressive role in all 91 matrilineal societies in this sample and in 29 out of 37 of the rest. (That is patrilineal, bilateral and dual descent societies.) Zelditch looks at the exceptions in some detail and finds that many of them are at least questionable in terms of the reliability of the evidence. However, he concludes:[60] 'Since there is no instinctive reason for the 'normal' sex allocation *some* variation which is valid should be expected.' Parsons clearly feels that Zelditch's evidence supplies strong support for his own case although he is not explicitly concerned here with detailed cross-cultural analysis.

Parsons's main concern, however, is with the modern American family. Here he suggests that only one member has an occupational role and that is the adult male. (Women are involved in their expressive roles in the household and minors do not work as a central life activity.) He is expected to have a job and would probably be subject to censure if he did not have a job through no fault of his own. He is expected to be a good provider. His occupation determines the social status of the family as a whole. This, then, is the instrumental role, linking the family to the outside world and maintaining it as a viable entity in that environment. He is, as we have seen, socialized into this role through transferring his identification from the mother to the father.

There are two sources of strain in the masculine role. In the first place there is the increasing specialization of occupational life which may mean that the work is deprived of much or any intrinsic satisfaction. Second (and this presumably applies to the women as well), there is little chance of easy social intercourse—especially in mixed company—outside the family. For the adult married man, therefore, work and home form two interrelated dimensions of a single role.

The woman, in the context of the nuclear family, plays the expressive role. She is responsible for the internal maintenance of the domestic unit, the care of the children, the emotional support of her husband. In recent years, Parsons suggests, she has had some support in the performance of this role from the growing 'professionalization' of her work. Housework has now become a quasi- (and unpaid) occupation. Many of the facets of her daily work are the subject of courses at school and college, books and magazine articles. This is true not only of the more physical tasks—cooking and housework—but also of the more subtle and vital 'human relations' side of her role.

Yet there are strains in her role too. For one thing, very young children are not, according to Parsons, treated very differently on the basis of sex.[61] In the second place, there is the problem of the overall egalitarian ideology in American society to which men and women are exposed in the schools and the media. There is the possibility, therefore, of a strain between two or more conflicting expectations, one relating to her role as a woman and the other relating to her 'role' as a person. In an early paper Parsons felt that there were two directions in which the woman might be relatively emancipated. In the first place she was becoming emancipated from 'traditional and conventional restrictions on the free expression of sexual attraction and impulses'.[62] This seems to mean chiefly the adoption of the external manifestations (in terms of dress, cosmetics, etc.) of the 'glamour' role. Second, the woman can achieve some appearance of emancipation from housework through a 'common humanistic element'. This means, chiefly, the taking up of 'cultural' or other 'serious' interests. Both these forms of 'emancipation' are not, of course, running counter to the overall expressive role; rather they are a reinforcement of that role.

In more recent writings Parsons suggests that this emancipation might even go further and there is perhaps less emphasis on the strains in the woman's role. She is marrying earlier and having fewer children so that she spends less time overall in child-bearing and rearing. She is freer to take on other roles in life including paid employment outside the home. Parsons feels, however, that this work will be a job, ancillary to the main source of income, rather than a life-time career.

This differentiation of sex role is functional for the individual and for the system as a whole. He writes:[63] 'There is much evidence that this relative definiteness of status is an important factor in psychological security.' This psychological security is important not only to the parents but also to the children seeking role models. Uncertainty in sex-role definition is not only damaging to personalities but is also a threat to the social system as a whole.

Summary

It is hoped that this account of Parsons's approach to the family has shown the intimate interconnections between the various arguments, the fact that this represents part of a total theory and not a collection of separate generalizations. We find that as societies evolve they undergo a process of structural differentiation. In this process the family becomes a more separate and more specialized institution, fulfilling more specialized functions. True, the family has lost some of its traditional functions—economic (in a productive sense), educational, religious and so on—but this does not mean, contrary to what some critics might argue, that the family has become functionless or a more or less useless 'survival'. Rather it has come to specialize in the functions of 'socialization' and the emotional support of adult members of society. The family now functions more indirectly for society. It is relatively isolated and this relative isolation is functional for the demands of a modern industrial society. Yet no family stands alone. The parents, particularly the father, do not merely occupy familial roles but have roles in other parts of the wider social system as well. Furthermore, while socialization is one of the prime functions of the family, the growing child is never socialized entirely within his family; account must also be taken of the school and peer group as socializing agencies.

As a unit, and in common with all small groups, the family is differentiated along two axes: the instrumental-expressive axis and the vertical power axis. This leads to a four-fold role structure. The child is socialized within this framework, at first through intensive interaction with the mother and later through participation in the whole family system where he learns to differentiate between the sexes, between the generations and between the family and external non-family. The instrumental male leader of the family is the main anchor between the family and this external world and the male child has to be pried loose from his primary attachment to his mother and learn to identify with the father. There is therefore an intimate inter-connection between the socialization process and the division of roles between the sexes. Parsons feels that this family structure is more or less ideally suited to the tasks that it has to perform and that it is unlikely, although not impossible, that any substitute will be found.

Criticism

It will be clear that the scope of Parsons's theorizing is so great that a book could be devoted to a critique of his theories alone. Here I shall confine myself to what I consider to be the main critical points that might be levelled at his analysis. Many of the particular details could also be subjected to critical analysis by, for example, evaluating them against empirical findings but, for the most part, I shall leave these details to one side.

a The scope of his analysis As the titles of his books make clear, Parsons is seeking to outline a general theory of society and the part that the family plays in any wider system. Yet, apart from an implied evolutionism inherited largely from the classic dichotomies developed by Spencer, Durkheim, Tönnies and others and some comparative or cross-cultural references, Parsons is in fact concerned largely with the modern American family. Even where this is not made explicit (as is the case in his essays on the American family) his references are almost invariably to the modern American family. He is writing for an audience which will nod with recognition at his references to 'the bald-headed row' and 'milque-toast' husbands.

One may go further and state that Parsons is not only just concerned with the modern American family but more narrowly with the modern American *middle-class* family as Rodman, a sympathetic commentator on his work, acknowledges.[64] In his essay on the kinship system of the USA, Parsons notes the following possible exceptions to his analysis: the rural family system, the upper-class family system and the lower-class, particularly but not exclusively black, family systems. Together, one might assume, these add up to a large body of exceptions. Further, as Parsons notes few specific surveys or studies to support his analysis of the American middle-class family, one might expect that his evidence derives from a perceptive but selective interpretation based to a large degree on personal experience.

Similar doubts may be expressed in relation to Parsons's analytical approach to the four-fold role structure of the nuclear family. It has already been noted that the experimental groups on which this analytical framework is based were as far removed from family groups as it is possible to imagine, that is they were single sex, close in age, and transitory. Furthermore it is a matter of common sense observation that a considerable proportion of families do not fall into the neat symmetrical pattern of mother, father, daughter and son. There are large families which Parsons suggests may form a different social system. There are fatherless families which, in some parts of the world, form the characteristic family unit. Are *these* to be treated as possibly pathological 'deviations'? And there are families where all the children are of one sex. The last point is not necessarily a frivolous one for it has been noted that the degree of sex-role identification is affected by the structure of the 'sibling group' in terms of sex and age. Brim, the author of this study, concludes that 'cross-sex siblings will have more traits of the opposite sex than will same-sex siblings, and that this effect will be greater for the younger as contrasted with the older siblings.'[65]

It is not a complete answer to these criticisms to say that Parsons is concerned with the development of a general theory and that these empirical references should be taken as being illustrations rather than proof of this theory. The problems raised by these many exceptions to his general model are so numerous as to call the whole model into question. It may be suggested that a distinction may be made between Parsons the essayist and commentator on the American social scene and Parsons the grand theorist. In the former capacity he is often insightful, suggestive and stimulating. In many respects these insights (which should of course be examined against more systematic research) are independent of and are neither helped nor given added strength by his more abstract and systematic theorizing.

b The problem of over-systematization Perhaps one of the most frequently used words in Parsons's vocabulary is 'system'. He is concerned with establishing the intimate inter-connections between the cultural system and the personality system. It is a daring project and one which should not be dismissed out of hand for it raises some of the most difficult and fundamental problems to be faced by the social sciences. Yet it is also true that his systematic approach often raises these problems without really solving them. Is our understanding of society and personality greatly enhanced by the multitude of two-by-two or four-by-four tabulations that proliferate in the pages of *The Social System* and *Family: Socialization and Interaction Process*? Too often this appears like the mechanical application of a technique of analysis rather than the development of a comprehensive theory. There is always the danger that such analytical boxes will be created and then the author will seek round to find observations to fill them rather than to have a real dialectic between theory and research.

One aspect of this over-systematization is what Baldwin calls Parsons's 'rigid insistence upon isomorphism'.[66] This is seen in Parsons's system sub-system approach. The personality can be seen as a system but also as a sub-system in relation to the family. Similarly the family may be viewed as a system or as a sub-system of the wider social system. Sex-role differentiation and the processes of binary fission in socialization to a large extent depend upon the prior adoption of this framework for analysis. It is difficult to take exception to this framework in a general sense; the problems arise when we examine Parsons's attempts to see complete structural and functional parallels at each level. This has the effect of 'over socializing' the personality and reifying the collectivity by almost treating it as an organism like an individual personality. Thus families or organizations are treated in some respects as if they were personalities faced with similar functional problems. As Baldwin notes, 'The requirement that the four sectors of society must correspond to the father, mother, brother and sister in the stylised nuclear family seems almost completely gratuitous.'[67]

c The passive approach to socialization One unfortunate effect of this over-systematization is the tendency to treat socialization as a more or less one-way process flowing from the 'socializing' agents to the 'socialisee', the child. While the title of the main work refers to an 'interaction process' it is difficult to see any genuine *inter*action as far as socialization is concerned. The very metaphors used betray a singularly mechanical and unilateral model. The incest taboo 'propels' the individual from the nuclear family, families are 'factories' which produce human personalities, the child may be likened to a pebble 'thrown' by the fact of birth into the social 'pond'.[68] The basic attributes of the child of plasticity, sensitivity and dependence provide the 'fulcrum for applying the lever of socialization' and so on. Such metaphors at best show a strong unilateral bias and at worst betray an astonishing lack of sensitivity to human creativity and variability.

Any adequate account of socialization should adopt a truly interactive approach. While some possible components of such an approach will be elaborated later, I shall note some of the implications of this statement at this point. In the first place, the theory would take into account the fact that in spite of the great power difference between parent and child there is genuine interaction in their relationships from the earliest moments. Or there may be a 'reflexive' interaction, that is the parent interacting with herself through the child.

Thus a child may lift up his arms in order to balance himself, faced with the difference in height between his face and his mother's face. The mother may interpret this as a desire on the part of the child to be picked up and will respond accordingly. The child will then respond to this and so on.[69] Second, the process of socialization itself may flow both ways; an extreme example of this is where the children of an immigrant family, through their greater participation in the culture through school and peer group, socialize the parents into the values of the new society. Finally, in place of the dyadic and binary divisions presented by Parsons, we would replace a much more complex and dynamic system involving triadic relations between parents and siblings. This will be discussed at greater length in the chapter on Laing.

d The unitary character of the wider society The last criticism may be summed up by saying that Parsons fails to give full justice to the complex patterns of mediation that take place within the nuclear family. A similar criticism may be made of his analysis of the family in modern society. Whether we are considering the general theoretical question of the family as a sub-system or whether we are considering the specific historical question of the family in modern industrial society it still appears that there is little mediation between the family and the 'outside world'. There are no classes, no regions, no religious, ethnic or status groups, no communities.[70] The outside world is treated as an undifferentiated environment in which the family is placed.

e The static approach All the foregoing points, in one way or another, underlie what is perhaps the most common criticism levelled at Parsons, namely his apparent 'static' bias. 'Static' may, itself, have a variety of meanings. In the first place it may mean an absence of movement. Up to a point Parsons may be acquitted of this charge. He recognizes that the family is an institution which has change built into it, that members grow up, leave the family, form other families, die and so on. While, as we have seen, it is possible to criticize Parsons on the basis that his movement is all in one direction, he cannot be properly criticized for a static approach in the sense of a lack of movement.

In the second place, 'static' may mean 'ahistorical'. Here the critics are on stronger ground. It is true that Parsons places the family of today in a broadly evolutionary perspective and is aware of the changes that the family has undergone over time. But a truly historical approach takes account not merely of change but the specific cultural circumstances of that charge. Gross categories such as 'industrial society' which do not take into account the variety of historical experiences encompassed under that label tend to become empty and likely to obscure rather than to illuminate. This was, in effect, the burden of the last criticism. To analyse the family as a sub-system within a larger social system is in effect to prejudice the issue and to argue that it is of relative unimportance what the particular historical experiences were that shaped any particular interrelationship between an institution and its context.

There is a third meaning of static and one which is perhaps more important than either of the other two. It can be said that Parsons's work is static in that it ignores the *potentiality* for change. Here we are constantly left with the impression that what is *must* be because of the vital functions which are being fulfilled. It is possible, but not very likely, that a substitute to the nuclear family might be found, but it would have to have more or less the same sort of four-fold role structure. Some marginal adjustments to the position of women may be possible but that cannot go very far; a 'job' rather than a 'career'. That Parsons shows little concern for the range of human variability and potentiality is illustrated in the following passage:[71]

> Put very schematically, a mature woman can love, sexually, only a man who takes his full place in the masculine world, above all in its occupational aspect, and who takes responsibility for a family; conversely the mature man can only love a woman who is really an adult, a full wife to him and a mother to his children, and an adequate 'person' in her extra-familial roles.

Such a quotation appears to betray an almost dehumanized and mechanical view of sexual relationships. It also appears to undermine any possible criticisms one would wish to make of the present 'occupational system' and the way in which it may possibly undermine and threaten human (including sexual) relationships rather than to enhance them. It is true that Parsons and his associates occasionally give recognition to the possibility of alternative ways of doing things. Thus 'For simplicity we will refer to mother and child but recognize that "agent of care" is the essential concept and that it need not be confined to one specific person: it is the function which is essential.'[72] However, such possible alternatives are never seriously explored and the total impact of the work is to provide a justification for the prevailing family and economic system.

f Sex roles Perhaps the sharpest illustration of Parsons's static approach and the one most open to criticism (certainly from the feminist movement) is his approach to sex roles.[73] It is here that his oversimplified mapping of the expressive-instrumental differentiation on to the sex differences leads him to making some of his most questionable statements. In this analysis, Parsons does claim the support of empirical evidence in the form of Zelditch's cross-cultural comparison. The chief findings have already been noted; here we will make some criticisms of Zelditch's overall approach. In the first place there is the often-discussed weaknesses of this kind of cross-cultural evidence. We have the problems of the reliability of the initial evidence, the comparability of different pieces of work and the categories used and the reliability of the chosen sample. At the very least cross-cultural material of the kind that Zelditch is using must be treated with a degree of critical discrimination. Here Zelditch adopts a rather curious procedure. When he finds exceptions to the predicted patterns he subjects these exceptions to more detailed critical scrutiny. In some cases he finds that we may have reason to suspect the original data. I am prepared to accept his critical notes on the work of, say, Margaret Mead; the point is he does not subject (or is not seen to be subjecting) the findings which support his case to the same critical scrutiny.

Zelditch's study does at least note these apparent exceptions in some detail and does not attempt to explain them all away in terms of inadequate data. There is some indication, further, that he is prepared to remove any element of necessity about the relationship between instrumental-expressive and male-female. Thus he writes:[74] 'if mother's brother is called a "male mother" the content of these two roles will be assumed equivalent.' And in a passage already quoted he argues that there is no 'intrinsic' reason for this identification. Parsons also does not appear to be completely convinced of the necessity of this relationship but merely notes that as a result of biology and (presumably) long centuries of cultural conditioning any alternative arrangements seem unlikely.

But is the expressive-instrumental distinction all that meaningful or valid in the first place? Is it true that clarity is required in this respect and that one cannot perform both roles? In this argument there are at least two definitions. In the first place there are the formal definitions which have already been given. In the second place there are the 'operational' definitions which are used as intermediaries between the 'raw data' and the concepts. Thus Ego will be considered the 'instrumental' leader of the nuclear family if the reports show him to be 'boss-manager of the farm, leader of the hunt etc. Ego is the final court of appeals, final judge and executor of punishment, discipline, and control over the children of the family'.[75] Similarly, the 'expressive' leader is 'the mediator, conciliator, of the family; Ego is affectionate, solicitous, warm, emotional to the children of the family; Ego is the "comforter" the "consoler", is relatively indulgent, relatively unpunishing'.[76] Zelditch recognizes that many ethnographic reports might be a little imprecise on these details and so offers a variety of more direct indices. Thus, for example, Ego will be considered as the instrumental leader if 'Alter shows respect to ego; the relations of ego and alter are constrained, reserved: alter on occasions indicates hostility towards ego'.[77] Again the difficulties of evaluating ethnographic material on this basis must be enormous. However, it may be suggested that in introducing this further indirect index an element that was not in the original definitions has been introduced, namely one of hierarchy between the instrumental and the expressive leader.

Slater makes some telling criticisms of the 'instrumental-expressive' distinction although his case is weakened by a tendency, in at least part of his argument, to equate this distinction with the extent to which strictness or leniency is demonstrated. Thus strictness is equated with an instrumental orientation, leniency with an expressive orientation. Such an interpretation could possibly be drawn from Zelditch's paper (thus reflecting again on some of the inherent vagueness in the distinction) but is surely not the main point of the distinction. Slater doubts whether the distinction as a whole is all that meaningful and questions whether there is necessarily an opposition between the two such that one individual cannot perform both types of role. He also suggests that socialization and personality development is, in modern American society, likely if anything to be retarded where there is a sharp division between father and mother along this dimension. Possibly this instrumental-expressive distinction was a thing of the past and that we are now moving towards what he describes as a 'de-differentiated family'.[78] We may accept that any social entity has problems of fulfilling the tasks that are required of it (although it is not always easy to determine what these tasks are) that is it has the 'external' problems of relating to its environment. We may also accept, for the sake of argument at least, that the same group will be faced with 'internal' problems, that is, problems of creating and maintaining harmony and co-operation within the unit. If we accept this (and I am not personally convinced of the usefulness of stating the problem in these terms) a variety of possibilities are opened up. First, *both* functions can be performed by one person. Zelditch merely asserts that this cannot be the case but does not offer any substantial proof for this assertion. Slater notes, on the other hand, 'In many cultures one parent, usually the mother, is both more expressive (nurturant) and more instrumental (demanding).'[79]

Slater also suggests that small group studies show a positive rather than a negative correlation between the two roles. Second, some *tasks* may be a mixture of expressive and instrumental functions. It may be suggested that the consumption activities of the modern nuclear family contain a mixture of expressive and instrumental functions. Third, these functions may be performed by different people at different times, according to the demands of the situation. In other words there is a clear differentiation of *functions* but not of persons associated with these functions. Dual-career families may represent a possible example of this kind of pattern. Finally, individuals may specialize in the performance of these kinds of roles, that is the pattern suggested by Parsons and Zelditch. But it must be stressed that this is only one possible pattern and there is little evidence to suggest that this is a necessary pattern. Certainly we cannot necessarily say that this fourth pattern is inevitably associated with sex differences.

When it comes to discussing the distribution of roles according to sex, therefore, Parsons appears to take what *is* as an indication of what, almost certainly, *must* be. It is true that he never quite commits himself to a statement of this kind but it is also true that he never seriously considers any alternative patterns. This is seen most clearly when Parsons examines the directions along which 'emancipation' might take place. For the most part these represent an elaboration, perhaps even an intensification, of the expressive role:[80]

> This situation helps perhaps to account for a conspicuous tendency for the feminine role to emphasize broadly humanistic rather than technically specialized achievement values. One of the key patterns is that of 'good taste' in personal appearance, house furnishings, cultural things like literature and music. To a large and perhaps increasing extent the more humanistic cultural traditions and amenities of life are carried on by women. Since these things are of a high intrinsic importance in the scale of values of our culture, and since by virtue of the system of occupational specialisation even many highly superior men are greatly handicapped in respect to them, there is some genuine redressing of the balance between the sexes.

This woman is still with us; in the advertisements of the Sunday supplements. It may be a little unfair to evaluate this passage, written in 1943, from the standpoint of the feminist movements of the 1970s although it is likely that even thirty years ago this passage might have seemed a little quaint. What is alarming here is the limitations of the author's cultural horizons. This picture might have been appropriate for some 'university wives' but it offers little or no hope for emancipation on the part of 'blue collar' wives, later to be analysed in depth by Komarovsky.

The limits of Parsons's emancipation seem to be at the level of a 'job' rather than a career. Again, as in the case of his analysis of the socialization process, social actors are playing their part according to some prearranged script. They passively respond to societal demands rather than critically and creatively assess and perhaps negate these demands. The possibility of the enlargement of human choice, the transcendence of the 'given', is not given any serious attention in Parsons's approach to the family. Societies may change but human actors, either individually or collectively, seem to have little part in the direction of that change.

g Parsons's optimism Such an approach might lead us to suppose that sociology had replaced economics as the 'dismal science' were it not for the fact that Parsons's account is permeated with an overall optimism and faith in the American system. It is true that there will be strains, tensions and deviations but there appears to be nothing that society cannot handle. Contradictions, or even serious dysfunctions, do not make an appearance in his work. The optimism can be seen in his faith that the strains in the woman's role can be overcome through the adoption of the 'glamour' or 'humanistic' styles of life. A similar optimism can be seen in his treatment of the position of old people in society. In the Parsonian world the young are encouraged to leave their family of orientation and strike out on their own. The major anchor of status and identification (both directly for the male and indirectly for the family as a whole) is the occupation, a basis of identity which is terminated on retirement. Furthermore, people are living longer. However, Parsons argues that now, on retirement, people are freer to take on new functions: 'A society which has been increasing its "production" of older people has at the same time been creating an increasing demand for their contributions.'[81] What he has in mind here are what he calls 'fiduciary and cultural' functions. Examples here may be 'judges and religious functionaries' and part-time or full-time positions on boards of directors. Again, at the very least, we see the limitations of Parsons's cultural horizons which do not seem to include the poor or even the only moderately well-off members of society. Again, also we see Parsons's faith in the self-regulating character of the American system, a system which may have problems but no contradictions.

There is, however, one point where Parsons indicates clearly the possible dysfunctional aspects of the modern American family. This is in a paper, written in collaboration with Renee C. Fox, on 'Illness, Therapy and the Modern Urban American Family'.[82] In this paper they point to some similarities between the position of the sick person and the position of the child in the family. The sick person is unable to perform his normal (adult) role. He needs to be cared for. There is a 'passive withdrawal' and the 'state of illness is partially and conditionally legitimised'.[83] This state is conditional because the patient is under an obligation to get well and to seek and accept professional care. If sickness can be seen as a way of opting out of one's role in the family then it is possible that to care for the sick person within the family might reinforce this process. This is because 'the American family apparently operates at high levels of emotional intensity'.[84] Family members are likely to over-react to sickness in one of two ways: they may either exaggerate the extent to which the member is ill and so reinforce his identity as a sick person or they may play down the seriousness of the illness and say that 'it is nothing really'. For this reason the family should most appropriately seek detached professional help outside in the care of its sick members.

Up to a point this paper may be seen as an illustration of the differentiation theme. The institution of the family is specialized in certain directions and other institutions (such as professional medical care) enter to take care of other functions. But the paper also reveals the potential instability of the modern American family. In the face of a relatively common occurrence such as illness, the family is shown to be extraordinarily vulnerable. The family, small and relatively isolated, is shown as an institution putting all its emotional resources into one basket. There is little leeway for it to cope with emotionally charged situations such as illness. In any other context this might be seen as a possible indictment of the modern nuclear family. In the context of Parsons's work it is an illustration of the inter-dependence between the family and other institutions.[85]

We end, therefore, with what may be seen as evidence of a critical component within Parsons's functional approach to the family. Other possible latent dysfunctions are to be found in his work as, for example, where he notes how the child may be treated as a 'thing' or a 'possession' by his parents. Elsewhere he refers to the American family as being in 'a delicate state of balance and integration with the rest of the social structure'.[86] The possibilities for an analysis in terms of contradictions are present in the functionalist analysis: had Parsons pursued his analysis along these lines his contribution to the study of the family, already considerable, might have been the more impressive and the more abiding.

Bell and Vogel

Bell and Vogel present a functionalist interpretation of the family which lies firmly within the Parsonian tradition. The reason for a separate reference here is that they give particular emphasis to the interchanges between the family as a system and other aspects of the social system. This approach is itself derived from the joint writings of Parsons and Smelser. They stress that their model, used as a framework for a collection of articles, is tentative and preliminary.

Bell and Vogel specify that in talking about the family they are dealing with the socially recognized categories of mother, father and child. Their chief focus therefore is on the nuclear family. In common with Parsons they accept the structural differentiation thesis and the argument that we may look at the social system, the family as a system and the personality as a system and that one must be careful to specify the level at which one is operating. Thus it is possible to consider the family as a system concerned with the problems

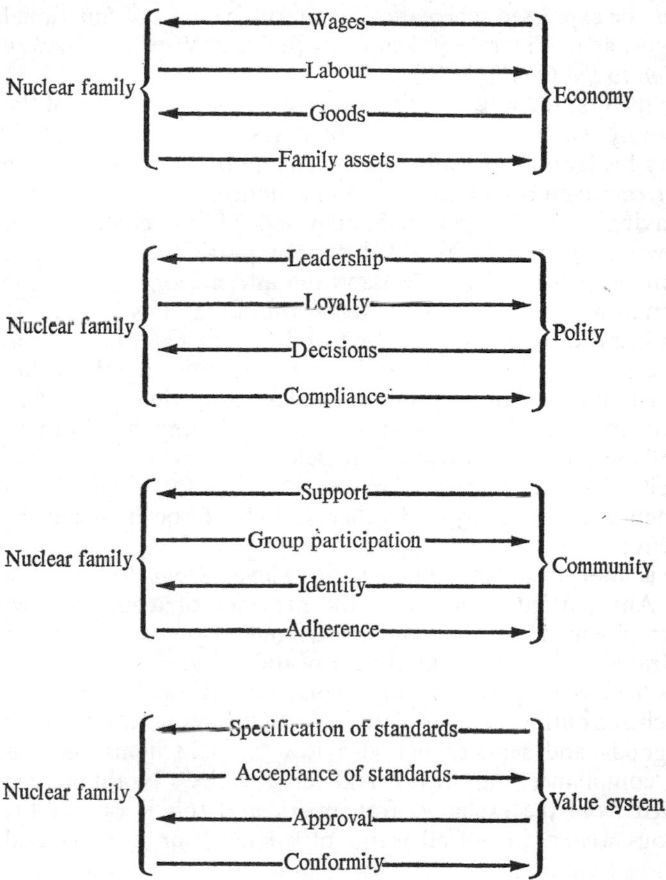

Figure 2

of task performance, family leadership, integration and solidarity of the family system and also to consider the personality as a system concerned with essentially the same problems. Thus the extent to which the father performs his role especially associated with the task performance problem (close to the instrumental role of Parsons) can be considered in terms of the functioning of his individual personality or the functioning of the system as a whole. Again we have a set of inter-connected boxes, although presented in simpler terms to those used by Parsons. At the societal level the basic problems of adaptation, goal gratification, integration and pattern maintenance can be identified by the institutions of the economy, the polity, the community and the value system respectively. The relationship between the family and these other institutions of society may be expressed schematically in terms of a set of functional interchanges, as in Figure 2 (taken from Bell and Vogel, *A Modern Introduction to the Family*, p.10).

To take the first set of transactions as an example, a member of the nuclear family works in the occupational system for wages. He is exchanging his labour for wages. In the sphere of consumption, the family (or one member of the family) exchanges the family assets (wages, savings, etc.) for goods. Similar sets of interchanges take place between the family as a sub-system participating in these transactions with the wider system and the internal workings of the family seen as a system. Most activities within the family have functional significance for the family itself and for the external system. A simple example is that of the father who occupies a role within the nuclear family and in the economy and a change in one (such as unemployment) will affect his position and functioning in the other.

Some of the difficulties involved in Bell and Vogel's approach—and indeed with other approaches emphasizing functional interchanges between the family and other sectors of society—may be listed briefly:

1 The isomorphism between the various levels seems to be a little too easy. Any particular problem—the presence of a maladjusted child, unemployment, divorce, retirement and so on—can be fitted into this framework with the minimum of difficulty.

2 This 'catch-all' quality is particularly underlined in the transactional scheme outlined above. Entering into this model are not only tangible goods and services but also less tangible items such as 'loyalty', 'compliance', 'approval' and 'conformity'. Nothing need be excluded from the exchange framework and this is one of the most serious weaknesses of all forms of exchange or transactional theory.

3 The reification of the entities, somewhat arbitrarily constructed in the first place, is particularly problematic. We need to ask in what meaningful sense can we say that the economy, the polity and the community and the value system are meaningfully bounded entities which can enter into this transactional system? How, for example, can the value system 'give' approval?

4 Similar problems, of course, arise when we consider the family as a bounded unit in this transactional scheme. They recognize that the interchanges may take place either with the family itself or an

individual acting on behalf of the family. This is a necessary qualification but one which seriously calls into question the whole framework which to a large part depends upon bounded or boundary-maintaining entities.

At best it can be said that Bell and Vogel, following a broadly Parsonian approach, have alerted us to the interconnectedness between the family and 'outside' entities and the way in which these interconnections have repercussions within the family itself. At worst the approach may be said to reify social entities and to mystify family relationships. In all fairness, however, it must be said that they provide us with one of the most useful collection of papers in the field and that the authors themselves recognize the tentativeness of their enquiry.

Goode

If Bell and Vogel follow Parsons particularly in attempting to trace the interconnectedness between the family sub-system and other systems/sub-systems, Goode follows Parsons largely in terms of the structural differentiation model. Here, however, Goode attempts to trace family changes and developments throughout the whole world. But Goode's functionalism is more an overall article of faith[87] than a commitment to the development of a fully articulated functional model.

Goode's functionalism has two major aspects. In the first place he provides a list of the basic functions of the family, somewhat akin to Murdock's original list.[88] We have already discussed the difficulties of listing functions in this way.[89] In the second place he adopts a more Mertonian approach to functionalism and argues that when one talks of the 'function of Y' we mean the *consequence* of Y in increasing or lowering the value of X.[90]

This approach is clearly much looser than harder versions of functionalism and Goode deploys it as a methodological directive in the investigation of a wide variety of problems. These are essentially problems of the 'middle range' and include such areas as the relationship between illegitimacy and the social structure, the pressures on a divorcee to remarry, the theoretical importance of love and, at a more general level, the relationships between industrialization and the family. If Parsons is the major theorist of the sociology of the family, Goode is its major craftsman and no discredit to Goode is intended in the use of the label.

It is unlikely that sociology will ever be without this mode of theorizing, nor is it necessary that it should be free of this style of approach. Indeed, in so far as his approach almost ironically demonstrates the relativity and historical contingency of such institutions as the conjugal family, love and divorce, it continues a strong critical stream that has never been entirely absent from sociological enquiry.[91] Yet the approach also implies an underlying conservatism at the same time. While Goode seeks to avoid the equation 'functional equals necessary' the overall picture is one of a highly interconnected social system where, at any one time, there are few alternatives between major social upheavals and marginal adjustments. This, coupled with the positivistic externalist stance implied in functional analysis, in practice is likely to be supportive of any existing social system rather than the reverse.

Goode's analysis of the relationship between the family and the industrialization process is perhaps most widely known as it has been reprinted in several places. While here Goode is dealing with society at a much more general level the same kind of functional argument can be clearly seen. Stated very briefly, Goode argues that throughout the world there is a tendency for the process of industrialization to be accompanied by the move towards what he calls the 'conjugal type' of family. He outlines the main features of this type of family, recognizing that it is an ideal typical abstraction: 'The most important characteristic of the ideal typical construction of the conjugal family is the relative exclusion of a wide range of affinal and blood relatives from its everyday affairs.'[92] The tendency is towards neolocality, there is a freer choice of mate, the descent system is multilineal and so on. We are familiar with the broad outlines of this family system as it corresponds very broadly with Parsons's relatively isolated nuclear family. Goode does however stress that this family system cannot be stripped right down to its nuclear bones but that grandparents will still have an important part to play.

Goode argues that there is a degree of fit or congruence between this family system and the process of industrialization. Again the main outline of the argument is familiar from Parsons's essentially similar account. However, Goode adds several important qualifications. In the first place he is careful not to assign any necessary causal priority to either the changes in the family or to industrialization. Second, he points out that change will take place at different paces and from different starting points. Thus the industrialization process may be associated with a fall in the age of marriage in some parts of the world and a rise in the age of marriage in other parts. Third, Goode assigns some importance to the impact of ideology which may have an independent or intervening effect.

Goode's analysis, partly as a result of the many qualifications and cautions that he introduces, is characterized by a certain vagueness. This vagueness is enhanced by the rather general use of the term 'industrialization' and the way in which it becomes blurred with bureaucratization and urbanization. What is left after going through his impressive collection of material from throughout the world is some fairly indefinite notion of fit between the two but little else.

In general many of the problems associated with Parsonian functionalism may also, but to a markedly lesser degree, be associated with the work of Goode. There is the tendency to a relatively optimistic equilibrium model,[93] a tendency to underplay possible contradictions and dysfunctions and the problem that functionalism often leads to statements which are difficult to either prove or disprove. The relative lack of systematization in Goode makes this last problem a particularly thorny one. However, these weaknesses are counterbalanced by a stronger sense of empirical and comparative material and a recognition of the importance of features such as the class structure in the analysis of the relationships between the family and society.

Vogel and Bell

We have already considered the overall functional framework within which Bell and Vogel present their collection of papers. However, included among this collection is a paper by the editors which reflects a different style of functional analysis.[94] The object here is not to present the details of the particular problem under examination but to use this paper as an illustration of a slightly different style of functional theorizing to the ones that have been considered up to now. On the whole this paper may be seen as an example of 'partial' functionalism; that is a functionalist orientation is used to attack a particular problem without being over-concerned with the wider implications of a functionalist model.

Very briefly, the authors consider the ways in which a particular child in the family—an emotionally disturbed child—can be used as a scapegoat between parents. They outline some of the sources of tension which lead to this scapegoating process (perhaps the parents come from different ethnic backgrounds) and the way in which a particular child is selected as a scapegoat. A typical example of this scapegoating procedure is where one parent encourages one sort of behaviour and the other parent encourages the opposite form of behaviour. The child will become induced to taking on a scapegoat role and hence reinforce the likelihood that this role will continue.

Vogel and Bell consider some of the possible functions and dysfunctions of this scapegoating process. On the functional side, the scapegoating process helped to stabilize relationships between the parents by diverting the tension between them on to the child. This enabled the parents to live up to the standards set by the wider society in terms of their roles 'as steady workers and relatively respectable community workers'.[95] But perhaps the family did not live up to the standards as satisfactorily as other members of the community and so the family might become in its turn a scapegoat for the community as a whole. The scapegoating enabled the family to maintain its overall solidarity.

At the same time certain dysfunctions are created. The child—if he is a bed-wetter, for example—may require special care and attention. Further, the child may fight back and put further strains on other members of the family, particularly the mother. This may lead to the family seeking professional help. Outside the family, the dysfunctions of the child become even more apparent particularly in the school situation, for example. Finally the presence of a disturbed child may ultimately act back on the parents in such a way as to exacerbate their original conflict. The parents may start to blame each other for the child's disturbance and so on. Vogel and Bell conclude: 'In short, the scapegoating mechanism is functional for the family as a group but dysfunctional for the emotional health of the child and for his adjustment outside the family of orientation.'[96]

What Vogel and Bell demonstrate here is that a functionalist approach can be used usefully to examine particular problems if certain things are borne in mind. In the first place it is necessary to specify the 'for whom' or 'for what' in any statements about function. In the second place it is necessary to specify the dysfunctions—again making clear 'for whom' or 'for what'—of any given pattern of action. It is true, however, that there is still a somewhat arbitrary air about the whole procedure and it may in clumsier hands lead to a recitation of 'the good news and bad news'. Finally, it is clear that the adoption of this mode of approach does not necessarily commit the author to an overall functional view of society.

A note on role theory and functionalism

Role theory, in common with functional theory, has had a key part to play in the development of sociological theory in general and in the sociology of the family in particular. Yet, also in common with functionalism, its central position is now much less secure and some sociologists are arguing either that we should severely delimit the problem areas encompassed by role theory[97] or that we should abandon the concept altogether.[98] Furthermore, it would appear that there are as many versions of role theory as there are of functional theory and that many of the problems associated with the latter are also to be found in the former.[99]

Very generally it may be argued that there are two main strands in the development of role analysis. The first strand emphasizes role in terms of positions in the social structure, the way in which these positions are articulated and integrated into the social system and the way in which individual actors are selected for or socialized into these roles. This form of role theory is clearly congruent with and often part of a wider functional theory. On the other hand, particularly in the work of Goffman, there is the more literal interpretation of the dramaturgical metaphor, the focus on the social actor playing his role, in some ways creating his role, in different situations. The focus here is more on the self and the presentation of that self although the element of constraint, central to the first version of role theory, is scarcely absent. To oversimplify considerably, the first version concentrates on the script while the second version concentrates on the player.

In one of the most interesting recent attempts to develop a theoretical approach to the family, Ralph Turner tries to integrate these two strands of role theory.[100] He is critical of functionalist approaches to the family, particularly of the way in which functional theory is insensitive to the rich variations in the patterns of family living, while recognizing the contribution that functionalism has made to the study of the family and, in common with other authors, while being prepared to list the functions of the family. A key distinction he makes is between viable roles and functional roles.[101] The use of the former term (the term derives from games theory) is intended to convey the notion of the actor in the family situation actively seeking to create the best position possible in the existing structure of domination and with the social resources available. This term is introduced in recognition of the fact that the functional roles (as developed, for example, by Parsons and Bales) give us little insight into what is actually *done*. Families, surrounded by a wall of privacy, have a strong tendency to develop unique systems of roles, worked out according to a process of bargaining. The functional roles, as it were, provide some of the basic raw social material but the viable roles represent these positions being actually worked out in a day to day process of bargaining, conflict and accommodation. The actor is given a fair degree of leeway in this process and there is a constant process whereby the functional roles are interpreted through the viable roles.

Turner's aim is clearly to provide a sociology of the family that is closer to the way in which the family is actually experienced by its members and which does justice to the considerable variation that exists in family forms and family interactions. In many respects he is successful in this aim. He gives close attention to the sources of conflict within the family and the ways by which conflict is conducted and resolved. He notes that socialization is not merely the establishment of patterns of conformity but also creates diversity. He has a useful section where he examines the strains in the conventional sex roles, particularly in the dilemmas associated with masculinity. Yet in spite of all this the overall perspective still remains largely within the functional paradigm with analyses of strains and conflicts rather than contradictions and with an underlying notion of equilibrium, derived in part from his interactional framework and its emphasis on reciprocity.

It is likely, therefore, that role theory in whatever form it may take is likely to give particular emphasis to the constraints over human conduct and hence to have close affinities with functional analysis. It is not intended to deny that such constraints exist in society and that it is important to recognize not merely how actors conform to these constraints but also how, in a more active sense, they *use* these constraints in order to evolve a more viable role. However, it is also important to examine the historical source of these constraints (as, for example, in the discussion of the roles of men and women) and with this the possibility of active control and change before role theory in the version offered by Turner can realize its critical promise.

Conclusion

The aim of this chapter has been to illustrate selectively some of the varieties of theoretical approaches that might be grouped under the general label 'functionalist'; in particular I am interested in presenting those theoretical approaches that have received fairly wide currency through their incorporation into textbooks. I hope that I have demonstrated that the term 'functionalist' can encompass a total theory (as in the case of Parsons) or a relatively looser orientation (as with the writings of Goode). Other writers differ in their degrees of 'hardness' and in the scope of their theories.

It might be thought that the differences between these theories are so great that it becomes almost meaningless to gather them all together under the overall label 'functionalists'. It will be noted, for example, that there is little agreement as to what the 'basic' functions of the family are, how many there are and to the extent and way in which they might or might not have changed. Yet it can also be argued that all these approaches, however various and even contradictory they might seem, present certain similar problems. Very generally, I shall group these problems under three headings: functionalism as an explanation, the problem of the relationship between the part and the whole and the political theory of functionalism.

1 The problem of functional explanations has been discussed at great length in the literature and it is not intended to provide an extensive treatment here. Very generally, the difficult problem that all functionalist theories of the family (or indeed of anything else)

are faced with is that the 'functions' are rarely unambiguous or obvious. The family is not a formal organization and there is no clearly laid down organizational charter telling people what the family is 'for'. If you ask people why they form families or what their family is for it is unlikely that you will be given a response in terms of its functions. Most likely, the 'explanation' given will be in terms of notions of tradition, morality or 'nature'. In the study of the functions of the family it might be said that all the functions are 'latent' functions. In making a statement that institution X performs a particular function in terms of Y, the sociologist is making a statement which is not open to either verification or falsification. It may seem plausible or few people might dissent from it but this is not the same as explaining a particular practice or institution.

Let us take the example of 'socialization'. All the theorists mentioned here would agree that this is one of the functions that the family performs and has always performed. However, there are difficulties here. It is true that all families perform the socialization function because, first, socialization is almost built into the definition of the family and, second, most people are or have been born and brought up in families. To elaborate the first point, if we define the family in terms of the socially recognized categories of mother, father, daughter and son we are already presupposing a high degree of socialization. And the second point implies that if people were brought up under some other institutional arrangements (say a commune), then socialization would be the function of that institution as well as or instead of the family. Further, while we may argue that all families perform the socialization function the converse is not necessarily true, i.e. that all socialization is performed by families. The functionalist explanation, therefore, poses one further question: why has this particular function (which all would agree is essential for society, indeed is part of any definition of society) become generally associated with the institution of the family? Most of the functionalists mentioned would probably concede that this is not a necessary law-like relationship (although the whole emphasis of the functionalist arguments often leads one to suppose otherwise) but remain on the whole unclear as to what the basis of this relationship is. And a similar kind of argument could be presented in relation to any of the postulated 'functions' of the family.

2 What all the functionalist accounts presented in this chapter have in common is the fact that they are concerned with the relationship between a part and a whole. The functions of the family are in terms of the wider society of which it is a part or possibly in terms of the members which are part of the family. Clearly any functional account must clearly specify the parts and the wholes very carefully and in many cases this has been done. However, we are faced with a

difficulty when it comes to defining the boundary of a whole. What, for example, are the empirical referents of Parsons's social system? In practice it would appear that his social system can be equated with the USA or any other national unit. However, the boundaries which the sociologist assigns, and must assign if he is conducting a functional analysis, are not necessarily the boundaries which would be assigned by the actors in the social situation under investigation.[102] Thus the individual may think in terms of his class, his community, his ethnic group, the Western world and so on. The part-whole relationship constructed by the actor (a relationship which may fluctuate according to circumstances) may not coincide with the part–whole relationship constructed by the functionalist. There is always, to some extent, an element of arbitrariness in the assignment of functions which attempt to relate a part to a whole. This is particularly clear in the case of the analysis of socialization where, as Danziger notes: 'The very term . . . seems to posit society as the goal-setter and active principle, leaving the individual as something that is worked upon, more or less successfully.'[103]

3 This raises the last general critical point which might be directed against these theories, that is in terms of their meaning as *political* theories. In making this point I am arguing that all social theories, however explicitly 'ideological' or 'value-free', have a political dimension. By this I mean that directly or indirectly, social theories give support to particular images of man and his position in society which are more or less conducive to change in that relationship. This is not to say that theories are, or ought to be, programmatic in the sense of outlining various things that ought to be done. What I am saying, and this is no novelty, is that the major theoretical streams in the social sciences in some way reflect on the ability of man actively to change his condition either by stressing the limits to that ability (as in the case with most social science) or the potentiality. Such theories also reflect on the ways in which man might change or be changed. Such a general statement is of course clearly true of racially based theories of man or behaviourism and is also true of functionalism.

In this context we may examine the alleged 'conservative' bias of Parsons or many functionalists. It is no answer to argue, as Hacker does, that Parsons is, in fact, politically a liberal.[104] It is highly likely that all the theorists we have considered are or were liberals in terms of the American political spectrum. What we are concerned with is the impact of the theories in terms of the wider definition of politics in the last paragraph. And here we can argue that functionalist theories of the family would fall at the conservative end of the spectrum in a variety of respects. In the first place they give emphasis to the limits of human activity rather than the potentialities. While they do not argue that function equals necessity there is, at the very least, a strong presupposition that functional equals highly important. There is an overall emphasis on harmony and equilibrium with a relatively small amount of attention given to dysfunctions or contradictions. At the very least, both aspects require equal attention, and, as the quotation from Danziger suggests, the theories tend to give priority to society or to the system as being the ultimate justification for a particular practice or institution. Even change, as we note in Goode's account of the family and industrialization, tends to be something which happens *to* people rather than something in which they can take an active, if perhaps not fully comprehending part.

It is unlikely that we shall ever do completely without functionalism. I hope that, in spite of the many serious criticisms that may be made of these theories in general and in their particulars, I have emphasized some of the merits of these theories. Certainly functionalism as a general approach can lead us into exploring hitherto unconsidered relationships, or explaining surprising findings. I have noted the possible critical element in some functional and role theories. As a mode of disciplined approach it has produced some useful and stimulating results—the work of Merton and Goode probably illustrates this at its best. I see the business of sociology as being that of understanding rather than explanation and in this process of understanding, functionalism may play a part but perhaps not the whole or even the main part.

2 Why kinship?

Introduction

We now shift from problems of macro-theory in the study of the family to an example of a problem of 'middle-range' theorizing. It is certainly not my intention to argue that the problem discussed in this chapter—the problem of the nature and significance of kinship in modern urban society—is the sole possible example of this level of theory. However, it is an important one and one which derives to some extent from the larger scale issues discussed in the previous chapter. It is a debate which has received full coverage in most of the texts and readers and is also one which raises important questions beyond the initial terms of reference. In its simplest terms this debate deals with the extent to which kin outside the immediate nuclear family have lost their significance in urban, industrial society. Is it at all meaningful to talk of a kinship or an extended family *system* in modern society? Or, conversely, is the relatively isolated conjugal family the typical family unit in modern society? This is not merely an academic debate; it has implications for many aspects of social policy including housing and urban redevelopment, the condition of old people in modern society and the re-location of industry. This chapter will examine some of the arguments on either side of this debate and will attempt to provide an overall evaluation. It is not my intention to provide a comprehensive survey of the literature but, rather, to concentrate on certain representative figures in the debate. The main argument is that these studies of kinship have on the whole become divorced from major issues in the sociology of the *family* and that this divorce has been to the detriment of the theoretical development of the field.

To a certain extent the debate was originally rooted in one of the central concerns of sociology in its historical development, the attempt to understand the fundamental changes that took place in

European society in the late eighteenth and early nineteenth centuries, the changes usually associated with the growth of capitalism, industrialization and urbanization. For Marx the main concern was the growth of classes and class antagonism, the worker selling his labour power to the capitalist. In such a society, a family-based economy would be an anachronism, something marginal and irrelevant to the main lines of historical development. The effect of capitalism was to weaken not only kinship ties and relationships but the institution of the family itself. Weber, similarly, traced the process of rationalization (partially associated with the growth and spread of the Protestant ethic) whereby the rational systematic deployment of labour replaced traditional ties and nepotism. Durkheim's model of organic solidarity stressed a society held together through mutual interdependence and the division of labour, and mediating between the individual and society were occupational or professional groupings rather than locally based communities or kinship units. The conjugal bond strengthened as the wider familial and kinship ties dwindled in some scope and significance.[1] All the major dichotomies which have become central concepts in sociology—community and association, traditional and rational, folk and urban—emphasize in different ways the dwindling importance of ties based upon blood or kinship and their replacement by more indirect, secondary and impersonal ties. Wirth's celebrated essay on urbanism as a way of life showed the development of urban society based on size, density and heterogeneity leading to an emphasis on secondary ties as opposed to primary ties and the growing transitoriness and impersonality of urban life.[2]

Parsons

It is against this broad background of the analysis of the qualitative differences between modern society and traditional society that this debate has taken place. But the specific point of reference for most of the protagonists was Parsons, in particular his essay on the kinship system of the USA.[3] In this essay, as in all of his work, Parsons was writing within the tradition of the main figures of European sociology but was referring to the specific situation of the USA. The main features of Parsons's arguments have been discussed elsewhere in this book[4] and only the specific points raised in this essay will be outlined here.

Parsons notes that anthropologists have been traditionally concerned with kinship in primitive societies and that there has been a lack of a similar anthropological perspective for the kinship systems of modern society. The kinship system of the USA is described by Parsons as being an 'open, multilineal conjugal system'.[5] There is no term outside that of 'family' (i.e. the nuclear family of parents and children) for any grouping of kinship. We talk of 'family' and an open-ended and unbounded body of 'relatives': 'Ours then is a "conjugal" system in that it is made up *exclusively* of interlocking conjugal families.'[6] The 'isolated conjugal family' is the 'normal household unit'.[7] The adult members of this isolated conjugal family are supposed to be economically independent of their own parents. Typically, when they marry they leave home and form a new conjugal unit. The main stress is on the conjugal tie between husband and wife which is expected to have precedence over any other tie.

While Wirth attributes the growing emphasis on secondary non-kinship ties in the process of urbanization, Parsons lays stress on the particular demands of the occupational system in industrial society. The occupational system demands that labour be recruited on the basis of achieved characteristics rather than on ascribed ties such as kinship. It demands mobility, both socially and geographically, and such mobility inevitably weakens the strength and salience of ties of birth and kinship. In a rational, industrial society there is particular stress on the conjugal bond (based on free choice and romantic love) as an emotional counterbalance to the impersonal ties generated in the occupational system.

Two points may be noted about Parsons's essay. In the first place it is not based on any empirical work, or at least no empirical work is specifically cited in this essay. It is largely an imaginative reconstruction and typification based upon the author's own participation in and membership of the system which he is describing. Second, Parsons argues that this system is most clearly to be found among the urban middle classes and that there may be exceptions to this picture to be found in rural areas, among the higher echelons of American society and among the urban poor. On both these counts Parsons can be, and has been, criticized.

The critics

Perhaps not the first case study, but almost certainly one of the most cited, to contradict this general stream of theorizing and its particular application in the writings of Talcott Parsons was the first Bethnal Green study by Young and Willmott.[8] They discovered a real reluctance on the part of their informants to leave the East End of London. This was not simply a function of long residence; this reluctance was also 'rooted in a lasting attachment to their families'.[9] They found that after marriage there was a strong tendency and indeed a desire to live close to (but not with) the wife's parents. The mother played a pivotal role in this kinship system and siblings kept up their contacts with each other through her. When she died, these contacts tended to fall off. There was a particular stress on the mother–daughter tie and clear evidence of a three-generational family system being maintained. Such a system was not merely based on sentiment or simple sociability but consisted of a high degree of mutual aid and support.

Bethnal Green has perhaps become a symbol of traditional working-class solidarity and it is worth pointing out that the authors of this first study noted similar findings in earlier studies. Peter Townsend, in an appendix to the paperback edition of the second Bethnal Green study,[10] is at pains to point out that this area is not some isolated cultural island but that his findings concerning the system of mutual aid support existing within three-generational families (contradicting the widespread supposition that old people were isolated in industrial society) were to be supported by several other studies in Britain and Europe.[11]

These studies of three-generational relationships among working-class families might easily be regarded as falling in with one of Parsons's expected exceptions to his general model, the urban poor. The expectation is, of course, that as living standards rise, as social and geographical mobility increases, so family life will come to approximate more closely to the isolated middle-class model. The persistence of ties of kinship in this case can be explained in terms of the need for mutual support and the persistence of some kind of community life. Similar findings and similar arguments apply to the maintenance and importance of kinship ties among immigrant groups[12] or among groups or regions where there exist different cultural, religious and linguistic traditions, often hardened by the existence of discrimination in the wider society.[13] Another of Parsons's predicted exceptions—that of the rural family—has also been extensively studied with similar results.[14] The persistence of kinship ties among upper-class families has also not gone unnoticed, and again this represents the third of Parsons's predicted exceptions to his general model.[15]

This list of findings, contradicting the general supposition that the relatively isolated conjugal family was becoming the typical unit in industrial society, could be extended considerably. Reiss, in a recent statement, provides a summary of some other American findings.[16]

> Recent studies have shown, however, that individuals do maintain relationships with their relatives. In Detroit it was discovered that about one-half of the population see their relatives once a week. Another sample in Los Angeles and one in San Francisco reveal very similar patterns. In each case there was more social participation with relatives than with co-workers,

> neighbors, or friends. Several studies have also shown that there is a great deal of aid exchanged among extended kin, particularly between parents and married children. In Detroit about 70 per cent of the wives in a sample indicated that they exchanged aid of some type with relatives. In a study of middle-class parents in New Haven, Connecticut, it was discovered that 79 per cent had established a pattern of providing aid for their married children. Another study in Cleveland indicated that about one-half of the respondents received help of some sort from parents and from siblings while 93 per cent provided some aid to parents and about 80 per cent to siblings. This aid may include financial assistance, help during illness or in emergencies, taking care of the children or just giving advice. Relatives are the first ones most people turn to for aid in emergencies. Schorr discusses the nature of this aid between adult children and their aged parents, showing that financial aid flows to the children from the parents, but that married children more often provide living quarters and other types of service for their aged parents.

Impressive in this list of studies is the reference to *middle-class* families. If the findings of the persistence of kinship ties in industrial society were confined to rural, lower working-class or to traditional upper-class families there would be little cause for surprise. Yet several American studies showed that even those groups most likely, according to Parsons's formulation, to exhibit the characteristics of the isolated conjugal family (that is the urban middle class) did not appear to conform to the theoretical predictions. In various articles and papers the work of Litwak and Sussman and Burchinall showed that their findings and the findings of other researchers contradicted all Parsons's theoretical assumptions.[17] It is true that industrial society requires social and geographical mobility; it is not true that such mobility tends to weaken ties between the 'adult-children' and their parents. No association was found between mobility and the strength of extra-familial kin ties or the belief in the importance of such ties. Indeed such ties aid rather than hinder geographical mobility and social mobility. The authors note the fact that help flows from the parents to the 'adult-children' and their families particularly during the period of the upswing of the latter's career or during the early years of married life. Such help is often concealed in the form of wedding or birthday presents rather than being provided directly, so as not to contradict the main ideal of financial independence from one's parents. They argue that it is not the isolated nuclear family which is the characteristic unit of industrial society but what they describe as the 'modified extended family'. This is defined by Litwak as:[18]

> a coalition of nuclear families in a state of partial dependence. Such partial dependence means that nuclear family members exchange significant services with each other, thus differing from the isolated nuclear family, as well as retain considerable autonomy (that is, not bound economically or geographically) therefore, differing from the classical extended family.

Such a concept is perhaps best handled by the use of network analysis rather than an analysis in terms of bounded groups. The authors present their conclusions with an air of finality rare in sociological investigation: 'Understanding of the family as a functioning social system interrelated with other social systems in society is possible *only by rejection of the isolated nuclear family concept*.'[19] And:[20]

> In a more recent empirical study . . . the evidence on the viability of an existing kinship structure carrying on extensive activities among kin is so convincing that we find it unnecessary to continue further descriptive working order to establish the existence of a kin network in modern urban society.

Similar findings have been produced for Britain. Bell found that middle-class spiralists (i.e. those who were both geographically and socially mobile) were not necessarily isolated from their kin, and analysed in some detail the mechanisms of aid flowing from parents (usually on the husband's side) to married children, usually in the early years of their married life. Perhaps the most detailed study of relatives and kin among the British middle class has been provided by Firth and his colleagues.[21] They examined the main features of kinship ideology and the kinds of terms used to designate kin. They looked at the various factors in kinship knowledge such as 'kin-keepers' or 'pivotal kin'.[22] There is a detailed examination of the kin universe, of kin named and unnamed, effective and non-effective, intimate and peripheral. The general picture they provide is of an open system with considerable scope for free choice and selectivity, largely expressive rather than instrumental but definitely a *system*. It is not just a collection of people who happen to be related to each other. Again in these two studies the picture of the relatively isolated nuclear family is contradicted in studies of the British middle class.

At this point the main features of the findings relating to kinship in urban society may be summarized:

1 The term 'isolated nuclear family' is misleading and inaccurate in relation to the modern urban family. A more appropriate term is the 'modified extended family'.

2 This modified extended family is not confined to working-class, rural or upper-class sections of society but is found among the mobile,

urban middle class, the grouping most likely to exhibit isolation according to the Parsonian formulation. This does not necessarily contradict Wirth's characterization of the urban environment; indeed perhaps *because* of the impersonality of urban life people are *more* likely to turn to kin—even kin some distance away—for help and for social relations.

3 The use of the term 'modified extended family' reminds us that we are not dealing with a bounded system. Out of the total possible number of persons in a kin universe only a few are 'selected' for more intimate relationships. This selection process is influenced by degree of relationship, geographical distance and personal choice, usually in that order of importance.[23]

4 Within the category of degree of relationship the order of preference (for a married ego) is normally parents, siblings and others. A large element of this modified system, therefore, revolves around generational relationships.

5 In the maintenance of kinship ties and the handling of flows of aid information and resources, women play the most important part. The importance of these last two factors will be examined in greater detail later in this chapter.

Evaluation of the debate

The stronger statements of Sussman, Litwak and others would seem to suggest that there is nothing further to be said and that Wirth and Parsons have been defeated through the cumulative weight of evidence. But sociological debates rarely end in such a decisive manner and in this case matters are far from being entirely settled. This is not merely a question of there being studies which point in directions other than the conclusions reached by Litwak and Sussman[24] nor the fact that there remain several residual problems such as whether upward mobility has a different effect on family and kinship ties than does downward mobility.[25] At least two recent studies could give support to both the Sussman/Litwak camp and the Parsons camp. The recent study by Firth and his associates certainly does not give us a picture of the middle-class nuclear family isolated from kin but his emphasis on the expressive and optional nature of many of these ties—'ascriptive friends' in Goode's useful phrase[26]—is not greatly at variance with Parsons's overall analysis of the family in industrial society. Similarly, Adams's study of kinship in urban society explicitly attempts, on the basis of his evidence, to give credit to both sides in the debate.[27]

Parsons himself has noted that the two approaches are complementary rather than contradictory[28] (a conclusion echoed by Adams) and it would appear that there is a certain amount of misunderstanding and ambiguity on both sides. Three sources of ambiguity may be noted: (a)Ambiguities around the meaning and degree of 'isolation'; (b) ambiguities concerning the level of society involved; and (c) ambiguities concerning the definition of 'kin'.[29]

(a) The extreme case of the 'isolated nuclear family' hypothesis would be where Ego marries, moves away from areas where his and his spouse's families of orientation live and has no further contact with these families of any kind. Such a situation is not impossible, but the fact that it would normally be regarded an occasion for regret or negative comment by others indicates that it is neither desired nor normal. Parsons, of course, has never proposed such an extreme version of his thesis, and the emphasis is on the 'relative' isolation of the nuclear family. The term 'relative' implies some kind of comparison so that we must immediately ask 'relative to what?' There could be various bases for comparisons namely:

1 Generational comparison, i.e. comparison between Ego's generation and his parents' generation and/or grandparents' generation.

2 Longer-term historical comparisons, such as that between pre-industrial and industrial society. One variation of this may be the comparison between the urban and the rural family at a given point of time, assuming that the direction of change is towards greater urbanization.

3 Comparisons between 'modern' societies and 'traditional' societies at a given point of time. Again there is a simple evolutionary assumption here.

4 Comparison between kin and various sets of non-kin, such as workmates, friends and neighbours.

5 Comparison between a theoretically desired 'normal' level or a statistical average and certain actual levels.

Given that the basis for the comparison implied in the word 'relative' is not always clearly stated and that different writers may be using different standards of comparison, this indicates there is considerable scope for misunderstanding and ambiguity in this debate. What is clear is that the demonstration that Ego and his spouse maintain some kind of relationship (through visits, telephone exchanges, etc.) with their parents and siblings does not in itself prove or disprove the Parsons thesis.

Further scope for ambiguity lies in the fact that it is often difficult to apply any precise weighting to the various indicators of isolation or its opposite. A relatively isolated person might be: (a) a person who knows the names and addresses of relatively few of his kin; (b) a person who interacts *infrequently* with his kin; (c) a person who interacts with *few* of his kin; (d) a person who gives to or receives little or no assistance from his kin; (e) a person who does not wish to interact with his kin; (f) any combination of these or other indicators. What is clear from the cumulative evidence is that geographical *separateness* is not the same as a *sense* of isolation and that a lack of regular face-to-face interaction does not necessarily mean isolation in any sense other than this. Again we are left with plenty of scope to argue for either Parsons or his critics or both.

(b) The second source of ambiguity is one recognized by both Adams and Parsons. Adams notes that Parsons is concerned with the functional centrality of kinship as an institution the relationship between the part and the whole, while Sussman and other critics of Parsons are concerned with the functioning of the part.[30] Parsons himself puts forward a similar argument to justify his contention that the two approaches to kinship in urban society are complementary rather than contradictory. He is making a comparison at the cultural or societal level between the USA and pre-industrial cultures noting that in the former extended kinship elements do 'not form firmly structured units of the social system'.[31] Kinship units, for example, do not on the whole form corporate groups or units of production.

This ambiguity reflects one of the central ambiguities of functional analysis which we have already noted,[32] namely the question of for whom or for what a particular institution is functional. Nevertheless, the expression of this ambiguity does clarify the differences between Parsons and his critics and does show the possibilities of a reconciliation between the two perspectives. Litwak and Sussman have shown a modified extended family system functions for individual families and for individual family members. This argument does not contradict Parsons's assertion that the kinship system is not functionally central for society as a whole. Similarly Parsons's argument that the family in modern society functions indirectly for that society[33] does not contradict but, if anything, reinforces his critics' detailed analysis of the help pattern among middle-class families. It is likely that both parties have been guilty of overstatement—a reader of Parsons's earlier essay on the kinship structure of the USA might be forgiven if he found Sussman and Litwak's findings 'unheralded'—but that beneath much of the apparent contradiction a considerable measure of agreement is to be found.

(c) Probably the most important ambiguity, however, is over the use of the term 'kinship'. In anthropological literature the term 'kinship' usually refers to those relationships established by birth and descent (including fictitious relationships). The term affinity is used for relationships established through marriage although in practice the distinction is often of little importance. In the studies of kinship in Western urban society, however, the term 'kinship' is usually used to cover 'relatives', that is relatives outside Ego's nuclear family of procreation. (The lay informant is more likely to use a term like 'relative' rather than 'kin' to indicate such relationships.) Within the 'kin universe' some attempt is made to distinguish between kin who are merely recognized and those who are actually part of an effective network of exchange and reciprocity.

In practice, therefore, the word kin when it applies to modern urban society often has a relatively narrow referent. The analysis usually begins with Ego. Ego is married and has children who are themselves unmarried.[34] The analysis continues by looking at the relationships that exist between Ego and Ego's spouse and their respective families of orientation, especially the parents. Adams's finding that the order of ranking in terms of contacts, affection and obligation—parent(s), then age-near sibling and then, a long way off, best-known cousin—are probably neither atypical nor surprising.[35]

The chief focus of attention, then, is on the relationship between married child—or 'adult child'—and parent(s): 'Thus it is primarily for parents, and secondarily for siblings, that the concept of the "isolated nuclear family" fails to hold among the residentially mobile.'[36]

If this be true—and most studies would seem to support Adams's general picture with some variation—then the central area of controversy disappears. Goode, for example, deliberately uses the term 'conjugal family' to take into account the fact that in strict terms the 'isolated nuclear family' does not exist to any large degree: 'At a *minimum* two members of each unit are tied to other units through a common member of a given nuclear family.'[37] This is echoed in Townsend's theoretical chapter to the Penguin edition of *The Family Life of Old People*. Townsend notes that the marriage of, say, a son does not merely start a new family life cycle but creates three new relationships and changes several others.[38] Simply because a new conjugal relationship is created and a new residential unit is established does not mean that existing *relationships* are severed. To oversimplify a little, if we view the modern kinship system as consisting of a set of interlocking nuclear families, then Parsons concentrates on the nuclear family aspect while his critics concentrate on the interlocking aspects. Under these circumstances it might be better if the term kinship were replaced by a term such as 'generational relationships'.

Wider issues

Sociological debates—the debate over the relationship between Protestantism and capitalism is a striking example—often have implications far wider than the particular points raised by the various protagonists. In this case it can be seen that the debate has raised important questions about the relationships between the family and society, especially a changing society, and the problems of urban society and social mobility, questions which have practical as well as theoretical implications. Yet clearly the continuation of such a debate may also direct attention away from other issues or may serve, indirectly, to obscure other issues. We have seen how the putting forward of relatively exaggerated claims on both sides tended to obscure the fact that there was not all that much difference between the two perspectives. The tendency to conduct the debate in terms of 'kinship'—usually with one or two nods in the direction of anthropological writings and statements regretting the absence of similar studies in industrial society—tended also to isolate the arguments from the mainstream of writings on the sociology of the family. Thus, for example, the often noted fact that women are usually most involved in the modified extended family is not always systematically linked to a discussion of the position of women in the family and the society. It was one of the virtues of Parsons's original analysis that he did attempt to place his account in a wider analytical framework and to make connections between different sections and levels of the social system, a virtue which tended to become lost as the debate became more focused on to the particular arguments on behalf of the modified extended family as opposed to the isolated nuclear family.

Four interrelated wider issues will be dealt with here: (a) the methodological weakness of many of these studies; (b) the lack of a systematic analysis of kin as opposed to non-kin; (c) the tendency of the debate to have the effect of playing down conflict within the modified extended family and to contribute, indirectly, to the 'family as a success story' theme; (d) the relative lack of attention to the question as to the wider meaning of kinship, as to *why* these particular patterns exist and are maintained.

(a) Many of the studies cited in this debate are based on the use of some kind of social survey technique. Samples are taken, on a random or a non-random basis, usually in a particular urban area. Adams's sample, for example, was white, married (only once) for twenty years or less, living in Greensboro, North Carolina. He interviewed 467 females and 332 males:[39]

> If the husband was at home, he was ordinarily interviewed in preference to the wife. Approximately once in every four cases the wife was interviewed in the evening, even though the husband was available, in order not to under-represent working wives. All interviews were conducted in private, i.e. the spouse was not present as the questions were asked. The predominance

of females is explained by the greater likelihood of their being home.

Litwak's study on geographical mobility and extended family cohesion was based on a survey of 920 white married women in Buffalo, New York.[40] Firth and his associates carried out a more detailed intensive unstructured set of interviews with a smaller non-random sample of couples in two areas of London.[41] Bell carried out a survey of two Welsh middle-class housing estates but was also one of the few students of kinship to include case material and analysis in his account.[42]

This list could be extended. The main point is that most of these studies were carried out using some variation of interviews based upon random or non-random sample surveys. The central problem that this raises—and this is not a problem confined to kinship studies[43]—is that the basic unit is the individual or individual household while the questions asked and the problems discussed deal with *relationships*. This particular problem is exacerbated where, as is the case in the Litwak and Adams studies, the sampled units are individuals, not even married couples (just women in Litwak's case). The authors talk of a kinship *network* but never follow up the intricate connections and links that the concept of network implies. It is rather like listening to a telephone conversation at one end of the line only.

The other problem associated with sample surveys of all kinds is that, for the most part, they are based on verbalized responses in an interview situation. (Usually the interviewer visits his respondents at home.) It is certain that considerable care was taken in the preparation of the questions and the training of the interviewers. I am not, unlike some sociologists, convinced that material collected this way is totally invalid; for example, *variations* in the response to particular questions may provide interesting and useful data. Yet a relatively relaxed chat about kin in an interview situation (that is a non-kinship situation) is not the same as living through kinship crises and events. The emphasis is generally on measurement as opposed to meaning.[44] In evaluating responses to questions such as 'How close would you say you feel to your mother?' (Adams) or 'Generally I like the whole family to spend evenings together' (Litwak) how far are we warranted in treating these as cues to actual conduct? How far are these ideological statements, applied to particular cases or how far are they expressions of what the subject thinks the interviewer ideally expects are the morally 'correct' answers? It is not that researchers are necessarily wrong to use these techniques—in many cases they may be the only techniques available given limited time and resources—but that there is a marked absence of critical reflexivity on the part of the researchers in relation to their techniques used. Rarely do we find a critical self-examination on the lines of 'what kinds of responses are these, what do they mean and in what ways do they relate to the issues under discussion?'

These problems have particular applications in relation to the study of kinship in urban society. If it is the case, as several authors argue, that the modified extended family system is maintained through a sense of obligation, then it is highly likely that this sense of obligation will be manifested in the interview situation. Conversely, it may not be thought to be 'proper' to discuss openly conflicts and antagonisms within the kinship network in such an interview situation. Thus the use of the method of social surveys as applied to this particular problem may reinforce the overall functionalist perspective (or more exactly eufunctionalist perspective) examined in a previous chapter.

(b) A second problem is that the kinship studies rarely provide an equally systematic examination of the importance or otherwise of non-kin. To be sure most of these studies show that the respondents often spend more leisure time with relatives than with friends, neighbours or workmates and that they are more likely to call on a relative in times of emergency. Yet alternative patterns are possible. To provide a personal illustration of this, a few years ago in my department there was a considerable amount of exchange of baby equipment and clothing between some of the younger married members of that department, as well as mutual baby-sitting. It is likely that there were certain preconditions for this, namely a relatively cohesive work situation, geographical distance from kin and a set of people at similar stages of their work and family life cycle careers. Such preconditions do not always exist in this combination and even where they do these particular exchanges need not necessarily take place, but it does illustrate the possibilities of alternatives to kin being mobilized in ways similar to the patterns described by Litwak and Sussman. In a very different context Michel, in a study of French working-class families living in furnished hotels, found that relationships of proximity replaced the role that kinship might be expected to play in other sections of society. A particular combination of social class, work experience and living conditions (there was little opportunity for relatives to live with these families) contributed to the development of this particular situation.[45] The point is that the studies of kinship in urban society ask detailed questions about kin but tend not to ask equally detailed questions relating to categories of non-kin.

In this connection, Litwak and Szelenyi have provided a suggestive theoretical statement which incorporates kinship groups, neighbourhoods and friendships in a more general discussion of primary groups in industrial, urban society.[46] They counter the argument, implied in the writings of Wirth, Simmel and Tönnies, that such primary groups are doomed in modern society. Just as the modified extended family system can survive in spite of—or perhaps because of—increased social and geographical mobility, so too can neighbourhood groups and friendships. There is a tendency for such groups to perform different functions and to operate in different ways: nevertheless they are still of significance:[47]

> What we are suggesting is that friendship ties tend to rest on free choice and affectivity; neighbourhood ties, face-to-face contact; and kinship structures, permanent relations. There is no reason at any moment in time why all these primary groups could not overlap—friends may be neighbours and family members at the same time. However, the main point of our discussion is that there are pressures in an industrial society for each of these groups to separate.

This article provides a valuable initial statement, opening up the field of discussion to include significant sets of non-kin.

(c) One of the major arguments in the analysis of the family in modern society is the argument that, far from disintegrating and losing its functions, the modern family has made a remarkably successful job in adapting itself to modern society. This 'family as a success story' theme will be considered in more detail in the next chapter; here I shall analyse the way in which these kinship studies have contributed to this theme.

It has been noted that the analyses of kinship in modern society have often taken their cue from the observation that there is a lack of investigation into this field as compared with the rich accounts of primitive societies. Some of the authors—Firth, Schneider, Goodenough, for examples—are in fact anthropologists. However, it would seem that in many cases the anthropological model has not been taken all that seriously. In the first place, as we have noted, these studies of kinship in modern society are based on social surveys using the individual or the individual household as the basic unit. In contrast, anthropological studies have more commonly looked at a society or section of society as a whole, thus obtaining what is so often lacking in these sociological accounts—an analysis of *relationships*. It has been argued convincingly that it is not impossible to continue some of the best traditions of social anthropology in the study of complex societies.[48] Second, and following from this, anthropological accounts of kinship have typically included analyses of conflict, of disputes, their causes and the way in which attempts are made to resolve such disputes. To refer to two studies included in volumes already mentioned in this chapter, the family may be viewed as a centre of 'hatred and discord' as well as of 'affection and integration',[49] and the same forces that entail obligations may also engender possibly lethal antagonisms.[50] In the analysis of kinship in modern urban society, however, such accounts play a very minor role. The chief concern seems to be—and this again unites Parsons with some of his critics—to show that the modern family is functionally adapted to the demands of modern society and that this is true whether one calls it a conjugal family (Goode), an isolated nuclear family (Parsons) or a modified extended family (Sussman and Litwak). Conflict, where it is recognized at all, appears to be an idiosyncratic feature perhaps attributable to some person rather than any structural failure ('I am afraid that we just don't get on so we do not see much of each other'). The possible exception to this general statement is the presence of accounts of mother-in-law conflict. On the whole, however, the emphasis here has been to point out that the conflict in this respect is less than might have been expected in the light of traditional mother-in-law jokes.

What is the reason for this relative neglect of conflict in the analysis of kinship in modern society? As we have suggested it may be a function of the research tool typically adopted, the social survey. Such methods may be more likely to elicit ideal expectations rather than actual on-going relationships. Or it may be that, as Parsons has maintained all along, kinship is not all that central so there is not really very much at stake for serious conflict to be generated. If, however, we agree that by kinship in urban society we usually mean generational relationships, this argument carries much less weight, for generational relationships would seem to have a fair degree of conflict embedded in them. Indeed, the traditional mother-in-law problem may in part be interpreted as an expression of a contradiction between generational relationships and conjugal relationships. Whatever the reason for this neglect the overall effect has been to contribute, in most cases indirectly, to the 'family as a success story' theme.

(d) The final criticism is one which will form the main point of the rest of this chapter. The studies cited have shown that Ego and his spouse typically not only maintain contact with their respective parents and siblings but that a considerable flow of help and assistance moves between them. These findings gave rise to the concept of the modified extended family. However, the analysis appears to stop there and does not, on the whole, go on to ask about the meaning of these findings. Why is kinship (even in this somewhat limited sense) important, why do people turn to their kin for support at times of crisis? If it is true that there is an element of choice in the system, why do people more often than not choose kin? In the following pages I attempt to relate these questions—and their possible answers—to some wider anthropological discussions on the nature of kinship.

Why kinship?

It may be useful to follow Colin Bell's advice at this point[51] and consider some recent anthropological discussions on the nature and significance of kinship. Put at its simplest the debate revolves around the question as to whether there is an isolable entity which can be given the label 'kinship' as apart from other kinds of social relationships. Further, if such a labelling be possible and the word 'kinship' can be meaningfully used, to what sphere of human activity does the label refer? It might be argued, therefore, that if we are able to provide an adequate description of the word 'kinship' we are some way to explaining its persistence and importance in any particular situation.

One set of responses to these questions would be to locate the institution 'kinship' in that area of social relationships more or less closely shaped by the facts of 'biological relatedness and/or sexual intercourse'.[52] Kinship, therefore, relates to fundamental 'natural' processes; in a sense it might be seen as looking beyond the purely 'social' and may reflect 'biological and psychological parameters of human social existence'.[53] At the very least there is an overlap between the facts of biology and the social institutions of descent and kinship.[54] The deep and pervasive significance of kinship can be traced back to these basic facts.

The notion that the term 'kinship' refers to sets of relationships rooted in fundamental biological and psychological processes can be easily linked to another theme, namely that kinship is distinguished by its particular tone and emphasis on expressiveness, on obligation or on what Fortes calls the principle of 'kinship amity'. He refers to the rule of 'prescriptive altruism which I have referred to as the principle of kinship amity and (which) Hiatt calls the ethic of generosity'.[55] The stress is on 'inescapable moral claims and obligations'[56] and a degree of trust that is not automatically possible with non-kin. For an insightful example he cites the fact that the Tallensi distinguish clearly between the involuntary bonds of kinship and voluntary, optional and flexible ties.[57] Fortes, like Levy, would appear to lay stress on the fact that these generalized, normative and obligatory relationships derive their tone from the inescapable fact that one does not choose one's own parents, and the particular quality of the ties between parents (especially the mother) and children.

We are now one step or more away from biology and basic psychological processes, but it would appear to be clear that, in the last resort, the unique quality of kinship relationships is to be attributed to these factors. Other authors give stress to the peculiar 'difference' of kinship from other forms of relationship. They may note the peculiar 'richness' of kinship[58] relationships or point out the common derivation of the terms 'kindred' and 'kindness'.[59] In all cases the emphasis would appear to be on something which is irreducible to any other kind of relationship, such as economic or political relationships.[60]

Such a view, however self-evident it might seem, has not gone unchallenged. Beattie, replying to Gellner, argues that kinship is not to be equated with genealogical relationships. To say that a particular social relationship is one of 'kinship' tells us nothing about its actual content; it is an idiom, not a further category of social relationships.[61] Barnes, in the same set of exchanges, notes, for example, that the conventional distinction between the 'pater' and the 'genitor' is not so self-evident as it might seem. Given, as Strindberg's 'Father' was ready to recognize, that the fact of physical paternity can never be proved absolutely, even the 'genitor' is a social category, that is one who is recognized for practical purposes as being the biological father.[62] What those who replied to Gellner are saying in effect is that biology in itself can tell us nothing about *social* relationships. Further, we should not treat 'kinship' as a separate thing but see it at work in particular contexts, political, economic, ritual and so on. This line of argument reached its most iconoclastic in a recent Association of Social Anthropologists symposium where the editor flatly declared that there was no such thing as kinship. Other contributors, more or less influenced by Wittgenstein, came to the same conclusion.[63] In a very different tradition, the Marxist anthropologists stress the notion of kinship as an ideology, as a superstructure particularly related to such factors as land as an instrument of labour and the control over women necessitated by such an economy.[64]

Clearly it would be difficult to provide an adequate synthesis which would do justice to all these varying accounts. If, however, we treat these accounts not so much as scientific laws or hypotheses but rather as refined typifications of accounts of the meaning of kinship which are available to and used by members of a given culture, then some degree of synthesis may be possible. Such a synthesis might include the following points:

1 Terms such as 'kinship', 'kindred', 'descent' and 'relatives' have something to do with biological relationships. They are names given to sets of relationships which are seen by members of a society to have some connection with assumed or actual biological relationships or with relationships (such as fictive kinship) which are assumed for certain purposes to have the same practical consequences of

'actual' biological relationships. To say this is not to commit oneself to any form of biological determinism and tells us nothing about the content or meaning of such relationships. It merely states that, in a very general way, there is some degree of overlap between the fundamental facts of sexual intercourse, marriage and procreation and the social relationships that fall under the category of 'kinship'.

2 Members of a given society have certain ideas about what these relationships entail and these ideas shape and define the social reality of kinship. Kinship thus provides an idiom for ordering a wide variety of relationships which are not necessarily 'purely' kinship in the sense outlined above. Ideologies develop around the nature and significance of kinship but these ideologies do not themselves necessarily derive from the basic biological facts in any clear or deterministic sense; indeed we may say that the ideology gives meaning to sets of ties which would otherwise be socially meaningless.

3 These relationships and the meanings and values that are attached to them are used selectively in a variety of contexts, including contexts which are analytically separate from the sphere of kinship. A process of selective use serves to distinguish which members of a kinship universe are significant for particular purposes. Selectivity also operates in the process whereby kin and non-kin are chosen and used for different purposes.

4 While the ideology of kinship may encompass a variety of themes, an important one will be the theme of obligation. This derives from, but only in so far as it is mediated through various ideological prescriptions, the apparently inevitable and inescapable nature of kinship. We should not see the idea of obligation as stemming inevitably from the 'facts' of kinship. Rather we should see it as a particular appeal which is often legitimized by being associated with familial or kinship relationships. Kinship, it might be said, is closely associated with the rhetoric of obligation but, since there are often competing obligations within the kinship universe as well as between kinship and non-kinship relationships, this association does not in itself tell us anything about a particular social event nor does it enable us to predict the outcome of a particular event.

It might be felt that these discussions, often developed in the context of an argument about kinship in pre-industrial societies, have little relevance for the discussion of kinship in modern urban society. However, it has been noted that in many cases a plea is made for the adoption of an anthropological perspective on our own society and that in some cases the individuals who have conducted investigations into kinship in modern society have themselves been anthropologists (Firth, Schneider). Furthermore, since it has been suggested that we should view the various theories about the nature and significance of kinship as theories which are available to 'lay' members of a given society, it might be useful to see what kind of theories are present and used in our own society. The studies cited often give direct or indirect indications about kinship ideology as well as providing analytical accounts of the nature and importance of kinship in modern society.

It is clear, for a start, that notions of obligation and sentiment which are in some ways peculiarly if not exclusively attached to 'relatives' (to use the widely cited everyday term) are notions which are available within our society and not merely externally imposed interpretations of the meaning of kinship. Stress is often laid on the normality or naturalness of turning to kin first in times of need ('blood is thicker than water') and any attempt to ask 'why' might be thought to be unnecessary or even slightly subversive. Kinship, then, has a taken-for-granted quality; reference is made to 'what everybody knows' or 'what everybody does around here'. Several studies record statements similar to the following one recorded by Adams: 'My parents and sister are the only ones I can really count on.'[65] Kinship, in these lay terms, appears to be a Durkheimian 'social fact', something unassailably real.

It has in fact been argued that it is in modern society, perhaps particularly in the middle-class sections of modern society, that kinship takes on its 'purest form', that is a form uncontaminated by any instrumental considerations. This is a version of the 'structural differentiation' argument whereby the institution of kinship becomes specialized; its rhetoric is in terms of nature and obligation and its domain is the field of intensive expressive relationships. Reiss places this argument against the background of the relative anonymity of urban bureaucratic society: 'The function of these extended kinship relationships appears to be basically those performed by primary friendship relationships; personality satisfaction including a sense of belonging, companionship and security.'[66] Firth and his colleagues lay particular stress on this expressive character of kinship relationships among his middle-class London respondents, and Adams, in his study, pays emphasis on 'keeping in touch' rather than coping with actual needs.[67] In most cases, it would appear, kin do not *have* to get together or associate with each other. If they do, it is largely because they want to and they want to, not merely for some actual or imagined future benefits but because of the intrinsic nature of the relationship itself. Yet we are still faced with the problem of explaining why it is that kin are apparently chosen out of a wider set of possible relationships (as well as of explaining why some kin rather than others) for these particularly expressive reasons.

Perhaps at the opposite end to these expressions couched in verbalized expressions of ideal 'natural' expectations and obligations are the accounts which stress the content of what is actually gained out of these relationships. Thus Sussman *et al.* stress the patterns of help in middle-class families, flowing from the parents to the married children. Such help often assists the children to maintain a middle-class style of life or perhaps to advance up a career ladder. Bell's account of the family life of middle-class spiralists presents essentially the same kind of argument. At different levels of the social structure and later in the life cycle help may flow from the married couple to the retired parents. Or, in the case of international or intranational mobility, ties of kinship may provide valuable lines of communication relating to such important matters as housing and job opportunities.[68] Such ties may build up over time and become elaborated with each new move, each new foothold established in the new environment.

The stress here, therefore, is on the content of the relationships. Kinship ties are not seen as abstract lines on some genealogical chart but actual living relationships established and developed, elaborated over time and sustained through constant *use*. The content of kinship ties may include concealed or open financial payments, common residence, assistance during crises, more regular patterns of assistance such as baby-sitting or shopping, exchanges of visits, gossip or information. It is important to note that the content of these relationships is not merely in terms of material goods or assistance. Gossip or information may be as much an important part of the content of a kinship relationship as the mobilization of actual goods and services.

Such 'instrumental' relationships usually are seen as existing within some framework of reciprocity. This may be a reciprocity within the context of the life cycle, taking place over time. Thus middle-class parents may help their married sons in the early stages of their careers in the unspoken hope that such assistance may be returned when they themselves have retired. Or such reciprocity may be more immediate and visible. Townsend notes: 'they received help because they also gave it, or had given it, in the comparatively recent past.'[69] A typical pattern is the aged parent who lives with or near her married daughter. Her daughter may help with the shopping, visits to the doctor, etc. and may, in return, receive baby-sitting help from her mother whilst she goes out to work.

The most sophisticated attempt at a sociological explanation of the importance of kinship in an industrializing society to appear in recent years has been Anderson's analysis of the nineteenth-century working-class family in Lancashire.[70] Anderson opposes the over-simplified thesis that industrialization leads to disruption and seeks to explain the persisting importance of kinship ties in early nineteenth-century Preston by an exchange model derived in large part from the theories of Blau and Homans. Important elements in his model are what he calls 'psychic profit' and reciprocity under which he includes both the timing of reciprocity and its certainty. While recognizing the importance of values about kinship he argues that in the long run at least there has to be a fair measure of congruence between values and the prevailing optimal bargains that might be struck. His work is based on detailed historical reconstruction, analysing, for example, the fact that while it was economically possible for children to leave home and strike out on their own yet it was the case that a high proportion of the aged were supported by their children. He analyses the exchange relationship that developed, particularly in response to the 'critical life situations', those situations such as death or unemployment where the resources of a single couple and their children were often inadequate to meet the particular crisis unless aid was forthcoming from some other source. It must be remembered that many of these families were near the margin of poverty so that there were strong and powerful incentives of an instrumental kind for kin to develop some kind of exchange relationship with each other. Yet, given the prevailing uncertainty and the difficulty of predicting the future, such exchange relationships were often of a short-term nature. Kin were turned to in these and in other situations because, unlike neighbours, there were more 'ascribed and enduring links between actors'.[71]

There are difficulties with Anderson's analysis, indeed with exchange theory generally, which cannot be explored in any detail here. For example, it is important to ask to what extent the formal models match or reflect the lay understandings of the situation. How far, in other words, do actors in fact understand the situation with which they are confronted as actually being one of exchange and choice? Yet it is clear that Anderson is asking the right sort of questions in, for example, considering the complex relationship between values and instrumental relationships and in attempting to evaluate the reason why kin were chosen as opposed to neighbours. Towards the end of his book he notes that a more non-calculative involvement might become possible with the increase of affluence and the growth of the welfare state.[72] It is clear, therefore, that the nature and significance of kinship is not something fixed and eternal but something which is highly flexible and derives its meaning as much from the context in which it operates as from any 'inherent' qualities. Anderson recognizes this also when contrasting the relatively closed circle of obligation, reciprocity, constraint and sanction which operated in the rural areas from which many of his families originated and the relatively open system where, while all the elements of obligation, values, and instrumentality were present, they did not form such a coherent or mutually reinforcing system. The fact that the meaning of kinship may differ at different levels of society is also argued by Farber where he contrasts the interest in the 'symbolic family estate' at the higher levels with the emphasis on mutual support in face of scarcity and need at the lower levels and argues that the different meanings assigned to kinship at different levels function in subtle ways to maintain the social structure.[73]

A variety of explanations for the continuing importance of ties of kinship, as defined in this particular context, have been outlined. There is the lay explanation, 'blood is thicker than water'. There are two sociological explanations largely in terms of the functions which these relationships perform for the members and, indirectly, for society as a whole. Some sociologists stress the instrumental functions, the importance of reciprocity and mutual aid. Others give emphasis to the expressive functions, arguing that visiting and 'keeping in touch' are themselves the main rationale and that the more instrumental considerations are secondary. The notion of obligation is a common feature to all these explanations. Very generally it may be argued that the lay explanation overstresses the ideological dimension and does not pay much attention to the content of the relationship while the two sociological explanations attempt to grasp the content but fail to explain adequately why it is that kin should be emphasized in this way.

The difficulty with the explanations offered so far is not so much that they are wrong or even that they are incomplete. The objection is that they direct the investigation in one particular direction and tend to obscure alternative perspectives. The lay perspective appears to give emphasis to a positive sense of duty—people *ought* to help their mothers or children—although there may be some ambiguity in this sense of duty, an ambiguity which points to constraints as well as to positive reward. The sociological perspective tends to emphasize eufunctions as opposed to possible dysfunctions. This approach fails to examine the implication of the following criticism of Homans, presented by Adams: 'If . . . two individuals are not free to dissolve a social relationship because of location or obligatory necessity, the association between consensus affection and interaction no longer holds.'[74] What follows is an attempt to provide some of the elements which I consider ought to be taken into account in an evaluation of kinship in urban society.

In the first place we must remind ourselves of the kinds of relationships we are discussing. 'Kinship' in the way it is used in these discussions usually refers primarily to generational relationships. The chief line of relationship emphasized in these studies is that between parents and married children. Next come sibling relationships and finally come other kinship relationships. Consequently any explanation of 'kinship in urban society' must locate its focus on the sociology of the family rather than the often more abstract notion of kinship or concepts of kinship derived from the study of other societies.

The kinship universe as a whole is a variable, unbounded one with a high degree of selectivity and indeed ambiguity at the edges. But at the heart of this universe is the tie between parents and married child and this is much less ambiguous and voluntary in character. It is here that kinship has its most 'built in quality' to use Firth's terms.[75] He notes: 'One of the most significant factors of kinship is that it consists of social relationships the ultimate basis of which is independent of the choice of the central individual involved.'[76] Firth's emphasis gives due recognition to the sense of obligation we have already discussed, the sense of 'naturalness', 'taken-for-granted' quality of many of the ties examined in these studies. The analysis of kinship in modern society must give recognition to the tension between choice and obligation which lies at the heart of these relationships. Doubtless Parsons is right to emphasize the achieved universalistic character of many or most role expectations in modern society. Such expectations are emphasized in school, in the media and at work. But they are not the whole story and while they may not conflict in these latter spheres they may come into conflict in the area of home and domestic relationships. The closer to the heart of the kinship relationships the greater the emphasis on obligation. Or, to put it another way, considerations of distance (social and geographical) and personal liking are less likely to confound this sense of obligation, the nearer one gets to the parent–married child relationship.

The reason for this must, in part, lie in the process of socialization itself. The central dilemma of the socialization process in modern society is in its dual nature. On the one hand it is a process of socialization into a society whose dominant ethos is not based on kinship or familistic ties. On the other hand the process of socialization itself involves intense and prolonged relationships with significant others, mother and father.[77] While, if we are to follow Parsons's account, successful socialization necessarily involves the gradual movement beyond these particular ties (until Ego himself marries and starts the whole process over again) it is doubtful whether the contradiction here is ever completely resolved.[78] It is also likely that the process of socialization is not merely a matter of the inculcation of societal norms and values in a rather generalized sense (the sense usually presented in text-books) but also involves directly and indirectly socializing the child into recognizing the particular values of the family and parenthood itself. It is also highly likely that the parent sees the children, not simply (if at all!) as beings to be socialized in the general societal sense but rather as projects, or extensions of his or her own project. Thus, for example, we have the almost poignant dilemma of the middle-class parents who wish to stress the virtues of independence and initiative in their children but only within certain fairly clear limits, at least as far as career and marriage are concerned.[79]

Adams writes on the basis of his findings:[80]

> It almost seems that living in the same city with one's parents makes frequent interaction imperative, living over 400 miles apart makes frequent interaction impossible, while being in different communities but within 100 miles leaves room for a modicum of personal choice.

This, allowing for some scaling down of distances necessary in British society, is a useful point and it emphasizes the varying situations and structures of opportunities that may exist. At one extreme we have the working-class community situation. Here, through lack of opportunities, education or finance, couples fail to move far away from the community in which they were brought up. Consequently they live near one or both sets of parents and see these parents—and perhaps other kin—frequently. Frequent interaction may not, as Homans suggests, produce liking but it may make avoidance or a break that much more difficult even in the absence of positive liking between one or more individuals and one or more set of parents. An environment of relative or absolute poverty provides the background for a set of mutual exchanges and aid. Thus we have a situation of low mobility opportunities, low income, proximity to kin and frequency of interaction all reinforcing each other. At the other extreme we have a situation where both members of the couple have moved far, geographically and socially, from their families of origin, are relatively affluent and have no instrumental need for kin. Nor perhaps do they desire to associate regularly with their parents, their siblings and the families of their siblings. They have greater desire and scope for the exercise of choice in their personal relationships, and these relationships may or may not include kin. Yet this distance does not mean that they have severed all ties with kin altogether (although this is possible) or that parents no longer enter into their personal projects. Similarly, the close proximity of parents in the first extreme does not, of course, mean the absence of conflict.

These idealized extremes (perhaps representing Bethnal Green and Crestwood Heights respectively) suggest that we should take account of the varying structures of resources, the varying balances and mixes of opportunities and constraints that exist in a variety of family situations. These constraints are not just physical in the sense of geographical distance or lack of money but may also be internalized and perceived as a sense of obligation. Such an approach would give recognition not only to the complexity and diversity of family situations but also to the possible built-in elements of contradiction and conflict in these relationships themselves.

Two further points, again emphasizing the built-in element of conflict in the situation as well as the possible positive functions, may be briefly mentioned. The first is to emphasize that we are dealing, in the main, with generational relationships. Generational conflict is usually understood in terms of conflict between parents and adolescent children. There are possibly good reasons why there should be an emphasis on this form of generational conflict but there is no reason to suppose that it is absent later in the life cycle.[81] Yet certainly many of the reasons given for this 'earlier' form of generational conflict are still present later in the life cycle. Such reasons include the rapidity of social and technological change, the different socialization and educational experiences and the societal emphasis on achieved as opposed to ascribed characteristics. That these parents with whom middle-class (and other) families exchange goods and services are also of a different generation is a point not usually given full recognition except perhaps under the particular heading of 'the mother-in-law problem'.

Another point which needs to be emphasized in the explanations is the greater degree of involvement of women in this modified extended family system. To be sure the studies emphasize the fact that the woman usually has a greater store of kinship knowledge, that she is more likely than her husband to keep up these ties and that the tie between mother and married daughter is often of particular importance. The reason for this is often expressed in the form of some variation on the rhyme:[82]

My son's a son till he gets him a wife,
My daughter's a daughter all her life.

Townsend speaks of the 'special unity between grandmother, daughter and daughter's child'.[83] Young and Willmott note that daughters 'still follow their mothers and inherit the same occupation' unlike their more mobile husbands.[84]

An alternative version of the preceding accounts of the modified extended family would, therefore, be that it is part of a system which exploits women by maintaining them in a subordinate position. I am not, at this stage, concerned with the correctness or otherwise of this assertion;[85] what is, however, disturbing is that it is highly likely that this preceding statement would be labelled 'ideological' whereas the more orthodox interpretation in terms of 'expressive' and 'instrumental' roles would not. Furthermore, the apparent strangeness of this assertion is in part a reflection of the separation of 'kinship studies' from studies of their aspects of family life, particularly the roles of men and women.

If, however, we attempt to make these connections then a host of interesting problems follow. To what extent are women constrained, not merely by their role in relation to their husbands but also by their role in relation to their parents and kin? To what extent will greater societal change in the respective roles of men and women affect this 'modified extended family' as well as the 'nuclear family'? There is some evidence to suggest that, to a limited extent at least, the occupational involvement of women need not necessarily work against the traditional domestic role of women but may reinforce it. Thus in many working-class districts the close proximity of the mother enables the married daughter to go out to work while her mother baby-sits at least for part of the day. The role of the grandmother in the 'liberation' of Soviet women has been noted by several authors and an article on the family in contemporary Czechoslovakia notes some possible paradoxes and contradictions in this situation:[86]

> The growing employment of women without adequate supply of institutional facilities for child care, or without the possibility to hire paid help, leads at least to a certain degree to the strengthening of the traditional family pattern in which three generations or the nuclear family with other relatives live together and the kinship in general plays a rather important role.

Noting that many of the women who require help from the extended family in this way are often white-collar in occupational status and often better educated than their parents, he concludes:[87]

> In socialist countries the social and economic conditions of running the households and organizing child care, combined with a high rate of women's employment, strengthens the social functions of kinship. This may lead to new kinds of tensions, as closer functional ties between generations are observed mainly in those families where the differences of attitudes and values are likely to be greatest.

It would be interesting to find out what happens in American or British middle-class families where there may perhaps be greater use of unrelated but paid domestic help (again female!). At this level does the greater occupational involvement of women mean a loosening of extended kinship ties? Or is it the case that the liberation of women requires something more fundamental than their greater participation in the labour force, even at professional levels? Again, these are important questions but ones likely to be by-passed in the debate over kinship in urban society.

Conclusion

It has been suggested that if we regard the modified extended family not so much in terms of kinship analysis but rather in terms primarily associated with the three-generational family then, first, the debate over the kinship system in urban society assumes less importance and, second, further perhaps more important problems come to light. These problems point to contradictions within the socialization process, conflicts of generations and relationships between sexes. In short a link is made between this particular debate and many of the major concerns in the sociology of the family. Of course, in this re-emphasis, something will be lost. The analysis of relationships between siblings remains an important and still relatively unexplored area although this could possibly be treated as an extension of some of the earlier mentioned problems.[88] Thus the family system in which the child is socialized involves not merely the parent–child dyad but often the parent–child–sibling triad. The way in which such relationships are carried over in the later stages of the life cycle is an important area of analysis. Also likely to suffer neglect with this re-emphasis on generational rather than kinship relationships are relationships with categories such as aunt, uncle and cousin. On the other hand, if we remove the analysis of generational familial relationships from the total field of kin in the way suggested—a removal which would appear to be justified by the evidence—than the relative importance or otherwise of these other sets of relationships may be thrown into sharper relief. Again, however, since it is likely that Ego's relationships with aunts, uncles and cousins is, to some extent, mediated through his relationships in his nuclear family of origin, then the analysis of these more remote sets of kin can be placed in the context of these more immediate relationships. Doubtless there are other problems which may not be adequately handled with this re-orientation that I have suggested but the overall shift may direct our attention to sources of conflict and contradiction within the family rather than to an overemphasis on the positive functions of the modified extended family system. Such an emphasis has, as we have suggested, contributed indirectly to the argument that the modern family is adequately—perhaps even perfectly—adapted to the demands of modern society. This theme will be taken up in the next chapter.

3 The modern family: a success story?

> The widespread pessimism about the family is difficult to sustain in the face of the material assembled in this chapter. Although much of the life of the family can be seen only through a glass darkly, there is enough clear evidence to warrant its description as one of the twentieth century's great success stories.[1]

> Our society has created the myth of the *broken home* which is the source of so many ills, and yet the unbroken home which ought to have broken is an even greater source of tension as I can attest from bitter experience.[2]

Introduction

The previous two chapters have outlined two major themes in the sociology of the modern Western family: the theoretical analysis of the family in terms of functionalism and the empirical issue of the structure of the modern family, in particular the issue as to whether the 'relatively isolated nuclear family' is the typical domestic unit of modern society. These are not, of course, the only concerns that have attracted the attention of family sociologists. But they appear to be two central concerns, and many other themes can be related to them. Both the topics of mate selection and husband–wife relationships—two important themes not directly tackled here—can be seen in the context of a society which emphasizes the importance of love and free choice and lays great stress on the conjugal relationship as against any other familistic or kinship ties.

The main rationale for treating these two problem areas was not in terms of an interest in functionalism or kinship as such but rather to demonstrate the way in which such concerns have been directly or indirectly supportive of a familistic ideology. At best the treatment of these topics has tended to divert attention away from a critical analysis of the modern family; at worst it may become directly supportive of certain kinds and patterns of family living. Betty Friedan, for example, has shown how many of the functionalist arguments and many of the 'findings' of family sociologists have been incorporated into college courses supporting 'the feminine mystique'.[3] The point is not that sociologists of the family should give a united cry of 'down with the family' but that the reasons why such a cry can and might be made be given at least the same critical attention as the thesis stressing the possible functions of the family. Indeed a sociology committed to the enlargement of human responsibility, control and freedom should do no less.

Undoubtedly, the impact of family sociologists on familistic ideology is both a two-way and an indirect process. It is not enough to say that this is just another manifestation of bourgeois ideology; such statements are more likely to obscure than to explain. The mediations between a particular body of theory, research and knowledge and actual ideology and practice have to be examined in considerable detail. To refer to Friedan's account again, she notes how the works of Margaret Mead have often been selectively interpreted to support an ideology probably very much opposed to what Mead herself stands for.[4] Bodies of data or 'findings' do not stand in a simple one-to-one relationship with ideology or public policy but are more frequently used as resources from which differing and often opposing protagonists can draw support. The percentage of marriages ending in divorce, for example, can be countered by presenting the larger and usually unwritten percentage of marriages which do not end in divorce.[5] A more recent example may be cited in the interest in 'mate-swapping' or 'swinging'. The 'traditional' view would be to regard this practice as further evidence of the decline of the family; more functional-minded sociologists might see this in terms of a process of adaption to changing conditions and, as the title of an article called 'the family that swings together clings together' indicates,[6] view it as supportive of the institution of the nuclear family.

The functionalist arguments and the debate about the isolated nuclear family have been incorporated into a wider debate, that relating to the alleged decline in the family. Such a debate is clearly one involving an interrelated set of arguments about facts and values. Logically speaking there are four possible positions on this issue:

1 It may be argued that the family is in decline and that this is to the detriment of society. Thus it will be argued that the decline of the family brings with it a whole host of other social evils such as delinquency, lack of discipline, drug abuse and so on. This is a view commonly held by certain 'moral entrepreneurs' in society.[7]

2 It may be argued that the family is in decline and that this is either all to the good or a natural stage in the evolutionary history of mankind. Barrington Moore appears to approach this argument,[8] and it has its parallels in 'rationalistic' views of the obsolete character of religion in a scientific age.

3 It may be argued that the family is not in decline and that this is all to the good. This is more or less the position of Fletcher, McGregor, Aron and, to a large extent, Parsons.

4 It may be argued that the family is not in decline and that this is to the detriment of the individual and society. This is the most common 'radical' perspective and is identified with the writings of Laing, Cooper and radical feminists.[9]

Of course, important debates cannot be pigeon-holed so readily. It will be apparent that the very word 'decline' is as much an evaluative word as the more direct evaluations of this alleged 'decline'. In so far as the word decline is taken to mean a shrinkage in terms of structure and function there is a direct link between this debate and the two preceding chapters. However, the alleged 'decline' is usually seen in more moral terms, dealing with a decline in the quality of relationships within the family. Thus it may be argued that marriage is no longer a solemn or sacred undertaking, that children no longer respect their parents and old people are no longer cared for and so on.

In practice it would appear that the main lines of this debate have been conducted between a popular view as to what is happening to the family (or perhaps a professional view as to what the popular view is) represented by alternative 1 and a sociological perspective represented by alternative 3 in the above scheme. Alternatives 2 and 4 usually appear on the sidelines or, indeed, are involved in a different area of discussion altogether. Two particular sociological views will be underlined here: those of Fletcher and Aron.

Fletcher and Aron

Both Fletcher and Aron wish to demonstrate that the family is not in decline but that, rather, it is well adapted to the demands of modern society. Indeed, Fletcher at least would argue that the modern family is *better* adapted to the needs of individuals and society than it was in the past and would appear to give support to the view, already cited, that the modern family is 'one of the twentieth century's great success stories'. There are differences between Aron and Fletcher: Aron appears to accept the relatively isolated nuclear family argument and regards middle-class city dwellers as the 'most representative areas of modern civilization'[10] while Fletcher would probably deny this. Aron is examining the main characteristics of modern—particularly European—society in terms of the major concerns of the founding fathers of sociology. His description of the modern family is in a direct line from Durkheim's brief analysis of the conjugal family.[11] Fletcher, on the other hand, is conducting a polemic from a humanist standpoint against clergymen and educators who maintain that the family is in decline and that this decline is a major source of many of our problems. Yet the measure of agreement between these two sociologists is, on the whole, more impressive than any differences. Generally speaking these two authors can be taken together (along with several others including O. R. McGregor, Parsons and the analysts of the modified extended family) although the emphasis will be laid on Fletcher who presents the more detailed argument.

Fletcher writes in the introduction to the revised edition of his book: 'I believe that the family has *not* declined: that the family is *not* less stable than hitherto; and that the standards of parenthood and parental responsibility have not deteriorated.'[12] In order to maintain this argument, Fletcher continues, we must have facts and we must have an historical perspective. In order to argue that the family has or has not declined we must examine the family in the recent past, not as some ideal typification or 'Rebecca Myth' but as it actually existed. Fletcher skilfully shows, first, that there was not one Victorian family but several and that on almost any measure of family worth, strength and functioning one would care to devise, the modern family compares favourably with its predecessors. He draws our attention to the adverse conditions of the working-class family life, the overcrowding, the child labour, the insanitary conditions and so on. He points to the sexual licence of the upper and middle classes.[13] As for the middle classes, often held up to be the model of the Victorian ideal, Fletcher reminds us that the middle-class household was based on the subservience of women and the existence of a large body of servants. Since these times the status of women has improved, legally, economically and socially, there has been a great increase in the standard of living for the working population, improved housing and sanitation. People are living longer, marrying earlier and having smaller families. The modern family is now supported by the social services. He considers that on all these, and many other counts, the family situation of today is much preferable to its Victorian counterpart.

Looking at the modern family, Fletcher attempts to demolish what he considers to be widely held myths. For example, the figures do not show the institution of marriage being threatened by divorce: 93 per cent of marriages at the time he is writing will not end in the divorce courts and the high peak was reached in the war and immediate post-war periods. Sixty per cent of divorces (1957) were in marriages that had lasted for over ten years, a high percentage of divorces were between childless couples or couples with only one child and the overwhelming majority of divorced persons will remarry.[14] On other matters he cites evidence to show that mother's going out to work does not have a disadvantageous effect on the children and the family as a whole and that old people are not neglected by their families. Fletcher concludes:[15]

> There is little doubt, then, that the 'essential' functions of the family, centred upon sexual relationships, parenthood, and home making, are fulfilled far more satisfactorily in the modern family than they were in the family of the distant or the recent past.

More than that, however, the family performs some important 'non-essential' functions as well. They perform economic functions as consumers, educative functions, health functions, religious functions, recreational functions and so on. To some extent the argument becomes a little over-assertive at this point. Thus, in relation to the political function or the function of government, he writes:[16]

> The members of the modern family are now, therefore, drawn far more closely into the tasks of government than ever before. They enjoy far greater degrees of responsibility for government, and, correspondingly, far greater demands are made upon their capacities for responsibility.
>
> This function has considerably increased in effectiveness and in importance in the modern family.

No real evidence is cited for this and it is not asked whether these governmental functions are carried out by families or by individuals who happen to live in families. Fletcher's general conclusion is that modern society makes greater demands on the family and the family is well able to meet these demands. On the whole, these trends will continue. Aron echoes this conclusion although giving stress in a Durkheimian way to the rise of individualism which at one and the same time threatens and puts greater demands on the conjugal family and provides the basis for greater personal realization and development. The modern family 'often gains in loving cohesion what it loses in stability'.[17] The family is an emotional counter-balance to a rationalized bureaucratic society, a 'Gemeinschaft' in a world dominated by the principle of 'Gesellschaft'.

Many of Fletcher's points are well taken and on the whole his book (the revised edition of which has to date run into five printings) is a well argued, thoughtful and humane contribution to a field often seen as being highly emotionally charged. If it has encouraged its readers not to accept at face value many of the prevailing notions about the family it has done a service. However, Fletcher's concern—perhaps stressed more in the first edition—to provide an attack on the moralists who predicted gloom and disaster perhaps led him to create a few new myths about the family. In particular, of course, he gave popular weight to the functional approach to the family and to the idea that the family was very well adapted to the needs of modern society. Ignoring, for the moment, the problem that to say that an institution is well adapted to the needs of modern society may be the greatest possible indictment one could make of that institution, this approach does tend to conjure up the 'happy family' image. It is true that Fletcher does draw our attention to some of the possible excesses of family life. He notes, for example, that families may become too inward-looking and, in a memorable passage, writes:[18]

> Hence the family is that group within which the most fundamental appreciation of human qualities and values takes place—'for better for worse': the qualities of truth and honesty, of falsehood and deceit; of kindliness and sympathy, of indifference and cruelty; of co-operation and forbearance, of egotism and antagonism; of tolerance, justice and impartiality; of bias, dogmatism, and obstinacy; of generous concern for the freedom and fulfilment of others; of the mean desire to dominate—whether in overt bullying or in psychologically more subtle ways.

Fletcher does give recognition to the dark side of family life, perhaps indeed more recognition than most other family sociologists, but the impact of the book as a whole is almost certainly to give great weight to the myth of the happy family, the family as a success story, a myth as potentially dangerous as its opposite, the myth of the declining family. In the rest of this chapter, which serves as a link between the two sections, I shall outline some possible dysfunctions of and contradictions within the family.

'Dysfunctions' of the family

Merton defined 'dysfunctions' as 'those observed consequences which lessen the adaption or adjustment of the system'.[19] Keeping within the assumptions of functional analysis for the moment we may ask to what extent the family may be said to have these 'dysfunctions'. Some of these dysfunctions have already been indicated; others, using a different terminology, will be examined later. The rationale for this section is to illustrate the possible reasons we may have for doubting the simple account of the 'modern family as a success story theme' which in part derives from functional analysis and the debate over the 'isolated nuclear family'.

The first possible dysfunction to be considered is at the level of the individual, assuming that we may treat the individual as a 'system'. It may be argued that while the family may be functional for society as a whole, it is, or can be, dysfunctional for the individual. The effective functioning of the family in society and the cohesion of the family as a unit may be at the expense of one or more members of that family. This may be illustrated in terms of the two axes of the family structure, generation and sex. In terms of generation, the relationship between parent and child may be an exploitative one, involving the projection of parental aspirations, concerns, uncertainties and conflicts on to the immature child. This was illustrated in the account of Vogel and Bell's analysis of the 'child as a scapegoat'.[20] The writings of Laing, Cooper and Esterson have highlighted a considerable body of research concerning the role of the family system in the aetiology of schizophrenia.[21]

It might be noted here that this indicates one way in which the 'isolated nuclear family' can, in certain sections of the community at least, be reconciled with the evidence for the modified extended family. While it is true that, for the mobile urban middle class, geographical separation does not necessarily mean isolation from kin, it does have implications for the functioning of the immediate family. Parents do not, under these circumstances, play out their parental roles against a permanent 'audience' of other kin. To a large extent they are the sole agents directly responsible for the socialization of the child; there are few legitimate checks or counterbalancing forces in the neighbourhood, the wider kinship network or among friends. In urban society, children, it may be assumed, rarely have any direct access to kin outside the immediate nuclear family. It may also be suggested that this question of the visibility of kin (particularly grandparents) and the possibility of their playing a role in the socialization of the child (so that the child is not simply a parental object) may be one of the important differences between the working-class family and the more mobile middle-class families. Green's well known article on 'the middle-class male child and neurosis' (where a direct comparison is made between Polish families in small communities and the urban middle-class family) may to some extent be interpreted in this light. Thus, if Green is correct, the middle-class mother is able to manipulate love 'successfully' because she has, to a much greater extent, the larger burden of responsibility in the socialization for the pre-school child. She does not carry out this process against an audience of others.[22]

The dysfunctions 'inherent' along the other axis of family life, that is in the relationship between the sexes, have been much more extensively examined and will be looked at more systematically later in this book.[23] Here it may be suggested that the successful functioning of the family in modern society and the reiteration of the supporting familistic ideologies may be at the expense of the aspirations of women in society. It is true that Fletcher argues that the improving status of women in society is part of his whole argument that the modern family is well adapted to the demands of modern society. Much of this is undeniable but the question is to what extent does the emphasis on the family as a functioning unit in society necessarily place boundaries on the role and aspirations of the woman? And if greater emphasis is given on the family and its role in modern society—partly perhaps as a result of the wide reading of books like *The Family and Marriage in Britain*—will not the tensions and frustrations surrounding these boundaries become all the greater?[24]

We have suggested that the effective functioning of the family in society may possibly be dysfunctional for one or more of its individual members. One aspect of this, and one which is receiving increasing attention, is the theme of violence in the family.[25] A high percentage of murders and violent assaults take place within the confines of the family. Considerable publicity has been given in recent years to the 'battered baby syndrome'. These darker aspects of family life, while for a long time recognized by poets and novelists, have yet to be fully incorporated into textbooks on the sociology of the family.

I have noted some of the ways in which the family, while functioning adequately in terms of society, might be dysfunctional for one or more of its members. The family itself might also be seen as being dysfunctional for some aspect of society as a whole. Fletcher has noted that the family may become too inward-looking and its members to be too much withdrawn from effective participation in other areas of social life as a result of their overinvolvement in the family. This is indeed implied in Parsons's and Aron's arguments that the family serves as an emotional primary counterbalance to the rational bureaucratic demands of the major institutions in the wider society. Outside work, the main area of involvement in modern society is the family. Most socializing takes place between members of the modified extended family and most leisure-time activities are undertaken within the home with other members of the family. The relatively low participation of individuals as citizens in the various agencies of local and national government and in voluntary associations directly concerned with these wider concerns of citizenship must be and has been recognized as a problem for a formally democratic society.

One aspect of this, and one which has not received much direct attention as yet, is in the growing area of concern relating to the environment. Environmentalists note that this is concerned with three interrelated problems: the problem of pollution, the problem of population growth and the problem of pressure on natural resources, that is food and raw materials. It can be argued that the family can be seen as a major institution through which many of these world-wide problems are mediated. That the family is viewed as the major, indeed the only, locus of decision-making in relation to family size is widely accepted and indeed recognized in the United Nations Charter.[26] It may also be argued that the main economic function of the family in modern society recognized the family as the major locus for consumption decisions. It may be argued further that this is wasteful of resources (each household has its own vacuum cleaner, deep freeze, washing machine, etc.) and multiplies the amount of waste material and pollution. The family car, increasingly recognized as a major environmental threat, is perhaps the most dramatic symbol of this fact. Furthermore, given that the relatively privatized family is the major source of affectual relations in modern society, the possibility of effective participation in other agencies designed to overcome some of these environmental problems is thereby severely limited. These remarks are obviously highly speculative but perhaps point the way to a sociological understanding (as opposed to purely biological or ecological) of the problems of the environment which recognizes the mediating role of the modern nuclear family in the problems concerning the threats to life on this planet.

One final possible dysfunction of the family (and this is by no means an exhaustive list) also relates to this mediating role of the family. Countless studies of education and social class have pointed to the important mediating role of the family in maintaining the social structure. This is recognized by Aron:[27]

> It is the family as much as the nation that transmits the explicit and implicit norms of social class. Thus the exponents of tradition fear disintegration of the family, and the champions of social justice may view the persistence of it as an insurmountable obstacle to equality at the starting line.

The child is not born directly into society nor does the family stand alone. The family is located in the class structure of society and the child comes to understand the social structure and his position in it through the mediating influence of the family. The family indeed may be seen as one of the major factors perpetuating the class structure, simply because it is viewed as the major agency of socialization. Whether one regards this as a dysfunction or not of course depends to a large extent on how one views the class structure.

It is likely that this list of possible dysfunctions of the family could be extended further. But, if we accept that functional analysis has considerable logical and methodological weaknesses, then the analysis of the dysfunctions of the family tends to perpetuate these weaknesses. It points indeed to some of the ambiguities of the functional analysis of the family but still accepts some of the assumptions of functional analysis. Moreover it raises the problem of evaluation and weighting. How do we weigh and evaluate this function as against this dysfunction? To what extent are we justified in assuming that possible dysfunctions for the individual are outweighed by possible functions for society as a whole or vice versa? Can we assume that these dysfunctions of the family are a matter of social pathology —something that happens in particular 'problem' families—or should we argue that function and dysfunction are two sides of the same coin and are manifested in a variety of ways in all families? Fletcher would presumably argue that over the past hundred years or so the positive functions of the family have assumed greater importance and the dysfunctions have assumed lesser importance. Thus, for example, the patriarchal family with the emphasis on control of family property and descent has assumed less importance with the growth of democratic society. Whatever conclusion one comes to, it is surely incumbent on those sociologists who wish to adopt a functionalist perspective on the family and who argue that the modern family is well adjusted to the demands of modern society to recognize fully the possible dysfunctions of the family and to give full weight to them in their analyses.

Contradictions in the family

It is because of the difficulties involved in functional analysis that in place of the term 'dysfunctions' I propose to use the term 'contradiction'. This is defined by Esterson in these terms: 'Contradiction in a social system may be defined as the experience of simultaneous affirmation and negation within the system in respect of an issue.'[28] The term contradiction is used in preference to 'dysfunction' for the following reasons:

1 The term 'dysfunction' often appears to carry the connotation of something that is residual, pathological or unusual. Certainly in relation to the study of the family it has been treated in this way, as something which may be present but which is not really to be expected in the ideal typical model. At the very most the term 'dysfunction' is used to indicate something which may or may not be present. The term 'contradiction' on the other hand, implies something that is 'built into' the situation.

2 The term 'dysfunction' also carries with it the implication that this is something that may be removed or alleviated through remedial action. This follows from the first point. A contradiction is resolved dialectically bringing about a major change in the system of which it

is part. The term 'contradiction' is therefore more dynamic and includes the notion of change at its heart: 'The basic cause of development of a thing is not external but internal and lies in its internal contradictions.'[29]

Contradiction is also to be distinguished from 'conflict'. 'Conflict' is often too ambiguous a term; it may be manifest or latent, individual or collective, overt or covert. Conflict may also be seen as something which is pathological or residual or as something which can be overcome within the existing system without a major change in that system. Conflict may be a manifestation of contradiction but it is not the same thing. A contradiction may exist in a system without there being any overt manifestations of conflict.

The basis for there being contradictions in the modern family lies in the fact that it is at one and the same time part of a wider system and a relatively bounded system in its own right. No family stands alone, yet for theoretical purposes we may treat it as if it stands alone and its members may in some respects regard it as an institution that stands alone. The major relationships which constitute the family—marriage and parenthood—have a legal basis and reference may be made to the law when these relationships are challenged or in doubt (parental authority or bigamy for examples). The tendency for the nuclear family to equal the household emphasizes the notion of a unit bounded in space. Yet families are not encapsulated units and are part of the wider society in all kinds of ways. At any one point of time the members of a family occupy roles and have identities outside the family or which overlap with roles and identities within the family. And over time, individuals move 'out of' one family situation into other roles and other family situations.

With this general point in mind we may locate some of the contradictions within the modern family. In the first place we may note the contradiction between the fact that the family is seen as the main agency of socialization and the fact that part of this socialization is in terms of roles outside the family. As we have seen, the family is seen as the main legitimate agency of primary socialization. At the same time this socialization is in terms of roles and identities outside the family. Parsons would argue that the main way in which this contradiction is 'resolved' is through the fact that the adult male is both father and 'breadwinner', that it is through identification with the father that the male child comes to assume these 'external' roles. This may possibly work in a relatively stable economic and social situation such as a farm family, for example, where the son inherits not merely the family farm but the identity as farmer as well. It is less certain that this can take place fully in modern society where the occupational structure is constantly changing and where much of the father's work is invisible to the male child. The other aspect of this is the 'Freudian dilemma', the fact that the child is brought up in an intensive and almost total environment and is yet at the same time expected to sever himself from this environment and assume new identities in new families and new extra-familial situations. Parsons assumes that this transition is made relatively smoothly; others, such as Laing, for example, assume that the transition is never fully made. Yet another aspect of this dilemma is that between the 'demands of society' and the fact that the family is based on individual—or what are perceived as individual—projects. Couples are expected to marry on the basis of love and children are seen as the 'completion' of this married state. Yet the complete realization of these individual adult projects may be at the expense of the children in whom the 'wider society' has an interest as potential workers, citizens, etc.

The second major area of contradiction within the family lies in the fact that the major roles or functions within the family are also related to identities in the modern society. The roles of husband and wife are both part of and different from the roles of men and women. There is a dialectical interplay between these roles in the wider society. Were it the case that there were complete overlap between the familial roles and the societal roles then there would be no contradiction. However, simply because it is not the case or not felt to be the case that a 'woman's place is in the home', a contradiction exists within the modern family between the societal expectations and the actualities of family life. The contradiction is felt particularly acutely by the woman but is not confined to her. A similar analysis may be made of the fact that the identities 'old' and 'young' have a familial generational referent and a societal meaning.

Thus within the modern family there are contradictions between the family as a unit and the family as part of a wider system and within the family, within the two major axes of familial structure, generation and sex. We may, therefore, accept the Parsonian model but attempt to treat it dialectically rather than functionally, to point to the contradictions inherent within this structure rather than simply accept its functions. These contradictions will be examined in relation to three main bodies of critical writing: the neo-Marxist writing associated largely with the 'Women's Liberation' movement; the existentialist writings of Laing, Esterson, Cooper and others, and the critical analysis of the relationships between sex and society.

This preceding account of dysfunctions and contradictions within the family has been too schematic, too abstract. Many issues have been ignored or skated over. For instance, is it true that contradictions can only be resolved through major structural changes? What are the relationships between general contradictions in society and particular contradictions within the family? The point that we have reached so far is that if we agree that the account of the family as a 'success story' is at best a partial account, we must look around for some alternative framework of analysis, a framework that does not lean upon, at least not exclusively, the functionalist tradition. In directing our attention to the possible sources of contradiction within the family it is to be hoped that some of the possible routes to this goal can be marked out. We must now see where some of these routes take us.

process [illegible]
[illegible]
[illegible]
[illegible]
within the [illegible]
[illegible]
takes us.

part two

4 R. D. Laing: the politics of the family

Introduction

Popular culture may sometimes come closer to the darker side of family living than academic social science. The American 'private eye' story, for example, often shows the investigator attempting to unravel a tangle of wealth, corruption, violence and, binding all these together, a guilty secret at the heart of an influential family. Often the detective (like the analyst) may find that the trail leads back to the very person who hired him in the first place. Or there is a sub-genre of horror movie (illustrated by *Les Diaboliques*, *A Taste of Fear* or *Hush, Hush, Sweet Charlotte*) where two or more members of a family or closely related set of persons conspire to drive another person mad. Such popularly expressed myths convey, in common with all myths, a form of social reality. Such myths certainly, in a dramatic form, echo some of the central concerns of Laing and his associates and remind us that not all the streams of popular culture maintain the model of the 'happy family' to be found in many television series. Perhaps it was the *Forsyte Saga* that most clearly illustrated to millions of people the two-edged character of family life; one edge is warm, protective and fiercely loyal while the other edge is destructive, narrow and ultimately violent.

This, then, is a glimpse at the world of R. D. Laing and the general picture that emerges is clear enough. The difficulties arise when we attempt to isolate the diverse, and perhaps contradictory,[1] elements that go to making up this overall picture. There is the influence of Sartre, first the Sartre of *Being and Nothingness*, in *The Divided Self*, and second the Sartre of *Critique de la raison dialectique* in some of Laing's more recent writings on the family. There is Freud and Sullivan and there is the influence of symbolic interactionism, particularly the work of G. H. Mead and Goffman. The critique of modern advanced industrial society closely parallels that of Marcuse and the discussion of dyads and triads in the family reflects, even if it does not derive its inspiration from, a major stream in formal sociological thinking from Simmel, through Coser and Caplow to some modern games theorists. Among the other influences on Laing we may note Bateson's notion of the 'double-bind'. All these influences, together with Laing's own research and experience, merge into a unique, vivid and sometimes frightening synthesis. To attempt to disentangle some of these strands without, at the same time, losing sight of their essential interrelatedness will be one of the main tasks of this chapter.

It must be recognized that Laing's own style does not assist us in this task of reanalysis. In one place his style may be directly reflective of William Blake, in another place he will use the austere language of set-theory. He is particularly fascinated with the interactive 'knots' that develop in everyday life, the spirals of perspectives that develop in even the simplest situations. As we shall see, this stylistic difficulty, which I suspect most readers encounter in reading Laing, is not entirely accidental. His style, in part at least, may be seen as an attempt to give full recognition to the implications of an existentialist perspective on social interaction.

Such an approach, however, presents some difficulties for an attempt to interpret or reassess Laing's approach. For one thing, the very process of reanalysis and resynthesis may involve the reification that Laing is seeking to avoid. I am aware that, as a sociologist, my selection and interpretation of Laing's material is almost certainly likely to be different from a similar process of reanalysis conducted by a philosopher or a psychologist. I have responded to those features of his work which appear to be of help to me as a sociologist interested in the family. This inevitably involves selection, perhaps even distortion, but I hope that I have not done any great violence to the main themes with which Laing is dealing.

One possible distortion may arise from the fact that I have treated Laing as a representative figure here. A full treatment would require an assessment of the differences and similarities between the closely associated figures of Laing, Esterson and Cooper. Esterson, for example, has presented a clear outline of some of the major features of Sartre's recent writings that have influenced this 'group'[2] while Cooper has developed a more sustained critique of the institution of the family.[3] Reference might also be made to the work of Ackerman, whose insights into the theory and practice of family therapy clearly antedate the more radical perspectives of Laing.[4] Reference must also be made to the work of Henry and to the closely related perspectives (particularly the discussions of schizophrenia and the family) collected by Handel.[5] Out of all these and many other similar and associated perspectives Laing has emerged, possibly against his will, as a kind of 'symbolic leader'. Students who in the early 1960s might have been seen discussing *The Power Elite* or *The Sociological Imagination*, are now more likely to be seen reading Laing's *Politics of Experience and the Bird of Paradise*. As a symbolic leader, Laing has probably suffered the same fate as Marcuse, McLuhan or perhaps, more recently, Althusser, and may be more discussed than read, becoming part of that process of defining 'us' against 'them' which Laing so pointedly describes. To some, Laing may be empty, derivative and perhaps even dangerous; to others he is the touchstone of radical commitment. Serious assessment may be resisted by both sides.

In my discussion I shall attempt first to outline some of Laing's main themes which seem to me to be most relevant in the study of the family. For the most part I shall be relying fairly heavily on *The Politics of the Family*,[6] a collection that includes a revised version of a series of talks given through the Canadian Broadcasting Corporation together with three earlier papers on the family. I shall also be referring to some of his earlier work and the books of Cooper and Esterson already cited. I shall then consider what I feel to be some of the main criticisms that may be levelled at Laing's approach. Finally, I shall consider some of the main themes again in the light of these critical observations.

The main themes

In *The Divided Self*, Laing attempted to provide an existential account of the schizophrenic experience.[7] He was less concerned with providing a clinical explanation of this condition than with describing the structure and meaning of this experience and hence also with challenging our conventional notions of the borderlines between madness and sanity. Some references to the family background of schizophrenics appear in this work but these are dealt with in more detail in *Sanity, Madness and the Family* which he wrote with A. Esterson.[8] Strictly speaking, Laing and Esterson are not saying that the family backgrounds of persons defined as schizophrenics account for their condition; rather they are suggesting that many of the apparently bizarre and meaningless aspects of schizophrenic behaviour can be understood as meaningful in the context of family experiences. In investigating these family backgrounds, Laing is led to consider the structure of experiences within 'normal' families. Two other major themes, the social psychology of interpersonal perception[9] and the existentialism of Sartre as represented in his *Saint Genet*, *Problem of Method* and *Critique de la raison dialectique*,[10] combine with this critical evaluation of the condition defined as schizophrenic to provide the main sources for his discussion of the family in *Politics of the Family*. Over the next few pages I hope to examine some of the main themes that Laing developed in the course of his journey from *The Divided Self* to his more recent examinations of the institution of the family itself.[11]

1 Laing, as we have noted, adopts an existentialist approach to the study of the family, in particular the existentialism of Sartre. While what this means in practice should become clear during the more detailed examination of the themes, one or two general points about what is meant by an existentialist approach in this context may be in order. In the first place, the notion that the social (or 'behavioural') scientist stands outside his 'data' in a one-way observer–observed relationship is challenged. There is always a dialectic between the two, unlike the relationship between a scientist and a non-human organism. To understand schizophrenia, for example, we should look beneath and beyond the clinically applied labels and formal lists of symptoms; rather we should look at the process whereby these labels come to be applied, often with the active participation of the 'objective' professional psychiatrist.[12] We should strip away the 'vocabulary of denigration'[13] implied in this labelling procedure and seek to understand the inner meaning of the schizophrenic experience.

This approach has implications when we come to examine the family experience of persons defined as schizophrenics. Again, we have the question of the dialectic between observer and observed in the study of the family. The family as it appears to the 'observer' may be different from the family as it appears to each of its members—simply through the fact of its being observed and being aware of its being observed. The fact that in the process of investigation we can talk of this '*family*' as a social entity at all may be an outcome of the dialectic between the relationships between the members of the family on the one hand and their relationships, separately and together, with the outside world on the other.

The family, then, is more than the sum of its individual members. At the same time it is not a metaphysical 'group' entity, however much its members may be mystified into believing that it is. Laing, therefore, is trying to avoid the pitfalls of both 'methodological individualism' on the one hand, and 'holism' on the other.[14] Perhaps a key concept here is that of the 'project':[15]

> The most rudimentary conduct must be determined at one and the same time in relation to real, present factors which condition it and in relation to a certain future object to which it attempts to give birth. This is what we call the project.

The family is not merely to be understood in terms of the present relationships of its members nor even of those present together with their past relationships, but also in terms of its future, the projects of each of its members, projects which, in the context of the family, are bound up with each other. Perhaps this is most clearly seen in the process which is usually, and rather over-simply, defined as 'socialization': 'We must remember also that we live our childhood *as our future*. Our gestures and roles are taught and learned in the perspective of that-which-is-to-come.'[16]

The existential approach to the family is, of course, apparent throughout Laing's writings. It should become more apparent in our examination of the various threads in his argument and in Laing's use of terms such as 'series', 'intelligibility', 'praxis' and 'process'. Put at its simplest, it might be said that Laing attempts to give full recognition to human freedom while showing the limits to and constraints on that freedom, the terrible paradox that my freedom is bound up with your freedom. Perhaps this is most apparent and yet also most obscure in the context of the family. (Consider: 'You must decide for yourself, dear' or 'I don't care what he does after leaving school so long as he's happy'.) The language of conventional social science when it comes to examine the family either gives too little scope for freedom or too much. Thus it may define some ideal typical construct of 'romantic love' which in a true Durkheimian fashion is external to and coercive of the individual without examining the multiplicity of meanings assigned to this concept, the multiplicity of uses to which it may be put. Or it may talk about 'mate selection' in terms of some purposive rational behaviour (within the limits set by religion, social class, ethnicity and locality) without asking how it is that individuals are 'selecting mates' in this particular way in the first place. Such approaches tend to distance us from the family and, to some extent, contribute to the process of mystification. Laing attempts to get closer to the heart of family living.

? The first step in understanding Laing's approach to the family, therefore, is to be found in his investigation into the family lives of persons defined as 'schizophrenic'. This is not, in itself, a new departure,[17] and Laing himself recognizes the pioneering work of Bateson and Sullivan in this field. He notes that ' "Schizophrenia" runs in families, but observes no genetically clear law.'[18] Over the past few years, as Laing records, there has been a shift from a focus on the 'schizophrenogenic' mother to the family as a whole. Now, it is increasingly likely to be recognized that 'not only the mother but also the total family situation may impede rather than facilitate the child's capacity to participate in a real, shared world as self-with-other'.[19] Yet, as Haley argues, there is a danger in this shift from the mother to the whole family system if it also implies that we now tend to treat the family as a mysterious 'whole'.[20] We need to specify and examine more clearly the actual nature of the relationships within the family which contribute to the development of 'schizophrenic' symptoms.

This shift of focus from the 'disturbed' to the 'disturbing'[21] is not entirely an exercise in tracing the 'causes' of schizophrenia. Given the existential approach and Laing's critical account of the very nature of the condition defined as 'schizophrenia', a simple cause–effect model would scarcely be appropriate. Rather the main argument is that the experience and behaviour of 'schizophrenics'—often apparently bizarre and meaningless to the outside observer—can be understood in the context of the patients' own family experiences. One of the more readily intelligible illustrations provided by Laing is the case of Jane who was 'absorbed in a reverie of a perpetual game of tennis'.[22] This particular internalization of her family was very similar to the structure of relationships within her family as they were observed by the analysts. Thus her father and his mother were ranged against her mother and her mother's father. These two halves of the family did not communicate directly to each other but used Jane as a 'go-between'. Jane had lost the link between her own reverie and her 'real' family life. This is a relatively simple illustration; similar accounts are given in greater detail in *Sanity, Madness and the Family*.

Clearly, the whole field of the nature and aetiology of schizophrenia is a controversial one and it is not the intention of the present work to enter into this debate. Rather, it is the aim to assess the significance of these accounts for the study of the family. In the first place, Laing seems to be saying that the gap between 'normal' and 'abnormal' families is not all that great and that detailed accounts of what we may like to call 'abnormal' families can illuminate our understanding of all families. In the second place, Laing is, as we have argued, concerned to shift our attention from the role of the mother (stressed in some of the earlier literature) to the family as a whole, without, at the same time, reifying that entity. He is, therefore, seeking to develop a language, a set of tools, with which we may understand the complexity of intra-familial relationships. Some of the major items in this language will be outlined in the following pages.

3 How can we approach this complex structure of relationships within the family? In the first place, any family group may be seen as a set of dyadic relationships; thus in a family group of four members there are six possible dyadic relationships. From the social psychology of inter-personal relationships we are aware of the complex 'spiral of interpersonal perception' within any one of these dyads.[23] John may love Mary and Mary may love John. But does John think that Mary loves him and does Mary think that John loves her? And does John know that Mary thinks that John loves

her? And does Mary know that John thinks that Mary loves him? The complexities of these simple dyadic relationships become readily apparent and Laing and his colleagues have developed their analysis of these relationships with considerable subtlety and depth. The family can be seen as being a particularly important arena for the playing out of these dyadic dramas, with all the possibilities for confusion, misunderstanding, manipulation and attempted manipulation and yet also the possibilities for understanding and mutual growth. Laing focuses, for the most part, on those relationships that appear to spiral off into complete misunderstanding and worse. His world is a familiar one in modern drama and the cinema:[24]

> And one of the most hellish whirligigs of our contemporary interpersonal alienation is that of two alienated loves, two self-perpetuating solitudes, each in emptiness feeding on the other's emptiness, an inextricable and timeless confusion, tragic and comic—the ever fertile soil of endless recrimination and desolation.

Yet complex as these dyadic relationships are, they do not fully or adequately define the complexity of intra-familial relationships. Our reference to the family as a set of dyadic relationships may give a misleadingly static picture of family life. Superficially it may not appear very different from the Parsonian model of family roles distributed around the two axes, expressive-instrumental and authority. However: 'each person does not occupy a simple definable position in relation to other members of his or her own family'.[25] If we wish to understand a particular person in a simple four-person family we must see him or her not only in the context of the sets of dyadic relationships that have been outlined but also in terms of triadic relationships. These dyadic dramas are played out in front of an audience. There are all the possibilities of shifting alliances, of playing off one against the other, of conducting one set of relationships through another. Thus the growing alienation between a husband and wife may be expressed not directly but through the children as in mutual accusations of neglect or of 'spoiling' the child. Within the context of family life, our roles change as, in different encounters, we become different 'others-to-others'.[26] Thus the family is an arena for a complex set of dyadic *and* triadic dramas and games.

This analysis of the complexity of triads and dyads in the family derives not so much from Simmel's analysis of the formal properties of these relationships and his recognition that the progression from two to three is a qualitative progression rather than a simple additive process, but rather from Sartre's existentialism. Laing, in his account of Sartre's *Critique de la raison dialectique*, points out that 'reciprocal and triadic relations are the starting-point or basis of all relations including all forms of reification and alienation'.[27] He goes on to outline some kinds of reciprocities, positive and negative (taking the forms of exchange or conquest).[28] He then goes on to argue that the third party is necessary to unify the dyad. The outside observer may give unity to two others who are unaware of each other's presence. Or two people may become aware of their dyadic unity in relation to a third party. The dyad only becomes a relationship in the presence of a third.

Within the family these triads must be seen as the key relationship. The individual family member internalizes these sets of relationships and makes a synthesis of the interaction of the others. The others also synthesize his synthesis and so on. Furthermore these relationships are not confined to a simple four-person family group but are of necessity—since each married person is part of both a family of orientation and a family of procreation—carried over generations. There is the process of *projection*, the mapping of one set of relations on to another set of relations. Thus a child may be likened to a father or a brother—more than this he may be 'induced' to embody these others—perhaps dead or unknown others in his life. These dyadic and triadic dramas are therefore carried over from one generation to another. It is at this point that Laing attempts to reconcile what Sedgwick regards as irreconcilable: the perspectives of Freud and Sartre. Like Freud, Laing sees family dramas being repeated, with slightly different casts, from one generation to another. Using Sartre's approach to the 'third' he shows the complexity of overlapping family structures through which these dramas are accomplished.

It may be asked what is peculiar to the family in this particular discussion of dyads and triads. For many of the processes which are being described such as the role of the third and the spiral of inter-personal expectations may be found in all kinds of group and two-person interactions and not merely in families. Laing would probably make three points in elaborating an answer to this question. The first is that the family is a much more pervasive unit than all other groups or institutions in our society. Married or single, with or without children, the family, either of orientation or of procreation or both, always has an influence. Even dead persons may serve as models for as yet unborn children. Closely related to this is the fact that the family involves more sustained and more intensive interactions than we find elsewhere. Often it is difficult or impossible to withdraw from these situations where even silence may be understood to be a response. Finally, the family is a major agent of socialization within our society. The culture of a particular society or group in society is largely mediated through the family. This means that a large part of the most intensive form of family living is concerned with the socialization of young children, a process which is much more than formal or explicit instruction. Typically, the child does not choose the family into which he is born. He is introduced into a world which is, in the first instance, constructed for him and appears as a 'given'. The parents—and other adults or older siblings —can for a large part set the rules of the game. They can lay down the normative expectations and the appropriate sanctions and they can define the reasons for these expectations. A large number of the cases studied by Laing and Esterson seem to include parents who are able to define the world as a place of extreme danger to their children. Thus at one and the same time a parent may be creating a particularly binding form of relationship to the child (that of a protector) and also defining the nature of the outside world for the child. Thus these dyadic and triadic relationships are carried out in a context where the self comes to be defined, a context where there is a unique and intensive dialectic between the family and one's own identity. The family is experienced as a system in which one *is*: 'To be in the same family is to feel the same family inside.'[29]

4 Discussion of the previous theme indirectly raised the problem of the definition of familial boundaries. While it is clear that there are several overlaps between Laing's account of family structure and the structure of other group and interpersonal situations, there are also senses in which the family is distinct from these other structures. Some of these were analysed in the last section. Here we look at the way in which families come to define their own boundaries and their *series* and *nexus*.

The *series* is a passive group structure; it derives its 'unity' not from the fact that its members have any mutual concern for each other as fellow group members but from the fact that the group is externally constituted. Its members are interchangeable units. Examples of a series are a group of people at a bus stop (an example provided by Sartre) or a group united through some external *serial object* such as public opinion, the red menace or the Jews.[30] In the context of the family we can see seriality in the cases of families which achieve their unity through a constitution of 'them' or, more specifically, 'the neighbours'. By 'neighbours' it is not meant this specific neighbour to my right or left but a constituted, generalized set of 'neighbours' perhaps constructed at a time of crisis such as the coming of a coloured lodger or the pregnancy of an unmarried daughter.[31] The members of the family possess their unity only through the construction of these external processes. Finally: 'In this collection of reciprocal indifference, of reciprocal inessentiality and solitude, there appears to exist no freedom. There is conformity to a *presence* that is everywhere *elsewhere*.'[32]

The *nexus* on the other hand is a fused or bonded group where the members are bonded together on the basis of reciprocity, mutual concern and the internalization by each member of the other members seen as fellow group members. In *Sanity, Madness and the Family* Laing defines the *nexus* specifically in terms of family relationships:

> that multiplicity of persons drawn from the kinship group, and from others who, though not linked by kinship ties, are regarded as members of the family. The relationships of persons in a nexus are characterized by enduring and intensive face-to-face reciprocal influence on each other's experience and behaviour.[33]

In the previous section we looked at the complex structure of dyadic and triadic relationships within the family. Each member interiorized a synthesis of these relationships and of their own syntheses of the relationships in which he was included. Each lives in the social field of the other. What holds the family together is not a common goal in some clearly defined instrumental sense but rather the continued presence of the others. Each member is part of the group and is, therefore, part of each other. Out of this complex develop conceptions of family loyalty. In extreme cases families may come to live in 'family ghettos' maintained by terror. This is seen where the external world is perceived and presented as one of danger and where these phantasies of external terror become the basis of terror within the family. We are approaching the double-edged nature of family living: on the one hand the 'highest ethic of reciprocal concern' on the other the generation of terror, phantasy and domination.[34]

Thus we have the *series*, the spurious unification through the construction of a set of unnamed others, and the *nexus*, the actual unification of the group through sustained, mutual interaction, support, obligation, involvement, loyalty and terror. Both appear, in Laing's writings, as kinds of traps. In the first the individual is responding to some unnamed 'others' and unspecified 'them'. In the latter, the individual is bound by loyalties and obligations which he may not fully understand or recognize. The family may be a group of saints or a group of gangsters; in either case the bonds of overlapping reciprocities and obligations will be the same.

It is not entirely clear whether Laing views these terms as indicating alternative modes of family living or whether both aspects may be found within the same or similar families. Certainly, the family described by Esterson appears to be an example of serial relationships. There is little mutual concern for its members as persons; rather its unity is constituted by references to 'public opinion' or to obscure dangers such as 'coffee bars in Chelsea'.[35] But it is also possible to see a dialectical relationship between the two. The mutual concern of the members of the nexus may be strengthened or constituted partially on the basis of a serialized set of others. In both cases, however, we see the process of the delineation of familial boundaries not in terms of some categories established by the external sociologist or analyst but as an accomplishment of the members themselves.

5 This work of drawing boundaries is not simply a matter of marking off the family—'*my*' family—from the non-family but it is also at the same time the work of constituting and understanding the wider social world. A binary structure of relationships and perceptions is one which is internalized at an early age through the socialization process within the family. Thus the perception of the world in terms of our family/the outside world, in terms of them/us, parallels other kinds of distinctions we make—inside/outside, good/bad, male/female, white/black, Jews/Gentiles. What Laing appears to be saying here—and I shall discuss this further in a critical evaluation later in this chapter—is that we learn to make these elementary and ultimately often destructive distinctions within our family in our early years.[36] This process of making binary distinctions in terms of family relationships is important in another way. This process of dividing the world up in terms of them/us, a distinction based upon the family (' "our" family'), points out the crucial role that the family plays as the *mediator* of wider cultural and social relationships and points to the way in which this mediation takes place.

To a large extent this discussion of the family as a mediator derives from Sartre's chapter in *The Problem of Method* on mediations.[37] Here Sartre is conducting a dialogue with orthodox Marxism. Crude Marxism tends to explain social phenomena mechanically in terms of the relationships of groups of persons to the means of production, in short in terms of a class analysis. While Sartre recognizes his debt to the Marxian tradition—indeed he argues that we are all working within this tradition—he also points out that this does not take us close enough to social processes as they are lived and experienced by individuals. This can be seen in the analysis of works of literature and their authors. Orthodox Marxists would tend to analyse these in terms of the class position of the authors; Sartre would argue that this is only the beginning of a true account. In his summary of *The Problem of Method*, Cooper paraphrases Sartre in these words: 'Undoubtedly he [Valéry] is a petit-bourgeois intellectual, but every petit-bourgeois intellectual is not Valéry, and this sums up the heuristic deficiency of contemporary Marxism.'[38]

In particular, such an analysis of an author and his work needs to consider that author's family background. It is not enough to say that this person comes from a petit-bourgeois family but we should also see the way in which the family mediated and selected certain aspects of petit-bourgeois culture. To do so we must look at the structure of triadic and dyadic relationships within the family, the relation between this family of procreation and the two families of orientation and so on: 'The human being learns how to structure his perceptions, particularly within his family, as a sub-system interplaying with its own contexted sub-culture, related institutions and overall larger culture.'[39] There is no simple one-to-one mapping of middle class/working class on to the dichotomy our family/them, although the two are not unrelated. Laing is directing us to examine the subtle and complex mediations that take place within the family and between the family and the constituted external world.

Conclusion and summary of main themes

The child is born into a highly complex segment of social structure, far more complex than might be predicted on the basis of numbers alone. The elementary nuclear family of mother, father and children represents a complex interacting and fluctuating system of dyadic and triadic relationships. But no nuclear family stands alone; each mother and each father are themselves part of their respective families of origin. A complex drama is repeated from generation to generation and it is extremely difficult for any one actor to disentangle the complex threads and knots that extend across the generations. In the process usually described as 'socialization', the growing individual internalizes these complex patterns of family structure and learns to identify with them. To understand the role of the family in the formation of personality we must consider not merely the individual actors—the dominant mother or the authoritarian father—but the complete web of familial relationships over generations.

The process of 'socialization' also involves the growing delineation of familial boundaries. Through these immediate and inescapable experiences in the family, the growing child learns to mark off his family from other families, from the 'world outside'. Distinctions such as good/bad, black/white, our people/your people develop in the process of socialization. This can be seen as a dialectical process. The world outside may be seen as being alien, as containing unnamed terrors and pitfalls. The only refuge from this alien world is the family itself, the family which defined the outside world as hostile in the first place. And so the grip of the family is tightened and there is a further twist in the dialectical spiral.

To Laing, therefore, the significance of the family is two-fold. In the first place the family, as the first unit with which the newly born child comes into contact, represents a major element in the formation of personality. This in itself, of course, is scarcely new; what is new is Laing's treatment of the family in terms of these dyadic and triadic relationships rather than as either a collection of individuals or as a reified whole. In the second place, the family is a major mediator between the individual and society. Elementary distinctions and interpretations of the social world, such as those in terms of ethnic group or class, for example, are made and reinforced in the experience of family living.

It should be clear that, while Laing accepts the generally held view of the family as an important, perhaps the most important, unit in social life, his evaluation of this importance is very different from that of many sociologists or psychologists. Indeed, much of his writing can be seen as a critique of many of the prevailing interpretations of the family, although this critique is not often made explicit. One place where an explicit attack is made is in *The Politics of Experience*:[40]

> In much contemporary writing on the individual and the family there is the assumption that there is some not-too-unhappy confluence, not to say pre-established harmony, between nature and nurture. There may be some adjustments to be made on both sides, but all things work together for good to those who want only security and identity.
>
> Gone is any sense of possible tragedy, of passion. Gone is any language of joy, delight, passion, sex, violence. The language is that of the boardroom. No more primal scenes, but parental coalitions; no more repression of sexual ties to parents, but the child 'rescinds' its Oedipal wishes.

Laing continues this critique by examining the notion of 'adaption' so often used in family studies and asks the question, itself a major theme of his writings: 'Adaption to what? To society? To a world gone mad?'[41]

Such a critique is, of course, not merely one of current writings on the family but also of the institution of the family itself. This is especially marked in Cooper's attack on the family. In particular it might be said that the family represents a constant assault on the self; it is perhaps the most total of total institutions. To Laing the family is, among other things, an institution where 'normal' parents get their children to love them by terrorizing them.[42] It is an institution where for the rather bland term 'socialization' we may read 'training obedience', a dangerous link in a chain leading from the family to soldiers or officials unquestioningly following orders.[43] 'Dysfunction' would be too mild a term to describe Laing and Cooper's account of the disastrous effects of the institution of the family.

Some critical points

I have, in the past few pages, attempted to present Laing as fairly and as faithfully as possible with few overt comments or interpretations of my own. At the very least it can be said that he presents a particularly original and provocative combination of the various themes and sources previously cited and outlined. Taken together his writings, together with those of his close associate David Cooper, represent one of the most closely argued and consistent attacks on the institution of the family and especially on the prevailing near consensus among social scientists on the significance of this institution in modern society and its 'functions'. Laing's attempts to do justice to the complexity of family relationships, to try new methods of approach (such as the use of the language of set-theory) which may or may not prove to be useful, command respect. Laing is not merely a polemicist (although he clearly is that as well) and his analyses and concepts should prove to be stimulating even to those who do not accept his conclusions or some of the implications of his work.

Before proceeding to a critical examination of some of the main points of Laing's argument it is worth spending some time looking at two features which are inevitably tied up with these arguments: his style and his method. It has already been mentioned that Laing's style is both polemical and, at times, obscure. It is difficult to express his ideas in terms other than his own. His verbal spirals and knots parallel the interactive spirals and knots that he is attempting to analyse. His sentences and paragraphs are often short and sometimes apparently without the normally accepted phrases and transition passages linking one stage of the argument to another. Such literary devices may occasionally mystify the reader and will almost certainly infuriate the academic scholar, more used to the orderly progression of a scientific paper in a learned journal.

Laing's answer, almost certainly, would be that this style is deliberate, first as an attempt to capture the depth of the reality of family life and perhaps, second, as part of his attack on more orthodox social science. The conventional scientific paper rarely reaches the public and often distances itself from its subject through the language of the particular discipline and through the techniques of measurement and analysis. Laing's approach is a direct assault on the problem, an attempt to minimize the barriers between scientist and object, and between reader and writer. Such an approach is consistent with a desire to capture and understand family life as it is experienced by family members.

While accepting the strength of this argument[44] and agreeing that the accolades of the scientific profession need not be the sole criteria of worthwhileness, it still remains true that Laing could make a few more concessions to the more orthodox reader. It is not so much the fact that Laing uses, in the conventional scientific sense, unusual language, but that he often combines Freudian or existentialist jargon with his own particular prose style. Perhaps more serious, however, is the assertive 'take-it-or-leave-it' tone of much of his writings. Martin, a not wholly unsympathetic critic, writes of Laing's method of 'random accusation and sloganized virulence, which destroys the possibility of genuine discussion'.[45] The combination of the language of prophecy with the language of analysis is not necessarily to be despised—Marx, after all was a master of it—but it does sometimes present some formidable difficulties to those who wish to assess the work in question.

This leads us to a second preliminary criticism, that of Laing's method and use of sources. It will be remembered that Laing's early researches were into the family lives of persons defined as schizophrenics. In his later writings, Laing appears to shift from talking about the families of schizophrenics to talking about *the* family while still, in many cases, using the same kind of case material for illustrative and demonstrative purposes. Some illustrations appear to come from (unnamed) accounts of 'normal' families but we can find few actual examples based on systematic research into such families.

The answer to this possible criticism is clear enough. In his existentialist account of schizophrenia, Laing is constantly challenging the validity of the term itself and, beyond this, the validity of lay and professional distinctions between madness and sanity, between normality and abnormality. In part this is a polemical statement—normal families send their sons to fight in Vietnam, build fall-out shelters and so on—and partly a suggestion that the patterns of interaction in schizophrenogenic families is in essence similar to that in families not thus defined. While such families clearly do not represent a random sample of families in a given cultural milieu they do represent a strategic sample. Patterns observed in the family life of schizophrenics can provide us with heightened models of family experience which can be found elsewhere. The approach is rather like the approach of a court of enquiry after a major accident or disaster. Such enquiries almost invariably reveal patterns of deviance and neglect which have gone on some time before the accident under investigation. How it is that certain persons come to be *defined* as schizophrenics is a separate question, just as is the one as to how a particular accident took place. The parallel is, of course, defective in some respects but does, I think, illustrate Laing's strategy.

It need hardly be said that it is highly important that research, inspired by Laing's orientations, into 'normal' families be carried out.[46] At present what we have is a set of highly imaginative and suggestive orientations. We may look at our own families or at the families of friends or neighbours and recognize the truth of much of what Laing is saying. Or we may look at some imaginative fictional accounts of family life—the television quartet *Talking to a Stranger* for example—and note how many other writers have been sensitive to the same patterns. Or, indeed, we may look at some existing accounts by sociologists and others of family life and reinterpret them in the light of Laing's observations. *Crestwood Heights* and *Blue-Collar Marriage* are two possible candidates here and I shall be considering these and some other cases in the concluding chapter.

One problem in the investigation of all aspects of family life is the problem of bias. This is, of course, nothing peculiar to these studies but it does take on a new significance in the kinds of studies needed here, where the investigator attempts to probe a little deeper than the verbalized responses to formal interviews. There is always the danger that the author will end up by telling the reader that this *is* what is going on, rather than in *showing* the reader what is going on and suggesting that the author's interpretation is a plausible one. Consider the following exchange from *Sanity, Madness and the Family*:[47]

> Mother: She's brought people home—when she's been ill she's brought people home that she normally wouldn't tolerate, you know, these beatniks.
> Father: There have been writers and God knows what.
> Mother: People have come home and requested to be put up for the night.
> Interviewer: You don't approve of writers?
> Mother: Oh, it isn't writers—no, no—of course we approve.
> Father: I approve.
> One notes again how contradictory is her mother and father's attitude—oscillating between implicit expressions of disapproval and explicit avowals of approval.

Here, it might be suggested, Laing and his associates are perhaps not taking the existentialist approach far enough in seeing the investigator as part of the socio-psychological system under investigation. This perhaps represents, in sharpest form, the contradiction between the analyst-patient relationship implied in traditional Freudian analysis and therapy and the dialectical relationship between observer and observed implied in the existentialist approach to the study of human behaviour. This contrast is perhaps most marked in Esterson's book where there appears to be a lack of integration between the presentation of the case material and the theoretical approach outlined in the second part. It may be argued in the case above that the oscillation 'between implicit expressions of disapproval and explicit avowals of approval' is in fact the result of the interruption 'you don't approve of writers?' Some kind of rapport between interviewer and subject had, presumably, already been established. After the interviewer's question, the subject might have wondered if he might not have indirectly insulted or offended the interviewer. After all, was he not a middle-class person, a professional person, perhaps even a writer or a friend of writers himself.[48] In this case, of course, Laing and his associates do provide us with enough information to suggest an alternative interpretation of this particular incident and, it is also true, that this is not an isolated incident upon which the authors are intending to build their case. What is perhaps needed in this kind of research is, first, a more explicit recognition of the active role of the investigator in the situation under investigation and, second, the provision of enough material, reports of interviews, extended cases, etc. to enable the reader to make alternative interpretations of the situation under examination.

I now turn to some specific critical comments on Laing's work.

1 The first is the general lack of any clear social or temporal location of his families, a criticism that has been made strongly by Martin.[49] It has been noted how Laing generalizes from the families of persons defined as schizophrenics to talking about *the* family in general and that this progression, while open to abuse, is clearly of some strategic value. Of less certain value, however, is the failure to 'place' these families in any social or cultural context. We know something about the socio-economic background of the families described in *Sanity, Madness and the Family* but we know little about the location of 'the family' about which he writes in, say, *The Politics of the Family*. We assume that these families are located in modern Western capitalist societies.[50] He appears to assume that similar things are going on in advanced communist societies and, since we have no clear statement to the contrary, many of his generalizations would appear to apply to all families in all societies at all times. It is clear, however, that even within a single modern capitalist society such as Britain, the USA or Canada there exist considerable differences between families according to social class, religion, ethnic group, region and so on. Laing would appear to regard all these differences as incidental, as not seriously affecting his central argument. To be fair to Laing, he does recognize the problem. In *The Divided Self*, for example, he suggests that Western psychoanalysts tend to be 'gauche' where it comes to handling wider sociological material while Soviet analysts may be more 'gauche' in dealing at the inter-personal level.[51] In *The Politics of the Family* there is a brief recognition of 'different pluralities in a pluralistic society'[52] and he also has an approving reference to the work of Speck who attempts to place and analyse individual families in the

context of a network of wider non-familial relationships.[53] I shall later suggest ways in which a case that Laing presents could be located in a particular social and cultural context. Perhaps, however, this criticism is less serious in the context of *The Divided Self* where Laing is presenting the outlines of an existentialist approach to madness. More serious, however, is the point where Laing comes to talk about *the* family in general with no clear guidelines as to what is essential and what is incidental in the analysis of and the 'placing' of such families in time and social space.

In a sense it might be suggested that Laing is turning Sartre on his head. In his *Problem of Method*, Sartre analyses the problem of 'mediations'. At its simplest, the argument is that an analysis purely in terms of a Marxian definition of social class is an incomplete analysis. The sociologist or the historian must analyse the particular way in which class values and experiences are mediated through specific institutions such as the family, religious sect, community, etc. Laing, although clearly influenced by the later Sartre—as we see in *Reason and Violence*—almost appears to reverse this approach by stressing the family as a source, not merely of particular features of individual personality but also of fundamental ways of perceiving and orientation to the social world. The family itself appears, for the most part, to be detached from any particular social, historical or cultural context. It is Sartre without Marx.

To illustrate this general criticism (and also incidentally to illustrate some of Laing's major preoccupations) let us look at some aspects of a case presented by Laing in some detail. My aim is not necessarily to provide any 'missing dimension' which Laing overlooks in his account; rather it is to suggest at what points in his account a discussion of factors outside the immediate family situation might, in a more general way, increase our understanding. The case is that of 'Julie' described in the final chapter of *The Divided Self*.[54] I am not presenting all the details of this 'clinical biography'—used here merely for illustrative purposes—and the reader should refer to the original for these.

Julie had been in a mental hospital for nine years since the age of seventeen. She was a 'chronic schizophrenic'. She felt that she was not a real person and that she was trying to become a person. She was worried that she might be too destructive and was beginning to be afraid to touch anything. She felt that her mother was smothering her and would not let her live. This was in spite of the fact that her mother was always encouraging her to go out, to meet more friends:[55]

> However, the basic psychotic statement she made was that 'a child had been murdered'. She was rather vague about the

> details, but she said she had heard of this from the voice of her brother (she had no brother). She wondered, however, if this voice may not have been her own. The child was wearing her clothes when it was killed. The child could have been herself. She had been murdered either by herself or by her mother, she was not sure. She proposed to tell the police about it.

Laing interviewed the members of Julie's immediate family circle. In building up a 'clinical biography' he constructed three phases in Julie's life history: a phase when she was 'good', a phase when she became 'bad' and a phase when she was 'mad'. Laing's account of this good-bad-mad sequence derives largely from his interviews with the mother.

In the 'good' phase Laing presents a set of statements made by the mother:

> 'Julie was never a demanding baby.'
> 'She was weaned without any trouble.'
> 'She was clean from the moment that nappies were taken off at fifteen months.'
> 'She always did what she was told.'
> 'She was never a trouble.'

Laing argues that these statements, seen by the mother as indices of 'normality', in fact implied an extreme denial of autonomy to the child.

In the second, the 'bad' phase, two major changes took place. The mother shifted from organizing every detail of her daughter's life to encouraging her daughter to go out and make friends. The daughter, for her part, did not respond in the expected way to these suggestions. Instead she did nothing. She was untidy. She cherished a doll, long after her mother thought it desirable for a girl of her age. She began to accuse her mother of never allowing her to develop as a person. This phase developed from about the age of fifteen. During this phase Julie's sister recounts an incident with her father:[56]

> Despite her father's distance from her and his relative inaccessibility, Julie had seemed fond of him. He occasionally took her for a walk. On one occasion Julie came home from such a walk in tears. She never told her mother what had happened. Her mother mentioned this to me to say that she was sure that something awful had taken place between Julie and her husband but she never discovered what. After this, Julie would have nothing to do with her father. She had, however, confided to her sister at the time that her father had taken her into a call-box and she had overheard a 'horrible' conversation between him and his mistress.

In the final 'mad' phase, Julie developed the idea that her mother was trying to kill her. The major incident involved the loss of her doll (called 'Julie Doll' by the daughter). The mother had insisted that the doll should be given up and one day the doll had gone. It was never known whether the mother or Julie had disposed of the doll. Julie accused her mother and her mother denied the accusation. Julie was then told by a voice 'that a child wearing her clothes had been beaten to pulp by her mother, and she proposed to go to the police and report this crime'.[57] This incident was 'probably the efficient cause in the transition from being bad to mad'.

Laing is careful not to identify the mother as the sole 'cause' of Julie's condition. Instead he directs our attention to the total pattern of interactions within the family. There is the older sister, defined as being a 'difficult' child by the mother. She played an important role as a big sister—a 'Sister of Mercy'—in Julie's fantasies. There was the father, somewhat withdrawn from the family situation and having the minimum degree of relationship with his wife and children. He was defined as a 'sexual beast' by the mother.

I am aware that I have not done justice to Laing's existentialist account of this case but I hope that I have outlined the main features in order to suggest points where an analysis of social facts might be appropriate. There is, first, the notions and practices of child-rearing that are apparent in this account. Anthropological and comparative evidence demonstrate that not merely do child-rearing patterns (attitudes to weaning, excretion, punishment and reward, etc.) vary between and within cultures but also that there exist varying definitions of the nature and status of childhood. In particular there are differences in the way in which childhood is regarded as a separate and unique phase of development or whether it is regarded very much as a preparatory stage for the assumption of adult roles. It is likely that all cultures have elements of both these emphases but to differing extents. More important, for this particular case, is the way in which parents in a particular sociocultural environment come to define infants and children as 'good' or 'bad', 'difficult' or 'easy', 'normal' or 'abnormal'. An analysis of these differing patterns within a society in terms of some index of social class is almost certainly too crude. What we need is an analysis based on, say, Bott's insights into the relationships between family and social networks, showing how particular sets of parents come to develop some kind of consensus about these definitions of 'good' or 'bad' as they apply to particular stages of infancy and childhood.[58] It is clear from Laing's account that Julie's mother considered that her definitions of 'not demanding', 'no trouble', etc. were 'normal' definitions, that is, presumably, her definitions were not too much at variance with those which prevailed in her particular social circle.

It may be, therefore, that if we are to have a full existentialist account of the backgrounds of persons defined as schizophrenics (or indeed, of any other persons) we need to look beyond the immediate family ties to the wider social network of kin, neighbours and friends in which a particular family is placed. Other factors, absent from Laing's account, may be noted briefly. We know little about the father apart from his (assumed) sexual relationship outside marriage and his apparent remoteness. In particular we know nothing about his occupational background. This is not to make the over-simple formulation of occupation equals class position equals particular socialization pattern. It is rather to make the point that for most families in our society the father represents the major point of articulation between the world of the family and the world of work. Family life cycle and work career are closely linked in all kinds of ways and we need to examine the subtle interconnections between them. To what extent, for example, is the father's remoteness in this particular case related to or exacerbated by a work situation which effectively removes him from the home for long periods of time? Finally we may note several other factors which might be significant: type of community, religious body membership, effective membership of any other voluntary associations, income, type of dwelling and so on. We are not proposing a simple additive model (occupation of father plus type of network plus kinds of power relationships within the family equals a particular kind of outcome). Rather it is an interactive model whereby particular features of the 'external' social world are selected, interpreted and shaped within a particular family structure of interactions. In treating the family as a 'mediator' it is also important to know 'what' is being mediated.

Our account need not stop there however. Such an interactive model of the family within a meaningful segment of the social world needs to be placed in a wider historical context. What are the features of Western capitalism, industrial, urban, bureaucratic society which make certain sets of options and life chances more real or meaningful? In what way are particular choices limited or unevenly distributed throughout society at a particular point of time? Again, it would be nonsensical to make a simple extrapolation by fiat from Western capitalism to schizophrenia; but an account of schizophrenia or of any other form of behaviour labelled 'deviant' that did not include a reference to the structure and culture of capitalist society would be incomplete.[59]

It may be considered that we are making heavy weather of a particular case which is already full of complexity. Laing, as a clinical biographer, in limiting his attention to a particular case in its family setting is probably correct to state that there is a point beyond which, for the present purposes, he cannot or is unwilling to take his analysis. Such a limitation, however, becomes less justified when, as is the case in the later works, he moves on to talk about the family in general.

2 Laing's failure to handle, systematically, the wider sets of relationships within which the family is placed is demonstrated paradoxically in those more polemical pieces where he attempts a critical analysis of modern society. I am thinking of his contribution to the *Dialectics of Liberation* conference and his *Politics of Experience* where, as Sedgwick aptly notes, 'his language becomes at once both *more socially committed* and *more mystical*'.[60] I must confess to finding this section of his argument, where he attempts to link his insights into madness and the family with a wider social critique, the most obscure and the most unsatisfactory. I shall attempt to disentangle some of the strands of this social critique which, on the whole in my opinion, tends to fall below those of Henry or Marcuse (both of whom also contribute to the *Dialectics of Liberation* volume).

a Analogies The argument that sane people carry out bombing raids over North Vietnam while insane people are those who are successfully labelled as such and who are subsequently committed to institutions quickly became part of the rhetoric of the New Left. As rhetoric—and rhetoric is never 'empty'—it works reasonably well but it fails to specify the links between the interactional definitions of madness and the macro-level political processes. In a recent interview, Laing has denied that he ever said that it is the world that is mad and not those who are labelled as mentally ill[61] although it must be admitted that his polemic sometimes appears to approach this position.

A more complex and obscure analogy appears in his contribution to the *Dialectics of Liberation* collection.[62] Roughly it goes something like this. The mother looks at the child and sees herself as if in a mirror. Yet she imagines in seeing herself that she is actually seeing the child and not herself. In fact it is not even herself that she is really seeing in the child but the self that was seen by her mother and by her mother's mother and so on. We literally 'lose ourselves', our definition of self and other in this 'spiral of alienation'. Similarly in international relationships we see ourselves in Them, the enemy, but fail to recognize ourselves. As in witchcraft we attribute to Them 'exactly what We are doing to Them'. Again, this is a powerful passage but the obscurities remain. Is Laing saying that processes of international relationships are similar to or analogous to the dialectic of interpersonal alienation between mother and child?[63] Or is he saying that in the family situation we have the very seeds of these wider political processes? Again, the leap is made from one level to the other without any clear indication as to how the leap is made.

b Irrationality and intelligibility Earlier in the same essay, Laing makes the simpler point that the apparent irrationality of the schizophrenic can be made intelligible in the context of his family. Similarly the apparent irrationality of the family can be rendered intelligible in the context of the wider social system and so on to the world system. This may possibly be Laing's way of indicating a degree of scepticism about any possible partial solution to the problems he describes;[64] it certainly fails, once he goes beyond the family, to provide any clue as to how we might relate the politics of the family to other political processes.

c Socialization More simply still the links between family processes and wider political processes may be established through what is conventionally described as 'socialization'. In the first place it is in the family that the child first learns the values of obedience and the acceptance of violence. In this respect the family is often extremely successful in carrying out its 'functions'. At a more complex level, as we have seen, it is in the family and through the complex psycho-social patterns within the family that the child learns to make the simple binary oppositions between mother/child, our family/your family, us/them, good/bad, white/black and so on. Again the parallels with the Parsonian approach—although not the evaluations—are striking. In the family the child is induced by the parent to accept a particular identity. Further, parents not only teach their children to map certain values on to themselves but they also teach their children to map certain values on to appropriate 'others'.[65] Is there any escape from this process, for even those hostile to racism talk of 'racialists', even those hostile to authority talk of 'pigs', even those hostile to violence talk of 'hardhats' and 'skinheads'?

But, even if there does not appear to be a simple alternative or solution to the dilemma that Laing proposes, perhaps there are other forces at work at the same time and from the same source. The processes of opposition and mystification which Laing describes are countered, not merely by writers such as Laing himself but by 'lay' expressions such as 'they are just like us, really' or 'we are all the same under the skin'. People often appear to be able to hold both sets of perspectives at the same time. It is interesting to note, moreover, that these more universalistic perspectives, stressing similarities rather than differences and otherness are sometimes expressed in familistic terms. 'Their' soldiers have loved ones at home just like 'our' soldiers, 'their' mothers and children suffer just like 'our' mothers and children and so on. These human expressions may be labelled as being sentimental or politically naive but they appear to be as much part of human interpretations of the social world as are the expressions of opposition, hostility and mistrust. And if the latter can be readily attributed to primary experiences in the family, why not also the former?

It might be noted in passing that Laing's argument is not all that different from the formulations of the 'culture-personality' school with the exception that Laing is less concerned with the differences between cultures as with the basic similarities in the structures of thought across cultures. At its simplest the culture-personality school (represented by Mead, Kardiner, Linton and others) assumed that personality was largely formed in early childhood; particularly important were the practices of weaning, bladder-control, etc. Similar cultures have similar child-rearing patterns, therefore similar cultures have similar modal personalities. While the implications and conclusions of Laing and the culture-personality school are very different, the structure of the argument being presented is very similar. Both, of course, derive much of their inspiration from the insights of Freud.

The major difference, of course, is that Laing pays little attention to the specific culture in which the family is located, except in so far as particular cultures (not necessarily nations) derive their identity of 'us' against 'them' through these fundamental experiences within the family. We are led back to the earlier criticism that Laing ignores the specific social, cultural and historical conditions in which a family is located and this neglect leads to much of the obscurity in his argument about the alleged links between the processes of induction in the family and the ways of understanding and perceiving the social world in terms of simple binary oppositions. We may coin the term 'familial determinism' (on the analogy of 'economic determinism') for Laing's analysis. Economic determinism is usually criticized on the grounds that it is 'economic' (and hence gives little or no attention to other factors) and that it is 'deterministic' in that it assumes a simple one-way causal process. We have already considered in this context Laing's excessive attention to the family as against other factors; we shall now look more closely at the deterministic side of the argument.

3 Laing's account of the family, although concentrating on the totality of family relationships, focuses specifically upon the major roles structured around the process of socialization, namely the parents and child. It might be said that Laing takes a fairly orthodox model of socialization (involving interaction with significant others, the growing process of abstraction from specific rules and punishments to more generalized rules, and so on) and gives it a radical twist. Yet he shares in many of the weaknesses of the more orthodox

models of socialization namely: (a) The relative failure to examine systematically the role of others or factors outside the immediate parents and (perhaps) siblings; (b) The tendency to adopt a fairly unilateral model of socialization flowing from parent to child. The child appears to be shaped totally by his experiences within the family.[66]

We have already examined the first weakness in relation to Laing's work. We find little attempt to locate the family in time or in social space. Yet even in Laing's own examples we can see the influence of factors outside the family at work. Let us take the process whereby the categories good/bad are mapped on to certainly socially relevant categories within society, a process which Laing implies to be derived from the family. At the very least we can see the culture defining which categories within society become socially relevant, why, for example, the 'otherness' associated with colour of skin is much more sharply defined than the otherness associated with colour of hair. To explain why this is so, of course, we have to examine a whole complex of economic, historical and social structural factors. It is clearly not enough merely to say that a reified 'culture' does this or defines that. It is also clear that things are somewhat more complex than a simple matter of defining certain sets of others as 'good' or 'bad'. While to a child in a WASP family, Blacks, Poles and Catholics are all 'others', each would appear to be an 'other' in different ways and the rules that apply in relation to one grouping might not apply, or might not apply with the same force to another grouping. Intermarriage with representatives of these three categories might be frowned upon but not, presumably, to the same extent for each case. Furthermore, high educational or economic status might compensate more readily in the case of a Pole or of a Catholic than in the case of a Black. The point is made that the mapping of the social world is often more sensitive than a simple nominal either/or distinction but may also take in ordinal factors (greater or lesser than) which may themselves vary according to specific circumstances. While the family plays an important part in this mapping process, we must also examine the culture to see what is being mapped and to what extent.

This point has already been made in a slightly different way when it was argued that the family is 'located' in history and social space. But the 'outside' world not only impinges upon the family by virtue of the fact that the family is 'located' within it but also by virtue of the fact that the growing child, in common with other members of his family, will come to participate in systems outside his family and that his sphere of significant others will come to include members of his peer group, his school teachers and, later, his employer and workmates. To be sure, these others are also mediated through the family. In all kinds of subtle or not so subtle ways the parents will select, approve or veto members of the child's circle. Teachings about evolution, religion or history will be filtered, countered and reinterpreted in the family. But to admit this is still to recognize that there is *inter*action and that, increasingly in the course of a child's life, others outside the family present alternative and possibly radically different interpretations as to what is going on. The language of reference group theory or role theory may be inadequate in some senses but it at least enables us to locate some of the countervailing forces outside the family.

Thus the familial deterministic model as presented by Laing can be criticized by locating the family within its social context and by outlining the various sets of others who may and often will contribute to the socialization process. We may modify this deterministic model in a second way by stressing the interactive character of family life, by suggesting that the growing child is not merely a passive recipient of parental definitions but, very quickly, learns means of resistance or redefinition. Consider the following imaginary but perhaps not unlikely exchange:

Child: This bloody train won't go.
Mother: Don't use that word.
Child: What word?
Mother: You know what word.
Child: You mean train?
Mother: You know very well what word I am talking about.

In this fictitious exchange the mother brings up the infringement of a taboo and, in accordance with the taboo, cannot use the word itself. In terms of induction it might be assumed that the implication is that nice children, people like us, do not use words like that. The child, however, successfully deploys his awareness of the taboo against his mother. To complicate matters further, it may be that the child is copying his father in using expletives against the failures of the inanimate world. Furthermore it is not a total victory for the child. The mother has reaffirmed her position as one who is competent and able to define what is taboo for younger members. Further, the absent father may be secretly pleased at the way in which the child is adopting him as a role model.

This is a simple, perhaps highly selective example, although I suggest that it is probably closer to family life than one of Laing's own examples, that of a mother holding a child out of a window. What the *sources* of these patterns of resistance are need not detain us at this point. The child may learn them from other children, from older siblings or he may be exploiting differences within the parental camp. These patterns of resistance on the part of the child, small and partial though they may be, are almost certainly an important part in the development of the child.[67] Laing's parents, on the other hand, appear to be particularly skilled at what Goffman, writing in another context, calls 'looping', that is the cutting off, by the superior, of even the most slight path of resistance on the part of the subordinate.[68] In the example already discussed, the mother might interpret her son's resistance as yet further evidence of his 'badness' and may say as much to a neighbour or other family member who happens to be present at the time: 'There, that's him all the time. I don't know what's come over him lately.'

Laing, therefore, while contributing to the shift in focus from the mother to the family in interaction has perhaps not carried the interactive perspective far enough. We need also to examine the roles of others outside the family in the socialization process and the patterns of resistance and selection that take place on the part of the socializee. Furthermore, it is worth pointing out that an existentialist and interactionalist perspective should consider *all* the relationships within the family. In Laing's work the central relationship appears to be that between the parent and the child. The emphasis tends to be on the traps into which the child is forced rather than on the traps in which other adult members of the family find themselves caught. All this needs to be considered in a cultural and social milieu. It needs to be noted, in conclusion, that socialization need not and does not always merely flow from parent to child but may also flow in the reverse direction.[69]

4 Laing presents us with the dark, unspoken side of family living, a side too readily played down in much of the text-book discussion of the 'functions' of the family. At the very least, therefore, it is a useful corrective to some of the more bland impressions that we might receive from these sources. The family is a destructive exploitative institution as much as it is the reverse. Further, it provides the background for some of the fundamental and dangerous ways in which we come to understand and divide the social world in terms of 'them' and 'us'. The obscurity of the links in this argument have already been noted, but one final question must be this: to what extent are these 'dysfunctions' inherent in the institution of the family itself or to what extent are they true for all groups? Ultimately there appears to be a profound pessimism in the writings of Laing:[70]

> Let there be no illusions about the brotherhood of man. My brother, as dear to me as I am to myself, my twin, my double, my flesh and blood, may be a fellow lyncher as well as a fellow martyr, and in either case is liable to meet his death at my hand if he chooses to take a different view of the situation.

It is, I suspect, for this pessimism, for the emphasis on the dark side of family living, that Laing has been most severely criticized. Largely as a result of this emphasis he has been accused of being ultimately 'violent and totalitarian'[71] and of perhaps being too much influenced by the visions of his patients.[72] And yet Laing is also, more recently, quoted as saying:[73]

> I think that my picture of the family that has been published remains an extremely partial one. Some of the happiest and most fulfilling and rewarding and pleasantly memorable experiences in my life have been in families in which I've lived myself.

Laing is almost certainly a more complex, more paradoxical, perhaps more tragic thinker than either his admirers or his critics are prepared to recognize.

We should not, therefore, expect Laing to provide us with any easy answers to the dark questions that he proposes. Certainly, to date, he has given us little indication as to any possible ways out of the dilemmas he describes. Should we abolish the family?[74] But would not its most likely alternative, some form of commune, manifest just the same kinds of problems and dilemmas? Communes—particularly those which have attempted any major changes in the institution of the family—have throughout history encountered the hostility of the outside world. Through this hostility, the identity of the commune members has been sharpened and the outside world in its turn comes to be treated with hostility, contempt or indifference. This is particularly marked, of course, where there is an absence of any major structural change in the rest of society. Further, we may ask, to what extent is this dichotomous world view necessary at certain points of time? To what extent is the emancipation of the Blacks, of women,[75] of the proletariat, dependent upon a definition of the Whites, of men, and of the bourgeoisie as 'the other'? Laing would appear to argue that all these dichotomies are destructive, perhaps of the whole human race, given the power of modern weapons and organized forms of warfare. Marxists would argue that these polarizations are necessary in order to ensure the ultimate emancipation of the whole of humanity. This is perhaps the profoundest ethical dilemma of our day and it is perhaps a tribute to Laing's imaginative perspective that we may be brought to consider such questions through a study of the family. Yet we must also ask, in the way that Laing does not, to what extent are these dilemmas inextricably linked with the family or to what extent is the family merely an arena where these dramas are played out, perhaps in their most heightened form?

Conclusion

On all kinds of grounds Laing's account of the family may be challenged. Furthermore, these criticisms are not merely the criticisms that might be asked by orthodox social science and which might account for his relative absence from the footnotes of learned journals. Orthodox social science would ask for the evidence. It would ask for the hypotheses to be stated with greater clarity, in a testable form. It would ask for a clearer presentation of a model. Clearly, there are problems of evidence in the writings of Laing. It is true that we need more accounts of the lives and interactions of 'normal' families and that we need, more clearly, to specify the relationships between these families and the outside world. But it is likely that even if we were to formulate Laing's theories in a more testable form, the nagging doubt that something had escaped and eluded the scientist would remain.

Yet it is not enough to say that Laing is a visionary or a mystic, a person whom we may read as inspirational literature then to return to more mundane forms of enquiry. For one thing, that response only leads to the kind of dichotomy that Laing is talking about, between them and us, between those of us who have the privileged insight and those of you who cannot see beyond those slide-rules. There is already enough sectarianism of this kind around the field of the social sciences and it is doubtful whether it has served humanity well. For another thing, if Laing is saying something important about the family and modern society—as I believe he is—it ought to be possible to translate it into other terms, to examine critically what he is saying, perhaps even to apply his 'findings' to the construction of a new and better society.

Let me, tentatively, list some of the important features of Laing's work on the family, particularly in relation to the more orthodox sociological perspectives:

1 He has provided a radical, critical perspective on the family which, at the very least, provides a valuable counterbalance to the mainstream functional writings on the family. In the language of these writings he has analysed and described in graphic terms the dysfunctions of the family, both for the individual and for society as a whole.

2 He has made a valuable contribution to our understanding of what Handel calls the 'psychosocial interior of the family'.[76] Such an approach avoids the static tendencies in role or reference group theory while also avoiding talking about the family in a reified holistic fashion. Further, it notes that the family is more than a collection of individuals but a complex set of interactions. Particularly useful here are his analyses in terms of dyads and triads

and his account of the dialectic between the 'internal' relationships within the family and the 'outside' world. The role of myth and fantasy in family living is also usefully examined as is the way in which familial dramas carry over from generation to generation.

3 Laing's approach comes closer to family life as it is actually experienced than do many of the more orthodox presentations. At the same time he attempts to link his study of the family with a concern for wider problems of society as a whole. This marks the beginning of an existentialist account of the family.

Yet curiously there are affinities between the work of Laing and the approaches of Parsons that are outlined in Chapter 1. There is the same scant regard for history, although here it would seem that Parsons shows the greater willingness to 'place' the modern family in some kind of socio-cultural context. There is the same tendency to see socialization as a one-way process flowing from parents to children. Here what is tragic for Laing is functional for Parsons. Even Laing's accounts of the development of binary perspectives on the world echo Parsons's accounts of the process of binary fission involved in the socialization process. (It will be remembered that both acknowledge a debt to Freud.) And finally, both see little prospect for radical change. With Parsons this is largely because of his suspicion that the fundamental features of sex-role division and socialization have some biological foundation and are therefore subject to definite constraints on the amount of change that is possible, while with Laing it would appear that it is a fear that the knots have become tied too tightly for us ever to escape. In a sense, Laing represents the dark side of the functionalist model rather than its radical antithesis.

However, it would be a distortion to argue that Laing is merely filling in the unwritten dysfunctions of the functionalist perspective. For one thing Laing would reject the very language in which this assessment is made. More importantly, he has encouraged us to look critically at the family, and especially at our own families. If his argument seems to be shocking, distorted or frightening this is perhaps only because we have become too used to the relatively bland images of happy families, an image which orthodox social science has played a considerable part in creating.

Lawrence perhaps said it all clearly some forty years before *The Politics of the Family*:[77]

> For in the family there was a whole tradition of 'loyalty'; loyalty to one another, and especially to the Mater. The Mater, of course, was the pivot of the family. The family was her own extended ego. Naturally she covered it with her power. And her sons and daughters, being weak and disintegrated, naturally

> were loyal. Outside the family, what was there for them but danger and insult and ignominy? Had not the rector experienced it, in his marriage? So now, caution! Caution and loyalty, fronting the world! Let there be as much hate and friction *inside* the family as you like. To the outer world, a stubborn fence of unison.

Perhaps it is time that social science took the poets seriously.

5 Women as a social class

Introduction

Undoubtedly, one of the main challenges to the mainstream sociology of the family has come from the body of writing associated with the Women's Liberation or radical feminist movements. This challenge is both direct and indirect; it is direct in that most of the authors under this, admittedly general, umbrella spend some time in attacking the functionalist bias in family studies and the way in which this forms part of a patriarchal ideology, and indirect in that all programmes for the liberation of women explicitly involve a radical attack on, or at least a sharp questioning of, the institutions of marriage and the family. These movements, therefore, raise sharply the possibility that the family is not to be seen merely as a universal 'given' or as a cultural necessity but as something that can be actively and critically evaluated, acted upon and changed or abolished. It is this explicit linking of theoretical analysis and active practice that distinguishes most of the current feminist writings from most earlier texts, including the influential *The Second Sex*.[1]

The incorporation of these new feminist writings into a book on the sociology of the family might be offensive to some feminists. In the first place it might be argued that, just as it is impossible for a white person to write about the 'black experience' so too it is impossible for a man to write about the experience of being a woman. In the second place, it might be taken as an example of 'repressive tolerance' to treat these writings, which are often basically manifestos for revolutionary change rather than scholarly texts, as merely a source of 'ideas'. It is for the reader to judge whether these criticisms are valid or not. For my part I feel that the dangers in ignoring these writings are greater than the dangers involved in treating them seriously. Furthermore, it is to be hoped that this chapter in some modest way will serve as a corrective to the 'sexist' bias in much writing, not merely in the sociology of the family, but in sociology generally.[2]

The common approach to the study of men and women in society is through the use of the concept of 'role'. There have been two opposite consequences of this common usage. In the first place the concept 'role' implies some differentiation between culture and biology and hence serves to show the possibility of cultural variation and change. The role of a mother is to be distinguished from the biological fact of motherhood, the role of a father from that of fatherhood. There is no simple one-to-one relationship between male/female (biologically based distinction), man/woman (social roles) and masculine/feminine (cultural typifications of personality differences between men and women). To some extent, therefore, the role analysis serves potentially as a basis for freeing men and women from a purely biological determination of their positions in society.

In practice, however, the opposite seems to have been the case and, while clear differentiations between biology and culture are made, the concept of role has almost taken on the mandatory character of a biologically based determinism; instead of 'biology is destiny', 'role is destiny'. The use of the role metaphor has come to stress the script-determined performance, the relative solidity and fixity of cultural prescriptions and expectations.[3] The emphasis becomes one of conformity to or deviation from certain culturally determined role expectations rather than the possibility of changing these expectations themselves. Thus role analysis, often allied to a functionalist analysis, comes to overemphasize constraint and conformity rather than potentiality and change. Furthermore, the vagueness of much role analysis and the doubtful explanatory power of some of its concepts leads me to avoid this particular approach here. As I write a woman passes pushing a pram and carrying a shopping bag. Is she carrying out her role as a wife, a mother, a woman, a housewife or as a consumer? Were I to do the same would I be seen as enacting the role of a father, a housewife, a husband or a consumer, or would I be seen as some kind of deviant, someone departing from my role as a father, husband, man, breadwinner, etc? And if we apply the 'correct' or 'agreed' label, would it make any difference, would it really explain anything? To be sure, constraints on behaviour exist and role analysis often usefully draws our attention to these constraints. To be sure, also, people carry out certain performances in accordance with the expected expectations of the other. But these undoubted insightful benefits do not completely eradicate the air of arbitrariness that sometimes accompanies role analysis and for these reasons I chose not to use these concepts, except in a metaphorical or shorthand sense.

In its place I choose to consider women as a social class.[4] I do this for several reasons. In the first place, the very use of the term 'class' implies inequality and exploitation and therefore comes closer than role analysis to the central concerns of the Women's Liberation movement. In the second place, it shows one of the main ways in which Marxism, often lying outside the ambit of most texts on the sociology of the family, can be seen as playing a vital part in the development of theories of the family. In the third place, the analysis of the relationships between men and women in terms of social class, while necessarily incomplete and inadequate in some respects, may throw up links between the sociology of the family and other areas, particularly social stratification, to the benefit of both. Just as most analyses of politics do not include 'sexual politics'[5] so too it would seem that most analyses of social stratification exclude an analysis of sexual stratification.[6] Finally, an analysis in terms of class—at least in taking this as a starting point—draws our attention to the complexity of the links between men and women in the context of the familial roles and those between men and women in the wider society.

Not all the writers referred to in this chapter take a Marxian or class perspective. In attempting to treat de Beauvoir, Millett, Firestone, Greer, Friedan and Mitchell under the same head I am obviously doing violence to the unique contribution that each one makes to the overall field. De Beauvoir presents the most complete theoretical analysis, Mitchell provides a terse Marxian guide to action, Millet gives an impressive literary account of major 'sexual politicians' and Greer and Friedan, in their different ways, provide trenchant accounts of the woman's experience. There are, undoubtedly, important differences between all these writers, but all of them, and others, have in some way contributed to the central theme of this chapter.

Marxism and the family

The contribution of Marxism to the study of the family is, on the whole, an indirect one. While the relevance of Marx and Engels's analysis of the class struggle and the nature of capitalism are still live issues, it is unlikely that many contemporary Marxists spend a great deal of time looking through the details of Engels's reinterpretation of Morgan's theories on family evolution.[7] There are several possible reasons for this relative neglect, at least until fairly recent times. In the first place, apart from Engels's work, there is little systematic analysis of the family in capitalist society nor accounts of its place in socialist society. And Engels's own work is probably seen as containing too much nineteenth-century grand evolutionary speculation into matters for which there is either little evidence or little opportunity for obtaining such evidence. Many of these relatively fragmentary statements about the family that appear in the works of Marx and Engels often seem to be contradictory and certainly reflect, and perhaps even contribute to, uncertainty within the socialist movement itself about the nature and future of the family.[8] On the one hand there are those who argue that socialism necessarily implies the abolition of, or radical change in, the family. On the other hand there is the argument that socialism would entail the development of true family relationships based upon love and mutual respect and freed from the exploitative character that they assumed under capitalism. Both positions could be justified by reference to Marxist texts.

What one derives from the analyses of Marx and Engels, fragmentary as they are in this respect, is not so much a detailed, documented case as a general orientation. This is similar to Firestone's argument that we should use the *methods* of Marx and Engels rather than concentrating on the particulars of any one text.[9] In the first place, in Engels's work on the family we are forcefully reminded of the family as a *changing* institution. He quotes Morgan approvingly:[10] 'The family represents an active principle. It is never stationary but advances from a lower to a higher form as society advances from a lower to a higher condition.' In this emphasis, Engels showed his particular debt to Morgan and to other evolutionists such as Maine and Bachofen. Even if most anthropologists would now accept Westermarck's judgment that the assumption (in Engels and Morgan) of an early stage of primitive promiscuity is 'one of the most unscientific ever set forth within the whole domain of sociological speculation'[11] and would probably also reject the assumption that society has moved through the stages of Savagery, Barbarism and Civilization, we are still left with the emphasis on the family, not as some eternal given, but as something which is subject to change. Yet merely to say that an institution changes would be to say very little. Where Engels departed from his sources, particularly Morgan, was in providing a distinctly causal analysis to this evolutionary approach. Harris's phrase 'diachronic causal functionalism'[12] has more than an element of truth in it, emphasizing the fact that the family changes in association with changes in the economic base. The family is, therefore, to be treated as a dependent variable.

The other main reason why we should take Engels's account seriously is again not the result of any particular details in his argument but in his stress on the exploitative relationship between men and women that lies at the heart of the modern family and in its recent origins. Engels argued that the dominance of the male was not an inevitability but was associated with particular historical conditions, especially the growth of private property as an institution.

For private property to be passed on from generation to generation the man needed to exercise greater control over women, since paternity could never be unambiguously determined. Thus, Engels argues, monogamy 'appears as the subjection of one sex by the other, as the proclamation of a conflict between the sexes entirely unknown hitherto in prehistoric times'.[13] This was 'the first class antagonism'. Furthermore, as the separation between domestic and civic society continued, so the position of the woman in society declined. Her role became more and more ancillary to that of the male, focused as it was on the narrowing sphere of the home. Yet, under capitalism, contradictions were appearing in her role, contradictions which could ultimately threaten the existing system. Capitalism saw in women a useful supplement to the labour force, a reserve army of labour which could make a profitable contribution during expanding times and could also keep the general level of wages down. But this introduction of women into the world of work—that is paid employment outside the home—threatened their subordinate status. Similarly, the bourgeois notion of marriage as a contract also implied an agreement between equal partners and hence pointed to a contradiction between ideal and reality.[14]

That reference is made to the contribution of Engels in almost all the major current radical feminist texts is a tribute less to his elaborate and questionable evolutionary scheme than to his devastating and critical analysis of the family under capitalism. Writings on the position of women in society, however, hardly constituted the mainstream of socialist thought during this intervening period. The main moderate or revolutionary organizations—unions and parties—became dominated by men, and the main issues of work, unemployment and war were, by and large, traditionally 'male' interests. August Bebel continued the tradition of Engels in his book *Women: Past, Present and Future* and gave close attention to the situation of women under capitalism, subtly linking the objective conditions with imaginative understandings. Two quotations may give the flavour of Bebel's work:

> Servitude which lasts for hundreds of generations ends by becoming a habit. Inheritance and education teach both parties to regard it as the natural state.[15]
>
> Whilst marriage is so exclusively the one response of women, to which she is bound to cling with every fibre of her nature, it is only natural that love and matchmaking form the main subject of her thoughts and talk.[16]

Again, it is only fairly recently, particularly in Mitchell's writings, that Bebel has been given much attention.[17]

Yet the influence of Engels through Bebel and, more recently, de

Beauvoir, has not been so simple as this account might have suggested. To be sure, the attack on marriage as an exploitative relationship continues and certainly the general Marxian perspective that the identities 'man' and 'woman' are not abstract eternal realities or fixed biological entities but are historical realities continues to provide the main link between the radical feminist movement and the socialist movement generally. However, there were ambiguities within Engels's writings which underlie many of the debates which take place within the feminist movement today. The question is one of causality. Engels writes that the determining factor is: '*in the last resort* the production and *reproduction* of immediate life'.[18] Engels, although he has been increasingly criticized for his materialist bias, does appear to give some recognition to causal factors other than the mode of production. Thus the class division between men and women can, to some extent, be seen as an independent factor. This consideration has taken on greater importance as critics realized that the assumption of some primitive matriarchy was at best a dubious assumption and that Engels's account of how patriarchy took over was sketchy and obscure. The evident difficulties that socialist societies have had in overthrowing patriarchal attitudes —in Russia the working women still did the housework on their return home and 'machismo' is still alive in Cuba[19]—also gave rise to the feeling that the sexual division of labour was perhaps more fundamental than had been imagined. To date the most radical response to this challenge has been that of Firestone who attempts to use, but also to widen, the method of Marx and Engels so as to develop a 'materialist view of history based on sex itself'.[20] This is not to commit the older errors of treating the division between the sexes— and therefore the subordination of the female to the male—as some fixed biological necessity—but rather to argue that it is only with the development of industrial society that the *possibility* of culture transcending biology becomes apparent, a possibility that will be realized through the sexual class struggle. In a sense, therefore, to Firestone the sexual class struggle is *the* struggle and not one which is subordinate to others. Millett's notion of sexual politics and patriarchalism, although less systematically developed than the arguments of Firestone, conveys essentially the same idea, that the sexual class division is something which is deeper and more fundamental (although not therefore inevitable) than the Marxian class struggle.[21]

Thus the main influence of Marxism on the study of the family has been to emphasize the historical determination of sex roles and identities and the exploitative relationship at the core of the marriage institution, roles and relationships that can be transcended through revolution. Yet ambiguities, omissions and weaknesses in the original texts have led women writing within the same tradition to look more closely at the nature and forms of sexual exploitation. These re-examinations have led to further ambiguities and uncertainties, some of which will be developed later in this chapter.

Relationships of inequality, subordination and exploitation

The American news magazine *Newsweek* describes Angela Davis arriving in Moscow 'in a clinging sweater and no bra' (11 September 1972, p. 28). That, in 1972, a leading publication can still refer to a black revolutionary as a sex object might be an example of the pervasiveness of sexism or of a particularly nasty triple put-down (black, revolutionary and female). The arguments of the Women's Liberation movement draw their strength from the perception of the fact that its central concern is not just a matter of sex discrimination in employment but something more far-reaching and challenging. The particular importance of the links between objective situation and subjective experience will be examined in the next section. Here we will consider the implications of a class analysis of the 'role' of women in modern society.

As I have noted, the conventional sociological analysis here is conducted in terms of 'roles'. A typical example, based on cross-cultural evidence, is provided by Goode:[22]

> However, in three-fourths or more of societies for which information is available, women carry out these tasks; grinding grain, carrying water, cooking, preserving food, repairing and making clothing, weaving (of cloth mats and baskets), gathering food (nuts, berries, herbs, roots etc) and making pottery. All these tasks can be carried out while remaining close to the children or the hearth.
>
> In most societies men are assigned these tasks: herding, hunting and fishing, lumbering, mining and quarrying, metal-working, making musical instruments, manufacturing ceremonial objects, wood-working and house-building.

Parsons's discussion of the functional division of sex roles between the instrumental and the expressive elaborates on this theme but does not give recognition, as Goode does, to the fact that, whatever it is that a man does, his tasks are almost everywhere accorded higher prestige than the tasks assigned to women. Goode also reminds us of the cultural nature of these prescriptions. The making of musical instruments or ceremonial objects does not normally require physical strength and can, in theory, be carried out at home within sight of the cradle but are in fact normally defined as 'men's work'. Such a sexual division of labour of course still persists. It exists in the home, between home and work and in the world of work. Neither the allocation of tasks within the home nor the distribution of men and women in the labour force is what might be expected on the basis of chance alone. In spite of the increasing participation of women in the labour force the basic structure of male/female, instrumental/expressive and work/home still holds good. Many of the occupations where women are found to predominate—nursing, teaching, textiles, light engineering, secretarial work, air stewardesses, etc.—may be seen as extensions of the domestic expressive role.[23]

This is not, in spite of the veiled ideological assumptions of the instrumental-expressive polarity, a question of 'separate or different but equal'. At work women may be paid less for the same or similar work, or may be effectively excluded from higher paying positions. 'Male' occupations generally have higher prestige than 'female' occupations and where a once male occupation becomes 'feminized' the status of that occupation normally declines. Lockwood argues that one of the problems facing the 'black-coated worker' is the overall decline in the status of clerical occupations due to the increasing employment of women in these positions.[24] A recent study examines the feminization of the bank-teller's role in the USA. Since the Second World War the tradition of male dominance in this occupation has been broken and consequently the status of this occupation has declined. The job itself has fewer career prospects and the women are partially attracted by the glamour of the job, a potentiality recognized by the employers as they attempt to move away from the sober nineteenth-century image of banking where solid masculine respectability was identified with financial reliability. Now sexual banter may take place across the counter between teller and customer, reaffirming the respective sexual roles of the participants in this interaction.[25] In a similar, but slightly higher status occupation, Greer quotes some managerial expectations of the 'girl-in-a-million, the perfect private secretary', including the use of a deodorant, the ability to make good tea and coffee and the expectation that she should 'always look beautiful but not provocative'.[26] An instructive 'deviant case' is provided by the male nurse who is often redefined as 'doctor' by others in everyday encounters and finds that he constantly has to prove his masculinity.[27]

Similarly, the work at home is accorded low status. Indeed it could be argued that the status of housework has declined as the separation between home and work has become more marked, as many of the domestic tasks have become more mechanized and as more women have entered the labour force for at least part of their lives. In radio or television shows where women telephone in or are interviewed one often hears some variation on the theme of 'I am just a housewife'. The job is unpaid and carried out in relative isolation from others, with the exception of the children who may be defined as 'getting in the way'. With a split between home and work we get a 'loss of an objective standard by which to measure oneself and one's actions'.[28] Status is not a fixed thing, a static evaluation, but an ongoing accomplishment. Where there are relatively few others who are in a position to evaluate one's work and activity, one's status and identity becomes much less certain.

Thus, if the analysis in terms of roles leads one to suppose that the roles of men and women are 'different but equal' one runs the risk of confusing ideology with actuality. Yet even if we recognize that many of the things that men and women do are differently evaluated this perhaps only touches the surface of the problem. There may be increasing female participation in prestigious occupations such as those associated with the media and publishing. They may be paid the same and yet there may still be sexual exploitation. The question of the relationship between men and women is not merely one of 'who does what' but also of 'who *is* what', although of course the two are closely related. A dramatic illustration of this is provided by an event which took place in Edmonton, Alberta, in 1916. A prisoner was found guilty but the defending counsel challenged the legitimacy of the sentence by asserting that the woman magistrate was not legally a person. While this particular case was satisfactorily settled, the argument as to whether the word 'person' included females in the terms of the British North American Act continued for several years after at the level of the Canadian Supreme Court.[29]

The attempt to analyse the roles of men and women in class terms takes account of this relationship between being and doing. In the first place it emphasizes that we are dealing with a dynamic relationship not a static prestige ladder. In the second place we are reminded that this is one of subordination of the woman and exploitation by the man. And finally we are reminded of the pervasiveness of this relationship. It is this which distinguishes class relationships (whether sexual or economic) from more particular relationships such as occupational roles.

The use of the term 'exploitation' might give rise to some concern in this case. It is not, of course, implied that all husbands beat their wives (although the fact that we talk about wife-beating rather than husband-beating might give us some reason to pause) or that any deliberate, systematic pattern of cruelty is assumed to exist. The term is used in its dictionary sense: 'to utilize for one's own ends'. In this sense, exploitation is unavoidable in all kinds of human relationships. What is special about sexual exploitation is this totality and pervasiveness. We are looking at a generalized lack of reciprocity between the sexes.

This is clearly stated in de Beauvoir's account of woman as 'the Other', one whose identity is defined not in her own terms but in terms of men. Unlike the term 'male', the term 'female' imprisons her in her sex. The girl grows up in a world which is defined for her, a circumscribed world whose boundaries are delineated in a variety of ways. 'Little girls are made of paper' I can recall hearing a mother admonishing her son as he battled with his elder and taller sister. Later in life marriage—and love—become her chief destiny, again unlike man's experience of love and marriage. She is involved in what de Beauvoir calls the 'melancholy science' of managing a man. After her children have grown up, she still remains defined by her sex. In a chilling phrase de Beauvoir writes: 'With no future, she still has about one half of her adult life to live.'[30]

For the woman, therefore, there is a contradiction 'between her status as a real human being and her vocation as a female'.[31] The existence of a contradiction indicates that we are not dealing with a closed system but with something that has within it the possibility of developing its own change and revolution. Often, however, woman flees from the potentiality of change and choice in bad faith. In common with other exploited groups, there is a high degree of complicity on the part of the woman in her own exploitation. She may enjoy entertaining her men, being the power behind the throne or considering herself to be the power behind the throne.

All the authors cited here show in one way or another how this sexual class relationship is supported by myths, language and ideology. There are the myths of 'the eternal woman', 'good and bad women', 'feminine evil' and 'feminine power'. These are not only myths generated by men for their own support but are also propagated and accepted by women themselves. Television comedy shows and commercials abound with examples of the use of 'feminine wiles' or 'intuition' for the manipulation of the man about the house. The woman appears to 'win', but only in the short run, for the very weapons which are available for her use are determined for her by her position as a woman. Similarly, everyday speech reflects the same patterns. Greer notes how most of the terms for sexual intercourse in popular use are unilaterally male orientated terms, emphasizing male initiative, domination and penetration. Similarly many terms of abuse have female connotations either in their use as generalized insults or as terms applied to women in a derogatory way. Many of these terms of abuse can be seen as being linked to myths about women. (Thus the terms 'old bag', 'old hag', etc., are linked to myths of feminine evil.)

Finally, and at a more elaborated level, there is ideology. Just as, in Marxian analysis, the class system is justified and legitimated by reference to the ideology of free enterprise, so too is the sexual class system legitimated by reference to an ideology. This ideology has many elements, rarely fully articulated, but all pervasive. There are notions of female sexuality derived from a range of sources including the teachings of the Church, Freud and D. H. Lawrence. There are notions of the woman's true role derived again from religious teachings, from the writings of child psychologists and functional sociologists. Ideology should not be identified with any one particular writer or set of writers. While Freud, Lawrence and Erikson have all been cited as 'enemies' of Women's Liberation, the more sensitive accounts of their works point to ambiguities and depths in their writings that allow them to transcend any crude ideological definition. Again these writings can be reinterpreted to counter the ideologies which derive from them. Firestone attempts to re-examine Freud's notion of the Oedipus complex in terms of power.[32] Erikson's distinction between inner and outer space may be seen either as a statement about the 'eternal' nature of man and woman or as a statement about their roles under particular historical circumstances.[33]

The term 'ideology' has a wide range of uses and meanings and it is not always certain whether it has much value in a sociological discussion. There is often an element of arbitrariness involved in assigning the label 'ideology' to a set of ideas, beliefs, etc., just as there is often an element of arbitrariness involved in the assigning of the label 'role' to a particular set of practices. Yet it can be said that the use of the term 'ideology' carries with it its own dialectic. To use the term is to discover, or claim to discover, the hidden, concealed connections between social position and social legitimations. To some extent, it is the sociological parallel of the psychologist's 'rationalization'. The use of the term is a challenge both to the persons whose positions are defined by that ideology and to those who are in the position of defining these others. This is not to say that there was no such thing as 'sexism', 'male chauvinism' or 'patriarchalism' before these terms were used but that the use of these terms is itself a stage in the refinement and evolution of these terms.[34]

So far in this section I have noted the dimensions of class analysis as they apply to women: subordination, exploitation and ideology. Yet I have not mentioned what most modern feminists would consider to be the major institution responsible for this class position, that is the institution of marriage and the family. This is the major arena in which the sexual class struggle is seen to take place. This is the institution whose essential character, it is maintained, would be threatened by any radical change in the role of women. The major roles for which the woman is socialized from childhood are those of wife and mother. These roles constitute her primary project, her main source of identity. In this her existence is contrasted to that of the man. Any serious political analysis of the role of woman and the ways in which it might be changed must consider deeply the institutions of marriage and the family.[35] The implications of the class analysis of the position of women in society for the study of the family will be considered later in this chapter.

The objective and the subjective

Robin Morgan, in her introduction to the collection *Sisterhood is Powerful*, argues that the Woman's Liberation movement is the first movement to base its politics on experience.[36] Mitchell also stresses the importance of the 'politics of experience', a phrase taken from the title of one of Laing's most widely read books. Stated in these terms the argument seems to be a little unfair to all previous revolutionary political movements. The influential writings of Baldwin, Malcolm X, Cleaver, Fanon and many others are full of immediate accounts of what it is like to be black or oppressed in a white or colonial society. And while it may be true that the working-class movement has, to a large extent, become institutionalized in reformist political parties and trades unions, it is still true that the tone and strength of much working-class protest, even today, derives not from an abstract discussion of human rights but the direct experience of deprivations and inequalities.

Yet it is probably true that the Women's Liberation movement lays greater overt stress on experience than most other movements. The phrase 'gut reaction' is a common one in the literature and there is often a refreshing suspicion of revolutionary or Marxist jargon which, it is felt, often serves to stand in the way of direct experience rather than as a means for its expression. The reason for this emphasis lies in the pervasiveness of woman's experience, the *basic* quality of her role. The writings associated with the Women's Liberation movement are not merely accounts of inequalities in education or in the occupational sphere or of overt 'prejudice' but also of the routine everyday experiences of being passed by men in the street, of seeing one's image presented in the media, of housework and sex. Here, of course, the closest parallel is not so much the working class as the black experience which also has this pervasive character, such that boarding an integrated bus may be as much part of the black experience as boarding a segregated bus. So too, on a perhaps more trivial level, is the experience of going into a formally 'mixed' bar as much part of women's experience as being excluded from one marked 'men only'.

Stress is laid on the unequal character of this experience. It is not simply one of 'sex roles', the use of which term implies some degree of equality of experience. As Simmel notes:[37]

> If we express the historic relation between the sexes crudely in terms of master and slave, it is part of the master's privilege not to have to think continuously of the fact that he is the

> master while the position of the slave carries with it the constant reminder of his being a slave. It cannot be overlooked that the woman forgets far less often the fact of being a woman than the man of being a man.

And de Beauvoir points out that a man would not think it necessary to set out to write a book on 'the peculiar status of the human male'.[38] The fact that the problem is defined as one facing women is *part* of the problem. The fact that we talk about the position or role of women in society and much less frequently of the role or position of men in society underlines the point and reinforces the reasons for the stress on experience in the liberation of women.

One important area where this analysis of experience has been particularly fruitful has been that of 'love' and 'romance'. The conventional text-book approach to the question of love has been to see it in the context of 'mate selection'. It is argued that, in modern industrial society, love is the basis for mate selection and that this emphasis is functional for that system in that this society demands relative freedom of movement, a weakening of kinship ties and so on. Authors then normally go on to point out the fact that this 'love'—formally free and purely personal—is in fact circumscribed by limitations in terms of ethnicity, religion, social class, locality and so on. Love does not conquer all.

This conventional picture, while it is probably correct enough, does not go to the heart of the matter and in fact emphasizes the absence of a strong critical tradition within family studies. The conventional analysis of love in Western society minimizes the fact that the love relationship is an unequal one. Greer argues that the search for love on the part of a woman is 'guided by a search for security',[39] a fact which gives love a quality of anxiety and a lack of true, easy spontaneity. A more detailed critique of love in relation to women is provided by Firestone. Love, she argues, is 'the pivot of women's oppression today'.[40] It takes place within a framework of an unequal balance of power. The woman invests more in the relationship and is more dependent upon the outcome. Romance reinforces the sexual class system. Eroticism, a major component of romanticism, operates in one direction only; woman is the 'love object'.

Perhaps the most interesting part of Firestone's analysis of love is her discussion of the 'sex privatization of women'.[41] This is a process 'whereby women are blinded to their generality as a class which renders them invisible as individuals to the male eye'.[42] It can be seen that a very subtle sexual game is being played here. Sexually, women are treated as interchangeable. A girl is a 'date', a 'good screw', a set of statistics under her picture in the middle of a Sunday newspaper. At the same time, in the love encounter she is treated as if she were the only one that mattered. This privatization serves to obscure the fact that women are treated as a 'generalized other' and so their exploitation continues. This privatization is not something which is confined to the sexual encounters and experiences (for example, bottom-pinching in Rome) which Firestone describes, but also applies to other areas of the woman's experience. Housework, carried out in separate houses or flats, is a privatized work experience. Childbirth is something which both unites and divides women. In modern society the experience of childbirth as something privatized is reinforced by the circumstances under which it usually takes place.[43] Wedding rituals also have this character of sameness and uniqueness. A relatively narrow range of ritual elements are called upon (confetti, the wedding photographs, the telegrams, etc.) but the event is given uniqueness by the participants themselves reflecting on '*their* wedding'.[44] Thus many experiences of women—love, sex, marriage and childbirth—have this privatized character.

In the classical Marxian analysis of the development of class-consciousness, the movement from a class-in-itself to a class-for-itself, it is clear that the mere fact of exploitation is not enough. A relationship has to be perceived as an exploitative one and this implies identifying both one's fellow members of the exploited class and one's exploiters. The possibility of change and overthrow of the exploiters has also to be recognized. The development of working-class consciousness was seen as being aided by the increasing concentration of workers in large factories and particular quarters of the growing cities and, later, by the development of specifically and exclusively working-class organizations.

Thus the classical Marxian analysis gives full recognition to the complex dialectic between subjective and objective in the development of class-consciousness. In the case of women the difficulties can be seen immediately. Given the argument of Firestone that one of the main methods of sexual exploitation is through the privatization of the woman, how is she to overcome this and develop a class-consciousness on the basis of the model suggested above? It is this dilemma which has given rise to the emphasis on 'consciousness raising' in much of the contemporary Women's Liberation literature. The emphasis is on the organization of small groups, normally confined to women, which meet together to share experiences, to come to trust each other and to realize their common cause. These groups are not, it is strongly argued, therapy sessions or encounter groups. In these kinds of encounter sessions individuals (or couples) come together and then leave as individuals or couples. In consciousness-raising groups the emphasis is on building up a basis for revolutionary societal change not on personal adjustment. Thus the subjective and the objective are dialectically linked.[45]

The macro- and the micro-

A similar, but separate, concern of stratification theory to that of the relationship between the subjective and the objective is that of the relationship between levels of analysis, roughly the relationship between the 'macro-' level and the 'micro-' level. In terms of the analysis of social class the problem may be stated as the relationship between structures and events on the shop floor or in a particular community and the wider national or international patterns of stratification. Students of industrial conflict find that they need to explain the relative *absence* of conflict rather than its presence. In terms of Marx's or Weber's analysis of social class we may find all kinds of reasons for the overt expression of conflict at the shop-floor level, but we find that these theoretical insights are not enough to enable us to understand the relative absence of conflict. Similarly it would be misleading to regard every industrial dispute as simply a manifestation of the 'class struggle writ small'. A more sensitive account of social stratification would have to take into account the interplay between the local and the national and the international levels and the ways in which one shapes, modifies or cuts across the other.

This would appear to be a long way from the position of women in society. But here again the problem of the complex relationship between the levels is to be found. The role or identity of the woman —her status as the 'other'—is not merely a product of her position in the family or her position in the 'wider society' but of the interrelationships between both of these. While it is true that marriage, the home and the family form the major areas of a woman's life (and hence should form the major areas for change) it is also true that the role of a woman in modern society is not simply the role of a wife plus the role of a mother plus the role of a daughter plus the role of a sister and so on. In other words her identity is not simply a sum of domestic-based identities. Similarly to talk abstractly about 'the role of women in society' is to run the risk of reifying society and of ignoring the concrete institutions—particularly but not exclusively the family—in which this role is defined. Thus, to give an example, the process of socialization of the girl is not simply a matter of adopting the mother as a role model. It is true that she is the closest and often the most immediately observable role model. But there are also educational experiences, images presented to her in the media, the experiences of friends and neighbours. Of course, these experiences or models do not always come to the girl directly but are filtered through her experience of her mother and perhaps her elder sisters. Such models may contradict; the educational aspirations offered to the girl at school may be deemed inappropriate or unrealistic by the mother. Just as an analysis of social class in the normal sense should—but often does not—include an account of the complexity of the relationships between the various levels, so too can the analysis of women as a social class remind us of the way in which the domestic and the societal inter-penetrate, reinforce and possibly contradict each other.

The dialectics of liberation

The title of this section is taken from a revolutionary symposium held in London in 1967, some of the contributions to which were brought together in a collection edited by David Cooper.[46] The fact that none of these papers directly or even indirectly referred to the position of women in society and the way in which this might be changed is in fact a symptom of the growing concerns of the Woman's Liberation movement largely since that time. Recent writings of liberationists are full of accounts of the way in which women were assigned a subordinate status in left-orientated or revolutionary movements. The development of separate radical feminist movements is a measure of a general disenchantment among women with many left-orientated radical groups.[47]

To talk of liberation and the process of becoming liberated we must have some clear idea as to what this liberation might mean. It will be clear that among feminists generally and among their supporters both male and female there are a variety of different goals and different ways of achieving these goals. One goal, probably associated with the more moderate wings of the movement, is towards greater equality between men and women. The emphasis in practical terms is on increasing the participation of women in employment at all levels; the methods used to achieve this goal are the fairly orthodox ones of pressure group activity aiming at legislation on equal pay, abolition of sex discrimination, etc. It is realized here that, given the interdependence of men and women, home and work, this is not enough. As well as seeking ways in which to incorporate women more centrally into the world of work, ways must also be found of bringing men back into the home. This may imply, for example, a closer examination of segregation in school curricula. A new relationship between husband and wife will be worked out on the basis of equal or shared participation in work and decision-making.[48]

The literature has a range of variations on this theme. The approach of Margaret Mead, although sometimes a little obscure, appears to approach this model. She stresses the variety of ways in which cultures can structure sex roles and points to the dangers of having too rigid a division between male and female in terms of stereotyped role and temperament. The dangers are in terms of a loss of human potential and the continued presence of intolerance against the 'deviants' of either sex. Rather obscurely she stresses the importance of developing the 'authenticity of one's own sex'.[49] What she appears to be in favour of is a greater range of allowable expression on the part of members of both sexes. Similarly she is in favour of a greater range of experimentation in family arrangements and the greater freedom of divorce. Another, more recent, book also appears to support this moderate position. Janeway's study of social mythology *Man's World, Woman's Place* suggests that the emergence of the working wife as an accepted feature of the social landscape possibly means that a new equilibrium can be worked out within the marital relationship.[50]

The radical perspective differs from these more moderate approaches in a variety of ways. In the first place the goal is not the equality of sex roles but their abolition, not just the abolition of male privilege but sex differentiation itself.[51] In the second place this perspective would argue that this abolition of sex roles is impossible without the abolition of the institutions of marriage and the family as well. And finally, this liberation is not to be won through the orthodox methods of influencing existing political leaders and political parties and legislation but through collective action on the part of women themselves. Even other radical political groups are rejected, as we have seen, partly because of some women's experiences of rejection by these groups and partly because it is felt that the identity of women provides a more authentic base for radical action than other identities such as 'black', 'workers' or 'socialist'. Firestone directly emphasizes the analogy with the classical Marxist perspective on social class when she argues that women must seize control over the means of reproduction.[52] Purely individual solutions are rejected. To go out to work is merely to encounter exploitation in another sphere. The 'dual-career' families analysed by the Rapoports may be a possible solution for a few middle-class couples but cannot be a solution for women as a whole.

The process by which this revolutionary change is to be accomplished has already been defined. The stress is on the dialectic between theory and practice, between action and consciousness. Theory, in that it relates to direct experience, leads to the raising and sharpening of consciousness. So too action which may achieve a particular goal (such as the opening of an all-male establishment to women or the opportunity to present a radical supplement to an established women's magazine) also raises the consciousness of those participating the particular demonstrations or activities. The main enemy is not just male oppression but also 'tokenism', the granting of some limited objectives to a limited number of women, thereby splitting the movement. It was this surrender to tokenism, it is argued, that led to the loss of momentum on the part of earlier feminist movements.

Some parallels

This model of the process of revolutionary change will be a familiar one for it has generally been developed and applied by a variety of revolutionary groups and in a variety of situations. Many of the notions of 'consciousness', 'unity of theory and practice', 'tokenism', etc., will be familiar to those who are or who have been involved in other left-orientated groups. Throughout the writings, indeed, the militant feminists point to parallels between their situation and the situations of other exploited groups. One feminist makes the point explicitly: 'Racism, anti-semitism, imperialism, and sexism are at heart the same: all posit Manichean ideologies which divide the world in two and assign the oppressed the worst part.'[53]

The most common parallel is usually stated to be that between the situation of the blacks in the USA and that of women, expressed dramatically in Yoko Ono's statement that 'woman is the nigger of the world'. Much of the rhetoric appears to be taken over directly from the black revolutionary experience: use of terms like 'sexism' and 'Auntie Thomasina', adoption of new names and so on. Most of the writers cited in this chapter at some stage or another use the black analogy and, in an earlier period, Gunnar Myrdal makes the parallel in reverse by comparing the position of blacks (the subject of his study *An American Dilemma*) with that of women.[54]

The parallels between the position of women and that of the working class have already been suggested in the title of this chapter and form the main argument here. The argument is sometimes advanced, however, that the struggle of women is perhaps the most fundamental of all. In the first place it encompasses the largest proportion of the population. (Unless one takes a world view and uses the labels 'non-white' or 'coloured' and includes both men and women under these headings.) In the second place it could be argued that it is the most deep-rooted of all the forms of oppression. Speculations about early matriarchal systems apart, it would appear that women have been dominated throughout history and that, even after a socialist revolution, their position does not automatically improve except with considerable further struggle. Finally, as we have argued, it is perhaps the deepest and most pervasive form of exploitation and is manifested in all areas of social life.

Doubtless this general model of the dynamics of exploitation and revolution could be applied to a wide range of other situations. Firestone, for example, suggests that children are in a similar position to that of women ('women and children first') and that the liberation of the former would entail the liberation of the latter. Certainly both imply a radical attack on the institution of the family. Firestone and others (following the pioneering study of Aries) trace how childhood has become a separate identity in Western society, an identity reinforced by schools and other educational institutions. Here again we see links between the objective and the subjective and between the immediate environment of the home and the school and the wider society. Sociology, by generally treating children as 'socializees', may also be guilty of playing a part in defining this separate exploited identity of childhood. We may speculate further and consider that old people in society are also in an analogous position. With the institution of retirement and the stress on work as the major source of identity, old people have been assigned a subordinate and invisible place in society. Furthermore, as is the case with women, they are presented with unflattering self-images in the media, either as wise old sages on a pedestal or as irritable, forgetful or foolish figures of fun. Further, just as most sociology is implicitly 'male' sociology so also it tends to be 'young sociology'. The key areas of work and occupations, education and deviance all deal with young or young adult populations. Similarly, the study of the family with its emphasis on socialization, mate selection, marital relationships and the like tends, like the society in which it is placed, to push the old to one corner. It is entirely appropriate that de Beauvoir should have recently turned her attention to the position of the old in society.

Doubtless these speculations could be continued into a variety of spheres. What is of interest is the similarity of the model being adopted. This is a bi-polar power model stressing the dialectical process whereby the exploited become aware of their position and of the identity of the exploiters and through developing this dualistic model become the main agency of social change. The Marxist model of the class struggle is now removed from its particular materialist base, anchored in the mode of production, and given a more generalized meaning in terms of the struggles of all kinds of oppressed peoples. Perhaps this is, in fact, in keeping with the spirit of the opening lines of the Communist Manifesto.

Some difficulties

I have looked at the major writings of the contemporary feminist movement and I have attempted to present their case in their own terms. However, I have selected one theme, the approach to women in terms of social class, as the main organizing principle of this chapter. The approach seems to me to have at least two or three virtues. In the first place it shows the major direct link between the approaches of Marx and Engels on the family and the contemporary radical feminist writings. In the second place, it seems to have some advantages over the more widely used approach in terms of social role and, from the other end, may also provide an insightful supplement to approaches to *social* stratification, few of which specifically mention sex as a form of stratification.

In summary, therefore, the approach of 'women as a social class' implies the following:

1 A dyadic relationship between the sexes of inequality, subordination, oppression and exploitation.

2 Through the development of various contradictions in society this relationship is increasingly *experienced* as being one of inequality and exploitation. Among these contradictions we may note those arising out of the extension of educational and occupational opportunities to women as well as to men and the extension of the franchise. A contradiction thus develops between the 'role' of the woman in the home and her identity in the wider society.

3 Out of this experience and through the growing organization and awareness of women collectively will develop the main agent for the overthrow of the sexual class system and its replacement by a society where roles are not allocated on the basis of sex. There is thus a unity between the analysis presented by the leading radical feminists and active participation in the process of change.

In this section I shall outline what I consider to be some of the difficulties of this approach. In attempting this I shall take this outline as a *model* seriously and spend less time arguing about the particulars of the approach as an *analogy*. I shall focus on what seem to me to be some substantial problems in this analysis, the possible answers to which may advance our theoretical understanding. In short these questions are (a) whether women are a caste or a class, (b) the question of the source or origins of the sexual class struggle, (c) the role of men as the oppressor, (d) the relationships between the sexual class struggle and other class divisions and (e) the extent to which this broadly Marxist-based analysis might be supplemented with material derived from other traditions, in particular the Weberian and the interactionist approaches.

a Class or caste? One difficulty which might be raised in connection with this class analysis is the question of individual social mobility. The class model of society always allows for the fact that some individuals may rise or fall and become part of the proletariat or the bourgeoisie. Indeed this may be seen as one of the features differentiating class society from other systems of stratification such as feudalism or a caste system. However, what is the equivalent of social mobility in the sexual class system? It is true that individual women may rise to high positions in, say, the occupational or political spheres but they do not, as a result, become men. Indeed they become exemplary figures used to 'prove' the openness of the system while in fact masking the continuing oppression. They, more often than not, will be judged not as members of parliament or as company directors but as women who hold these positions. In some cases it will be suggested that they reached their positions of eminence by a denial of their femininity (thus serving as a warning to others) or through the assertion of feminine wiles or sexuality. Either way, they are judged as *women*, just as blacks who rise to positions of eminence are still often judged in terms of their ethnic origins.

This fact raises the possibility that the analysis might be in terms of *caste* rather than *class*. Betéille characterizes caste in these terms:[55]

> As a system of relations it is marked by a division of society into groups which are ranked in an elaborate hierarchy. As a system of values it is characterized by the legitimacy it accords to social inequality and the importance it assigns to the ideas of purity and pollution.

While sexual stratification can hardly be said to generate a model of an 'elaborate hierarchy' it undoubtedly has this all-pervasive character. Anthropological accounts are full of descriptions of ritual taboos surrounding menstruation, taboos which are not absent today. The *British Medical Journal* of 1878 contained a long correspondence as to whether the curing of hams by women who were menstruating caused the hams to go bad[56] and the popular term 'the curse' still carries with it some connotations of pollution and ritual danger. So, too, the continued segregation of some clubs and bars may still carry with it some notion of women being in some state of ritual danger. Women, in certain situations (such as the priesthood) are defined as in some way being 'out of place', a general characteristic of all forms of ritual pollution and defilement.[57]

Undoubtedly there are gains and losses to be had in the use of a caste model of sexual stratification.[58] Perhaps, indeed a fuller model might be found in the examination of the dynamics of caste and class in sexual stratification. Perhaps the main reason for adhering primarily to a class model here is that this model, at least in the Marxist tradition, contains within it the analysis of the sources of change within itself. A similar analysis in terms of caste might, therefore, contain some useful insights into sources of stability and resistance to change within the system.

b The origins of the sexual class struggle The Marxist analysis of class clearly locates the origins of class and the class struggle in the ownership of the means of production and, more specifically, in the development of capitalism. A class system, therefore, is located in specific concrete economic and historical conditions. What, however, is the origin of the *sexual* class system? It is not enough to locate this in the development of capitalism, for sexual stratification can be seen to both precede and continue after capitalism. If the analysis of women as a social class is to be more than just an analogy and to be an analytical and indeed revolutionary tool, this question of the origins of the sexual class system must be tackled.

I have already noted the difficulties involved in assuming some point in human history when an earlier matriarchal system was overthrown by a patriarchal system. Yet, on the other hand, it might appear that to locate the source of sexual stratification in biology might be to recognize that there are fixed bases for male-female differentiation of role and therefore some limits to the degree of equality that can be obtained or to the extent to which it is possible to abolish sex-based roles altogether. De Beauvoir is critical of the notion that the subordination of women can be justified by reference to biology. The existence of biological differences (such as in the capacity to bear and suckle children and some small differences in physical strength) provides an 'insufficient basis for setting up a hierarchy of the sexes'.[59] Relative physical strength or weakness is not an absolute quality but depends upon the extent to which particular human projects define strength or weakness in physical terms as being relevant criteria. Thus, if it is the case that on average women are weaker than men and if some jobs require greater physical strength than others, then it is likely that these jobs will contain a higher proportion of men than women. However, this is not, in itself, a sufficient basis for a wider system of social stratification.

What of the reproductive role of women? This might appear to be a more fundamental basis for sexual stratification and might appear to set limits to the extent to which sex roles might be abolished. In reply it could be argued that while biologically the fact that women bear children is a basis for biological *differentiation* it only becomes a basis for social *stratification* under particular historical conditions. Various authors have emphasized the historical conditions under which paternity, succession and property become important conditions limiting the role of women[60] while others have stressed the role of man the hunter (a role that he has occupied for the best part of human history) necessitating the physical movement of the man and therefore the complementary necessity for the woman to remain at home caring for the children.[61] As society has evolved past this hunting stage so too has society evolved beyond the strict necessity for a differentiation between men and women, based on the latter's child-bearing capacity. However, by this time, men have acquired such a dominant position in society that, like all ruling élites, they seek to justify this position on eternal grounds and resist any serious encroachment on their positions and privileges. This account, although persuasive, does not fully explain why, in this original hunting stage of human history, there were not cultures in which some women at least joined in the hunting and some men stayed at home to protect the dwelling and the children.

Millett's account of 'patriarchal society' stresses the historical fact of male dominance together with its political character, and thus the fact that it is not rooted in essential human nature.[62] Firestone, more radically, seeks to enlarge the materialist interpretation of history by basing it on the fact of sexual differentiation itself. The origin of this sexual discrimination lies in the biological family. However, while the origins of sexual stratification are deep-rooted and all pervasive, one of the features of human society is that it is constantly transcending nature. Thus she writes 'we can no longer justify the maintenance of a discriminatory sex class system on grounds of its origins in nature'.[63] The contradiction in modern society is that woman now has the potential for control over her own reproductive functions but is still dominated by men. Firestone indeed argues that modern science together with communal arrangements for child-rearing renders it possible for the reproduction of the human species to be divorced from the traditional relationships of mother and father. Mitchell's criticism of Firestone's account is that, contrary to the title of Firestone's book, it is not really dialectical enough, that it presents a more evolutionary than revolutionary account of the position of women in society. Similarly she criticizes Millett for using the term 'patriarchy' too loosely, arguing that this is not in itself a mode of production.[64] A tendency to use terms like 'patriarchy' too loosely or to analyse the whole of human history in terms of the sexual class struggle carries with it the dangers of reification and mystification and fails to account for the particular historical circumstances under which sexual differentiation is used as a basis for stratification. Thus Mitchell examines the way in which, under capitalism, the role of the women as a *consumer* reinforces and gives particular meaning to her subordinate role in society as a whole.[65] Gough's reworking of the Marxian perspective would probably fit in most closely with Mitchell's approach. She recognizes the inherent difficulties involved in making any statements about the origins of the family and sexual differentiation and rejects as irrelevant to the feminist cause any search for a 'feminist Golden age'. She suggests that while the origins of the family and the sexual division of labour can be located in the hunting period of human history, this did not entail a class division. Class divisions and sexual exploitation sprang from the development of an economic surplus and the growth of the state which provided men with the basis for powerful roles outside the kinship group.[66]

Undoubtedly, the question of the origins and the basis of sexual stratification will continue to be debated for some while yet. Two general conclusions would appear to be in order. In the first place it is misleading to lay emphasis on biological universals as a basis for sexual stratification or to refer to unspecified periods of human history such as 'patriarchy'. Such accounts divert attention away from the various concrete historical circumstances that give rise to and meaning to these 'universals' and the particular structures and institutions through which exploitation and dominance are maintained. Such an approach ignores also the intimate interplay between the biological and the cultural. And second, following from this, undue stress on the past should not blind us to the possibilities in the present that can be realized in the future. We should consider not merely those biological and historical circumstances that have provided the basis for the subordinate position of women but also the features in our own society which press towards a transcendence of these limitations in the future. Such features include the possibilities for controlling reproduction, the declining importance of many features associated with the nuclear family and, perhaps above all, the growing consciousness of women themselves and their desire to transcend their situation.

c The role of men If women are the oppressed in the system of sexual stratification, then men are the oppressors; if women are the exploited, then men are the exploiters. How far and in what ways is it true? If it be true can the system of oppression be brought to an end? The answers to this set of questions have wide repercussions for the understanding of the nature of exploitation in a wide variety of situations. Again the force of this observation may be judged if we substitute the oppositions of black/white or colonized/colonialist for that of women/men. The black militants' argument that sympathetic whites should turn their attention to the analysis of white racialism rather than to 'the black problem' may also be applied in the case of radical feminists and their male sympathizers.

The most clear-cut alternative to the oppressed/oppressor model outlined above is that provided by Margaret Mead whose main theme is that both sexes suffer as a result of over rigid sex-role typification. She writes: 'Only if we perpetuate the habit of speaking about "the position of women" in a vacuum will we fail to recognise that where one sex suffers, the other sex suffers also.'[67] In particular the sufferers are the boy with artistic leanings at an all-boys school, the adolescent knowing that he is expected to initiate sexual relationships but unsure as to how to go about it, the father doubly trapped in a routine job and a family situation that requires him to support them by remaining at that job. If women make more suicide attempts than men, men make more successful suicide attempts and a variety of other conditions ranging from ulcers and heart complaints to alcoholism may be traced in part to the particular strains of the male role. The popular television series *Till Death Us Do Part* in a curious way illustrates this problem. Alf Garnett raging at the women around him, pouring insults on them and the 'feminized male' in the person of his son-in-law, might seem to be the complete parody of the male chauvinist. Yet, partly through the sensitive playing of Warren Mitchell, Alf appeared to be as much victim as victimizer, a prisoner in his own role, impotent in a world that demands potency.[68]

There may be two possible arguments against the case that both men and women suffer as a result of over rigid role typification. The first is that while it may be true that both men and women suffer as a result of this exploitative situation, women suffer more than men. In the last analysis it is the woman who is defined as 'the other'. The man's 'vocation as a human being in no way runs counter to his destiny as a male'.[69] Furthermore it may be argued that it is often a characteristic of the oppressor to implicate the oppressed, either by arguing that the oppressed is happy in her subordinate status or by erecting an elaborate mythology whereby the oppressors appear to be the oppressed. The oppressed themselves, through false consciousness, may come to accept this definition of themselves and come to express sympathy with their oppressors.[70] Second, it may be argued that this analysis in terms of losses suffered by both sexes tends to lead to a relatively facile attack on the 'system' without specifying the particular institutions through which this 'system' is maintained or the way forward through revolutionary change. Tactically, even if there be a strong measure of truth in the assertion that men suffer as well as women, the way forward is through the organization of women and the development of their consciousness and this involves defining the man as the oppressor. At a later stage, men may be involved in the struggle against a society based upon sex roles, but for the time being they should direct their attention to the sources of male sexism rather than seeking to become involved in the women's struggle.

This leads us back to the analysis of the women's struggle in terms of 'the politics of experience'. The phrase, while persuasive, does raise some thorny questions. Is it the case that it is only the experience of the oppressed which is valid? What of the experience of the man or the oppressor? If an analysis of his own experience leads him to conclude that he is in fact the oppressor, that he benefits from this situation and that he should seek by all means possible to maintain this position, is this to be judged a correct assessment? Or if his analysis leads him into the opposite direction, that he is not the oppressor and that he is, rather, a victim of the system, is this also valid or is he a victim of false consciousness and in fact seeking to maintain his position through arousing the sympathy of the oppressed? What, to refer to a different area, of the worker who defines capitalism as the best guarantee of his prosperity or whose 'experience' leads him to define coloured immigrants as the enemy? There is a danger in the analysis of politics purely in terms of experience that a facile relativism might develop or that politically expedient mythologies will replace deeper analysis.

This discussion has inevitably merely touched upon the problem but I hope that I have said enough to stress that it *is* a problem. Several concluding remarks should be made. In the first place the definition of man as the 'oppressor' does not mean that every man is a male chauvinist. The stress is on male institutions and male ideology rather than on individual males. Similarly it can be argued that individuals in the 'developed' world may not betray any overt signs, in word or deed, of racialism but may, through their continued enjoyment of and aspirations for a higher standard of living, participate in the exploitation of the third world. Men too derive benefits from their participation in a sexist society although they may not themselves manifest overt signs of male chauvinism. In fact, males may still betray 'unconscious' signs of their sexism in everyday interaction in so far as they treat women differently from men. Thus physical touching, even when not initiated as a sexual advance, may take place more frequently from men to women than from men to other men. Similarly casual terms of address such as 'love' or 'dear' may flow more readily from men to women than from men to men. Sartre's account of the 'look' whereby a person, the 'looked at', becomes aware of his being-for-others, while originally presented in the context of a general account of the human condition, has a special significance in the relationship between men and women.[71]

In the second place it is probably true that major political and social change is less likely to be achieved by appeals to some universal humanity than by appeals to the situation of some oppressed groups or categories. This involves defining the boundaries by which the oppressed can be identified and can recognize each other and, dialectically, how the oppressor can be defined and identified. Thus groups with ill-defined boundaries such as 'consumers' or 'ratepayers' tend to be less successful in mobilizing themselves for political change than groupings where the boundaries are more clearly defined. What is less certain is what happens when this definition has taken place. It may result in the overthrow of the oppressors or the mobilization of a wider public support for the oppressed leading to substantial concessions being made by the oppressor. Each situation has its own dynamics. The model in terms of oppressor and oppressed provides a valuable key to the analysis of social change but it needs to be applied concretely with full recognition given to the particular features of the situation under examination. In the present case we may note that the model presented in the analyses of the radical feminists, while certainly incomplete and certainly not one which is adopted by the majority of women, has already generated some change in action and policy and has certainly provided a challenge, forcing more and more individual men and women to examine their own situation in relation to each other. In some cases this examination may lead to what is usually referred to as a male (and female) backlash. In some other cases it may lead men (and women) to examine more closely the system of role typification under which they both suffer. In some other cases it may lead women to define themselves more sharply as the oppressed and to define the identity of 'women' as the major basis for social change. Perhaps in this situation, as in comparable situations, the analysis may proceed in a direction where it becomes possible to view men as, in various ways, both oppressors and oppressed:[72]

> The truth is that just as—biologically—males and females are never victims of one another but both victims of the species, so man and wife together undergo the oppression of an institution they did not create. If it is asserted that *men* oppress *women*, the husband is indignant; he feels that *he* is the one who is oppressed—and he is; but the fact is that it is the masculine code, it is the society developed by the males and in their interests, that has established woman's situation in a form that is at present a source of torment for both sexes.

d Other classes, other struggles In the analysis of the relationship between men and women in terms of oppressor and oppressed it has been noted that this involves defining sex as a major basis for opposition and mobilization. However, bearing in mind that this class analysis of the situation of women was derived from the analyses of different situations altogether, it will be readily noted that there are other potential bases for identification and mobilization. Within modern industrial society we may note two major ones, economic class and ethnic status.[73] We might also include generation and, if we take a global view, the opposition between the 'third world' countries and the developed world. Within the developed world, however, the major bases for mobilization have been the identities 'working class' and, more recently, 'black'. Combining these with sex differentiation a property space table may be constructed (Table 1).

TABLE 1

	Men		Women	
	Black	*White*	*Black*	*White*
Working-class	BWCM	WWCM	BWCW	WWCW
Middle-class	BMCM	WMCM	BMCW	WMCW

Ignoring for the moment the difficulties involved in using the distinction working class–middle class (as opposed to the more Marxian distinction between bourgeoisie and proletariat) and the fact that the status of 'working-class women' might be viewed either as a status in its own right or as a status deriving from that of a husband, it can be seen that we have here the possibilities of cross-pressures or cross-cutting ties of the kind analysed by anthropologists and political scientists. Thus militant black women, confronted by the widely quoted statement of Stokely Carmichael that 'the only position for women in SNCC is prone', are placed in a situation of conflicting cross-pressures. So too are working-class women, confronted with the fact of male dominance in the union movement and most left working-class political movements or parties. Mitchell, in probably the best brief account of the problem of competing bases for identity, contrasts the positions of the 'radical feminists' and 'abstract socialists'. She concludes that 'both positions are possibly right together, both are certainly wrong apart'.[74]

These distinctions would appear to be leading us in the direction of an analysis of the relationship between cross-cutting ties and social order as argued, influentially, by Gluckman: 'how men quarrel in terms of certain of their customary allegiances but are restrained from violence through other conflicting allegiances which are also enjoined on them by custom.'[75] The parallel, although formally attractive, would I think be misleading. The clue to the difference lies in the word 'custom'. In the cases which Gluckman analyses, the notion of custom always to some extent directs us back to an overriding society or social entity which provides the major source of legitimation. This is not the case in the 'class' struggles under examination here for in these struggles there is no overriding source of legitimation. 'Custom' if it is referred to is often viewed as the ideological support, the set of mystifications, used by those who are in power. This is particularly true in the case of women where there are many references in terms of the 'customary role of women' or some similar phrase which provide the legitimations for the exploitation of one sex by the other. The analysis in terms of cross-cutting ties cannot therefore lead us to suppose with any confidence that the conflict will be contained or will in some way contribute to the maintenance of social order. What it does lead us to suppose, however, is that the patterns of conflict in advanced society will be more complex than any one model might indicate.

Excluding, then, the cross-cutting ties argument there are two further possibilities. The first is that one opposition will be defined as being more strategic or inclusive than another. It has already been shown how Firestone argues that the sexual class struggle is the overriding struggle and this is echoed by several other feminists. Logically, there is something to be said for this. As we have seen the sexual class struggle appears to be all-pervasive, it involves half of humanity, occurs in all societies and at all periods of history. Others may define the economic class struggle as being the decisive force because it directs our attention to the particular forms of exploitation at a particular historical period. In capitalist society, it will be argued, the class struggle is primary and the major source of the ultimate liberation of all humanity. Others may cite the international class struggle, the struggle against imperialism as being the major historic struggle and the major source of identification for countries of the third world and oppressed ethnic minorities in the developed world.

A distinction should perhaps be made between the individual and the societal level. At the societal level it is possible to argue about, and perhaps to assess, which struggle is primary. At the individual level, the 'choice' will not merely be one of rationally assessing competing claims but also in terms of one's own experiences, autobiographies and networks of relationships. Our analysis must proceed at both levels, at one level examining the process whereby certain boundaries are drawn as potential bases for identity and mobilization and, at the other end, by showing how particular individuals through their personal careers come to defining one set of boundaries as being more salient in terms of their experiences than another.

The second possibility is in terms of some hypothetical 'index of oppression'. Thus ranging from least oppressed to most oppressed we have WMCM to BWCW. Put like that such an analysis would probably be too formal to excite much attention although it does remind us that the oppressors may be divided as much as the oppressed and that the oppressor in one situation may be the oppressed in another. Furthermore, the fact that radicals are not neatly pigeon-holed into exclusive boxes bearing the labels 'women,' 'black', 'working-class' and so on means that there are always people within these movements who will call the attention of their fellow members to the patterns of oppression in other situations. Thus, within the radical feminist movement there have been individuals and groups concerned with tackling the problems faced by black or working-class women. The position of women may be raised as an issue in working-class movements and so on. The existence of these cross-pressures does not merely mean a tendency to fission and sectarianism (although it has probably meant that as well) but also provides for the possibility of links being made between different sections of 'the struggle'. Perhaps Gluckman's analysis may be applied to the oppressed although not to a society, which embraces both oppressors and oppressed, as a whole. Mitchell outlines the complexity of the situation clearly:[76]

> Dialectical materialism posits a complex (not dualistic) structure in which all elements are in contradiction to each other; at some point these contradictions can coalesce, explode and be overcome but the new fusion will enter into contradiction with something else.

e Alternative approaches All revolutionary movements need to have some theoretical explanation as to why it is that not all those placed within the boundaries of the 'oppressed' support 'their' movements and may indeed be actively hostile to these movements. This is particularly true with the Women's Liberation movement which has attracted a lot of hostile comment from women themselves. The following quotation may be a little more extreme than some but it contains many of the themes raised by women in opposition to the feminists:[77]

> Mark you, I'm not against everything you in the movement stand for. If you can achieve equal pay for equal work, I say bully for you. But for heaven's sake tread with care in your demands for equal job opportunities. How would you like to be stranded in such all-male preserves as garbage collection, sewer inspecting and mining? Total equality with men might also mean saying goodbye to many of the nice things they do for us, and I don't mean holding doors open or fetching our drinks at parties, charming though these may be. I am thinking, rather, of those joe jobs like putting up storm windows and getting rid of a bat in the house.

The problem, in literature on the working class at least, has usually been defined as being one of false consciousness or, less flatteringly, 'snobbishness'. Yet, as Lockwood has argued,[78] such an approach merely redefines the problem rather than solves it.

The problem is not, of course, one of explaining why women (or anyone else for that matter) do not support a particular platform or subscribe to a particular ideology. Rather, it is of explaining why it is that women do not more often come together to seek collective alleviation of their common deprivations, whether by revolutionary or reformist means. Part of the answer may lie in the isolation and fragmentation of their experience through the isolation of housework or indeed of many of their work experiences. But this explains the limitations on choice and not why a particular choice is not taken when it is available. Here part of the answer may lie in the possibility that she has alternative bases for identification.

Weber's definition of class and his elaboration of the concept of status have been widely used in analyses of social stratification as either an alternative to or as an elaboration of the approach of Marx. Very briefly, two important points were raised by Weber. In the first place his definition of class—'the typical chance for a supply of goods, external living conditions and personal life experiences, in so far as this chance is determined by the amount and kind of power, or lack of such, to dispose of goods or skills for the sake of income in a given economic order'[79]—potentially generates not just a dichotomous conflict model of social class such as we find in the Marxist approach but also a model which allows for any number of classes arranged in an hierarchy. Second, his approach to status 'determined by a specific positive or negative, social estimation of honour' points to a system of stratification which may coincide with or cut across his definition of social class. Classes *may* develop according to the Marxist model but this is not the only possibility. Stratification in modern industrial society appears much more complex with the aid of the additional tools provided by Weber.

Such an account would appear to be of little relevance for our analysis of sexual stratification. Surely, it will be argued, stratification by sex could only generate a two-fold model? But to argue thus would be to confuse the biological facts of sex differences with the cultural definitions and meanings assigned to these differences. It may be argued that while one of the ways in which women (and possibly men as well) experience their position in society is in accordance with the model of 'women as a social class' and that perhaps more women will experience society in this way as this definition becomes more available, this is not the only possible mode of experience. Men and women may experience their sex roles not directly but as mediated through other particular groups and categories of which they are members. Thus the identity of a woman may be mediated through her position in the economic class system, her membership of particular voluntary associations, her location in the community and so on. Primarily, of course, her identity will be mediated through the institution of the family but again this institution does not stand alone but is located in a particular class and community setting. In many cases the family will be the only institution through which her identity is directly mediated; this is particularly true of working-class wives who do not themselves go out to work.[80] Thus women can be located in society not merely in terms of their position in the sexual class system but in terms of other class and status systems, not all of which will be dichotomous, and in a status hierarchy. Opposition to collective attempts to change or alleviate her condition may lie either in the fact that, as a result of her membership in various status groupings, the identity as a woman may not be a particularly salient one or in the fact that her position in some alternative stratification system provides her as an individual with the identity that she seeks.

The situation may be complicated further if we consider the interactional dimension. This approach would argue that what is important is not so much the possession or non-possession of certain characteristics or personality traits but the extent to and the way in which these traits are realized, accentuated or muted in particular encounters, interactions or more or less lightly structured situations. Thus, to give a simple example, there is a difference between biological or chronological age and the extent to which age is realized as a relevant property in a given situation. A person defined as 'old' in one situation might be defined as being 'young' in another. Similarly, encounters may be more or less structured around the fact of sex differences, accentuated, say, at a dance or at a party and muted (although probably never absent) at a seminar or a prayer meeting. Identities such as 'masculine' or 'feminine', therefore, may be seen as being dependent rather than as independent variables, whose relevance is determined by the structure and culture of the situation rather than in terms of the possession of characteristics on some absolute basis.

The interactionalist approach cannot of course replace these other approaches—it does not tell us how or why sex is selected as a relevant characteristic in a large number of situations—but it does provide a useful link between the analysis at the cultural and societal level and the analysis at the personal or subjective level. It may explain, or take us some way towards explaining, why some women support the radical feminist movement and why some others do not. Thus many radical feminists left the male-dominated socialist or new-left groups because they found that they were being defined as women (or more accurately 'chicks') in situations where they felt that this definition ought to have been inappropriate. The interactionalist approach also underlines the vicious circle which confronts women in some top positions. Women are in a minority in these positions, therefore they are more likely to be judged on the basis of their sex rather than in terms of the particular demands of the position, therefore women are more likely to be closely scrutinized when they apply for these jobs, therefore women are in a minority position . . . Vicious circles, however, can also be virtuous circles and this account suggests that the cycles can be put into reverse by the recruitment of more women.

To conclude: it is not argued here that the approach in terms of 'women as a social class' is an invalid one. Indeed, it raises many important issues that are often left obscured by the more familiar approach in terms of sex roles. But it is an approach which needs to be combined with other approaches derived from the mainstream of sociological enquiry, namely the approaches of Weber and the interactionalist schools.

Conclusion: implications for the family

We have strayed some distance from the sociology of the family and have looked, all too briefly, at theories of stratification, revolution and politics. This has been necessary. While many of the mainstream approaches to the sociology of the family include a discussion of sex roles, particularly within the family, it is doubtful whether anyone reading these, for the most part functionalist, accounts could have predicted the growth of the body of theory and action around the radical feminist movement.

There is no doubt that these theories have implications for the sociology of the family, as the following quotations will illustrate:

> Individuals are not to be blamed for the failure of marriage: it is . . . the institution itself, perverted as it has been from the start. To hold and proclaim that a man and a woman, who may not even have chosen each other, *are in duty bound* to satisfy each other in every way throughout their lives is a monstrosity that necessarily gives rise to hypocrisy, lying, hostility and unhappiness.[81]

> If marriage and the family depend upon the castration of women let them change or disappear.[82]

> Patriarchy's chief institution is the family.[83]

> Even the modern nuclear family . . . necessitates male supremacy by preserving specifically human endeavour for the male alone while confining the female to menial labour and compulsory child care.[84]

Similar statements underlying the way in which the family is necessarily associated with the exploitation of women are to be found in all the texts cited in this chapter. In some cases (particularly those of Firestone and Mitchell) the attack is linked with Laing and Cooper's indictment of the institution of the family.[85] It would be a crude overstatement, however, to state that the radical feminists advocate the 'abolition of the family' in any simplistic sense. Mitchell argues that the family's dominant role in the exploitation of women is not to be overthrown by its 'abolition' but by the separation of its functions.[86] In a sense, therefore, the family will wither away rather than be overthrown. Actual immediate proposals are for a greater degree of experimentation and exploration in forms of living together and child-rearing—communes, modified extended families, couples in the context of a network of wider relationships, 'dual career' families and so on.[87]

The institution of the family, it is argued, maintains the sexual class system. This is because the 'essential functions' of the family—child-rearing, emotional support in an increasingly depersonalized world, etc.—clearly define a limited role for women. The differences in reproductive capacities are accentuated in the context of the family and provide the basis for the woman's basic role and function. While women may participate in the wider society—the world of work or voluntary associations—her ultimate status is still determined by the fact that she is defined as a wife and a mother. The distinction between 'inner' and 'outer' space should be interpreted in this context, that the man's role implies mastery of the world outside the family, the manipulation of things, people and symbols, while the woman's role emphasizes the expressive control over persons within the confines of the family.

One of the superficial paradoxes of this situation is that the radical feminist attack on the family in a sense supports the functionalist analysis outlined in Chapter 1. Both show a necessary interconnection between the role and status of women and the institution of the family. The differences are that the functionalists either do not explain this interconnection or suggest that it is a relatively fixed relationship in human society, while the feminists argue that the apparent universality of this connection does not imply its necessity. In terms of policy the implications of most of the functionalist positions would be that 'these interconnections are very deep-rooted and important for personality and for society so be careful when you seek to change things' while the feminist position implies that 'these interconnections are damaging to the personality and to society so we must restructure society as a whole'. 'Partial change', the feminists would continue, 'is not enough.'

Yet, *is* the connection between the modern family and the roles of the sexes so intimate as to warrant locating the source of the exploitation of women in the heart of this institution? To be sure there is evidence that this assumption was justified in the past and indeed in the present over a wide section of modern industrial society. But is this a necessary connection? The opposite case may be argued on theoretical and empirical grounds. Theoretically, we have seen how the functional analysis of the modern family involves the reification of that institution, blurring over a wide range of variation within a society and, even more importantly, the possibility for change and experimentation. What is missing is a perspective which examines how the individuals understand their own family situations and evaluate these situations, and the possibilities they see for changing their condition. It may be argued that the feminists also fall into the same trap and smooth over the differences in family situations and the possibilities that exist for change. At a more macro-level this involves developing a model of society where there is a *degree* of independence and autonomy in the various parts (sub-systems, etc.) so that change in one section does not necessarily imply and entail change in another. The 'system', therefore, has a degree of 'leeway' or 'give' in it; what is of course still open for discussion is the extent of this 'leeway' and whether it is enough to permit really radical change.

Empirically, and very inadequately, two sets of evidence may be called upon. In the first place there is the evidence best illustrated in the case of the 'dual career families'. These are defined as 'the type of family in which both heads of households pursue careers and at the same time maintain a family life together'.[88] This involves adjustment both in the spheres of work and family and does appear to represent a significant, if small, example of the way in which couples can, in the context of the family, exercise some degree of control over their life chances. It may be legitimately argued that this kind of control can only be found among the relatively privileged few who already have a degree of freedom in their (largely professional) work roles and incomes large enough to reduce considerably the burdens of domesticity. Thus all five families analysed in detail by the Rapoports had some form of domestic help at some time. Furthermore it will be argued that such personal solutions, open to the very few, are no substitutes for wider societal action to deal with what is a societal, rather than a personal, problem. Yet, while admitting these reservations, the accounts of dual career families indicate that there is some degree of leeway in the system and that the link between the institution of the family and the exploitation of women can be weakened—if not broken—for some individuals at least. The capacity for innovation in human relationships is one which should be given greater recognition in sociological accounts.

Other, still partial, sets of evidence may be used to ask whether major or revolutionary change necessarily implies the abolition of the family. Thus the Chinese communist experience is given sympathetic attention by some radical feminists. Morgan's anthology contains a sympathetic article on Chinese society,[89] for example, and it is likely that the Chinese revolution is a source of inspiration for the feminist movement as it is for many other radical and revolutionary groups. Yet, while the Chinese revolution has meant considerable gains towards equality between the sexes both in the wider society and the home (where, traditionally, women shared a subordinate status with children) and while the development of communes has meant the involvement of individuals and families directly in decision-making and societal involvement, it has not meant the abolition of the family. One recent visitor to China writes:[90]

> His family was encouraged to have a discussion involving his grandparents, mother and father, uncles and aunts, to contrast the bitter past with happy present: to tell how the poor and lower middle peasants had become masters of the country and now had previously undreamed-of riches in the form of bicycles, sewing machines and wristwatches.
>
> This was the first (but not the last) time that I was to be surprised by the continuing and indeed enhancing importance of family life in China. Later on, we were to hear about the role of similar family discussions in preventing and curing the tendency towards truancy in secondary schools.

This raises another issue, that is the extent to which the wider society may deliberately step in to curtail or enhance or to change the functions of the family. Again it may be argued that the Chinese experience cannot be transplanted directly to an advanced industrial capitalist society[91] but it still reminds us that the relationships between the family, the roles of men and women and the wider society are more complex than might appear in the writings of both the functionalists and the radical feminists.

Closer to the American experience, the development of communes among young people (a development welcomed to some degree by most feminists) has not necessarily entailed the abolition of sex roles. Thus one author has described some aspects of life among the 'Hippie' tribal families:[92]

> In the tribal families, while both sexes work, women are generally in a service role, such as waitress, masseuse, and secretary. Male dominance is held desirable by both sexes. The recognised dress is in a semi-rural or western style which emphasises sexual differences.

And[93]

> There is a lessening of firm identification toward any one role taken although the biological family roles are given prominence

over work roles. For example, the role of motherhood is given considerable emphasis and social support and approval.

In the urban communes described by Speck the girls seem to have the traditional status of 'chick', more or less passive appendages to the males.[94] There may also, of course, be communes directly associated with the feminist movement.[95]

It is not denied that the modern nuclear family is the main institution in Western society in which the exploitation of women takes place and that her position in that family to a large extent defines her position in other sectors of society. What is being suggested here is the complexity of this relationship, the possibility of there being change in the one without there being an equal or concomitant change in another. It should always be remembered that terms like 'family' or 'commune' are typifications of a wide variety of situations and have to be examined in the context of the culture in which they are placed and the meanings which the members assign to them.

To end this chapter on a critical note is not to deny the importance of the contribution of the radical feminist literature. They have shown the living importance of the Marxist tradition as applied to the study of the family and the relationships between the sexes, they have imaginatively explored all facets of a woman's life and experience and they have demonstrated the possibility of an analysis which is directed to change and the future rather than to the past or to a reified present.

6 Sex and capitalism

Introduction

We have considered two major critical streams which have direct bearing on the sociology of the family: the radical psychoanalytical approach of R. D. Laing and the critique of the family and of the 'roles' of the sexes presented by the radical feminists. There remains a third critical stream, one which is a little more difficult to characterize. It involves a searching examination of the relationship between sex and industrial or capitalist society, derives its impetus and inspiration largely from a fusion of Freudian and Marxian analyses and is particularly represented by writers within the tradition of the 'Frankfurt School'. This school, including among others Adorno, Horkheimer and Marcuse, stressed the inner 'psychic' dimension of exploitation under capitalism.[1] It is more difficult to characterize partly because of the different emphases and conflicting interpretations of this central problem and partly because the links between the institutions of the family and sex roles on the one hand and sexuality and capitalism on the other are rarely made clear or explicit. It is an area in which speculation appears to be uncontained and it is sometimes difficult for someone like myself, untrained in psychology, to provide a competent evaluation of many of the arguments.

For these reasons I am somewhat reluctant to stray into this field. However, there seem to be other, more compelling, reasons for giving at least some recognition to this aspect of the critical tradition. In the first place it presents a clear contrast to the treatments of sexual behaviour in the main writings on the sociology of the family where, for the most part, the main point of reference *is* the family and marriage and the sexual behaviour under examination is often labelled either pre-marital or extra-marital, and where the main emphasis appears to be the quantification of sexual experience in terms of how often, to what extent and with how many partners. Nowhere, perhaps, is the gap between the everyday world as experienced and understood by individuals and that world as measured and analysed by sociologists so apparent as in the realm of sexual behaviour. In the second place, the writings of the 'sexual radicals' raise, even if they do not answer, many important questions about the relationship between biology and culture and sexuality and society. And finally, these writings may provide some clues to the current renewed debate about 'permissiveness' and pornography. All these and many other questions are raised in this debate and, although it is unlikely that this chapter will provide many answers to these questions it is possible that it will place them in a framework rather wider than a simple opposition between the permissive and anti-permissive protagonists.

It should come as little surprise to note that the tradition of criticism within industrial society and directed against the human costs of the society should include within it an indictment of the sexual morality engendered by that society. Marx and Engels pointed a scornful finger at the bourgeois sexual morality: 'Our bourgeois, not content with having the wives and daughters of their proletarians at their disposal, not to speak of common prostitutes, take the greatest pleasure in seducing each other's wives.'[2] Men and women under capitalism were denied the opportunity to develop authentic sexual love relationships just as they were denied the opportunities to develop authentic social and communal relationships.[3] A critique of capitalist culture includes a critique of the sexual morality of that culture. Yet right from the start a deep ambiguity lay in that critique. Was it the case that authentic sexual love could only take place within the nuclear family based on monogamous marriage, and that capitalism tended, in all kinds of ways, to threaten and corrupt the family and marriage? Or was it the case that this particular form of family and marriage was very much part of that capitalist culture and the authentic relationships could only develop under conditions of complete sexual freedom? A second ambiguity was to develop later in this investigation of the relationship between capitalism and sexuality. If it were the case that capitalism was opposed to sexual freedom, what are we to understand by the apparent growth of that freedom in recent years? Has a new form of sexual exploitation developed along with developments within capitalism or is this a genuine, if incomplete, growth in sexual freedom? To what extent, therefore, does the sexual sphere of life have a degree of autonomy, a degree of independence from the particular economic base of the society in which it is placed?

Clearly in examining the diversity of attitudes towards sexuality in modern society a simple polarization between the 'permissive' and the 'conservative' is inadequate. Reiss, who distinguishes between those who hold a variety of standards of abstinence (including kissing and petting both with or without affection), the double standard, permissiveness without affection and permissiveness with affection,[4] is a useful elaboration but limited to the extent that he focuses on the act of pre-marital coition and does not take into account wider and more varied expressions of sexuality. In particular, it gives little recognition to the ideological dimension of these attitudes. We need to distinguish between, for example, the conservatives who argue that we have gone 'too far', the liberals who argue that we are going in the right direction and the radicals who argue that we still have far to go. Within the 'radical' camp, however, there is an interesting distinction between those who argue simply for complete sexual freedom and those who, like the conservatives, deplore many of the features of modern sexual expression (such as pornography and mate-swapping) but who argue that these are symptoms of wider societal corruption. A consideration of the contrasts and overlaps between these positions might throw some light on some of the ambiguities surrounding the relationships between sexuality and society which are to be explored in this chapter.

Such a discussion would appear to take us a long way from the sociology of the family. I hope to be able to show, however, that these debates are significantly connected with the institution of the nuclear family in modern society. In the first place, any definition of permissiveness will in some way be related to the institution of the family and the role of sexual intercourse within that family. Thus, generally speaking, a sexual practice is often defined as being the more deviant the further it is away from procreative sex within the institution of the family. Second, it is argued in several places that the family in capitalist society is a major agent of social control. Does the weakening of this institution—if it is weakening—mean the weakening of social control in society or is social control exercised in more subtle, more indirect ways? If sexual expression is partially removed from the exclusive domain of the family does this mean a weakening or strengthening of these subtle agencies of social control? In short, we are looking at the triangular relationship between sexuality, politics and the family which, in various ways, is the theme that links Marcuse, Reich, Reiche and perhaps also someone like Holbrook.[5]

In this chapter I shall not deal with each author separately but I shall attempt to draw together several themes which seem to run through this debate. These I place under the headings of 'sex and repression', 'sex and social stratification', 'sex and conformity'. I conclude by examining the relationship between these themes and the institution of the family and by raising some problems in this overall analysis.

Sex and repression

All the critiques of sexuality in capitalist society take as a starting point the writings of Freud on repression and civilization. Freud saw an inevitable antagonism between the instincts and civilization; culture in Marcuse's words involved a 'methodical sacrifice of the libido'.[6] This was expressed in Freud's terms as a struggle between the 'pleasure principle' and the 'reality principle'. The former was primary, instinctual and unrestrained while the latter involved recognition of the fact that the individual human organism lived in a natural and human environment and that some control of these basic primitive instincts was necessary both for the individual and for human society. The organized ego was the outcome of the successful control of the pleasure principle by the reality principle. Only in the realm of fantasy is the pleasure principle allowed free range of expression. Primary here is the control over sexuality, 'the sex instincts bear the brunt of the reality principle'.[7] The growth of civilization involves increasing sacrifice of the pleasure principle to the reality principle and hence an increasing sense of guilt. This was because the growth of civilization was dependent upon the increasing growth of the sphere of work which was, to Freud, essentially unpleasant and non-libidinal.[8] Work involved increasing organization and discipline and allowed little scope for the free play of instincts or the free expression of sexuality. This was in many ways a pessimistic picture and it was rendered more so by Freud's argument that there was no guarantee that this would be a successful accomplishment on the part of civilization. While some instincts would be sublimated and given expression in socially legitimate forms such as art, there was also the danger that the repressed instincts would break out in the form of destructive impulses. Thus civilization was under the constant threat from within, the threat that these destructive impulses would break out in the forms of violence, suicide, war and conflict.

This is necessarily a crude summary of Freud's argument but it forms the basic starting point for a critical approach to sexuality in modern society. Three particular problems have been taken up by some later writers: the apparently eternal ahistorical nature of Freud's concept of the reality principle; the differences at any one point of time between different groups in society in terms of their sexual expression and, finally, the possibility of sexual liberation.

It is clear that there is some simple evolutionary account of the development of civilization in Freud's discussion of the relationships between the reality principle and the pleasure principle. His analysis was at two levels, the ontogenetic and the phylogenetic. The ontogenetic was at the level of the individual who, in the process of becoming a fully socialized being from infancy, had to repress his instincts. A sociological account of this process is provided in the Parsonian model of socialization.[9] The phylogenetic was at the level of society, referring to the growth of civilization from the original state of the primal horde. These levels were clearly connected through the institution of the family in its dual role of enabling the infant to move through its basic psycho-sexual stages of development and of passing on the culture of the society in which it exists, a culture which includes the accumulated gains of previous generations. Yet apart from this there was little clear account of the particular features of any one culture that formed the basis for the reality principle. In short the emphasis was on an ahistorical civilization rather than on particular civilizations and particular cultures.

Reich was one of several 'neo-Freudians' who criticized the apparent culture-bound nature of Freud's analysis and tended, in contrast, to locate the particular source of repression in bourgeois (or more correctly, patriarchal) society itself. He was particularly interested in the relationships between the patriarchal family structure of bourgeois society, repression and an authoritarian régime. This involved a critical examination of Freud's notion of the ego. This no longer was to be seen as the successful outcome of the control of the pleasure principle by the reality principle but rather a distortion of man's basic nature. The Freudian unconscious suppressed the basic good instincts of man and was itself concealed and presented to the outside world by a mask of 'character' which was described as 'the artificial mask of self control, of compulsive, insincere politeness and of artificial sociality'.[10] Reich wanted to answer the question 'for what sociological reasons is sexuality suppressed by the society and repressed by the individual?'[11] and was therefore attacking the ahistorical nature of Freud's analysis. It was clearly also a critique of Marxists for failing to take into account the psychic aspects of exploitation under capitalism. Furthermore, in examining particular institutions, the patriarchal family, the authoritarian state, the class structure and ideology, he drew attention to the way in which repression was mediated through particular structures and institutions. The Freudian analysis was given political content. Also implied here was the possibility of true liberation, not merely the overcoming of repressive economic structures but also the revolutionary development of the possibility of true genital sexuality. This was to be seen in his well known emphasis on the importance of the true orgasm. Capitalism distorted man's capacity for true sexual expression, and hence any revolutionary programme had to include a programme for sexual liberation. In his political activity, therefore, Reich included working-class sex education and advice on contraception.[12]

Marcuse criticized Reich for presenting a much too simplified version of the relationship between sexuality and society and for seeing sexual liberation as a panacea for all ills, while recognizing the distinctive advance made in his linking of sexual repression with economic and political domination. Marcuse, like Reich, attempted to place Freud's general analysis in a particular socio-historical context and to link the political with the psychological. His aim was not so much to attack Freud's central argument as to build on it; thus, rather than rejecting the basic antagonism between the pleasure principle and the reality principle, he elaborated these concepts to give them their specific historical content. In this process Marcuse added two new concepts, that of the 'performance principle' and 'surplus repression'. Repression, to Marcuse, has two components: there is a level of basic repression which represents a necessary modification of human instincts which is required for the survival of the human race and there is a level of surplus repression. The surplus repression refers to those 'restrictions necessitated by social domination'.[13] If, following Marx, we see all hitherto existing societies as having a class base, then surplus repression is that repression which results from the domination of one class over another. This was not simply economic domination but psychic domination as well.

Just what was the link between economic and political domination and psychic—particularly sexual—repression? Part of the answer lay in Marcuse's use of the concept of the 'performance principle' which he defined as 'the prevailing historical form of the *reality principle*'.[14] Here Marcuse was attempting to capture what other writers might have called the 'basic personality type' of classical capitalism. The performance principle demanded a disciplined labour force, regular work habits, adherence to routinized time schedules, rational (in the Weberian sense) adherence to clear calculations of inputs and outputs both in terms of profitability and in terms of responsiveness to economic incentives, an emphasis on reason as opposed to passion or instincts, in short a combination of the rational economic man of classical economics and Weber's Protestant Ethic. Capitalism had little place for the spontaneous or the instinctual; free libidinal expression was reduced to the status of a leisure time or week-end activity. On the one side there was order, routine, economy and discipline and on the other side disorder, passion, the instincts; it is not difficult to see on what side sexuality fell.

However, Marcuse was faced with a problem. His account of the performance principle and surplus repression may have accurately—at least in a metaphorical sense—described the psychic conditions under classical capitalism. But it is doubtful whether this accurately reflects the situation under modern capitalism where it would appear that the expression of sexuality is actively encouraged, that all aspects of sex (not merely monogamous heterosexual sex) are openly discussed and sexual satisfaction is a major goal to be encouraged through manuals, education and therapy. One possible answer might be to suggest that however permissive society might be in the bedroom, the majority of the population still has to work for a set number of hours at fairly clearly specified tasks. Do what you like, this society might be saying, so long as you don't do it in working hours. However, Marcuse does not choose to place his main argument along these lines. Instead he introduces another concept, that of 'repressive desublimation'. In essence, what Marcuse is arguing here, is that the repression has appeared in another guise; it has not been reduced or abolished. This, of course, reflects Marcuse's overall interest in delineating the shift to more subtle, hidden forms of exploitation under late capitalism. The sexual liberation of late capitalism is a pseudo-liberation. In the first place its expression and encouragement is maintained and supported by large commercial interests, the media and advertising; it is not a spontaneous expression on the part of individuals. In the second place this 'repressive desublimation' weakens the ego, reduces the potentially revolutionary power of the pleasure principle and thereby serves as a powerful aid to the more subtle exploitation and manipulation of late capitalist society. This particular theme (which Marcuse deals with more fully in his later work *One Dimensional Man*) is taken up in more detail by Reiche. At this point the unsympathetic critic might, with some justice, wonder if Marcuse was not too obviously operating within a closed set of beliefs, whereby even contradictory evidence could be incorporated into the original framework without causing a major revision of the central argument.[15] Here the contradictory evidence would appear to be the greater degree of sexual freedom under late capitalism. Marcuse wishes to retain his original notion of sexual repression and capitalism and so elaborates the concept of 'repressive desublimation'. Here, as we shall see, part of the argument revolves around the extent to which the 'permissive' or sexual revolution is real or false.

In all fairness to Marcuse, it would appear that his theory of 'repressive desublimation' is an attempt to come to terms with some of the ambiguities of the 'sexual revolution'. Reiss, although tending to base his statement on surveys of pre-marital sexual practice, seems to sum up what many sociologists have concluded about the so-called sexual revolution of recent years: 'In short, there has been a gradually increasing acceptance of and overtness about sexuality. The basic change is toward greater equalitarianism, greater female acceptance of permissiveness, and more open discussion.'[16] Sherwin and Keller argue similarly, on the basis of surveys of American college students, that changes in attitudes are mistaken for changes in behaviour.[17] Less optimistically, Dreitzel suggests that the change in attitudes towards sexuality 'affects the public realm more than the private bedroom' and argues that the sexual revolution 'marks the advent of a new voyeurism'.[18] Even apparent signs of permissive sexual *practice*, such as more open forms of extra-marital affairs and 'swinging' may be found to possess their own rigid codes of behaviour and informal controls.[19] Thus Marcuse is attempting to make sense of a situation where sexual liberation is at best partial and where permissiveness seems to be more talked about than practised.

Reiche, writing more recently, presents what is essentially an elaboration of Marcuse's concept of 'repressive desublimation'. In common with Marcuse he argues that the basis of the attack must shift to an analysis of the processes of mental manipulation under late capitalism. Following Marcuse he delineates the character type required by early and classical capitalism. In Freudian terms this is an 'anal type' for whom work is a focal point of reference and who is driven by an inner compulsion. Under early capitalism sexuality was separated from work and took on the status of a leisure time reward, something which is quantified and given an exchange value.

Thus far Reiche has presented an elaboration of the basic analysis presented in *Eros and Civilization*. This is, as we have said, with reference to early and classical capitalism. Reiche goes on to present an elaboration of the later concept 'repressive desublimation'. He lists three factors in modern society which 'oppose the development of a genital character' in modern capitalist society:

1 'Insufficient preparation of genital organisation by the family and the outside world.'
2 'Alienating work which has adverse effects on sexual practice.'
3 'The overwhelming genital demands of society.'[20]

The first two controls were clearly present in early capitalism and, for some sections of the population, are still present under later capitalism. The last feature is a peculiar feature of late capitalist society. In a pseudo-democratic way the whole society is eroticized through the media. Sexuality is encouraged and 'in extreme cases the complete apparatus of the brothel has been taken over by marriage'.[21]

A pseudo-genital person is in a state of perpetual sexual tension. The normal course of sexual gratification is a state of unpleasant tension leading to release and pleasure, fore-pleasure leading to end-pleasure. For the pseudo-genital personality these sequences are fractured. He becomes a 'highly variable fetishist'.[22] For example Gillian Freeman in her survey of the 'undergrowth of literature' notes the importance of clothing in almost all specialized forms of pornography and stresses the continuity between what is normally regarded as 'hard core' pornography and material more generally available in children's comics and advertising. Thus the distinction between the world of Batman, Wonderwoman and Catwoman and the world of bondage and rubber fetishists is often difficult to discern.[23]

Reiche is clearly in agreement with Marcuse in casting doubts on the reality of the so-called 'sexual revolution' under late capitalism. For this reason he argues that programmes for sexual liberation, so enthusiastically espoused by Reich in an earlier period of German history, cannot have the same function for revolutionary movements as they did in the past. Indeed he urges the stressing of love and fidelity as defence techniques against the forces of repressive desublimation. For one thing such an emphasis might go some way to overcoming the gulf between the student movement and the working-class movement, in so far as one of the divisions between them is in terms of sexual practice. (Student radicals are defined as sexually promiscuous and leading a life of leisured luxury much in the same way as young aristocrats might have been defined in an earlier era.) Furthermore, the encouragement of fidelity and love would encourage —through effective sublimation—the development of a strong ego as a basis to oppose late capitalist society.

It should be clear that the authors discussed so far fall into neither the conservative nor the liberal categories of attitude towards permissiveness. They reject a notion of a simple linear liberalization of sexual behaviour and attitudes (or loosening of standards if one takes the conservative interpretation). While there is some recognition, from Reiche at least, that some genuine gains have been made in this respect, both Reiche and Marcuse are suspicious of the apparent manifestations of a 'sexual revolution'. Indeed, as we have seen, they suspect that this apparent increase in sexual freedom in fact masks an increase in manipulation.

All this makes nonsense of Holbrook's statement to the effect that: 'Presumably those who urge on us more pornography are following Marcuse in the belief that such symbolism can release us from the inhibitions imposed by society.'[24] In fact all three writers fall into the second category of radicals, those who are critical of many of the manifestations of sexual freedom in modern society and see the answer in a change in society itself rather than censorship or a return to a Christian standard of morality. Reiche writes disapprovingly of pornography, sex in advertising and infidelity and swinging among married couples. Whatever the ultimate revolutionary goal the present call is for love and fidelity among the young. Marcuse adheres to a more or less straightforward concept of 'perversions' although he does argue that the homosexual, for example, may have a critical role to play in late capitalist society. Reich too took his standard as true heterosexual love and argued that a revolutionary society would necessarily mean an end of pornography, foul language and all debased manifestations of eroticism.[25]

However all these writers talk of the possibility of sexual liberation, and it is this that distinguishes many of the post-Freudian radicals from Freud himself. Freud saw the conflict between civilization and man's instinctual nature as to a large extent inevitable. Sexual liberation was a matter of individual adjustment rather than societal change: 'It can more truly be said that analysis sets the neurotic free from the chains of his sexuality.'[26] On top of this there was the suggestion that society may have gone too far in its repressive demands and that there was the possibility that some of its stricter demands might be reduced or removed. Increased knowledge and increased truthfulness also have their part to play, but so long as it was recognized that such knowledge did not necessarily bring with it the greater power to control or negate the constraints of civilization. The correct stance in the face of what Trilling has called 'Freud's tragic sense of culture'[27] would appear to be one of stoic acceptance.

Clearly then, the Freudian left conceives of the possibility of sexual liberation that goes much further than is to be imagined from a reading of Freud himself. If 'civilization and its discontents' is rewritten as 'capitalism and its discontents' then this possibility of sexual liberation is inevitably linked with the possibility of liberation from capitalism itself. This is not merely a liberation from the 'anal' type of early classical capitalism (which has already been partially achieved) but also from the 'pseudo-genital' type of advanced capitalism. To these radicals sexual freedom would appear to mean a freedom from artificiality or commercially manipulated desires, a freedom from the perpetual state of tension suffered by this pseudo-genital personality type rather than a simple manifestation of 'anything goes'.[28] Sexual liberation is inevitably linked with political liberation and the one cannot proceed very far without the other.

Yet here we come up against a major ambiguity or perhaps dilemma in the analysis of the relationship between a sexual and a political revolution. In practice many revolutionary movements and revolutionary or newly liberated nations appear to manifest a markedly 'puritan' attitude to sexual expression and behaviour. Reich, indeed, devoted a considerable portion of his book *The Sexual Revolution* to analysing the causes for the failure of that revolution in Soviet Russia, thereby arousing the hostility of the orthodox Marxists as well as the orthodox Freudians.[29] Perhaps the most marked example of this is China, where while there have been considerable moves made towards equality of the sexes and the weakening of the traditional patriarchal family,[30] there is a considerable emphasis on monogamy and fidelity and extreme reticence in all sexual matters. Such an emphasis may be partially a matter of making a radical departure from earlier patterns of feudal or capitalist sexual exploitation and may also be seen as a manifestation of what Slater (closely following Freud) sees as an inevitable tension between dyadic libidinal withdrawal and societal libidinal diffusion.[31] While it might be argued that this 'puritanism' is a necessary emphasis in the building of a new society and that full sexual liberation may be reached at some stage in the future, the ambiguity of the whole concept of 'sexual liberation' remains.

Sex, class and exploitation

The interest in sexuality and repression in society represents the main concern of all three writers we have considered, and what follows in subsequent sections will be an elaboration on this theme. Here I shall take considerable liberties with the original arguments and suggest directions in which a sociological investigation of this problem might proceed, raising, in the course of this exploration, some possible criticisms of its original formulation. Here I shall take up the connections between sexuality, social class and exploitation.

It can be said that Freud did not entirely ignore this aspect of the problem and that relating to sex and social class was already present in Freud's writing. In *The Future of an Illusion* he notes: 'One thus gets an impression that civilisation is something which was imposed on a resisting majority by a minority which understood how to obtain possession of the means to power and coercion.'[32] He recognized that in this struggle between the pleasure principle and the reality principle some privations applied, necessarily, to all members of society while others appeared to bear more heavily on particular classes. Civilization is threatened when there exists within it a class that is suffering from too many of these specific deprivations. However, although Freud appeared to recognize that there was a strong class component to repression and civilization, his social analysis appeared to be closer to the 'élite' theories of Mosca and Pareto than to the class theories of Marx.

Combining the Marxian with the Freudian approach to the analysis of sex and class it may be argued that capitalism, at least in its early phases, presented a double assault on the sexuality of the working class. In the first place we have the equation, described graphically by Engels,[33] of brutalized working and living conditions and brutalized sexual relationships. Sex and drink, argued Engels, were the only means of personal escape from these conditions, and the long hours, physically exhausting working conditions and overcrowded dwellings inevitably meant that sex was brief and physical, a matter of unilateral taking rather than mutual giving, an isolated episode rather than something intrinsically bound up with a growing loving relationship. Outside literature, the best sociological account of sexual relationships under conditions of classical capitalism (even if in some places these conditions persisted into the twentieth century) is probably still *Coal is Our Life*:[34]

> Sex is something different from the relations between human beings, a matter of conquest and achievement, for the male individual. In such an ideology women can only be objects of lust, mothers and domestic servants. The sex-life of married couples shows the effect of this.

Slater and Woodside, writing in 1951, recorded the following evaluations of sexual experience on the part of working-class wives:[35]

> 'It's something that's got to be done and the quicker the better.'
> 'It's the one part of marriage I could do without.'
> 'He's very good, he doesn't bother me much.'

In the second place, at a deeper level, the very constraints of an urban, industrial society required a disciplined ordered rhythm of life very contrary to the freer instinctual flow represented by the libido. This characteristic was shared by the bourgeoisie for whom discipline and order were also prime considerations. As capitalism developed many of these differences between proletariat and bourgeoisie became blurred. The Protestant Ethic had become secularized and no longer occupied its central functional position, the worker needed to be encouraged in his role as a consumer as well as a producer and there was a convergence between some sections of the working class and the middle class. A mass sexual culture became more widely available through the media, cheaper forms of clothing, cosmetics and advertising. Possibly some of the traditional sexual links between the upper and lower classes—manifested in the seduction of the servant girl or employee by the master, or prostitution—declined or, through the availability of contraceptives, lost some of their fatefulness. The links between sexual and economic exploitation would appear to be less direct than they might have been in the classic period of capitalism.

Reiche is aware of the continuing fact of class differences in sexual experience within capitalism. He uses some readily available sociological findings for this purpose. Thus, for example, there is an association between the age at which one first has sexual experience and the length of schooling, the longer the period of schooling the later the sexual experience. Schooling is, of course, significantly associated with other indicators of social status such as occupation and income. Similarly it has been found that the higher one's socio-economic status the greater is one's chance for a happier sex life in marriage. And finally the upper and middle classes manifest more varied forms of love play in their sex life.[36] While it might be argued that the overall level of repression remains the same in spite of these different manifestations of sexuality, this material reminds us that it is important to examine the particular features of the social structure that mediate between the operation of the reality principle and the control of the pleasure principle.

Thus class differences in sexual experience continue to be of importance and must be taken into account if we are to consider the relationships between sexuality and modern capitalism. (One important intervening factor is, of course, differential access to methods of family planning.) Yet, as surveys by Reiss have shown,[37] the association between sexual experience and social class is by no means a straightforward one and if we are to proceed with this argument it will be necessary to elaborate a model of social structure more complex than a simple dichotomous proletariat/bourgeoisie or working class/middle class. We see these dichotomous models as being one of a set of possible bases for the mobilization of support and grounding of identity and as providing the source of many of the major themes in the history of modern capitalism. However, the development of a multi-layered class structure and the importance of status groups must also be included in these models not as strict alternatives in the sense that acceptance of the latter implies rejection of the former but different bases for identification and mobilization which might cut across/blur/or reinforce these older class models. It is this more complex model of social stratification that we have in mind when we consider some further possible interconnections between sexuality and the social structure.

Here the following points seem to be worthy of consideration and possibly further examination:

1 The notion of success as an important goal in present society has a sexual dimension which may or may not coincide with other dimensions of success. In this case it would be important to recognize that there is not one model of sexual success but several. There is the quantified Don Juan model of sexual success and there is the model of sexual adjustment in marriage. Somewhere between these models is the goal of sexual virtuosity which may or may not be within the institution of marriage but which precludes a simple quantitative approach to sex. It is likely that different sections of society hold different models of sexual success, possibly at different stages of their life cycle. However, common to all these and to other models is the notion that some form of sexual achievement is an important goal in society or, at least, an important component of any other valued goal.

2 Associated with the notion of sex as a component in societal

goals is the notion of sex as a source of status. It is unlikely that assumed or actual sexual experience will alone form the basis for the development of status *groups* (although certain patterns of sexual behaviour may be attributed to specific groups in society such as students or immigrants). The emphasis here is upon individual evaluations of status such as is to be found in 'the rating and dating complex', the 'slum sex code' and in male 'bull sessions'.[38] These examples demonstrate the importance of sexual experience as a basis for individual status ratings among young males and that one's own self-identity may be influenced by one's subjective assessment of the normal level of sexual experience in relation to one's peers. Negatively, and at a more general level, those who are assumed to fail to live up to certain expected, desired or 'normal' levels of sexual performance may be labelled 'frustrated', 'sexually deprived', 'men in raincoats', etc. Such labels may provide a rhetoric, a set of legitimations for understanding and ordering relationships within modern society.

3 The idea of sex as a societal goal and a source of status has been noted but the argument has assumed that sex operates independently. However, it is likely that the power of sexuality as a source of status is increased when it is linked with other dimensions of stratification. The word 'glamour' perhaps sums up more concisely than any other word a particular nexus of sexuality, wealth, prestige, power and life style.[39] As is often the case, there may be an incomplete relationship between the actual practices of certain defined groupings and the practices which are assigned to them by excluded outsiders. Pretty secretaries may be just that and no more in spite of the fact that they might be the source of inspiration for libidinous fantasies on the part of the sexually excluded, and there may well be some element of exaggeration in the assumption that social mobility through sport or show business necessarily brings with it a greater degree of access to and enjoyment of sexual resources. Yet the assumed association between wealth and sexual pleasure remains, although perhaps less in the form of a simple distinction between them and us, the excluded and the included. More and more people are perhaps able to savour the sexual ambiance of international air travel, Playboy clubs or their equivalents and various forms of entertainment.

4 Finally we may note the continued, although undoubtedly weakening, tendency for sexual partners to be selected from within class, caste or status group boundaries of varying degrees of clarity of definition. Even where the wide availability of contraceptive techniques effectively severs the links between sexual activity and parenthood (and hence usually marriage) it is likely that some formal and informal controls over the selection of sexual partners still exist. Elements of this pattern include not only limitations on the selection

of sexual partners who might become more permanent mates but also the sexual exploitation by the males of a dominant group of the females of a subordinate group, the attribution of sexual characteristics to the males and females of the subordinate group, notions of ritual pollution and so on. While such considerations may be less relevant within modern society, where many of the boundaries of class and status differentiation have become blurred or more individualized, they clearly still have relevance in terms of relationships between ethnic groups and in situations of colonialism or neo-colonialism.

That sexuality is a dimension and an often ignored dimension in social stratification can scarcely be denied. What does also seem to be apparent is that its association with patterns of social stratification, apart from situations of ethnic caste relationships, is far from being a straightforward one. Three possible relationships have been suggested here:

1 Where sex operates as a dimension of status differentiation which is to a large extent independent of other forms of evaluation. (Evaluation of sexual prowess or conquests between individuals who are, in most other respects, peers as in the case of the 'slum sex code'.)

2 Where sex operates as a dimension reinforcing existing status differentiations. (Caste relationships and, to a lesser extent, the glamour complex.)

3 Where sex, while not operating independently of other factors, tends to blur or add to the blurring of existing stratificational boundaries. (The glamour complex to a large extent.)

This analysis should be seen as being tentative and as being complementary to the earlier discussion which referred to Reiche's analysis of social class differences in sexual practices and experience. Furthermore, this analysis cannot be conducted apart from a consideration of two further themes: the question of the association between sexuality and conformity in post-industrial society and the position of women in that society.

Sex and conformity

We now pass to what is perhaps the most difficult part of the attempt to relate sexuality and capitalism: the alleged relationship between sex and conformity in late capitalist society. To put the matter more sharply we are asking to what extent is order maintained in capitalism, the patterns of class conflict and exploitation blurred over, through an increasing eroticization of everyday life? What role does sexuality play in the manipulation of consent? The argument, most closely associated with Marcuse and Reiche, has already been stated and may now be recapitulated with reference to the last section. Advanced capitalist society involves a shift to a greater concentration of economic and political power on the one hand and a growing blurring of class lines, at least in their overt and symbolic aspects if not in the underlying relationships of antagonism. There is a corresponding shift to the more subtle forms of manipulation of consent, part of which involves the manipulation of sexual symbolism. The nude pin-up has replaced the red flag. A somewhat similar target, although a very different kind of analysis and presumably a very different kind of solution, is offered by David Holbrook in his attack on 'sexual fascism'.[40] The components of this sexual fascism are a dehumanized attitude to sex involved when sex is 'separated from everything else that belongs to being human',[41] a passionate moral inversion and an over-masculinized taboo on tenderness, all of which is reinforced by the authoritarian tone adopted by many of the advocates of this so-called sexual freedom. Holbrook, however, makes little attempt to relate this particular syndrome to any particular historical or social conditions and certainly fails to point out any of the possible political dimensions of his attack.

It can be seen that, to a large extent, these critiques of sexuality in modern society are a specific application of a wider and long established critique of 'mass society', a society in which the old traditional working-class solidarities are seen as being eroded and replaced by a division between a ruling 'power élite' and a mass society. This question will be examined from two points of view: first from the point of view of the 'manipulated' and second from the point of view of the 'manipulators'.

Looking at the argument from the point of view of the manipulated the case would appear to consist of at least four interrelated propositions:

1 There is an increasing eroticization of more and more areas of life, and increasingly uniform and more generally accessible range of erotic material and sexual symbolism. The emphasis is on written, printed or photographed material (and more recently material performed on the stage) rather than an older, oral, semi-underground tradition. This material is not confined to specialist bookshops or cinema clubs but is more widely available and increasingly legitimized in terms of sexual happiness. We may take, at least for the purposes of argument, as given that there has been an increasing open eroticization of everyday life.

2 There has been a growing convergence of social classes, the emergence of a common middle-class life style. The best that can be said about this proposition (which appears to be a crucial one for Marcuse's argument) is that it is still not-proven. Modern industrial society remains in many respects as unequal as it was between the wars and, where there has been a growing overlap of incomes

between white-collar and manual occupations this has not necessarily entailed the adoption of a common style of life.[42]

3 This eroticization of everyday life is part of this common life style and is associated also with the growing stress on leisure and consumption in advanced capitalist society. It might be argued, therefore, that the preceding proposition need not necessarily be true but that the eroticization of everyday life serves to promote a pseudo-democratic view of the world. Sex, after all, is older than capitalism and one of the features of the 'erotic revolution' appears to be to promote the notion that this is what life is 'really' all about. It will be admitted (as Reiche does when he outlines some of the differences between social classes in terms of sexual enjoyment) that this sexual democracy has not yet been fully achieved. Not all members of society can afford to purchase *Playboy* or volumes of photographs demonstrating sexual positions, nor do they have the privacy or the energy (after bearing several children or working long hours) for the personal promotion of sexual harmony. Even so it might be argued that there is a greater degree of convergence in sexual life style at the middle levels of society, in the area encompassing the white-collar families and the more affluent sections of the manual working population. It would appear, however, that the growing homogenization of sexual life style has yet to be demonstrated and cannot merely be inferred from the apparent ubiquity of sexually 'liberated' literature. In fact different publications have different attitudes to sexual problems and behaviour and aim to appeal to slightly different readerships in terms of age and socio-economic status.[43]

4 This growing homogenization of sexual experience and stimuli leads to a greater degree of conformity and acceptance in advanced capitalist society. This is based on the assumption of a weakened ego structure as a result of this 'repressive desublimation' and on the alleged inverse relationship between dyadic (or narcissistic) cathexis and societal cathexis. Put simply this means that this apparent sexual liberation as well as blurring class differences weakens one of the main impetuses for revolutionary change (the repression of society in psychic terms) and seeks to promote a withdrawal into chiefly dyadic sexual relationships and away from the arena of class conflict and class solidarity. Such an assumption appears to imply a somewhat mechanical view of the relationship between personality and society, whereby energy expended in one direction (sexual activity) necessarily means a withdrawal from participation in some other area, in this case revolutionary political activity. Furthermore it smooths over the various patterns of resistance that are manifested within this supposedly homogeneous population.[44] Thus there is the populist appeal of many of the movements against pornography

which have working-class as well as middle-class support and which have, as a component to their attack, a reaction against 'them', the manipulators. In most cases this 'them' is perceived as a narrow intellectual élite rather than as a 'ruling class' or 'power élite'. At the other extreme we have the various patterns of resistance demonstrated in some sections of the youth culture whereby the deliberate and open flouting of sexual taboos is seen as an expression of collective hostility to the existing order (*Oz*, the use of four letter words in demonstrations, etc.).[45]

If the assumptions made about the 'manipulated' in this model of sexuality and conformity are often at best unproven, the same also applies, perhaps to a greater extent, on the part of the alleged 'manipulators'. The difficulties here are greater if only for the reason that it is so much more difficult to study decision-making at the top than it is to study attitudes at the bottom, and that similarities of social and educational backgrounds and postulated similarities of real interests do not necessarily mean identical interests when it comes to day-to-day policy decisions. The assumption that there is an entity called the 'ruling class', the 'power élite' or, more vaguely, 'the establishment' is not so much open to question as open to clarification and reformulation. Large differences in wealth, power and status within advanced capitalist society and the overlapping and concentration of interests based upon these differences can be demonstrated, but at the same time many of the conflicts and ambiguities within this apparently homogeneous 'them' need to be recognized and examined. In this particular case it is important to have knowledge of the variety of groups—advertisers, promoters of beauty competitions, publishers, model agencies, etc.—with an interest in presenting and sustaining certain sexual images.

If the assumption of a homogeneous ruling élite requires detailed and critical attention, even more so does the assumption that this élite is in some way interested in the sexual manipulation of the masses in order to maintain the existing system. What can be assumed is that the stimulation of consumption and commercial leisure activities is an increasingly important feature of modern capitalism and that sexual symbolism plays an important part in this stimulation. Sex is seen as being profitable, both directly (the sale of sex books, etc.) and indirectly (the use of sex to sell or to associate with other products or leisure activities). But the extent to which these particular forms of the exploitation of sex are a necessary feature of advanced capitalism is open to some question. For one thing it may not be sex as such that is being exploited; sexual symbols may be effective in that they are combined with other symbols (domesticity, wealth, power, etc.) and may derive their saliency from these particular combinations viewed in particular contexts. For another thing, the problem of drawing the line between the serious exploration of sexual relationships and the exploitation of sex is one of the most contentious areas in the discussion of pornography and censorship and the differences are often blurred, perhaps by other groups with different interests.

If it is difficult to place a meaningful label on all apparent manifestations of the sexual revolution in the arts, advertising, popular culture, etc., it is even more difficult to establish the links between this sector, the economy and society and other sectors such as the political, military or financial élites. In practice it would appear that opposition to many overt features of the 'sexual revolution' is just as likely to go hand in hand with an attachment to free-enterprise capitalism as it is that these features should in some way be connected.

It is finally difficult to see that there is any *direct* engineering of consent on the part of a ruling class through the use of sexual symbolism. For one thing the 'manipulators' may to some extent be themselves unaware of these connections. The use of fairly obvious sexual symbolism in a television advertisement for after-shave lotion may be as much a matter of a jokey wink, a nudge between 'men of the world', as a matter of direct subliminal persuasion. Furthermore, if the argument about the association between dyadic or narcissistic withdrawal and societal cathexis holds true then it may not necessarily be in the interests of the 'ruling class' to let the sexual revolution go too far. For the 'manipulated' are also producers as well as consumers and a wholesale embracement of sexual hedonism might be viewed as antagonistic to the orderly working habits which are presumably still required in advanced capitalism.

This is not to deny that there may be links between sexuality, advanced capitalism and consensus but that the links are more complex and indirect than the somewhat simple formulations of Marcuse and Reiche would seem to suggest. One possible intervening factor is the privatization of the family which some sociologists argue is a feature of this society.[46] The simple association of sexuality and conformity makes too many assumptions about the homogeneity of the ruling class and the ruled and assumes too much passivity on the part of the alleged 'masses'. There is in Marcuse, Reiche and, from a different standpoint, Holbrook, a low tolerance of ambiguity and an unwillingness to explore some of the more contradictory or ironical features of the manifestations of dehumanized sex which they deplore.

The role of the family

Marcuse may be criticized for having little to say about the family in his analysis of sexuality and repression in modern society. All he argued in *Eros and Civilization* was that the family had lost its major social functions. It was no longer a major economic unit in society and its functions were being lost to many outside agencies. Consequently there was a decline in the classical Oedipal crisis analysed by Freud —which, however wounding it might be, did guarantee some development of individuality, since no two family dramas were exactly alike—and the ego was now more likely to be prematurely socialized by the extra-familial agencies. Reiche follows Marcuse in this line of argument, stressing that the family appears to be breaking down and that there was little point in revolutionary activity being directed towards the erosion of this already declining institution.

Yet, of course, in the writings of Freud from which Marcuse derived his inspiration, the family played a vital role as the mediator between the individual and culture. Trilling expressed this in a memorable sentence:[47]

> By what he said or suggested of the depth and subtlety of the influence of the family upon the individual, he made plain how the culture suffuses the remotest part of the individual mind, being taken in almost literally with the mother's milk.

Later, as we have seen, Parsons was to take up this theme and analyse the intimate interconnections between the family system, the cultural system and the personality system. However, if Parsons was to develop Freud's analysis in a eufunctional direction, Reich was to stress the dysfunctional aspects of the mediating role of the family and to examine the repressive triangle of love, sexuality and marriage and their connections within the development of an authoritarian culture. He writes:[48]

> *The interlacing of the socio-economic structure with the sexual structure of society and the structural reproduction of society takes place in the first four or five years and in the authoritarian family.* . . . Thus, the authoritarian state gains an enormous interest in the authoritarian family: *it becomes the factory in which the state's structure and ideology are moulded.*
>
> *Man's authoritarian structure*—this must be clearly established —*is basically produced by the embedding of sexual inhibitions and fear in the living substance of sexual impulses.*

Reich is interested in investigating how it is that ideology appears as a material force in society and why it is that sex is suppressed by society and repressed by the individual. In place of the traditionally understood Marxian view of ideology which might be over-simply represented as:

Ideology ←———————— **Economic structure of society**

he develops a more complex model fusing the Freudian and the Marxian traditions. This might be represented as shown in Figure 3.

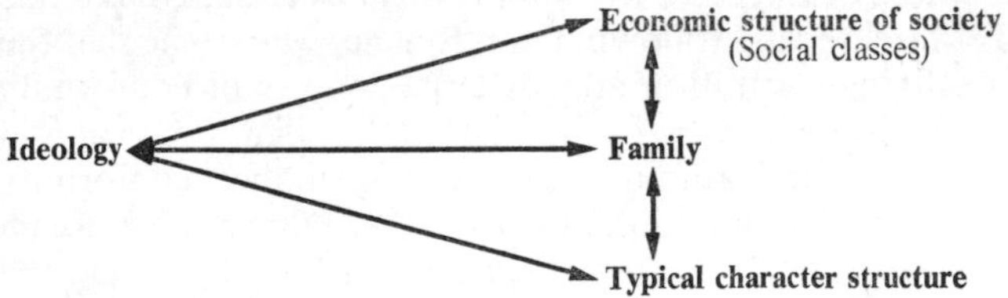

Figure 3

His particular concern is with the lower middle-class families who provided an important section of the social support for Nazi Germany. These families were patriarchal in structure and based upon the sexual suppression of women and children. In their occupational roles as petty officials they tended to identify with power and authority without, to any great extent, actually sharing in the full exercise of effective power. There was, as Weber might have said, an 'elective affinity' between this class's economic and political identification with the authoritarian régime and their sexual moralism, between sexual repression through the instrument of the family and the central notions of Honour and Duty. The choice to them appeared to be one between a compulsive sexual morality or sexual anarchy just as the political choice appeared to be between law and order and the rule of the streets. The state itself provided considerable ideological support for the family with the veneration of motherhood and certain patriarchal forms of family life.

Some support for Reich's analysis might appear to come from the members of the 'Frankfurt School'. The social psychological investigations into the 'authoritarian personality', Fromm's historical analysis of the 'fear of freedom' and Horkheimer's account of authoritarianism and the family all serve to round out and develop Reich's central arguments.[49] The general picture of the potential supporter of fascism, the person willing to surrender his freedom to an authoritarian régime, that emerges from these studies is one whose attitude toward his own family is a mixture of extreme rebellion and submissiveness. The more authoritarian subjects tended to be resentful of many actions and attitudes of their parents but also tended to have a more idealized view of them and tended to be more submissive to parental authority. In relation to their own families they tended to have an in-group (us versus them) orientation. Again, in terms of sexual relationships they held strongly dichotomous views, either fearing women or putting them on a pedestal. They tended to hold a sharp distinction between 'good girls' and 'bad girls', between the mother and the whore.

We have reached what appears to be a contradiction within a group of analysts who derive their inspiration from the same source and some of whom belonged to the same critical 'school'. On the one hand there is Marcuse, and following him Reiche, who argue that the family is a declining institution and that the sources of conformity and authoritarianism are to be found in extra-familial, political and economic agencies who, among other things, induce conformity through 'repressive desublimation'. On the other hand there is Reich and the researchers of the *Authoritarian Personality* who locate the source of authoritarianism and a willingness to accept fascism in the family structure itself, especially the lower middle-class family. Thus the same effect (conformity and authoritarianism) appears to be attributed to two opposed causes, namely the weakening of the family and the existence of a strong family structure.

One possible solution is that these authors were referring to different stages in the development of capitalism. Reich and Adorno *et al.* were particularly concerned with the lower middle-class families between the wars who came to accept fascism. Marcuse was more concerned with the period since the Second World War, with the more subtle processes of manipulation in late capitalist society during this period. Reiche is certainly talking about sexuality and capitalism in the 1960s. While the sexual repression of the classical capitalist period was very much maintained through the institution of the nuclear family, the apparent growth in sexual freedom was partially dependent upon the erosion of the family's traditional prerogatives in sexual matters. Thus in the development of a pseudo-genital façade, the main influences were the mass media and advertising rather than the family which became more and more a dependent variable, reflecting trends outside itself rather than remaining the major basis for personality formation. Possibly the researches of Adorno and his associates reflected a changing society with some individuals showing the marks of the old patriarchal family structure and values while others showed a shift, in their family backgrounds and orientations, to a more democratic but possibly weaker family structure. This apparently democratic family structure was in fact relatively powerless against the encroachments of socialization agencies outside the family.[50]

The argument would appear to be, therefore, that as sexuality becomes less and less exclusively centred on the institution of the family so the role of the family as an agency of repression becomes less central. If we wish to look for the sources of social control and manipulation in modern society we must look outside the family. The family would appear to be more victim than villain. And yet, on the other side, there are the very different conclusions of Parsons and Laing which, however opposed in overall orientation, appear to agree in the centrality of the family in the process of 'socialization'. It is also clear that still, in so far as any one agency is responsible for the socialization of children (legally, financially and morally in different ways and to different degrees) in modern society, that institution is still the nuclear family. Furthermore, ideologically, the family is still the main point of reference for the evaluation of sexual behaviour; we still, after all, talk of pre-marital or extra-marital sex. To accept the conclusions of Marcuse and Reiche we would have to accept that the extra-familial agencies are now strong enough to counteract the intensive socialization function of the family or that the family, in a more passive and uniform way, simply transmits these external influences. In either case some further analysis would seem to be required, either in the direction of explaining how the socialization function surrendered to these other agencies or in explaining the newly defined relationship between the family and society. This whole debate, which we have taken up at various points during this essay, about the centrality or otherwise of the nuclear family in modern society will be taken a little further in the concluding chapter.

The roles of women

If the apparent absence of any detailed discussion of the role of the family in the writings of Marcuse and Reiche is curious, even more astonishing is the almost total absence of a systematic discussion of the part played by women in the assumed relationships between sexuality and capitalism. This may possibly be one of the less desirable legacies of Freud. While it may just about be excusable for Marcuse not to have mentioned the exploitation of women in his *Eros und Civilization* it is less excusable for Reiche, writing a decade later, not to have mentioned the growing Women's Liberation movement.[51]

Yet in the examination of the relationship between sexuality and capitalism it is vital to give particular attention to the role of women in this process for several reasons:

1 The operation of the sexual double standard, particularly in classical capitalism. This implied not merely that virginity at marriage was expected of women but not of men but also the distinction between 'good girls' and 'bad girls', the unequal division of blame for sexual misdemeanour on to the woman and the role of prostitution in the support of the Victorian family. Such features, which are in several respects still with us in an attenuated form, incidentally throw some doubt on the effectiveness of the bourgeois family as an agency for sexual repression at least as far as the men were concerned.

2 Reich's analysis of the authoritarian family system clearly recognizes the importance of the subordination of women in this

patriarchal family structure. The patriarchal father suppresses not only children but also women. The authoritarian family system depends on the wife as a child-bearer rather than as a full social being, and emphasis is laid ideologically on 'the blessings of a large family'.[52] Thus the subordinate position of women is an integral part of Reich's analysis of the relationship between authoritarianism and the family.

3 But what of the 'sexual revolution'? In late capitalism, this apparent increase in sexual freedom was again a freedom which more often that not benefited the man rather than the woman.[53] In this connection the term 'sex object' is often used, a term which appears to imply the following interrelated and interacting themes:

(a) Woman as Being-for Others.

(b) This theme of Being-for-Others is publicly available and acts back to define and shape the woman's private identity.

(c) This public image of woman is normally in terms of prevailing definitions of sexuality. The process of objectification is given a further twist by the emphasis on particular parts—breasts, legs, thighs, etc.—of a woman's body.[54]

(d) These objectifications are further alienated by becoming possessions (oil paintings) or objects of consumption (pin-ups).[55]

(e) Further objectifications take place in the association of these images with other items of consumption either directly *for* women (fashion) or, primarily through advertising, the association of these images with themes of status, wealth, power, etc., thus reinforcing the theme of woman as possession. It cannot be denied, of course, that this eroticization of culture is not now wholly in terms of women for men but it is the case that the emphasis is still heavily in this direction.

It is not necessary at this point to repeat the discussion outlined in the previous chapter. What is important to emphasize is that if we are to attempt to outline a model of the relationships between sexuality and capitalism an integral part of that analysis must be the subordinate position of women. Furthermore, if we are to attempt to outline any model of a sexual revolution, again that account must clearly be one which considers this revolution in terms of the overall structure of relationships between the sexes and not merely in terms of an abstract increase in sexual freedom.

Discussion

I hope that this brief chapter has at least demonstrated that this particular section of the critical tradition does raise some important problems about the relationships between sexuality, the family and culture. These authors—particularly Reich and Marcuse—suffer as have other authors mentioned in this essay from either too easy acceptance or too easy rejection. It is the main contention of this chapter not that these authors have made important 'discoveries' about these relationships but that they have considered these relationships as being worthy of investigation. The remaining few comments will raise problems which I consider have not been adequately considered by the authors discussed here and which will, I hope, take the argument a little further.

1 In the first place there is the problem of defining sexual activity itself. Dictionary definitions revolve around the differences between the two sexes, being male or female, copulations, etc. Vance Packard quotes one definition that argues that sexuality is 'everything in each of us that has to do with being a man or a woman'.[56] Brown refers to Freud's widening concept of sex and offers the definition that includes 'any pleasurable sensation related to the bodily functions'.[57] Such definitions could, no doubt, be multiplied. The point about such definitions is that they provide little guidance when we are attempting to label a certain activity as being 'sexual' or not. Perhaps one of the major effects of Freud's writing, and its popular acceptance and diffusion, has been to widen the range of activities that might possibly come under the label 'sexual' and, at the same time, to induce a certain degree of uncertainty about this matter in any one particular case. Dictionary definitions, however, tend to have a bias in favour of adult heterosexual relationships. The analyses of infantile sexuality, repression and sublimation have, on the other hand, increased the sense of ambiguity as to what is or is not sexual. Thompson has noted the sexual imagery in some of the early Methodist hymns[58] and Freeman argues that there is considerable repressed sexuality in the beatings recorded in issues of the *Boy's Own Paper* published around 1900.[59] The way in which the urban landscape may be readily transformed into a jungle of sexual and phallic symbols need hardly be elaborated and is wittily illustrated in this quotation from Alfred Hitchcock: 'There are no symbols in *North by Northwest*. Oh yes! One. The last shot. The train entering the tunnel after the love scene between Grant and Eva-Marie Saint. It's a phallic symbol. But don't tell anyone.'[60]

The general point that arises out of this discussion is that a definition of sexual behaviour and sexual activity cannot begin and end with a dictionary definition but must examine the wider interactional and transactional processes that take place within a culture or sub-culture whereby a particular activity comes to be defined as 'sexual'. We should move away from the attempt to provide an absolute, biologically based and culture-free definition of sexuality while at the same time recognizing that definitions of sexuality are never wholly determined by a particular culture.[61] Much of the eroticization of the economy described by Marcuse and Reiche may not necessarily be a simple matter of 'more sex' but of more and more activities, things and persons being successfully accorded the label of 'sexual 'or 'sexy'.[62]

2 If there are ambiguities in the notion of sexuality itself there are even greater ambiguities as to what is meant by 'true' or 'perverted' sexuality. In the first place many of the writers mentioned here appear to be operating with some standard of true, non-exploitative, sexual expression against which to measure present sexual practices and standards. With Marcuse the emphasis appears to be on free genital sexuality although there appears to be some ambiguity in this respect.[63] Reich's definition of the orgasm—whereby sexuality under capitalism is found to be inadequate and distorted—is another example and Holbrook sees true sexuality as existing only within the context of a total loving relationship. The source of these standards, from which the critical examination of modern sexuality derives much of its power, might be some real or imagined primitive society, traditional moral or religious beliefs, wider conceptions of what it involves to be human, or some future liberated state. The parallel here is the discussion of 'alienation' whereby there is always some standard of 'non-alienated' man at least implied. What is implied here is some standard of non-alienated sexuality.

It is clear that all the writers mentioned are operating with some notion of non-alienated sexual relationships and that such a notion poses all kinds of difficulties. It might be easy—perhaps too easy—to dismiss such speculations on positivistic or even hedonistic grounds. Thus the notion of 'dehumanized sex' appears to assume that simple physical copulation (or the representation of that act) belongs to the sphere of animal behaviour and is only made human by the meaning which is assigned to it. Yet it is difficult to conceive of a situation in which sex is ever completely dehumanized in this sense; even the repeated descriptions of sexual acts in routine pornography may derive their rhetoric and metaphors from the culture in which they are placed.[64] Yet if we recognize that the sexual encounter, however 'private' it may appear, is placed in a particular culture and derives much of its meaning from a selective and heightened use of that culture we must also recognize that a part of that culture are its 'images of the future',[65] its concepts of what might or ought to be. Furthermore, the investigator of that culture, directly or indirectly, contributes to this stock of images, legitimations and rhetoric, a 'scientific' investigator such as Kinsey no less than a committed investigator such as Marcuse.[66]

What is being said, in a roundabout way, is that value judgments may be seen both *as* data and as contributing to and shaping that data. Thus many of the theories in this chapter could be redefined in terms of the rhetoric of sex, in terms of the way in which various groups or individuals define, understand and dramatically evaluate features of society as a whole in terms of sexuality. Similar observations apply to a discussion of 'deviant' sexual practices. Here the main directions of deviancy theory need to be incorporated into the analysis of sexuality in society. Instead of taking some absolute definition of 'perversion' (such as arguing that a sexual act is perverted to the extent that it is distanced from procreation) an examination of the 'labelling' process itself might be more revealing. This involves an examination of the 'labellers' as well as the 'labelled' and of the standards adopted by those who are labelled 'deviant' and their own standards of deviance and conformity.[67] Such an analysis is essential in modern society where there is no single clearly defined sexual code and where standards and practices tend to undergo redefinition in less than a lifetime.

3 Sex and the problem of order. This shift in perspective to an examination of those who label certain activities as perversions or deviant also raises questions as to the relationships between sex and the social order. One model of a 'traditional' society might be one in which the boundaries within which sexual activity is permitted or expected closely correspond to other boundaries which contribute to the overall maintenance of the social structure. The major lines along which these boundaries are drawn appear to be:

(a) Gender (the operation of the double standard, definitions of shame and honour, etc.).

(b) Age and generation. Here we consider the way in which full sexual status is accorded to those who are defined as and/or initiated into the status of adulthood. Reich noted that 'the sexual crisis of youth is an integral part of the crisis of the authoritarian social order'.[68] Simone de Beauvoir argues that the negative status of old people is often expressed in sexual terms.[69]

(c) Family and kinship. The operation of the incest taboo.

(d) Caste and class (see pages 181–5).

These boundaries are important features of the wider social structure and have wider political, social and economic significance, and the containment (ideal or actual) of sexual expression within these boundaries is a major factor in the overall maintenance of order.

This is not to say that all 'traditional' or 'pre-industrial' societies (to use two very inexact terms) are restrictive in sexual matters or that control is maintained through all these features of the social structure. What is being suggested is that where sexual activity was controlled, most of the effective enforcement of these controls was mediated through these particular features of the social structure. Thus in a society highly stratified in terms of age and sex (such as the rural Ireland of Arensberg and Kimball) effective control over sexual activity tended to reinforce these major axes of the social structure.[70] With the weakening of family based ties as a major component of a social structure based upon multiplex roles, the effectiveness of these channels in the maintenance of sexual controls was thereby also diminished. Perhaps also the importance of these controls in the maintenance of social structure was also reduced for the growing separation of the family and specialization of the family as an institution meant that a large part of what went on within the family became more of a private or individual matter with little consequence outside the family unit. In this light we may note the paradoxical element in Weber's analysis of the Protestant Ethic. Protestantism, in common with all rational salvation religions,[71] showed a marked hostility to the erotic sphere, seeing it as a sign of the animal and uncontrolled in man, the mark of original sin. At the same time the emphasis on universal brotherhood of believers rather than a kin-based community, potentially at least, laid the ground for the undermining of the very institutions that were, in many ways, best suited to the maintenance of sexual controls. To be effective, it might be suggested, sexual controls need to be mediated either through a strong internalized sense of duty instilled, say, through the active participation in the life and worship of a religious sect, or through a multiplex network of gossip, ridicule and possibly ostracism. With secularization (itself also a 'built-in' feature of Protestantism) the former set of controls weakened and with the growing separation of the family from other spheres of life and the processes of urbanization and industrialization the latter set of controls weakened also. To be sure the 'rationally regulated marriage'[72] served as the basis for the handling of the tension between rational asceticism and eroticism for some time but only so long as this marital relationship existed within the wider context of a religious brotherhood.

The point about this highly compressed discussion is that if we wish to talk about sexual repression in society we should not present a reified opposition between Society (or Culture) and the Individual but we should look at the particular features of the social structure through which this repression is mediated. This all too brief discussion has pointed to a shift in the source of these social controls (an analysis perhaps best presented, if indirectly, by Max Weber) and the ultimate weakening of these controls at least in terms of society as a whole. Now a variety of agencies act as controls over sexual activity (local and national government, ministers of religion, social workers, teachers, family and community as well as specialist 'experts' in sexual behaviour),[73] and not all of them act in the same direction.

4 We have noted the increasing difficulty of maintaining controls over sexual behaviour partly as a result of the increasing divergence

between the various sources of these controls. We have noted also how, in this complex society, the rhetoric of sex is used in a variety of ways and by different, often conflicting agencies. These observations point to a more complex relationship between sexuality and modern society than the one posited by Marcuse and Reiche. In fact Reiche presents a more subtle set of suggestions as to how we might characterize the relationships between sexuality and society than might have been indicated in this chapter up to now:[74]

> The contemporary task of psycho-analysis begins at the very point at which the majority of bourgeois psycho-analysts and Marxist politicians consider it should end: the determination of the tripartite relationship between the form of socio-economic organisation, the cultural expression and consolidation of this form of organization, and the way in which the individual reacts to both, either by adapting himself to them, or by changing them.

Reiche's account which notes, on the one hand, the divergence between classes in terms of sexual expression and, on the other, the growth of a contradictory tendency in terms of a 'mass sexuality' is probably more subtle than Marcuse's account of 'repressive desublimation'. Any account that does not recognize the seemingly paradoxical and contradictory trends in relation to sexuality and modern capitalism is almost certainly inadequate. A simple quasi-evolutionary account of the growth of sexual freedom is as misleading as an account which suggests the ever-increasing manipulation of consensus through sexual symbolism. The 'sexual revolution' may mean the increasing, if more subtle, exploitation of women. The sexual revolution may well enable individuals to discuss their sexual problems freely (in part by providing them with the language with which to do so) but may also play some part in creating new sexual problems such as, for example, creating anxiety through stressing some kind of standard of sexual adjustment, orgasmic fulfilment or whatever. The 'sexually inadequate' might possibly feel less inadequate in a society where the superior performance of the 'adequate' is less publicly in evidence.

5 Finally, this raises the problem about the relationship between sexual change and other forms of social change, between sexual liberation and other aspects of liberation. Many revolutionary or reformist programmes, it is true, carry little explicit reference to sexual freedom apart from indirect references to sexual equality and family planning. At least three possible revolutionary perspectives might be noted. In the first place there might be those who, implicitly accepting a model which shows sex and society to be weakly rather than strongly related, recognize the gains that have been made

in sexual freedom even under capitalism and who would argue that socialism would enable the complete realization of these trends and the elimination of some 'excesses' (such as pornography perhaps). Second, there would be those who would see in sexual behaviour some of the worst external features of an exploitative society and hence adopt a 'puritanical' stance to the prevailing sexual values. And finally, there are those who might argue that society still retains some or many sexual taboos and that the flouting or opposing of these taboos is both good in itself and a radical means of detaching the individual from society and its values. These positions do not, of course, include the varieties of radical feminist approaches which may coincide with or cut across the perspective outlined here. I would suggest that all these perspectives may be found among radical groups today and they derive, in part, from conflict in analyses of the relationship between capitalism and sexuality. Again, as well as investigating actual sexual practices and attitudes in contemporary society it might be worth while studying the rhetoric of sex, the way in which groups, especially radical groups, define themselves and distance themselves from the wider society in terms of sexual behaviour.

Conclusion

Thus the answer to the question asked by Reiche—'what has sexuality to do with class struggle?'—should be neither a flat 'nothing at all' nor the equally straightforward assertions of Marcuse. To argue that sex has nothing to do with capitalism would be to assert the existence of some unchanging, presumably basically biological, element in human life that was untouched by culture. At the same time it should be realized that we are dealing with an area of life—patterns of sexual expression and exploitation—which because of their prime focus on intensive dyadic relationships *appear* to possess and in some ways *do* possess a greater degree of autonomy than perhaps many other areas of life. The sexual class struggle—which we suggest is the main point of entry into the debate about sex and capitalism—should be seen *in the context of* but not determined by the economic class relationships. With these observations in mind we may perhaps begin to appreciate some of the confusing and paradoxical features of the modern 'sexual scene'; genuine advances both in the position of women and in sexual freedom together with increasing uncertainties and contradictions in these spheres; a nuclear family structure which at one and the same time appears to be both central and marginal; and the persistence of older patterns of sexual repression alongside new freedoms and new patterns of sexual exploitation.

Conclusion

The theories that we have been considering in the previous chapters have, for the most part, been what Cohen classifies as 'metaphysical' theories. Such theories, Cohen argues, are not strictly testable (unlike scientific theories) 'though they may be subject to rational appraisal'.[1] Such theories may be judged in, at least, two ways: in terms of the data that they generate and in terms of the 'images of man' that they generate. Rational appraisal should be related to both these considerations.

If we judge a metaphysical theory in terms of the kind of data that it generates we are to some extent attempting to transform part or the whole of such a theory into a scientific theory. We may find that a metaphysical theory leads us to consider certain features of the social world rather than other features, to make new kinds of connections, perhaps even to develop new techniques or methods for studying the social world. This aspect of sociological theory has received much attention and the whole argument is in practice spelt out anew every time a sociologist attempts to relate the particular concepts, observations, techniques he is using to some of the long standing concerns of sociological theory. Less attention appears to be given to the kinds of 'images of man' that are inevitably generated by a theory. Even an apparently neutral sounding statement of the 'if X then Y' kind in fact presents a particular image of man, an image more involved in causal processes rather than human praxis. We should note and remember that the language of sociology abounds in rhetoric and metaphors—role, actor, rewards, members, function, career and so on—and we should perhaps spend more time examining the way in which metaphors work than in examining the qualifications or disqualifications of sociology as a 'science'.

One thing is certain: it is through these metaphors that images of man are created, sustained or modified. In using them we are looking back at the culture from which they arose and 'forward' to the way in which their articulation gives greater solidity and definition to a social reality already present. When I investigate or talk about 'the role of the housewife' I am in some ways creating that role. But for the most part I do not create that 'role' (or function, or reward or career) out of nothing: the role metaphor already has particular salience in a certain kind of society. These connections between metaphor and 'reality' are not always straightforward or clear; they are themselves subject for further investigation. This is why 'reflexive sociology' should not be a specialized kind of undertaking carried out by people with an interest in sociological practice as a topic but should form an integral part of every sociological project.

Yet how are we to appraise the 'images of man' generated by a particular theory? It is after all a relatively simple matter judging a theory in terms of the data it has or might generate, as to whether such data are obtainable, what methods are required, how far the data relate to the theories and so on. All this would constitute a 'rational appraisal' of a theory. Yet it might appear that the image of man generated by a theory is a matter of value judgments, that it is not subject to rational enquiry in the same sense. As a first step in answering this question we would note that the mere explication of the kind of image being generated (admittedly no simple task) is itself a stage in the appraisal. We are, to some extent, exploring the latent implications of any theoretical statement, pointing to the kinds of pictures that appear to be coming across from a particular theoretical approach. The originator of the theory might well reply by saying that 'of course we know that people are not merely like this but that, for the purposes of my analysis, we may treat people or situations "as if" they worked like this'. He would argue that any disciplined study proceeds by recognizing certain limits, making certain assumptions, inevitably simplified in many respects. Yet in some cases the author does not explicitly state this (as in the case of some role analyses, for example), and even if he does introduce the 'as if' clause this is not in itself equivalent to saying that the argument is closed. Certain simplified assumptions might be felt to be in some way preferable ('closer to the truth') than others. Further, the 'as if' disclaimer gives little recognition to the way in which certain images of man do have wider implications and become part of the wider currency of debate, legitimations and rhetoric. One only has to consider the widespread diffusion of the 'naked ape' model (and its associated discussion of territoriality) or the 'games' model of inter-personal interaction.

Beyond the simple explications of the latent imagery of sociological theories we have the appraisal of these images. This would appear to be more a matter of value judgments but even here matters may not be so relativistic as they might seem. We can, after all, give reasons and produce evidence for the images we prefer even if such evidence may not be conclusive or may be subject to counter-claims. In many cases the claims and counter-claims will not be concluded in a zero-sum fashion with the removal of one from the field but with some kind of mutual recognition, involving a recognition of the difficulties involved in presenting one's own claim and the possibilities surrounding the other. In this book I have implicitly and, at times, explicitly rejected images of man which show the individual as being the relatively passive agent in the face of biological, psychological or cultural imperatives. This has caused me to question not merely the societally or culturally determined model of man implied in much functional and role analysis but also the relatively pessimistic models implied in the writings of Laing and Marcuse. Both these writers, while they give considerable recognition to the concept of the 'self' and are unwilling to accept the positivistic or functional images of man presented in orthodox behavioural science tend to present a picture of man almost, but not quite, totally controlled by forces outside him, either the mystified family or the subtle processes of manipulation of advanced capitalist society. Thus, in a way, there are some odd affinities between 'mainstream' and 'critical' theorists.

In place of these images I have attempted to substitute images which convey a picture of man the innovator, the creator, the person able to evaluate, reject or to change his environment, the person with the ability to say 'no'.[2] It is a picture of man with a future as well as a past, where that future, projected and imagined, influences the present as much as the past influences the present. There are clearly dangers with this kind of approach, particularly the danger of a facile optimism of being too hopeful when a child asks 'why should I?' or when a group of workers neatly bamboozle the foreman or the time-and-motion expert. Irony, ambiguity and tragedy are also part of the human experience: the foreman may know all the time what his workers are up to and the mother may welcome the cry of 'why should I?' thus binding the child closer to her. Yet if there is a danger that the image of man with a future may degenerate into an over-easy liberal rhetoric by ignoring the element of tragedy or irony in everyday life it is also clear that much orthodox sociology in the functionalist mode also has little place for these features either.

In this conclusion I shall explore these themes further using the family as a particular arena for the examination of sociological theory in this light. In many respects the family is a particularly appropriate area for this kind of approach. Apparently close to biological or functional imperatives, apparently universal and fundamental, the family as an institution seems to be the most resistant area of society to an interpretation stressing the ability of man to shape and use institutions rather than simply to be shaped by them. Yet, on closer examination, this apparently simple universal institution becomes more complex, more ambiguous, full of opportunities as well as constraints.

This chapter, then, will take up a set of themes which in part arise out of the preceding chapters together with this brief discussion about the nature of social theory. This is not intended to be a summary in the strict sense but rather the examination of some common problems as well as of some sources of division in the various approaches that have been outlined. Finally, although this is not the main purpose of the book, there will be a brief discussion on the future of the family.

The centrality of the family

Let us start with an apparently insurmountable problem: the fact that many different writers come to radically different conclusions about the place of the family in modern society. As will be shown, this is not simply a matter of a distinction between functionalist and anti-functionalist, between abolitionist or retentionist or between optimist and pessimist but more a matter of points of view that arise out of the intersection of these opposing positions. The following five positions—while certainly not exhausting the possibilities—reflect some of the main strands of argument presented in the preceding chapters:

1 The family is of decreasing importance in modern society. The first major blow the family suffered was industrialism and the overthrow of the traditional patriarchal structure. Since then the family has become smaller, weaker and less able to fulfil the few functions left to it. Many important functions have been taken over by outside agencies and the family has been eroded by the development of a 'mass society'. People cling to the form of the family and the ideology surrounding the family although the content has effectively withered away. To adopt Weber's memorable phrase on the secularization of the Protestant Ethic: 'the idea of duty in one's calling prowls about in our lives like the ghost of dead religious beliefs.'[3] We should not spend time in mourning the death of the family. Marcuse and Reiche would argue that the central problems lie elsewhere and Barrington-Moore would suggest that we should give the family a decent burial. Horkheimer, while sharing this general analysis of the loss of family functions and centrality is more worried by the apparent dangers of this and so would probably be classed with the pessimists.

2 The first group of pessimists would agree that the family has been declining in the way outlined by members of the first group but would also argue that the overall effect of this decline will be disas-

trous for social life generally. A modified version of this pessimistic perspective is presented by the contributors to the volume edited by Anshen, most of whom would appear to argue that the family has a vital role to play in social life generally, that it is under considerable strain in modern society and that the main solution is the strengthening of the democratic, open form of family structure. Less ambiguous and more pessimistic is Zimmerman; in a recent statement he argues 'when the ideological structure of the family system loses its virility and strength the social system generally gets into trouble'.[4]

3 Another, probably smaller, group would express pessimism not because the family is becoming increasingly marginal but because the family remains firmly at the centre. There are several overlapping arguments here, including the argument that the modern family is too well adjusted to a destructive culture and that the distinction between normal and pathological families would appear to be that in the latter the victims become too painfully obvious to the outside world. This group is pessimistic in that there appears to be little discussion of the way out in alternative family or non-family systems. Laing has presented little in the way of wide-ranging alternatives to the family so far and Henry adopted an even less ambiguously tragic stance in relation to the modern family.

4 If this second group of pessimists argue that the family is well—too well—adjusted to modern society—the optimists would support this argument but reject the tone. Their main argument, however, would be with those who argue that the family is in decline. Instead they would argue that the family has become more specialized but no less vital. Under this heading we would, of course, include Parsons together with Fletcher, Aron and McGregor. Also included here would be the supporters of the 'modified extended family' argument, whatever disputes they might have with Parsons over the structure of the family in modern society.

5 Finally we may note those who argue that the family is central but not essential and who would concentrate on the dysfunctions of the family rather than the eufunctions. Here we would include Reich with his analysis of the way in which authoritarianism is supported by the family structure and, more recently, the radical feminists who would argue that the abolition of the family as we know it is essential for the development of a society not structured around sex roles. While members of this group would support the critiques of the family provided by Laing and Henry they would be more optimistic about the possibilities of developing alternatives.[5]

How can we resolve these apparently different perspectives? Part of the answer must obviously be to examine more clearly what is being meant by such words as 'family', 'central', 'marginal' and so on. Yet it is clear that even greater specification of terms would not resolve the conflict between, say, a functionalist approach that leans heavily on the instrumental-expressive distinction and, on the other hand, the radical feminists who reject such a distinction and the analysis that follows from it. Moreover, it would seem likely that these differing perspectives and differing definitions are themselves *part* of the reality and that any attempt to freeze that reality by arbitrarily imposing one definition over another would be to impose one version of reality over others. These assessments and definitions are not merely the province of professional sociologists or family therapists but are also used and *lived* by 'laymen' in their everyday lives. (Including, of course, professional sociologists, etc., when they are 'living in the world'.)

It would follow also that such differences of opinion or interpretation are not likely to be resolved merely by an accumulation of more empirical material. What is important is the *kind* of material that we seek to gather; in particular we must ask does it seek to capture the multiplicity of lay meanings, definitions and understandings of the family in its approach rather than to impose certain externally derived definitions by fiat? Similarly, as we have seen in Chapter 1, the mere imposition of lists of functions on to a frozen entity called the family will not resolve these differing perspectives. In what follows I shall attempt to give recognition to the fact that there are not only many 'types' of family in modern society ('types' usually referring to an externally derived set of typifications) but that there are also many ways of understanding families. My family may be an imperfect but deliberately willed attempt to conform to some ideal of 'the Christian home' or it may be a series of traps, a thing out of control, threatening and stifling. I may wear my family lightly, ready to put it aside should the opportunity or occasion arise, or it may be an ever present cross to bear. My family may resemble the Mafia or the brittle ease of a Noël Coward comedy. These definitions, these understandings, these evaluations (which may well cut across class and status differences) must be part of my definitions, understandings and evaluations of family life. Furthermore, the diversity of these definitions itself arises out of a situation where the 'family' as an institution possesses a degree of autonomy in relation to the wider society.

The delineation of familial boundaries

In the chapter on kinship the difficulties and ambiguities in defining the kinship universe were mentioned. In our society there are no clear rules as to what we mean by 'relatives' or 'kindred'. By definition these are not bounded units since they are based on Ego's definition of the situation. Thus the picture of the kinship universe is one of increasing fuzziness at the edges and more definite, but still flexible, notions of duty, reciprocity, closeness (with the possibilities of conflict) nearer the centre. Moreover, this kinship universe is subject to change over time as a result of changes in one's own life cycle as an individual and as a member of two intersecting and changing nuclear families and changes in the individual and family life cycles of significant related others.

However vague and fluctuating this outer cloud of relationships might be, the inner nuclear core of parents and children would appear to be much more definite. At least that is the impression presented by, say, Laing on the one hand and Parsons on the other. Our dwellings, terms like 'family car' or 'family entertainment', and images presented through the media by advertisers, politicians and clergymen reinforce and maintain this definitive image of the family, one requiring the co-presence of parents and children and the relative absence of others. Yet, simply because this image is so widely disseminated does not necessarily mean that it always accords with subjectively understood reality. And, if indeed it is the case that many people understand and live their family this way for most of the time, we should perhaps regard this accomplishment as something worth investigating, a stimulus to our curiosity rather than something merely taken for granted as 'given'.

Some partial clues to understanding this aspect of family living are provided by Berger and Kellner in their interesting paper on 'Marriage and the Construction of Reality'.[6] This paper, which is an application of Berger's general concern in widening the sociology of knowledge to include everything that generally passes for knowledge, starts with Durkheim's insight that marriage serves as a protection against anomie for the individual. This is, however, too negative, they argue; we must look at the positive side of marriage and they suggest that we may see it as a 'nomos-building instrumentality'.[7] Reality is socially constructed. This everyday reality is not something fixed and 'out there' but something which is constantly being constructed and built up through conversation with significant others. Marriage, which in our society entails the coming together of two relative strangers who do not usually have a shared past, is a particularly crucial arena for the building of reality through conversation. A new reality is posited in the process of conversation and inter-personal relations within the marital relationship. In marriage the partners construct the present, reconstruct the past and develop a commonly projected future. In this phenomenological approach to marriage, possibilities become facticities. Clearly this kind of analysis can be extended to other relationships in the family and elsewhere. Berger and Luckmann present a similar account to the process of primary socialization. In this process, the outside world is presented to the child through the double filter of the immediate family and the position of that family in the social structure. Socialization may be viewed as a kind of 'confidence trick' where the outside world is presented as the reality to the child in a 'quasi-inevitable' way.[8]

Part of this reality which is constructed through marriage and the socialization process is the reality of the family itself, the boundaries, its members and its differences from other families. Thus the delineation of familial boundaries is not to be seen merely in terms of the imposition of a structure or set of terms devised by the analyst but in terms of the members themselves. The meaning of the family, the solidarity or fuzziness of its boundaries, is something which is built up, modified and redefined over time through living, talking and interacting in the family context. This world building is often extended beyond the boundaries of the immediate nuclear family to include significant members of the wider kinship universe. The naming of children may symbolically define certain significant ties and continuities beyond and outside the immediate nuclear family.[9] The use of kinship terminology in relation to non-related but significant adults may be part of the same process. Among other mechanisms or resources used in this process of reality construction we may note the following:

1 The major events and crises that go to make up 'family themes'.[10] These family themes may provide a central strand of experience for the family members—the prolonged illness or physical incapacity of one member, the use of a mentally handicapped child as a scapegoat or the labelling of a child as being 'bad' or 'difficult'—or they may be a set of shared experiences and events which are interwoven and periodically recognized, called upon and used in the business of socially constructing the everyday world of the family. A holiday, a move, a period of unemployment and many other events and minor crises may be woven into the particular history of a family and may be used, heightened in recall, in the process of constantly reconstructing the family and its boundaries.

2 The use of 'ritual in family living'.[11] Ritual may enter into family life in a variety of ways. There may be national or religious rituals that are celebrated and given particular meaning in a family context such as Christmas or Thanksgiving. There may be rituals associated with the individual or family life cycle—anniversaries, birthdays, weddings, etc.—which are again celebrated in terms of the family with the family as the main focus. There are rituals which are elaborations of daily routines, sometimes as a result of externally imposed timetables, such as going to work or school, mealtimes or bedtimes. And finally there are the more idiosyncratic rituals which are developed in the context of a particular family and which become

elaborated over the years. The father who brings home small gifts for the children on Friday night is an example of an elaboration of this kind.[12] Whatever the ritual, it is possible to view it as playing an important part in the social construction of reality and the delineation of familial boundaries.

3 The dwelling and the use of space. The authors of *Crestwood Heights* have provided a detailed analysis of the social meaning of the home and space within the home.[13] The house provides a solid representation of the family to its members and differentiates that family from non-family members. Family members have free access to the dwelling, while non-family members are admitted and selected on the basis of invitations, the use of door bells, etc. Certain rooms may be reserved for the entertainment of guests (when the family puts on a performance for non-family members) and to be treated fictitiously as 'one of the family' is often a matter of being allowed unmediated access through, say, the back door.

The use of family themes, ritual and domestic space are some of the mechanisms through which the family as a social reality is defined and redefined. Two further points must be noted. In the first place it would be wrong to see these mechanisms in simple functional (or eufunctional) terms. Bossard and Boll note that ritual may have its dysfunctional aspects and that mechanisms such as we have described may become desperate attempts to maintain a reality which is no longer appropriate. The clear dysfunctions of the scape-goating mechanism as part of the family theme have already been noted.[14] Second, it would be wrong to assume that these mechanisms serve to create the family reality as an undifferentiated whole. Rituals, as anthropologists have long observed, serve as much to emphasize divisions and separations as well as unities. The family meal, for example, may dramatize sex and age status divisions as well as the unity of that family. Children may not be accorded the same unlimited use of domestic space as adults; thus parents may implicitly claim free access to their children's rooms, a privilege which may well not be reciprocated.[15]

It will be recognized that while all families operate some boundary maintaining mechanisms not all families are equally successful in this process and, more positively, not all families present the boundaries in such clear forms. Laing's schizophrenogenic families, where the mother may seek to define the outside world as uniquely dangerous and seek to enclose the members of the family within its constructed boundaries, often with the collusion of other family members, represents one extreme rather than a model for all family forms.[16] The current debate about 'open families', while presented largely in terms of the equal participation of the husband and wife in home and work alike, may remind us of other possibilities.[17] In order to analyse the degree and kinds of openness or closure of families we need, of course, not merely to look at the processes of creating family worlds within the families themselves, but also at the place of the families in the wider society. Berger and Kellner recognize that their particular approach to marriage receives particular strength in the context of a society where family living is relatively 'privatized' and Henry makes much the same point in his detailed case studies. In a fascinating historical study, Sennett contrasts the two kinds of family living in the same residential area of Chicago at different periods in the late nineteenth century. In the early period there were upper-class families based on relatively open, wide-ranging networks of primary relationships. These families were replaced by more privatized middle-class families, whose family worlds were, Sennett argues, formed in defence against the urban and occupational worlds that they encountered.[18]

It is clear that future investigations into the family must recognize the variety of family experiences and the various ways in which families define themselves in relation to the outside world. One possibly fruitful classification has been developed by Ponsioen in a study of family change in the Netherlands.[19] He distinguishes between (a) patriarchal families; (b) open families within a closed village or neighbourhood; (c) the closed family in an open society; (d) the counterfeit family (where the ideal is the closed family but the reality falls short of this goal); (e) the boarding house type; and (f) the open family in the open society. Network analysis may be elaborated to distinguish not merely between close-knit and loose-knit networks but also between networks based primarily on kin and those based primarily on non-kin. Work in these directions could fruitfully involve a two-way process between the concepts analysts use to construct reality and the concepts actually used by actors in their daily business of living in families.[20]

Family and the family ideology

We have discussed the problem of the delineation of familial boundaries largely in terms of viewing this as an on-going accomplishment of the actors themselves and also as arising out of the interchanges between the family and the wider society. But we should note that these family boundaries are not merely neutral social facts but also that these boundaries have a normative dimension. Family boundaries and family relationships are shaped not merely by concepts or constructions as to what is but also by normative conceptions as to what ought to be. By using the label 'ideology' in this context (rather than 'norms', 'values', 'mores', etc.) we hope to convey the possibility that certain agencies are more specifically concerned with the generation of familial ideology, the relative (although admittedly long-term) contingency of this ideology and the possibility of there being 'deviant' or counter-ideologies. To label something as 'ideology' is to attempt to relativize the absolute, to bring out into the open what was previously thought not to exist. Ideology functions best when it does not bear the name 'ideology'; when the label ideology is successfully applied it has to begin to struggle for existence.

Nowhere is this more clearly seen than in the context of the family.[21] For here, in the process known as primary socialization, the adult who says 'don't' is at the same time asserting his right to say 'don't'. The rituals, use of space and family themes outlined in the last section recreate the particular family and the 'idea' of the family at the same time. Socialization is, for the most part, indirect and unobtrusive, as much a matter of silences as of conversations, of examples rather than direct instruction. Even when the outside world (school, peer group, the mass media) makes its presence felt and may provide alternative definitions as to what is and what ought to be, these experiences may, to some extent at least, be filtered through and appraised by the family. And, if the analyses of Berger and the authors of *Crestwood Heights* are correct, the family is increasingly to be seen as the central arena for 'normal' behaviour, for being one's true self, for letting one's hair down and so on. The family provides the main legitimate arena for the expression of sexual passion, anger, exhilaration, coldness, frustration, happiness and despair. Large scale bureaucratically organized and urbanized society, on the other hand, it is argued, can only take these emotions and passions in small doses, if at all.

There are a multiplicity of ways in which ideology and the family become interwoven. In some cases, the family and elements of family structure may be viewed as an ideal model for society as a whole. The 'patriarchalism' analysed by some of the radical feminists and by Reich refers directly to the process of mapping ideal sets of relationships from one domain on to another. Patriarchalism, then, involves two dominances, that of men over women and parents (particularly fathers) over children. These patterns of dominance are learned in the family, projected on to the wider society, encountered in the wider society and reflected back from that society on to the family. There is a strong reinforcing overlap between father and son, master and apprentice, head of the family firm or farm and heir to the estate. While today the patriarchal model of family and society is felt to be inappropriate, the relative power of familial symbols when applied to non-familial relationships—father, brother, sister, mother—is still maintained and tells us something about the ideal qualities of family relationships as well as about the ideal expectations of the particular situations—trade unions, religious orders—to which they are applied.

More explicit ideological formulations may be made about the nature of the family and its importance in the wider society. It has been noted that the various theories that have been cited as to whether the family is in decline and whether or not this decline, if it is occurring, is likely to have a damaging effect on society as a whole are not merely theories developed by sociological analysts but are also theories which are widely held and used by various agencies. In modern society these ideologies may be made most explicitly when the family appears to be under threat. Some of the concern about women and children working in the early nineteenth-century factories was not just about the hours and the working conditions but about the fact that they were there at all and these concerns provided an occasion to dramatize the values of family life and sexual relationships which, it was felt, were being threatened by this particular feature of the factory system. Similarly the proposal of legislation about divorce or abortion provides another occasion to dramatize particular familial values. Ideological statements, therefore, concern themselves with the nature and central significance of family life and the ideally expected quality of relationships within the family.

The examination of the source and effects of ideology in society is a complex business and involves many difficult problems which are, in many respects, central to sociological analysis. What is involved here is the attribution of a specific set of normative ideas to a particular group in society, the argument that these ideas become, in some way, more widely diffused and, finally, that they become part of the objective reality for a significant proportion of the population. To state the problem in these terms is to demonstrate the large amount of work that needs to be done in the analysis of the interconnections between ideology and society; clearly simple references to the ideas of 'the ruling class' can only serve as a starting point in this analysis. Berger and Luckmann, in their imaginative fusion of themes from Durkheim, Mead, Weber, Parsons and Schutz, have provided some valuable insights into the latter stages of the process, that is how ideas are sustained, internalized and projected in order to shape the facticity of the social world. They perhaps pay less attention to the notion of ideology in the Marxist sense, to the idea that particular groups or interests may have greater weight and power in the defining of everyday reality. What may be said in the analysis of this process is that, in connection with the family, ideological prescriptions would appear to have less work to do in so far as the family already is an on-going reality in some form or other, that most people live or have lived in families and that alternatives may often seem remote or identified with groups readily accorded the label of 'deviant' (religious groups, hippies, etc.).

There is not the space to pursue this topic further, only to state that the ideological dimension is an important, and often absent, part of the analysis of family relationships. Yet we may leave this theme with a contradiction. To say that there is an ideological dimension to family living which is not solely a product of the on-going business of family living itself is to say that there are agencies outside the family—churches, political parties, experts of one kind or another—with a particular interest in the family and its functioning (this interest is, of course, especially an interest in the 'younger generation'). Yet paradoxically, the assertion of some kind of outside interest in the family is to deny the priority of the family, is to challenge the exclusive legitimacy of family authority.[22] In many cases, it may be expected, this paradox is successfully obscured by projecting the ideal model of the family into the natural world, that is by attempting to place the family outside historical contingency. But in some cases this paradox may give rise to contradictory trends and definitions. Thus the English (and American) Puritan family stressed the concepts of order and unity but it was possible that these very ideas might be seen as having priority over potentially self-centred family relationships. Thus some of the more radical sects in the English Civil War discussed the possibilities of polygamy, marriage within forbidden degrees and feminism.[23] That these views did not 'succeed' is less significant than the fact that they were expressed and that they had their origin in the same set of values that attempted to set up the ideal model of the family. We should not necessarily dismiss the popular polemics that mock the practice of a celibate priest giving advice on the quality of family living (a kind of double-bind situation), but see in it the paradox arising out of a tension between rational world religions and the institution of the family, a tension which is often successfully obscured or contained but which sometimes is resolved in the living out of radical alternatives to the family.

Projects and the family

Up to now we have considered the family, more or less, as a whole, a whole defined by its members, by others and through ideology. To be sure an attempt has been made not to present the family as a reified whole, an entity with things like qualities existing over and against its members. At the same time we have not looked closely at the members of this family and the way in which the relationships between these members may be analysed.

The most commonly presented concepts for the analysis of family relationships are of course the range of concepts centring around the role metaphor. Some possible drawbacks in this emphasis have been outlined in one or two places.[24] At its best the dual origins of the role metaphor (in functionalism and in symbolic interactionism) serve to enable us to provide a dramaturgical analysis of the tension between the actor, his immediate situation and his culture. Yet even these dramaturgical presentations, while they stress the dynamics of this on-going tension, also present some ambiguities. In particular there is the concept of the self which sometimes appears to be nothing more than the sum total of masks presented to others on each different occasion or a mystical entity such as a 'real self' which lies apart from each and every presentation, a sense of awareness that 'this is not me' or 'this is the real me'. While experience teaches us that this latter notion of the self has something to recommend it (the experience of one's first interview for a job represents a dramatic illustration of this tension) we still have the question as to where this presumed 'self' comes from. At its worst, of course, the role approach ignores such problems altogether and the metaphor is taken to give priority to the script (that is the culture or the organization or the social system) rather than to the actor.

A more fluid, dynamic approach is to be found in those various approaches to the *politics* of family living. Here we are referring not so much to the coalition theories developed by Caplow (and derived from the work of Simmel)[25] but the existential psychoanalytical approach associated with Laing, Esterson and Cooper.[26] Here, it will be recalled, we viewed the family in terms of a complex set of overlapping dyadic and triadic relationships. Such an approach enabled us to handle not merely relationships within the nuclear family but also relationships over time between the interlocking nuclear families. But it was also noted that such an approach often fails to provide adequate links between the family and non-familial relationships and institutions and also fails to provide an adequate account of the place of the family as an institution within a wider historical and cultural framework.

It is suggested here that the interrelationships within the family might be examined in terms of *projects*. Here the concept is taken from Sartre although the interpretation may vary somewhat from the original presentation of the idea and some possible modifications to the original approach will be made. The term 'project' is intended to convey the following points:

1 In line with Sartre's original approach to social behaviour it implies that such behaviour cannot be conceptualized but can be comprehended.[27] The distinction is similar in spirit to the distinction between a sociology which seeks to place human action into predetermined conceptual categories and a sociology which aims at

an interpretive understanding of the actor.[28] The way in which the notion of 'project' differs from concepts normally understood will emerge later.

2 The emphasis on the 'project' implies an emphasis on the future. In Desan's words:[29]

> At the core of the inner contradiction of man lies a material or economic situation—here Marx is right—but this situation is not a frozen reality weighing upon a present event. It is, rather, a challenge *looking for the solution* in the future.

In this there is a sharp departure from the approach based on the concept of role where the emphasis is on the past (culture, social structure, etc.), the present (the situation) and the very near future (the anticipated response of role others). It also departs from much orthodox Marxism for similar reasons: it emphasizes the man making his own history rather than a more exclusive focus on the conditions over which he has no choice.

3 The project (or at least the main project) does not in itself have a content, but it refers to this future orientation, this constant dialectical process of negation and realization leading to further negation. Although the idea of the project is more specifically worked out (at least in terms more accessible to sociology) in Sartre's as yet untranslated *Critique de la raison dialectique*, there are clearly links here with his emphasis on an absolute freedom in *Being and Nothingness*. Particular projects must be realized in the context of this main project just as they are negated in the context of this main project.

4 It should not be thought that Sartre's approach is one which, unlike orthodox sociology, recognizes no constraints. As we have seen, Cooper points out clearly:[30]

> The most rudimentary conduct must be determined at one and the same time in relation to real, present factors which condition it and in relation to a certain future object to which it attempts to give birth. This is what we call the project.

Man is constrained in all the kinds of ways in which sociologists and Marxists have said he is but this is not the whole story. What is 'given' need not be accepted or one may choose to accept what is 'given'. Thus, in Chapter 5 we noted how sex roles, particularly the role of women, were determined by expectations in advance of actual encounters so that women employees, for example, were judged as women rather than as workers. This is a constraint which women may reject or accept.

We are led to consider these constraints, if we ask, as Desan asks, the question where does this project come from.[31] He suggests that however much Sartre might try to avoid it, his actual detailed accounts (of Flaubert for example) bring us back close to sociological and psychological factors. If we wish to analyse a particular life history in terms of projects it would seem to be unavoidable that considerations such as family background, educational experience, friendship and community would have to play a part, although probably treated with more subtlety than the average sociologist would treat them and more analysis than the average biographer would provide. The other alternative would seem to be to freeze the project in terms of an alienated, metaphysical dialectic, a mystification that Sartre is clearly also trying to avoid.

One set of 'factors' (to use a term clearly alien to Sartre's approach) which would have to be taken into account as limiting constraints is the existence of Others. In the *Critique* Sartre gives great emphasis to the factor of scarcity in the world and the way that this necessarily contributes to the overlapping of projects again providing a link with an earlier concern, namely the Other as a threat. In order to realize my project I need others who are themselves attempting to realize their projects through or with me. To accept my definition as a worker I need employers and fellow workers, to accept my definition as a man I need women, etc. Furthermore, the analyst is not a detached objective scientist but is also using this Other (in this case his 'subjects of research') for his own project.[32]

It may be suggested here that the family might be understood in terms of the projects of its members, the way in which these projects are realized or denied through the co-presence of others also seeking to realize their projects and the way in which projects become alienated, that is take on a life of their own and appear to confront the agent as an alien object rather than as the agent's *own* projects. Such an approach, it can be argued, gives recognition to the complexity of family living and a complexity which derives, to a large extent, from the central theme of change and the future which is built into the institution of the family. It is a complexity which also derives from the curious mixture of freedom and unfreedom which is at the heart of the family. This approach may also provide us with an opportunity to develop an approach to the family which does give some scope to human potentiality as well as to the constraints on human action and so moves away from the 'sociologisms' of many studies of the family in terms of, say, role theory.

There is not time here to consider all the implications of this approach, an approach which is by no means totally absent in family studies. Here I shall present a few illustrations from sociological studies. Consider the study of a Canadian middle-class residential suburb *Crestwood Heights*.[33] Family life here appears to conform, almost to the point of parody, to Parsons's relatively isolated nuclear family. The central family theme appears to be the career. This career has, at its heart, this tension between freedom and unfreedom which was mentioned earlier. On the one hand it appears to be freely chosen as a means through which, via the educational system, the individual is able to transcend his present situation. It is clearly an orientation to the future, located in the individual. The individual self, his identity,[34] his projects are clear to the individual and to others, often symbolized in the house and very visible styles of life. Yet it would also appear that this notion of the individual shaping his own destiny through his career is only part of the story. The career is worked out within the context of a large national, perhaps international, corporation which is bureaucratically organized. The career demands a measure of conformity at work and in terms of external life style: at the very least in order to pursue the career the individual must be prepared to move. Crestwood Heights, therefore, is not a final point of resting nor a point of origin but a stage in a 'spiralist' career, involving geographical and occupational mobility.[35]

This career is a central theme not only for the man but also for the rest of the family. The nature and significance of marriage is to some extent interpreted in terms of this centrality of career: 'A good match is of inestimable value to the man at the beginning of his career; indeed, it need only *appear* to be a good match to enable him to earn a certain measure of credit.'[36] This is not simply, or even primarily, a matter of marrying the boss's daughter. It is rather a matter of marrying someone whose social accomplishments and social ('expressive') skills are such that they enhance her husband's career. Thus the husband's project is realized with the aid of and through the wife; the wife's project is defined in terms of her husband. This reminds us that while, at one level, one might say that all projects are equal at another level there is considerable inequality particularly with respect to the way in which one actor is able to determine the project of the other.

The centrality of this project, the male career, is also shown in relation to the children.[37] The children are also supposed to pursue a career and parents attempt to develop and encourage the qualities of initiative and individual striving which they regard as being essential to get on in the world. The children (whose births, in accordance with the future-orientated rationality which forms the central theme of the book, are planned) are to some extent expected to be a continuity of their father's project. Yet this comes up against the other central notion of freedom of choice in job and in marriage. Several sections of this book are devoted to analysing the ways in which the parents overcome the particular contradiction between seeing the children as 'free agents' and, at the same time, as realizations of parental projects.[38]

The 'Crestwood Heights' study was carried out in the 1950s and perhaps it already seems to be a slightly alien world to many readers although many of the key features (the centrality of the career for example) are still with us. However, while on the surface Crestwood Heights appears to be relatively unruffled and self-perpetuating the signs of tension and contradiction are there in, for example, the women's sometimes reluctant acceptance of the role allocated to them and the lack of congruence between the way in which men and women define each other. In a recent study, upper middle-class couples who were considering or in some cases who had participated in some form of communal living or group marriages stated the reasons why they were attracted to this form of communal living. The men tended to emphasize such features as a desire to get away from the 'rat race' while the women emphasized getting away from the isolation of child rearing and over-dependence upon the husband.[39] Perhaps some of these respondents came from the equivalent of Crestwood Heights as perhaps also did some of the housewives whose 'problem with no name' formed the basis for Friedan's account of *The Feminine Mystique*.[40]

A very different picture is presented by Komarovsky in her *Blue-Collar Marriage*.[41] Here the career does not form the central family theme. For the men there is little notion or prospect of a career in the sense understood by the inhabitants of Crestwood Heights; 45 per cent of the men in her sample, while not wholly satisfied with their work situations, had no plans for upward mobility. In a sense the home and family itself was a major project. Many of the women saw marriage as an opportunity for escape or liberation from their parents. Yet while it is often assumed that the family is particularly central for women in a sense it was more central for the men than for the women. The women often had other members of their sex, kin, friends and neighbours to turn to while for the men, for whom as for the workers in Dubin's sample work was not a 'central life interest',[42] the family was the only source of primary relationships. A central ambition is to own their own home and the children are seen as holding the greatest hope for the realization of parental projects.[43]

Thus, in one sense, women attempt to realize their projects through their husbands just as the husbands attempt to realize theirs through their wives. Yet this is rarely completely successful. The husbands are expected to be the providers and yet often, inevitably perhaps, fail to live up to these expectations, and this failure sometimes causes resentment and frustration on the part of the wives. With considerable depth and sensitivity (demonstrating that research on the basis of social surveys can be insightful) Komarovsky shows the contrast and contradiction between the ideal of companionate marriage held out to *these* families as it is held out to more affluent sections of the American population and the actuality often marked by lack of communication and resentment.

Perhaps, however, the analysis of the family in terms of 'projects' has been better served by novelists than by sociologists. Sinclair Lewis's *Babbitt* and Wells's *Mr. Polly* provide two possible candidates for an extended examination in these terms. Yet sociological work is not wholly defective in this respect and it is hoped that this section has suggested, if not fully demonstrated, the possibilities that exist for the reanalysis of existing material in the light of this perspective.

Age, sex and the family

The term 'project' (like the term 'career') reminds us that, however complex the structure of dyadic and triadic relationships within the family, we cannot consider this complex set of relationships in isolation. Indeed functional theory and role theory also remind us of this unremarkable fact and provide us with a variety of conceptual tools with which to analyse the interrelationships between the family and the outside world. Such analyses—useful as they often are—tend, however, to posit some degree of functional fit or necessity in the relationships between the family and other institutions in society. Even approaches which stress notions such as 'role conflict'[44] appear to regard such conflict as being containable within the existing structure of institutions and adhere to some version of an equilibrium model. The approach in terms of projects starts with the recognition that ends, etc., which an individual attempts to realize within the context of the family are often different from and perhaps contradictory to the ends of other members of the family. Conflict and contradiction is therefore built into the model from the start rather than being something which is added after the establishment of the main theoretical structure. That certain projects may be realized in the context of the family or with or through other family members and yet which may owe their origin to something outside the family is the central way in which this approach recognizes the overlaps between the institution of the family and other areas of social life.

Yet the notion of careers or projects being realized in the context of the family may perhaps give too purposive a view of the family situation. The main feature of the family is that most people are born into one and that, for a large part of their life, the family appears as a 'given'. This is also true of two of the major bases of identity for the individual which are closely connected with the institution of the family, namely age and sex. The basic ascribed nature of these factors is one which has, of course, been stressed by all sociologists and enshrined in introductory textbooks. However, this emphasis has given an unfortunate air of necessity to the whole matter, and biological determinism or reductionism, even if it has been formally abolished, remains uncertainly at the edge of our vision.

It will be recognized, of course, that there are basic biological differences between the sexes and that ageing also is a biological process. It will also be recognized that societies differ to a marked extent as to how they handle this biological material, the extent to which and the way in which roles are structured around the facts of age and sex, the points at which age differentiations are made and so on. What perhaps needs to be recognized is the complexity and problematic nature of these relationships between biological differentiation and social experience. It is likely that this complexity is a marked feature of our present society.

In the first place we must consider the role of the family in the process of shaping and handling identities based upon age and sex. It is possible to describe the family as being the major arena within which the drama based upon age and sex is played out. Yet this is an attractive over-simplification. We must distinguish between situations where this drama, although carried out with and between family members, was as much a drama about politics or wealth as it was about family and family based identities and between the more modern situation where, as Ariès has noted,[45] the changing role of the family has contributed to a new emphasis on the elements of age and sex. Furthermore, the recognition that the kinds of emphasis given to the elements of age and sex—such as the emphasis on the growth of childhood as a separate and specialized social entity—may vary over time and between different societies itself implies a recognition that the family is not the sole agent in the generation of these identities. Hence our first problem is, as was suggested in the chapter on 'women as a social class', to locate the role of the family in the generation and maintenance of sexual and generational identities.

The work of Ariès and Parsons (sometimes seen as being opposed)[46] may be combined to highlight a paradox. Both, in their different ways and with different emphases and evaluations, point to the historical growth of the specialized nuclear family. Both, again with different emphases, point to the importance of the 'socialization function' in the growth of this more specialized institution. In terms of the identities based upon sex the family is 'central' in that, first, the major source of differentiation is between men and women on the basis of the importance of this socialization function and, second, that the family is a major institution within which individuals are socialized into the assumption of sexual roles and identities. Yet, if the family has become specialized in the way that has been suggested it also means that its members cannot meet all their needs within it and they must therefore participate in institutions outside the family and which give, of necessity, scant recognition to the salience of family identities. Even sex roles are subject to this contradiction between familially generated expectations and the relative lack of universality of these expectations.

In many ways, of course, attempts are made to justify ideologically the positions of woman in the wider society in terms of her familial based identity, but increasingly these claims are losing their power. Furthermore this influence (perceived or actual) is not simply in the direction of the family on to the outside world. The identities of male and female are presented, sustained and modified in the 'outside world' and reverberate back on to and into the family. In some cases these images and identities sustain the images and identities generated within the family; the women may learn domestic crafts, etc., at school while the male will be socialized and educated into his occupational roles, for example. But in some cases there may be clear contradictions. This is not simply a matter of the growth of occupational roles for women which in many cases clearly conflict with images of domesticity. Other images—such as certain sets of expectations surrounding the notion of male and masculine (a kind of modified *machismo*)—may also be felt to be inappropriate in the context of the development of a family specialized not only in terms of the socialization function but also in terms of 'human relations', 'sharing', 'companionship', etc. What, in short, is being suggested is a growing lack of fit between the identities based on sex as they apply in the family and as they apply in the world outside the family.

The question of age is, if anything, more complicated, if only for the reason that age boundaries are less visible and more difficult to define than sex boundaries. Again we see the basis of identities in the context of the family. The parent/child differentiation (again a key element in the 'socialization function') is of course a generational differentiation and one which is given constant emphasis and meaning in the context of everyday family living. At the same time a more subtle differentiation in terms of an age hierarchy between siblings may often be generated (recognized, for example, in differential 'bedtimes'). But again age and generational differentiations are also shaped and modified in the wider society, through school, classes within school, notions of 'experience' in the occupational world, ages defined as being relevant for particular purposes such as voting, getting married, conscription, buying alcohol, etc., and finally through legally defined notions of retirement age, pensionable age and so on. Again, there need not be a clear fit between the images and identities generated in the wider society and those which are generated and sustained in the context of the family. Simone de Beauvoir has shown how, like the woman, the old person comes to be defined in terms of the projects of the other—in this case largely the adult males in a society orientated towards the future and the realization of future projects. The wider society defines who are the old and what is to be their place and how we are to regard them.[47]

The location of the identities of age and sex both within and outside the family and the possibility of a 'lack of fit' between the various interrelated sources of these identities and their maintenance is part of the dilemma, referred to earlier in this chapter, between the simultaneous marginality and centrality of the family.[48] This ambiguous location of the sources of these identities also contributes to another dilemma, that between their apparent inevitability on the one hand and their accidental nature on the other. The family itself appears, to some extent, to be an inevitable, necessary institution and it appears thus because individuals are born into it and because the 'natural', inevitable and necessary nature of the family is part of a familistic ideology. If the family can appear in this way then identities such as those based on age and sex, which in part derive from the family and take on their sharpest definitions in family contexts, must also to some extent appear in this way. This nexus based upon biology, the family and age and sex would appear to have a powerful and necessary base. Yet if there are powerful sociological and ideological forces sustaining the apparent necessity of these identities there are also counter-ideologies and practices which challenge and call into question this apparent necessity. Research into the family, therefore, should take account of the fact that the major axes around which the family is organized—age and sex—are subjected to contrary pressures and counter-pressures and that what appears to be solid and immutable appears at the same time to be challenged and challengeable. What is 'given' need not necessarily be accepted and it needs to be accepted if it is to be recognized as given.

It must be repeated that this is not an attempt to develop a new theory of the family but rather to suggest some particular emphasis that might go into the study of the family in the future. In the first place it should be stressed that the definition of the family is itself problematic and that the investigator cannot be content with an approach based on legal definitions, on analysts' ideal typifications or on statistically normal patterns within a given culture. Some account—some considerable account—must be taken of the actor's own definitions of the boundaries of his family, and the way in which these boundaries might vary according to context or situation. This actor's definition of the family is not a once and for all accomplishment but a continuous process of creation and redefinition. The family, the idea of the family, other family members and resources are not 'just there' but are used and in being used are created and redefined. The sociologist, therefore, should concern himself with this everyday family work through the examination of ritual, of conversation, of the use of physical space and objects and family themes. Similar observations apply to the study of relationships within the family which should be viewed less as a 'once and for all' set of roles usually mapped on to biological relationships but, again, as identities which are constantly undergoing the process of definition, challenge and refinement.[49]

It is not enough to say that the 'family' is constantly being created and recreated in the ways that I have indicated. To say that everyday family life is socially constructed by its members is not to say that they have limitless resources with which to carry out this process of construction. Indeed, one of the central features of the family is its alienated processes, the sense in which family work becomes and appears as a 'given', as an arena of unfreedom, which is independent of the work of its members. Ideology from without and mystification and censorship from within serve to maintain this state of alienation. Families differ in their degree of alienation, their degree of effective control over family resources and their degree of openness or closure, and one of the tasks of a sociology of the family should be to explore the sources of these variations and the kinds of variations that are possible.

We are seeking, therefore, to 'locate' this family, to place it in a given culture and a given history. The resources—material and ideological—which are available to family members will differ within societies and across societies at different points of time as well as between the family members themselves. Another way of 'locating' this family is in terms of the 'projects' of its members for these projects are not merely 'of' the family although members seek to realize them within family contexts and through other family members. Finally, these projects take on a particular character within the context of the family partially because the family is organized around the major axes of age and sex, axes which derive much of their essence and legitimacy from being given their most intensive use within a family context and yet which are not wholly the exclusive province of the family.

Little of what has been said here is new. In the course of this book I have referred, not merely to 'critical writers' to some extent outside the academic orthodoxies, but also to existing empirical work and to existing theorists such as the ethnomethodologists, interactionists and phenomenologists. What follows is not an attempt to propose any radically new departures in family studies but to appraise what, in the light of the preceding discussion, would appear to be the most promising modes of enquiry.

a The detailed study of individual families We are already familiar with the work of Laing and Esterson[50] in the study of families of schizophrenic patients. Such studies have yielded not only valuable insights into the particular problems under investigation but have developed a variety of tools useful for the existential and dialectical understanding of family processes. In a similar vein, and in some ways more useful for the approaches to the family recommended here, is the work of Jules Henry.[51] Henry combines his anthropological background with insights derived from psychoanalysis and philosophy to build up a vivid and provocative account of modern American families. He is particularly insightful in his analysis of the everyday life of the family, its mealtimes, outings and rituals, the use of time, space and food at all times partly through the use of comparative understandings, relating these to wider features in the American culture. Further detailed understandings of the complexity of family life and the central importance of 'family themes' are found in Hess and Handel's studies of five American families.[52]

Similarly, we have useful and detailed accounts of the families of the poor in the writings of Coles and Oscar Lewis.[53] Lewis uses a variety of techniques combining intensive observation (tape recordings, observation, use of diaries, etc.) with social surveys. One weakness of Lewis's approach is the idea that the family may be treated as if it were a society and the implication that therefore one may use the same categories in studying a family as one might use in the study of a society (the economic system, the political system, religion, etc.).[54] His main emphasis is on approaching culture—the much criticized 'culture of poverty'—*through* the intensive studies of the family. Such an approach may divert our attention from important questions (such as the delineation of familial boundaries) which attach to the family itself.

Clearly such approaches present their own problems and dangers. This is not so much a matter of the 'representativeness' of such families (such studies draw our attention to the interrelatedness of phenomena and may provide the basis for further, more extensive study) but the practical problems of access. The work of Laing, Esterson, Henry and Hess and Handel was legitimized by their concern with studying families which were, in the first instance, defined as 'problem' families. Studies of poor families or families of different cultures or ethnic groups may be legitimized in the same way.[55] We lack comparable studies of 'normal' middle-class families and here, it might be supposed, the problems of this kind of study would be much greater. Perhaps one possible strategy would be to focus the study around 'normal' crises such as the birth of a first child. In all cases, of course, the study must be reflexive, taking into account the role of the investigator in the process of study not as something to be confined to a methodological appendix but as an inherent part of the study itself.

b Historical studies It is clear that if we are to focus on the study of change and process and if we are concerned with locating particular features of modern families in the culture in which they exist, greater use must be made of historical material. Such material may take one of two forms: the placing of the family in the context of large-scale processes of social change such as we find in the work of Ariès[56] or the more detailed investigation of particular family situations as illustrated in the work of Sennett and Anderson.[57] The relative absence of historical depth in sociological studies is of course a general problem and not one merely confined to the study of the family.

c Literary sources The uses of literary sources (novels, biographies and autobiographies) may be used, not just as an adjunct to the use of historical sources but as a resource in its own right. Such material might be of particular use in studying family processes over time and the intersections of individual projects within the family. Such investigations might also provide useful insights into the way in which certain 'ascribed' categories (such as those of age and sex) are given meaning in a family context or in the wider society.[58] Here, as in the use of historical material, such sources should be used reflexively, that is not merely as resources but as topics in their own right. The project of the novelist or the autobiographer must be incorporated into the projects of those characters he describes.

d Other sources Little mention need be made of the more orthodox modes of sociological enquiry such as surveys, interviews, statistical data, experimental data and content analysis. The bulk of the material used in, say, the *Journal of Marriage and the Family* is derived from these kinds of sources. While in many respects the use of social surveys or samples may often inhibit the kinds of questions that need to be asked about the family, such material cannot and should not be excluded. However, it is likely that the almost exclusive reliance on these methods has in many cases diverted our attention from important critical questions and may serve to reinforce uncritical models of the family.

The future of the family

Up to this point one important element in the theoretical approach to the family has been left out: the question of social change and the family. In general it would appear that the study of social change and the family—indeed one might say the study of social change generally—has suffered from two major defects. In the first place it has been isolated as a subject in its own right—perhaps under such a chapter heading as 'the family in historical perspective'—thus tacitly preserving the classical Comtean dichotomy between social statics and social dynamics. Change is not seen as an integral part of the subject under discussion.[59]

It must be agreed that there are extraordinary difficulties in not preserving some kind of distinction between social change and social structure if one is to adopt any methodological approach other than the historical. Studies based upon social surveys and observation almost necessarily concentrate primarily upon the here and now. In attempting to describe the family, indeed in even using the term 'the family', we are almost inevitably introducing an element of fixity and stability into our account. Yet the family, perhaps more than any other social institution, has change built into it. In the ideal family while there is similarity between roles in families at similar stages of their life cycles, the roles are much more diffuse than roles in most other institutions, much more all-embracing and consequently much more tied to the particular person who occupies them. Change in personal career and individual life cycle is inextricably bound up with change in the family life cycle. The birth of a child creates not merely parents and children but also grandparents, aunts, uncles and cousins. Death of a spouse creates widows or widowers, divorce creates ex-husbands and ex-wives and leads to second husbands and second wives and so on. The inevitable social processes of maturation, growth and ageing are both part of an individual's life career and form a core theme in the life of a family. Furthermore, such processes are not isolatable from the processes of change in the wider society. The problems of parents, themselves socialized in one period of time, attempting to socialize their own children growing up in what might be a radically different period of time has been seen as a key feature of what is called 'the generation gap'.[60] Thus the family, which so often is presented in relatively static, unchanging terms, terms which often unwittingly reflect ideological definitions of the family, is in practice built around the central fact of change. We may, of course, distinguish between those societies where the change often approximates to a series of repeating cycles within each family but where each cycle closely resembles preceding and subsequent cycles and between those societies where major structural change is taking place, thereby rendering each new domestic cycle as being to some extent problematic. In so far as our major concern here is with modern societies, the second model appears to be the most appropriate and it is here that the problems of an analysis focused on the very fact of change become particularly acute.

A second problem in the presentation of social change, particularly social change and the family, is that it is so often presented as something which simply happens *to* people. The conventional role model both reflects and contributes to this way of thinking about social change. In many cases, of course, change may appear in precisely this way to individual actors. Things may appear to be out of control, rehousing, migration, redundancy, inflation and many other features of modern society appear to take place external to individual families and to this extent the conventional sociological mode of interpreting social change may accurately reflect actors' understandings of the situation. Yet, just as the theories of bureaucratization and the 'iron law of oligarchy' may give rise to the accusation that sociology has replaced economics as 'the dismal science'[61] so too can it be argued that the conventional approach to social change reinforces the alienative effect of that change itself. Included in our accounts of social change there should be accounts of the way in which people themselves understand and respond to these changes, their very notions of change and images of the future and, what is most important, the extent to which and the way in which they have an active part in the creation of that change. It is perhaps not surprising that sociology, in spite of or because of its analysis of the 'changing roles of men and women' and 'social change and the family', was unable to anticipate the growth and strength of the Women's Liberation movement[62] or the renewed interest and participation in communal experiments in living.

It is at this point that the analysis of the family in terms of 'projects' might prove to be most useful. For 'projects' while they are shaping and developed according to the constraints within which they are born and the social resources that are to hand are also directed to the future. Even the tacit assumption that the future will not change very much—often implied in, say, marrying, having children or embarking on an occupational career—is an image of the future and this image of the future shapes present courses of action as much as the present is shaped by past experiences or present constraints. In a sense, therefore, the whole of the sociology of the family is about the future of the family and not merely some concluding chapter. Assumptions about the nature and significance of the family contribute to the future of the family and images of the future shape one's analysis of this institution.

There are, of course, various modes of treating the 'future of the family' as a topic of enquiry.[63] In many cases it is treated as a matter of accurately extrapolating current trends (demographic, legal, etc.) into the future. Or the enquiry may be guided by some notion of the irreducible functions of the family. In both cases, and in other more journalistic modes of prediction, the understandings and responses to the future of the actors themselves is reduced to a minimum. The future, like the past, is something which happens to people, rather than something which people themselves play a part in creating.

Yet in even asking the question 'what is the future of the family?' one is to some extent holding that institution up to question and is running counter to many lay (and sociological) interpretations of the family as something relatively impermeable to major change. The fact that one is asking the question about the future of the family is a major element in the analysis itself. Implicitly it involves the recognition that at least some features of the family are being called into question, that change is on the agenda. The context in which these questions are being asked is a context in which real change is taking place, in which challenges to the family as it exists are being issued (from the radical feminist movement, from communal experiments and from a variety of practices from 'swinging' to 'living together') and in which responses to these challenges and fears about the future of the family are being expressed. Whether we are concerned with conservative fears about the future of the family (and hence the future of civilization) or with radical notions of the abolition of the family, the analysis of the family and its future is embedded in an ideological debate.

Bound up with the notion of the future of the family, thereby implying that the identity of the family is in some ways problematic, is the notion of control. The notion of control, not by external forces or by organizational structures but by the actors most directly affected themselves, is a growing area of concern and practice in local communities, in industrial organizations and in educational institutions. It is also becoming a theme in the family itself, the institution which might seem the one furthest from the idea of rational control given its quasi-natural and quasi-inevitable status. The interlocking projects around the themes of 'family planning' (itself a radically significant phrase), 'careers for women' and so on are essentially dealing with this notion of control as, in some ways, ceasing to view the family in naturalist or inevitable terms. It should be stressed that this theme of control does not necessarily take us in the direction of the abolition of the family. It may imply the strengthening of the family (in either its nuclear or extended form) against the encroachment of state or bureaucratized authority or as an intermediary through which state resources to help the poor or the aged might be most effectively channelled. On the other hand it might imply the weakening of the family either through emphasizing the contradictions within the family or through positively stressing the development of 'open families', families as networks of interlinked domestic units[64] or of various forms of communal experiment.[65] The common theme in all these approaches and discussions is the notion of control in an institution often ideologically linked with the themes of nature and spontaneity.

Given the present variety of conflicting interpretations of the family and prescriptions for the future and given the centrality of the family in people's lives and imaginations if not in terms of necessary functions, the safest prescription for the future is some form of 'pluralistic' model. Varieties of forms of nuclear families, and modified extended families, will change, be strengthened or redefined alongside 'dual career' families, 'open families' and loose or tightly knit networks of families. Similarly the range of communal experiments will develop, ranging from completely economically self-sufficient communes with complex marriage or 'free love' to looser, more partial and more temporary arrangements.[66] A simplistic model might be to organize data along two axes, one differentiating between family and commune and the other differentiating between open and closed, as shown in Figure 4.

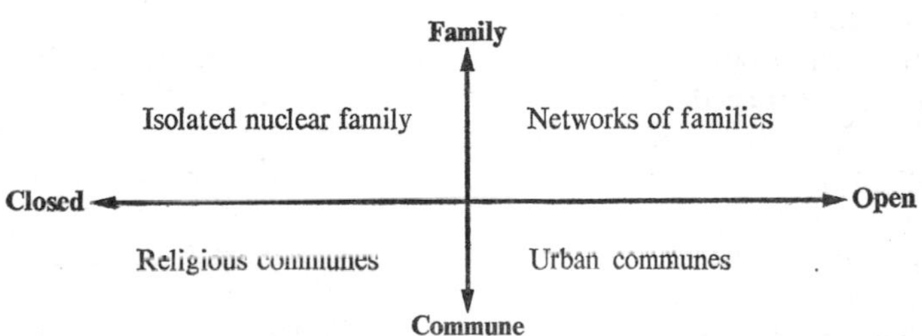

Figure 4

Alternatively these tentative classifications may be placed on a continuum ranging from closed families to closed communes with open families and communes overlapping in many respects in the middle. Much current discussion of the future of the family would appear to concentrate on development in this area of overlap and convergence, although not to the exclusion of possible developments at the extremes.[67] Sociological study should be directed to these areas of conscious change as a way of understanding the possible worlds of the future. It need hardly be stressed that such study should itself be critical in the same way as the study of more orthodox family forms should be critical. Contradictions in communal forms of living should be examined in the same detail as the examination of contradictions within the nuclear family.

What is the role of sociological theory in this discussion of the future of the family? Theory is often, at least popularly, opposed to practice, paralleling a distinction between thinking and doing. It is argued here, on the contrary, that theory is practice, a certain kind of practice perhaps, but still a matter of doing as well as of thinking. Theory, derived from a particular mode of reflecting about 'the real world', also creates that world. Part of the theme of this book is how certain theories about the family derive from and contribute to the maintenance and development of certain 'images of man'. Some of these images, particularly, but not exclusively, those derived from a functionalist tradition, introduce a degree of closure into these images. The emphasis is on constraints and limitations rather than on creation, innovation and potentiality. Such theories, as modern feminists have noted in connection with the functional analysis of sex roles, are at the very least congruent with a considerable body of prevailing practice.

To stress the need for alternative images of man, images of a more open character may easily develop into a naïve optimism or a warming rhetoric. Such emotional flag-waving may be at the expense of real theoretical work or effective political practice. The links between this book and actual practice are twofold. In the first place it was written in the belief that the sociology of the family—indeed sociology generally—could not proceed steadily in the same direction as it has proceeded for some years in the light of the challenge issued to it, particularly from the radical feminist movement. Yet the sociology of the family cannot simply proceed, either, by substituting one paradigm, one image of man, for another. Dialectically, in the confrontation between the old set of paradigms and the new, the old is incorporated into the new rather than being merely left in the wastebasket of outmoded theories. Similarly the newly constituted paradigm has within it the elements of its own reflexive criticism.

Second, the book, while it is not to be construed as making the case for the abolition of the family (itself a problematic slogan), is about a society where the possibility of such a course of action is recognized. The sociology of the family must, therefore, reflexively criticize its own legitimations, the boundaries of its own subject matter. There is perhaps nothing unique in this. The sociologist of religion is confronted with the process of secularization and the sociologist of organizations must take account of the argument that his very definition of his subject matter might presuppose a managerial orientation. Sociologists of deviance, race relations and development are aware of the ideological prescriptions that have often shaped, at least initially, the developments of these sub-areas in the first place. Yet it is likely that the sociology of the family, for reasons which have been stated in various forms throughout this book, has perhaps been most resistant to this critical reflexivity. The central reason is the way in which the institutions of family and marriage have been mapped on to basic biological processes and thereby given a degree of fixity and necessity which is perhaps denied to other areas studied by the sociologist. The critical approach to the sociology of the family would start from the assumption that this mapping is neither necessary nor inevitable and would be concerned with, among other things, examining the process whereby this mapping is successfully achieved on the part of members of a given social entity. The foundations for a critical perspective on the family are, as I hope to have shown, already present: not only in theories derived from a Marxian tradition but also in the recognition of the human costs as well as gains in family living as stressed by Laing and some radical feminists, in the various challenges to the centrality of kinship as a topic in anthropology and in the ethnomethodological practice of regarding the 'given' and the process whereby it is defined and successfully maintained as 'given' as itself problematic and a topic for investigation. Such critiques, although very different, demonstrate the precarious basis upon which the family exists and in so doing bring the family and its change, its abolition or even its maintenance within the ambit of human choice and human praxis.

Notes

Abbreviations

Am. Anth.	*American Anthropologist*
Am. Journ. Soc.	*American Journal of Sociology*
Am. Soc. Rev.	*American Sociological Review*
Brit. Journ. Soc.	*British Journal of Sociology*
Econ. & Soc.	*Economy and Society*
Journ. Mar. Fam.	*Journal of Marriage and the Family*
Journ. Royal Anth. Inst.	*Journal of the Royal Anthropological Institute*
New Left Rev.	*New Left Review*
New Soc.	*New Society*
Phil. of Sc.	*Philosophy of Science*
Soc.	*Sociology*
Soc. For.	*Social Forces*
Soc. Prob.	*Social Problems*
Soc. Rev.	*Sociological Review*

Introduction

1 Now published by Allen Lane.
2 William J. Goode, 'The Sociology of the Family', in Robert K. Merton, Leonard Broom and Leonard S. Cottrell (eds), *Sociology Today*, vol. 1, New York, Harper Torchbooks, 1965, p. 179.
3 In the introduction to *Changes in the Family*, UNESCO, 1962. I am grateful to Marijean Suezle for drawing my attention to this reference.
4 I am aware, of course, that there have been long and celebrated theoretical debates in the associated field of *kinship*. For reasons which I hope to explain I do not think that these debates have a great deal of bearing on the issues raised in this book.
5 Barrington Moore Jnr, 'Thoughts on the Future of the Family'. Reprinted in John N. Edwards (ed.), *The Family and Change*, New York, Alfred A. Knopf, 1969, pp. 455, 456.
6 Ralph Turner, *Family Interaction*, New York, Wiley, 1970.

7 The challenge of radical feminism has provoked at least three collections within recent months, each one dealing with different aspects of sexism and sociology, particularly sociology of the family. See: *Am. Journ. Soc.*, special issue on 'Changing Women in a Changing World', J. Huber (ed.), vol. 78, no. 4, January 1973; *Journ. Mar. Fam.*, special issues on 'Sexism and Family Studies', 1971; Hans Peter Dreitzel, *Family, Marriage and the Struggle of the Sexes* (Recent Sociology No. 4), New York, Macmillan, 1972.

8 Jules Henry, *Culture Against Man*, New York, Random House, 1963, p. 331.

9 J. R. Seeley, R. A. Sim and E. W. Loosley, *Crestwood Heights*, Toronto University Press, 1956; M. Komarovsky, *Blue-Collar Marriage*, New York, Random House, 1962; R. D. Laing and A. Esterson, *Sanity, Madness and the Family*, 2nd ed., London, 1970.

10 C. W. Mills, *The Sociological Imagination*, New York, Oxford University Press, 1959; A. W. Gouldner, *The Coming Crisis of Western Sociology*, London, Routledge & Kegan Paul, 1970; Dick Atkinson, *Orthodox Consensus and Radical Alternative*, London, Heinemann Educational Books, 1971; R. Blackburn ,'A Brief Guide to Bourgeois Ideology', in A. Cockburn and R. Blackburn (eds), *Student Power*, Harmondsworth, Penguin, 1969, pp. 163–213.

11 Blackburn has a brief section in his essay on 'The Family and Domestic Mystification', Blackburn, op. cit. pp. 195–7. Gouldner has relatively little to say on the family in his critical survey.

12 See Alan Dawe, 'The Two Sociologies', *Brit. Journ. Soc.*, vol. 21, 1970, pp. 207–18. Reprinted in Kenneth Thompson and Jeremy Tunstall (eds), *Sociological Perspectives*, Harmondsworth, Penguin, 1971, pp. 542–54.

13 Atkinson attempts to show the conservative core in some of the images of man presented by Marx and Marcuse. Atkinson, op. cit., ch. 3.

14 On reflexive sociology see Gouldner, op. cit., part IV. Also John O'Neill, *Sociology as a Skin Trade*, London, Heinemann, 1972; Dawe, *Soc. Rev.*, vol. 21, 1973, pp. 25–52.

15 O'Neill, op. cit., pp. 235–6.

16 See for example: John N. Edwards (ed.), *The Family and Change*, New York, Knopf, 1969 (especially part III); Herbert A. Otto (ed.), *The Family in Search of a Future*, New York, Appleton-Century-Crofts, 1970; Katherine Elliott (ed.), *The Family and its Future*, London, 1970. For an international and comparative look at change see William J. Goode, *World Revolution and Family Patterns*, New York, Free Press, 1970.

17 Wendell Bell, 'Familism and Suburbanisation: One Test of the Social Choice Hypothesis', *Rural Sociology*, vol. 21, Sept.–Dec. 1956, pp. 276–83, reprinted in Edwards, op. cit., pp. 101–11.

18 See R. N. Adams, 'An Inquiry into the Nature of the Family', reprinted in part in Jack Goody (ed.), *Kinship*, Harmondsworth, Penguin, 1971, pp. 19–37.

19 I have been deliberately selective in my choice of authors and themes, using them as representative of wider interests, rather than attempting

to cover the whole field. While this will inevitably involve some distortion I hope that the main argument will be clear enough.

20 C. Wright Mills, *The Sociological Imagination*, Harmondsworth, Penguin, 1970, p. 12.

21 Examples: Harold T. Christensen (ed.), *Handbook of Marriage and the Family*, Chicago, Rand McNally, 1966; Marvin B. Sussman (ed.), *Sourcebook in Marriage and the Family*, 3rd ed., Boston, Houghton Mifflin, 1963.

22 The title of a book edited by Gerald Handel, London, Allen & Unwin, 1968.

23 Quoted in Max Gluckman (ed.), *Closed Systems and Open Minds*, London, Oliver & Boyd, 1964, p. 12.

24 I was responsible for and wrote a chapter on the family in a text-book collectively prepared by the Department of Sociology at Manchester University. See Peter Worsley, *et al.*, *Introducing Sociology*, Harmondsworth, Penguin, 1970, ch. 3.

25 My sex may, it might be felt, also disqualify me from writing about the theories of some of the leading Women's Liberation authors. I take up this problem in a little more detail in Chapter 5.

1 Varieties of functionalism

1 The Open University, *Socialization* (Units 6–9 of Social Science Foundation Course), Bletchley, Open University Press, 1971, pp. 93–99.

2 Ely Chinoy, *Society*, 2nd ed., New York, Random House, 1967, pp. 139–41.

3 It should not be assumed too readily, either, that functionalism is dead in other areas of sociological enquiry. See, for example, Harold Fallding, 'Only One Sociology', *Brit. Journ. Soc.*, vol. 23, no. 1, 1972, pp. 93–101.

4 For a useful general discussion of the problem of order see Peter Worsley *et al.*, *Introducing Sociology*, Harmondsworth, Penguin, 1970, pp. 337–92.

5 Robert K. Merton, *Social Theory and Social Structure*, rev. ed., Chicago, Free Press, 1957, ch. 1.

6 Worsley, op. cit., pp. 134–7.

7 George Peter Murdock, *Social Structure*, New York, Macmillan, 1949, p. 197.

8 Ibid., p. 1.

9 Ibid., p. 1.

10 Ibid., p. 2.

11 Ibid., p. 10.

12 For some sharp criticism of this kind of comparative approach, see E. E. Evans-Pritchard, 'The Comparative Method in Social Anthropology,' in *The Position of Women in Primitive Society*, London, Faber & Faber, 1965, pp. 13–36. Also J. A. Barnes, *Three Styles in the Study of Kinship*, London, Tavistock, 1971, ch. 1.

13 See Alvin W. Gouldner, *The Coming Crisis of Western Sociology*, London, Routledge & Kegan Paul, 1970, pp. 336–7.

14 Murdock, op. cit., p. 4.
15 For longer and more sophisticated lists of functions see Open University, op. cit. and Ralph Turner, *Family Interaction*, New York, Wiley, 1970, pp. 217–21.
16 Rose Laub Coser (ed.), *The Family: Its Structure and Functions*, 1st ed., New York, St Martin's Press, 1964.
17 Ibid., p. xiv.
18 Ibid., p. xxviii.
19 Ibid., p. xiv.
20 Ibid., p. xvi. See also the reading from Malinowski in the same work, pp. 3–19.
21 Ibid., p. xvi. See also the reading from Lévi-Strauss in the same work, pp. 36–48.
22 Ibid., p. xv.
23 Ibid., p. xvi.
24 R. N. 'Adams, An Inquiry into the Nature of the Family', reprinted in part in J. Goody (ed.), *Kinship*, Harmondsworth, Penguin, 1971, pp. 19–37.
25 William J. Goode, 'A Deviant Case: Illegitimacy in the Caribbean', in Coser, op. cit., pp. 19–35.
26 P. G. Rivière, 'Marriage: A Reassessment', in Rodney Needham (ed.), *Rethinking Kinship and Marriage*, London Tavistock, 1971, pp. 60–2.
27 Probably the most concise and yet comprehensive discussion is to be found in R. Fox, *Kinship and Marriage*, Harmondsworth, Penguin, 1967, pp. 54–76. See also J. Goody, 'Incest and Adultery', in Goody, op. cit., pp. 64–81.
28 C. Lévi-Strauss, 'The Principles of Kinship', excerpt from 'The Elementary Structures of Kinship', included in Goody, op. cit., p. 48.
29 Coser, op. cit., p. xiii.
30 Thomas S. Kuhn, *The Structure of Scientific Revolutions*, Chicago University Press, 1962.
31 Gerald R. Leslie, *The Family in Social Context*, New York, Oxford University Press, 1967, pp. 238–47.
32 Robert N. Williamson, *Marriage and Family Relations*, 2nd ed., New York, Wiley, 1972.
33 Michael Anderson (ed.), *Sociology of the Family*, Harmondsworth, Penguin, 1971.
34 Turner, op. cit.
35 C. Wright Mills, *The Sociological Imagination*, New York, Oxford University Press, 1959; Gouldner, op. cit.; Dick Atkinson, *Orthodox Consensus and Radical Alternative*, London, Heinemann, 1971. For a useful collection of papers see Max Black (ed.), *The Social Theories of Talcott Parsons*, Englewood Cliffs, Prentice-Hall, 1961. For a brief but somewhat more sympathetic treatment see John O'Neill, 'The Hobbsian Problem in Marx and Parsons', in John O'Neill, *Sociology as a Skin Trade*, London, Heinemann, 1972, pp. 177–208.
36 See Hyman Rodman, 'Talcott Parsons' View of the Changing American Family', in Hyman Rodman (ed.), *Marriage, Family and Society*, New York, Random House, 1965, p. 263. For a historical

account of the process of differentiation explicitly using Parsons, see Neil Smelser, *Social Change in the Industrial Revolution*, London, Routledge & Kegan Paul, 1959.

37 Talcott Parsons and Robert F. Bales, *Family: Socialization and Interaction Process*, London, Routledge & Kegan Paul, 1956, p. 17.

38 Talcott Parsons, 'The Kinship System of the Contemporary United States', *Amer. Anthrop.*, vol. 45, 1943, pp. 22–38. Reprinted in T. Parsons, *Essays in Sociological Theory*, rev. ed., New York, Free Press, 1964. The quotation (in common with all subsequent quotations) comes from the *Essays* . . ., p. 178.

39 Talcott Parsons, *The Social System*, London, Routledge & Kegan Paul, 1964, p. 182.

40 Rodman, op. cit., p. 269.

41 Ibid.

42 R. F. Bales and P. E. Slater, in Parsons and Bales, op. cit., p. 302.

43 Parsons and Bales, op. cit., p. 404.

44 The details of this argument are presented in Talcott Parsons, 'The Super-ego and the Theory of Social Systems', *Psychiatry*, vol. 15, no. 1, 1952, reprinted in Coser (ed.), op. cit., pp. 433–49. All references will be to the Coser reprint. The cathectic orientation relates to the question of 'what the object means' in an emotional sense, the cognitive to 'what the object is' and the 'evaluative' means the placing of both the cognitive and cathectic aspects of an interaction in an overall scale of values.

45 For some suggestions on this point see James H. S. Bossard and W. P. Sanger, 'The Large Family System: A Research Report', *Am. Soc. Rev.*, 1952, p. 17.

46 Parsons and Bales, op. cit., p. 17.

47 Parsons, *The Social System*, p. 215.

48 This is, one would suspect, an account of a particular kind of therapeutic relationship, namely that within the Freudian tradition.

49 Parsons and Bales, op. cit., p. 49.

50 Talcott Parsons, 'The Incest Taboo in Relation to Social Structure', *Brit. Journ. Soc.*, vol. 5, 1954. Included in Coser (ed.), op. cit., pp. 48–70. The quotation comes from p. 60 of the Coser volume.

51 Ibid., p. 61.

52 Parsons and Bales, op. cit., p. 63.

53 Ibid., p. 105.

54 Parsons, 'The Incest Taboo . . .' in Coser (ed.), op. cit., p. 68.

55 Parsons and Bales, op. cit., p. 161.

56 Parsons, *The Social System*, p. 155.

57 Parsons and Bales, op. cit., p. 312.

58 Ibid., p. 314.

59 Ibid., pp. 307–51.

60 In ibid., p. 338, his italics.

61 While detailed criticism of Parsons's position will be taken up later, this is one argument that does seem to be particularly vulnerable to disconformation. One recent paper, for example, found subtle evidence of sextyping taking place in what was in many respects a progressive

Californian pre-school play group. See Carole Joffe, 'Sex Role Socialization and the Nursery School: As the Twig is Bent', *Journ. Mar. Fam.*, vol, 33, no. 3, 1971.

62 T. Parsons, 'Age and Sex in the Social Structure of the United States', *Am. Soc. Rev.*, vol. 7, 1942. Reprinted in Parsons, *Essays*. . . . The quotation is from p. 97 of the *Essays*. . . .

63 Parsons, 'The Kinship System . . .' in *Essays* . . ., p. 192.

64 Rodman, op. cit. He refers to Parsons's 'exposition of his view of the American middle-class family' (p. 263).

65 Orville G. Brim Jnr, 'Family Structure and Sex-Role Learning by Children', in Norman W. Bell and Ezra F. Vogel (eds), *A Modern Introduction to the Family*, rev. ed., New York, Free Press, 1968, p. 540.

66 Alfred L. Baldwin, 'The Parsonian Theory of Personality,' in Black (ed.), op. cit., p. 190.

67 Ibid., p. 170.

68 Parsons and Bales, op. cit., p. 36.

69 Example taken from an informal seminar paper presented by Harvey Sarles at Manchester in 1971.

70 It is not, of course, the case that Parsons fails to treat these items as topics in his work as a whole. However, in his specific work on the family these topics make a very fleeting appearance.

71 Parsons and Bales, op. cit., p. 22.

72 Ibid., p. 63.

73 References to the feminist critique of current sociology will be provided in Chapter 5. For a recent theoretical and empirical criticism of the instrumental-expressive continuum see Constantina Safilios-Rothschild and John Georgiopoulos, 'A Comparative Study of Parental and Filial Role Definitions', *Journ. Mar. Fam.*, August 1970, pp. 381–9.

74 In Parsons and Bales, op. cit., p. 319.

75 Ibid., p. 318.

76 Ibid.

77 Ibid, p. 319.

78 Philip Slater, 'Parental Role Differentiation', in Coser (ed.), op. cit., p. 370.

79 Ibid., p. 352. Once again one suspects that Slater and Zelditch are not necessarily talking about the same things.

80 Parsons, 'The Kinship System . . .' p. 194.

81 Parsons, quoted in Rodman, op. cit., pp. 277–8.

82 *Journ. Soc. Issues.*, vol. 13, no. 4, 1952. Reprinted in Bell and Vogel, op. cit., pp. 377–90.

83 Ibid., p. 378.

84 Ibid., p. 382.

85 It is perhaps worth noting that this essay contains little reference to the economic problems posed by sickness, an important consideration in a system dominated by private medical practice. This is perhaps a further illustration of the limitations of Parsons's cultural horizons.

86 In R. N. Anshen (ed.), *The Family: Its Function and Destiny*, rev. ed., New York, Harper, 1959, p. 260.

87 William J. Goode, 'The Sociology of the Family', in Robert K. Merton, Leonard Broom and Leonard S. Cottrell Jnr (eds), *Sociology Today: Problems and Prospects*, vol. I, New York, Harper Torchbooks, 1965 (originally published 1959).
88 William J. Goode, *The Family*, Englewood Cliffs, Prentice-Hall, 1964, p. 5. A more systematic approach is provided in his contribution to Merton, Broom and Cottrell, op. cit., where he examines the relationship between his functions and those of Murdock.
89 Pages 21–2.
90 Goode, in Merton, Broom and Cottrell, op. cit., p. 187.
91 In this connection it is interesting to note that Goode has recently turned his attention to the study of violence within the family. William J. Goode, 'Force and Violence in the Family', *Journ. Mar. Fam.*, vol. 33, no. 4, November 1971.
92 William J. Goode, *World Revolution and Family Patterns*, New York, Free Press, 1970, p. 8.
93 'I see the world revolution in family patterns as part of a still more important revolution that is sweeping the world in our time, the aspiration on the part of billions of people to have the right for the first time *to choose* for themselves. . . .' Goode, *World Revolution . . .*, p. 380.
94 Ezra F. Vogel and Norman W. Bell, 'The Emotionally Disturbed Child as the Family Scapegoat', in Bell and Vogel, op. cit., pp. 412–427.
95 Ibid., p. 425.
96 Ibid., p. 427.
97 H. Popitz, 'The Concept of Social Role as an Element of Sociological Theory', in J. A. Jackson (ed.), *Role* (*Sociological Studies 4*), Cambridge University Press, 1972, pp. 11–39.
98 M. Coulson, 'Role: A Redundant Concept in Sociology?', in Jackson, op. cit., pp. 107–28. See also Atkinson, op. cit., pp. 25–31.
99 I discuss some of the problems associated with the use of the term 'sex roles' in Chapter 5.
100 Turner, op. cit.
101 Ibid., pp. 187–97.
102 I have elaborated this point elsewhere. See D. H. J. Morgan, 'Theoretical and Conceptual Problems in the Study of Social Relations at Work', unpublished Ph.D. thesis, Manchester University, 1969, pp. 17–55.
103 Kurt Danziger, *Socialization*, Harmondsworth, Penguin, 1971, p. 14.
104 Andrew Hacker, 'Sociology and Ideology', in Black (ed.), op. cit., p. 291.

2 Why kinship?

1 E. Durkheim, 'La Famille conjugale', *Revue Philosophique*, vol. 41, 1921, pp. 1–14.
2 L. Wirth, 'Urbanism as a Way of Life', *Am. Journ. Soc.*, vol. 44, 1938–9, often reprinted.

3 Talcott Parsons, 'The Kinship System of the Contemporary United States' (1943). Reprinted in Parsons, *Essays in Sociological Theory*, rev. ed., New York, Free Press, 1964.
4 See Chapter 1, pp. 26–8.
5 Parsons, op. cit., p. 178.
6 Ibid., p. 180.
7 Ibid., p. 183.
8 Michael Young and Peter Willmott, *Family and Kinship in East London*, rev. ed., Harmondsworth, Penguin, 1962.
9 Ibid., p. 187.
10 Peter Townsend, *The Family Life of Old People*, rev. ed., Harmondsworth, Penguin, 1963.
11 For a summary and discussion of many of these findings see Ethel Shanas and Gordon F. Streib (eds), *Social Structure and the Family: Generational Relations*, Englewood Cliffs, Prentice-Hall, 1965.
12 See, for example, Firth's study of Italian immigrants in London, in Raymond Firth, *Two Studies of Kinship in London*, London, Athlone Press, 1956.
13 As shown, for example, in the work of Garigue in French Canada. See Philippe Garigue, 'French Canadian Kinship and Urban Life', reprinted in Peter Worsley (ed.), *Modern Sociology*, Harmondsworth, Penguin, 1970, pp. 123–35. Also Philippe Garigue, *La Vie familiale des Canadiens français*, Montreal, Les Presses de l'Université de Montréal, 1970.
14 For a summary of the main British studies see Ronald Frankenberg, *Communities in Britain*, Harmondsworth, Penguin, 1966, especially the first four chapters. For one particular American case study of rural-urban migration see James S. Brown, Harry K. Schartzweller and Joseph Mangalam, 'Kentucky Mountain Migration and the Stem Family', in Norman W. Bell and Ezra F. Vogel, *A Modern Introduction to the Family*, rev. ed., New York, Free Press, 1968, pp. 150–8.
15 Tom Lupton and C. Shirley Wilson, 'The Kinship Connexions of "Top Decision Makers" ', reprinted in part in Peter Worsley (ed.), op. cit., pp. 151–64. For an interesting American historical study see Stephen Birmingham, *Our Crowd: The Great Jewish Families of New York*, New York, Dell, 1967.
16 Paul J. Reiss, 'Extended Kinship Relations in American Society', in Hyman Rodman, *Marriage, Family and Society*, New York, Random House, 1967, pp. 204–9.
17 For useful summaries of these findings and theoretical arguments see Marvin B. Sussman, 'Relationships of Adult Children with their Parents in the United States', and Eugene Litwak, 'Extended Kin Relations in an Industrial Democratic Society', both in Shanas and Streib (eds), op. cit., pp. 62–92 and 290–323, respectively. These articles and other papers in this collection contain references to the main original studies.
18 Eugene Litwak, in Shanas and Streib, op. cit., p. 291.
19 Marvin B. Sussman and Lee Burchinall, 'Kin Family Network: Unheralded Structure in Current Conceptualizations of Family

Functioning', in John N. Edwards (ed.), *The Family and Change*, New York, Knopf, p. 147. Their emphasis.

20 Marvin B. Sussman, 'Relations of Adult Children with their Parents in the United States', in Shanas and Streib, op. cit., p. 63.

21 Raymond Firth, Jane Hubert and Anthony Forge, *Families and their Relatives*, London, Routledge & Kegan Paul, 1969.

22 Ibid., p. 139.

23 Anthropological use of the term 'kindred' referring to a set of relationships based on Ego and hence necessarily unbounded may convey what we have in mind here. See J. D. Freeman, 'On the Concept of Kindred', *Journ. Royal Anth. Inst.*, vol. 91, 1961, pp. 192–220, and William E. Mitchell, 'Theoretical Problems in the Concept of Kindred', *Am. Anth.*, vol. 65, 1963, pp. 343–54.

24 See for example Robert P. Stuckert, 'Occupational Mobility and Family Relationships', in Bell and Vogel, op. cit., pp. 160–8. This paper produces evidence to suggest that occupational mobility does weaken family and kinship ties.

25 For a summary of some of the arguments and evidence see B. N. Adams, *Kinship in an Urban Setting*, Chicago, Markham, 1968, pp. 168–75.

26 William J. Goode, *World Revolution and Family Patterns*, rev. ed., New York, Free Press, 1970, p. 76.

27 B. N. Adams, op. cit.

28 Talcott Parsons, 'Reply to his Critics', in Anderson (ed.), *Sociology of the Family*, Harmondsworth, Penguin, 1971, pp. 120–1.

29 For a recent critique of the 'modified extended family' argument covering much of the same ground see Geoffrey Gibson, 'Kin Family Networks: Overheralded Structures in Past Conceptualizations of Family Functioning', *Journ. Mar. Fam.*, vol. 34, no. 1, February 1972, pp. 13–23.

30 Adams, op. cit., p. 177.

31 Parsons, in Anderson (ed.), op. cit., p. 120.

32 See Chapter 1, pp. 54, 57–8.

33 See Chapter 1, pp. 26–7.

34 Students of the sociology of sociology might notice the possible congruence between this family and the likely structure of the sociologist's own family. The sociologist is probably writing at a time when his own family probably corresponds closely with this model.

35 Adams, op. cit., p. 166.

36 Ibid., p. 169.

37 Goode, op. cit., p. 70. His emphasis.

38 Townsend, op. cit., p. 246.

39 Adams, op. cit., p. 10.

40 Litwak included in John N. Edwards (ed.), op. cit., p. 74.

41 Firth, Hubert and Forge, op. cit., ch. 2.

42 Bell, op. cit., pp. 3–9 and chs 5 and 7.

43 Consider Coleman's argument that sample surveys often tend to focus on problems of 'aggregate psychology' rather than relational problems.

James Coleman, 'Relational Analysis: The Study of Social Organizations with Survey Methods', reprinted in Amitai Etzioni (ed.), *Complex Organizations*, New York, Holt, Rinehart & Winston, 1961, pp. 441–53.

44 For a vigorous, although perhaps overstated, criticism of much modern sociology from a symbolic interactionist perspective see Herbert Blumer, *Symbolic Interactionism: Perspective and Method*, Englewood Cliffs, Prentice-Hall, 1969, especially the first two chapters.

45 Andrée Vieille Michel, 'Kinship Relations and Relationships of Proximity in French Working Class Households', in Bell and Vogel, op. cit., pp. 311–18.

46 E. Litwak and I. Szelenyi, 'Primary Group Structures and their Functions: Kin, Neighbours and Friends', reprinted in part in Anderson, op. cit., pp. 149–63.

47 Ibid., p. 156.

48 For example Michael Banton (ed.), *The Social Anthropology of Complex Societies*, London, Tavistock, 1966; J. Clyde Mitchell (ed.), *Social Networks in Urban Situations*, Manchester University Press, 1969.

49 C. Lison-Tolosana, 'The Family in a Spanish Town', in C. C. Harris (ed.), *Readings in Kinship in Urban Society*, Oxford, Pergamon Press, 1970, pp. 173–4.

50 Robert A. le Vine, 'Intergenerational Tension in Extended Family Structures in Africa', in Shanas and Streib, op. cit., p. 189.

51 Colin Bell, 'Social Anthropologists on Kinship' (review article), *Soc.*, vol. 6., no. 3, 1972, pp. 457–61.

52 Marion J. Levy Jnr, in A. J. Coale (ed.), *Aspects of the Analysis of Family Structure*, Princeton University Press, 1965, p. 2.

53 M. Fortes, *Kinship and the Social Order*, London, Routledge & Kegan Paul, 1970, p. 251.

54 E. Gellner, 'Ideal Language and Kinship Structure'; 'The Concept of Kinship'; 'Nature and Society in Social Anthropology', all in *Phil. of Sc.* vol. 24, 1957, pp. 235–42; vol. 27, 1960, pp. 187–204; vol. 30, 1963, pp. 236–51.

55 Fortes, op. cit., pp. 110, 232.

56 Ibid., p. 242.

57 Ibid., p. 63.

58 M. Southwold, 'Meanings of Kinship', in R. Needham (ed.), *Rethinking Kinship and Marriage*, London, Tavistock, 1971, p. 48.

59 Freeman, op. cit., p. 209.

60 The approach of Schneider and Homans, viewing the institution of kinship in modern society as playing an essential part in the socialization process, may be associated with this perspective. Schneider, while he does not appear to adhere to a biologically based definition of kinship, is reluctant to view it as being merely an idiom in which other relationships are expressed. See David M. Schneider and George C. Homans, 'Kinship Terminology and the American Kinship System', in Bell and Vogel, op. cit., pp. 509–25. Also David M. Schneider, 'The Nature of Kinship', *Man*, vol. 64, 1964; *American Kinship*, Engle-

wood Cliffs, Prentice-Hall, 1968; and Schneider's contribution to the discussion edited by Coale, op. cit.

61 J. H. M. Beattie, 'Kinship and Social Anthropology', *Man*, vol. 64, 1964, pp. 101–3.

62 J. A. Barnes, 'Discussion: Physical and Social Kinship', *Phil. of Sc.*, vol. 28, 1961, pp. 296–9; 'Discussion; Physical and Social Facts in Anthropology', *Phil. of Sc.*, vol. 31, 1964, pp. 294–7.

63 Needham, op. cit. See, in particular, the papers by Needham, Southwold and Rivière.

64 Claude Meillassoux, 'From Reproduction to Production', *Econ. & Soc.*, vol. 1, no. 1, 1972.

65 Adams, op. cit., p. 89. Noted by Adams as a typical response.

66 Reiss in Rodman, op. cit., pp. 207–8.

67 Adams, op. cit., p. 88.

68 See the article by Brown *et al.*, which examines migration from rural Kentucky (James S. Brown, Harry K. Schwartzweller and Joseph J. Mangalam, 'Kentucky Mountain Migration and the Stem Family', in Bell and Vogel, op. cit.).

69 Townsend, op. cit., p. 61.

70 Michael Anderson, *Family Structure in Nineteenth Century Lancashire*, Cambridge University Press, 1971.

71 Ibid., p. 168.

72 Ibid., p. 178.

73 Bernard Farber, *Kinship and Class*, New York, Basic Books, 1971.

74 Adams, op. cit., pp. 63–5. See also Alvin L. Schorr, 'Filial Responsibility and the Aged', in Rodman, op. cit., pp. 186–97, for possible dysfunction.

75 Firth *et al.*, op. cit., p. 11.

76 Ibid., p. 11.

77 Homans and Schneider also give emphasis to the socialization process in their analysis of American kinship. However, they assume a high measure of congruence between socialization into learning the values associated with familistic roles and socialization into the 'fundamentals of (the) whole culture'. Schneider and Homans, op. cit. This paper contains a lot of useful information demonstrating the flexibility, variability and situational use of American kinship terminology. See also David M. Schneider, 1968, op. cit.

78 See Chapter 1 for a further discussion of Parsons's analysis of socialization.

79 See John R. Seeley *et al.*, *Crestwood Heights*, Toronto University Press, 1956, pp. 123–30, 395–402. Also David F. Aberle and Kaspar D. Naegele, 'Middle-Class Fathers' Occupational Role and Attitudes towards Children', reprinted in Bell and Vogel, op. cit., pp. 188–98. It is to be noted that Seeley *et al.* deny the importance of extended kin in *Crestwood Heights* and argue that it approaches the pure type of the isolated nuclear family hypothesis. It is not certain from the evidence presented whether they recognized the point emphasized by critics of Parsons, that geographical distance does not necessarily mean social isolation.

80 Adams, op. cit., pp. 37–9.
81 The best article on this is still probably Kingsley Davis, 'The Sociology of Parent-Youth Conflict', reprinted in Coser (ed.), op. cit., pp. 455–471.
82 This particular version comes from Young and Willmott, op. cit., p. 61.
83 Townsend, op. cit., p. 130.
84 Young and Willmott, op. cit., p. 188.
85 I discuss women as a social class in Chapter 5.
86 Jiri Musil, 'Some Aspects of Social Organization of the Contemporary Czech Family', *Journ. Mar. Fam.*, February 1971, pp. 196–206. Quotation from p. 204.
87 Ibid., p. 206.
88 See Elaine Cumming and David M. Schneider, 'Sibling Solidarity: A Property of American Kinship', *Am. Anth.*, vol. 63, 1961, pp. 498–507.

3 The modern family: a success story?

1 O. R. McGregor and Griselda Rowntree, 'The Family', in A. T. Welford *et al.*, *Society: Problems and Methods of Study*, rev. ed., London, Routledge & Kegan Paul, 1968, p. 433.
2 Germaine Greer, *The Female Eunuch*, London, Paladin, 1971, pp. 235–6.
3 Betty Friedan, *The Feminine Mystique*, Harmondsworth, Penguin, 1965, especially Chs 6 and 7.
4 Ibid., pp. 120–31.
5 As, for example, in Ronald Fletcher, *The Family and Marriage in Britain*, rev. ed., Harmondsworth, Penguin, 1966, p. 142.
6 Cited in Robert N. Williamson, *Marriage and Family Relations*, 2nd ed., New York, Wiley, 1972, p. 364.
7 A good selection of these views is provided by Fletcher in his appendix to the revised edition of *The Family and Marriage in Britain*, pp. 233–240.
8 Barrington Moore, 'Thoughts on the Future of the Family', in John N. Edwards (ed.), *The Family and Change*, New York, Knopf, 1969.
9 For a brief statement see Robin Blackburn, 'A Brief Guide to Bourgeois Ideology', in Alexander Cockburn and Robin Blackburn, *Student Power*, Harmondsworth, Penguin, 1969, especially pp. 195–197.
10 Raymond Aron, *Progress and Disillusion: The Dialectics of Modern Society*, Harmondsworth, Penguin, 1972, p. 108.
11 E. Durkheim, 'La Famille conjugale', *Revue Philosophique*, vol. 41, 1921, pp. 1–14.
12 Fletcher, op. cit., p. 16. His emphasis.
13 For an exhaustive and some might say exhausting account of the Victorian sexual underworld see Ronald Pearsall, *The Worm in the Bud*, Harmondsworth, Penguin, 1971.
14 There is a certain element of 'heads I win, tails you lose' in the use of divorce statistics among functionalist sociologists. Fletcher, on the

whole, is concerned to argue that the figures do not show what some people purport them to show. Parsons, on the other hand, writing about a situation where divorce rates are much higher, argues that the divorce rates show the high expectations that people have of marriage. Of course, both arguments could be right, but they raise the important question as to how high is 'too high', one which is virtually unarguable.

15 Fletcher, op. cit., p. 181.
16 Fletcher, op. cit., p. 182.
17 Aron, op. cit., p. 119.
18 Fletcher, op. cit., p. 27.
19 Robert K. Merton, *Social Theory and Social Structure*, rev. ed., Chicago, Free Press, 1957, p. 51.
20 See Ch. 1, pp. 53–4.
21 See Ch. 4, pp. 105–8.
22 Arnold W. Green, 'The Middle-Class Male Child and Neurosis', in Bell and Vogel, *A Modern Introduction to the Family*, rev. ed., New York, Free Press, 1968, pp. 618–27. Bott's analysis in terms of social networks, while originally developed in relation to *sex* roles, may also be analysed in terms of *parental* roles. See Elizabeth Bott, *Family and Social Network*, 2nd ed., London, Tavistock, 1971.
23 See Ch. 5.
24 The best descriptive account of these tensions and uncertainties is probably still Friedan, op. cit.
25 See the issue of the *Journal of Marriage and the Family* which deals with violence in the family—vol. 33, no. 4, November 1971, pp. 624–731.
26 See Garrett Hardin, 'The Tragedy of the Commons', reprinted in John Barr (ed.), *The Environmental Handbook*, London, Pan, 1971, pp. 47–65, especially p. 57.
27 Aron, op. cit., p. 119.
28 Aaron Esterson, *The Leaves of Spring: A Study in the Dialectics of Madness*, Harmondsworth, Penguin, 1972, p. 251.
29 Mao Tse-Tung, *On Contradiction*, Pekin, Foreign Languages Press, 1958, p. 4.

4 R. D. Laing: the politics of the family

1 Sedgwick maintains that there is a particularly sharp contradiction between the influence of Freud and the influence of Sartre and other existentialists. Peter Sedgwick, 'Laing's Clangs', *New Soc.*, 15 January 1970, pp. 103–4.
2 A. Esterson, *The Leaves of Spring*, Harmondsworth, Penguin, 1972, especially Part 2.
3 David Cooper, *The Death of the Family*, Harmondsworth, Penguin, 1972.
4 Nathan W. Ackerman, *The Psychodynamics of Family Life*, New York, Basic Books, 1958.
5 Jules Henry, *Culture Against Man*, New York, Random House, 1963; Jules Henry, *Pathways to Madness*, London, Cape, 1972; G. Handel,

Psychosocial Interior of the Family, London, Allen & Unwin, 1968. For further assessment see Robert Boyers and Robert Orrill (eds), *Laing and Anti-Psychiatry*, Harmondsworth, Penguin, 1972.
6 R. D. Laing, *The Politics of the Family and Other Essays*, London, Tavistock, 1971.
7 R. D. Laing, *The Divided Self*, Harmondsworth, Penguin, 1960.
8 R. D. Laing and A. Esterson, *Sanity, Madness and the Family*, 2nd ed., Harmondsworth, Penguin, 1970.
9 R. D. Laing, H. Phillipson and A. R. Lee, *Interpersonal Perception*, London, Tavistock, 1966.
10 R. D. Laing and D. G. Cooper, *Reason and Violence*, London, Tavistock, 1964.
11 The recent film *Family Life* seems to reflect the same shift. In its original version as a television play by David Mercer it was called *In Two Minds*.
12 There are clear parallels here between Laing's approach to mental illness and the labelling theory of deviance in sociology as represented, for example, in the writings of Becker. Howard S. Becker, *Outsiders*, New York, Free Press, 1963.
13 Laing, *The Divided Self*, op. cit., p. 27.
14 See John O'Neill (ed.), *Modes of Individualism and Collectivism*, London, Heinemann, 1973.
15 D. Cooper in Laing and Cooper, op. cit., pp. 51–2. His emphasis.
16 Ibid. His emphasis.
17 See, for example, some of the papers in Handel, op. cit. (especially items 14, 15, 21 and 22).
18 Laing and Esterson, op. cit., p. 17.
19 Laing, *The Divided Self*, op. cit., p. 189.
20 In G. Handel, op. cit., pp. 251–75.
21 R. D. Laing, *Politics of Experience and the Bird of Paradise*, Harmondsworth, Penguin, 1968, Ch. 5.
22 R. D. Laing, *The Politics of the Family*, op. cit., pp. 15–17.
23 Laing *et al.*, op. cit., p. v.
24 Ibid., p. 34.
25 Laing and Esterson, op. cit., p. 20.
26 Ibid., p. 20.
27 Laing and Cooper, op. cit., p. 109.
28 There are tempting and interesting parallels—as well as divergences—here, not merely with Simmel but also with Blau's theoretical statement *Exchange and Power in Social Life*, New York, Wiley, 1964.
29 Laing, *The Politics of the Family*, op. cit., p. 13.
30 Esterson, op. cit., pp. 37–8.
31 For a detailed account of this specific example see R. D. Laing, 'Series and Nexus in the Family', *New Left Rev.*, no. 15, 1962, pp. 7–14.
32 Laing, *The Politics of Experience* . . ., op. cit., p. 71, his emphasis.
33 Laing and Esterson, op. cit., p. 21.
34 Laing, *The Politics of Experience* . . ., op. cit., p. 74.
35 Esterson, op. cit.

36 An excellent fictional account of the way in which one's division of the world into them and us is generated and sustained within the family is provided in the beginning of Hermann Hesse's novel *Demian*.
37 London, Methuen, 1963.
38 Laing and Cooper, op. cit., p. 44.
39 Laing *et al.*, op. cit., p. 10.
40 Laing, *The Politics of Experience . . .*, op. cit., pp. 54–5. Laing is principally attacking T. Lidz here. (*The Family and Human Adaption*, London, Hogarth Press, 1964.) By implication, however, a whole body of social-psychological work is under attack for similar reasons.
41 Ibid., p. 55.
42 In D. Cooper (ed.), *Dialectics of Liberation*, Harmondsworth, Penguin, 1968, p. 27.
43 Ibid., p. 29.
44 See a brief discussion of language which may serve as a partial defence for Laing in Laing and Cooper, op. cit., p. 12–20.
45 David Martin, 'R. D. Laing', in M. Cranston (ed.), *The New Left*, London, Bodley Head, 1970, p. 205.
46 There have of course been analytically orientated studies that have used a sample of 'normal' families as a control group in the study of schizophrenia. For one good example of this kind of study see E. G. Mishler and N. E. Waxler (eds), *Family Processes and Schizophrenia*, New York, Science House, 1968.
47 Laing and Esterson, op. cit., p. 167.
48 A more blatant example, provided by someone close to Laing in spirit, where the author appears to sit in judgment on his subjects and to force an interpretation on the readers is provided by Jules Henry, 'My Life with the Families of Psychotic Children', in Handel, op. cit., pp. 30–46.
49 Martin, op. cit., p. 191.
50 Cooper makes this point specifically. Cooper, op. cit., especially pp. 5–30.
51 Laing, *The Divided Self*, op. cit., pp. 180–1.
52 Laing, *The Politics of the Family*, op. cit., p. 12.
53 Ibid., p. 49.
54 Laing, *The Divided Self*, op. cit., pp. 178–205.
55 Ibid., p. 179.
56 Ibid., p. 191.
57 Ibid., p. 194.
58 E. Bott, *Family and Social Network*, 2nd ed., London, Tavistock, 1971.
59 Ackerman, for example, refers to the 'extra psychic load' placed on the family in modern society. Ackerman, op. cit., p. 112.
60 P. Sedgwick, in Boyers and Orrill (eds), op. cit., 35.
61 *Guardian*, 27 December 1972, p. 12.
62 Cooper (ed.), op. cit., pp. 28–9.
63 He refers in the same passage to the 'amazing collective paranoid projective systems', ibid.
64 *Guardian*, op. cit.
65 Laing, *The Politics of the Family*, op. cit., pp. 117–24.

66 Cooper asks rhetorically 'when will parents allow themselves to be brought up by their children?' (Cooper, op. cit., p. 7.) In a sense this already happens.
67 For further patterns of resistance see Ralph Turner, *Family Interaction*, New York, Wiley, 1970, pp. 361–65.
68 Erving Goffman, *Asylums*, New York, Doubleday Anchor, 1961, pp. 35–7. The whole of Goffman's analysis of total institutions could be applied with profit to the analysis of families, particularly in this context, the patterns of inmate resistance.
69 I discuss this point more fully in the chapter on Parsons and the Parsonian approach to socialization. See Ch. 1, especially pp. 41–2.
70 Laing, *The Politics of Experience . . .*, op. cit., p. 79.
71 Martin, op. cit., p. 199.
72 D. Holbrook, 'Madness to Blame Society?', *Twentieth Century*, vol. 2, 1969, pp. 29–32. See also D. Holbrook, 'R. D. Laing and the Death Circuit', *Encounter*, August 1968.
73 *Guardian*, op. cit.
74 Cooper deals with communes in some detail. See Cooper, op. cit., pp. 46–67.
75 Women as such scarcely appear in the pages of Laing. They only appear in their most prominent roles as mothers and daughters. Perhaps Laing's studies, radical as they are, may not be wholly free from the label of 'sexist'. See next chapter.
76 The title of the book edited by Handel, op. cit.
77 D. H. Lawrence, *The Virgin and the Gipsy*, Harmondsworth, Penguin ed., 1970, p. 9.

5 Women as a social class

1 Simone de Beauvoir, *The Second Sex*, Harmondsworth, Penguin ed., 1972.
2 See Joan Huber (ed.), 'Changing Women in a Changing World', special issue of the *Am. Journ. Soc.*, vol. 78, no. 4, January 1973. The editorial focuses on the sexist bias in sociology. For the status of women in the sociological profession see Sylvia Fleis Fava, 'The Status of Women in Professional Sociology', *Am. Soc. Rev.*, vol. 25, no. 2, April 1960.
3 See Ch. 1, pp. 54–6.
4 For a slightly different approach to sexual stratification see Randall Collins, 'A Conflict Theory of Sexual Stratification', in H. P. Dreitzel (ed.), *Family, Marriage and the Struggle of the Sexes*, New York, Macmillan, 1972, pp. 53–79.
5 Kate Millett, *Sexual Politics*, New York, Doubleday, 1970, especially Part 1.
6 For an excellent account of the way in which women are treated in stratification studies see Joan Acker, 'Women and Social Stratification: A Case of Intellectual Sexism', in Huber (ed.), op. cit., pp. 936–945.
7 Frederick Engels, *The Origins of the Family, Private Property and the*

State, Moscow, Foreign Languages Publishing House, 1954. (Several editions available.)

8 For a good account of the ambiguities of Marxian analysis of the family and the way in which these ambiguities could be used to justify radically opposed positions see H. Kent Geiger, *The Family in the Soviet Union*, Cambridge, Mass., Harvard University Press, 1968. See also Juliet Mitchell, 'Women: The Longest Revolution', *New Left Rev.*, no. 40, 1966, pp. 11–37

9 Shulamith Firestone, *The Dialectic of Sex*, London, Paladin, 1972, p. 12.

10 Lewis Henry Morgan, quoted in Engels, op. cit., p. 50.

11 Quoted in Herbert A. Otto (ed.), *The Family in Search of a Future*, New York, Appleton-Century-Crofts, 1970, p. 88.

12 Marvin Harris, *The Rise of Anthropological Theory*, London, Routledge & Kegan Paul, 1969. A somewhat similar argument is presented in an unpublished paper by Peter Worsley, 'The Origins of the Family Revisited'.

13 Engels, op. cit., p. 108.

14 See also Herbert Marcuse, *Studies in Critical Philosophy*, London, New Left Books, 1972, pp. 128–43.

15 August Bebel, *Women: Past Present and Future*, London, Reeves, n.d., p. 7.

16 Ibid., p. 71.

17 Mitchell, op. cit., Juliet Mitchell, *Woman's Estate*, Harmondsworth, Penguin, 1971.

18 Engels, op. cit., p. 8. My emphasis.

19 M. P. Fogarty, R. Rapoport and R. Rapoport, *Sex, Career and Family*, London, Allen & Unwin, 1971, p. 81; Virginia Olesen, 'Context and Posture: Notes on Socio-Cultural Aspects of Women's Roles and Family Policy in Contemporary Cuba', *Journ. Mar. Fam.*, August 1971.

20 Firestone, op. cit., p. 15.

21 Millett, op. cit.

22 William J. Goode, *The Family*, Englewood Cliffs, Prentice-Hall, 1964, p. 70.

23 For detailed documentation see Fogarty *et al.*, op. cit., and E. Dahlstrom (ed.), *The Changing Roles of Men and Women*, London, Duckworth, 1967, especially Chs IV and V.

24 David Lockwood, *The Black-Coated Worker*, London, Allen & Unwin, 1958, pp. 122–5.

25 Jane E. Prather, 'When the Girls Move In: A Sociological Analysis of the Feminization of the Bank Teller's Job', *Journ. Mar. Fam.*, 1971, pp. 777–82. Doubtless similar changes could be observed, with a time-lag, in Britain.

26 Germaine Greer, *The Female Eunuch*, London, Paladin, 1971, pp. 123–4.

27 Henry Etzkowitz, 'The Male Sister: Sexual Separation of Labour in Society', *Journ. Mar. Fam.*, vol. 33, no. 3, August 1971, pp. 431–4.

28 Elizabeth Janeway, *Man's World, Woman's Place*, New York, Morrow, 1971, p. 170.
29 Canadian Department of Labour: Women's Bureau, *Women's Bureau '69*, 1970, pp. 10–11.
30 De Beauvoir, op. cit., p. 587.
31 Ibid., p. 359.
32 Firestone, op. cit., pp. 46–72.
33 Erik H. Erikson, 'Inner and Outer Space: Reflections on Womanhood', in Norman W. Bell and Ezra F. Vogel (eds), *A Modern Introduction to the Family*, rev. ed, New York, Free Press, 1968, pp. 442–63.
34 For a descriptive account of current and differing ideologies relating to the roles of men and women see Fogarty *et al.*, op. cit., pp. 102–11 and Dahlstrom (ed.), op. cit., Ch. 6.
35 See Juliet Mitchell, *Woman's Estate*, op. cit., p. 14.
36 Robin Morgan (ed.), *Sisterhood is Powerful*, New York, Random House, 1970, p. xvii.
37 Quoted in Viola Klein, *The Feminine Character*, London, Kegan Paul, Trench, Trubner, 1946, pp. 82–3. Klein's book has deservedly been reprinted recently.
38 De Beauvoir, op. cit., p. 15.
39 Greer, op. cit., p. 142.
40 Firestone, op. cit., p. 121.
41 Ibid., pp. 141–3.
42 Ibid., p. 141.
43 See Peter Lomas, 'Childbirth Ritual', *New Soc.*, 31 December 1964, pp. 13–14.
44 See Diana Barker, 'The Confetti Ritual', *New Soc.*, 22 June 1972, pp. 614–17.
45 For a fuller discussion of consciousness raising see Mitchell, op. cit., pp. 61–3. For some specific programmes see Morgan, op. cit., pp. 512–65 and Shulamith Firestone and Anne Koedt (eds), *Notes from the Second Year*, New York, Radical Feminism, 1970.
46 D. Cooper, *Dialectics of Liberation*, Harmondsworth, Penguin, 1968.
47 For brief analytical accounts of the growth of the American Women's Liberation movement see Jo Freeman, 'The Women's Liberation Movement: Its Origins, Structures and Ideas', in Dreitzel, op. cit., and Jo Freeman, 'The Origins of the Women's Liberation Movement', in Huber, op. cit., pp. 792–811.
48 For some general analyses broadly on these lines see Dahlstrom (ed.), op. cit. This refers to Scandinavian experience. For detailed accounts of a small number of case studies of husbands and wives who have worked out some kind of equality and balance between their spouses see Rhona and Robert Rapoport, *Dual-Career Families*, Harmondsworth, Penguin, 1971.
49 Margaret Mead, *Male and Female*, Harmondsworth, Penguin, 1962, p. 111.
50 Janeway, op. cit., p. 247.

51 For an imaginative account of what this might entail see Gloria Steinem, 'What It Would Be Like if Women Win', *Time*, 31 August 1970, pp. 24–5.
52 Firestone, op. cit., p. 19.
53 Ann Battle-Sister, 'Conjectures on the Female Culture Question', *Journ. Mar. Fam.*, vol. 33, no. 3, August 1971, p. 411.
54 Gunnar Myrdal, *An American Dilemma*, New York, Harper & Row, 1944.
55 André Betéille (ed.), *Social Inequality*, Harmondsworth, Penguin, 1969, p. 263.
56 Ronald Pearsall, *The Worm in the Bud*, Harmondsworth, Penguin, 1971, pp. 267–71.
57 For a fuller discussion see Mary Douglas, *Purity and Danger*, Harmondsworth, Penguin, 1970.
58 One influential article treats women in terms of an analysis of 'minority groups'. See H. M. Hacker, 'Women as a Minority Group', *Soc. For.*, vol. 30, October 1951, pp. 60–9.
59 De Beauvoir, op. cit., p. 65.
60 Ibid.; Engels, op. cit.
61 For two opposed interpretations of this period of human history see Ashley Montague, *The Natural Superiority of Women*, London, Macmillan, 1968; and Lionel Tiger, *Men in Groups*, London, Nelson, 1969.
62 Millett, op. cit. See also discussion of Reich in next chapter.
63 Firestone, op. cit., p. 18.
64 Juliet Mitchell, *Woman's Estate*, pp. 84, 90.
65 Ibid., p. 42.
66 Kathleen Gough, 'The Origins of the Family', *Journ. Mar. Fam.*, vol. 33, no. 4, 1971, pp. 760–71.
67 Mead, op. cit., p. 274. See also Steinem, op. cit.
68 A more detailed analysis—one of the few—of the role of men in society is to be found in Ralph Turner, *Family Interaction*, New York, Wiley, 1970, pp. 294–303. I have found that students—male and female—find it more difficult to write about the role of men in society than about the role of women.
69 De Beauvoir, op. cit., p. 691.
70 See Greer's analysis of male hatred and Friedan's discussion of the way in which mothers came to be blamed for a variety of ills in American society after the Second World War. Greer, op. cit., pp. 249–311; Friedan, op. cit., pp. 165–9.
71 Jean-Paul Sartre, *Being and Nothingness*, London, Methuen, 1957, pp. 252–302.
72 De Beauvoir, op. cit., p. 500.
73 For an analysis of some of the problems involved in this version of multiple group affiliation see Robert K. Merton, 'Insiders and Outsiders: A Chapter in the Sociology of Knowledge', *Am. Journ. Soc.*, vol. 78, no. 1, July 1972, pp. 9–47. Merton refers specifically to the overlaps between women/men and black/white. See also C. F. Epstein, 'Positive Effects of the Multiple Negative: Explaining the

Success of Black Professional Women', in Huber (ed.), op. cit., pp. 912–35.

74 Juliet Mitchell, *Woman's Estate*, pp. 94–5.

75 Max Gluckman, *Custom and Conflict in Africa*, Oxford, Blackwell, 1956, p. 2.

76 Juliet Mitchell, *Woman's Estate*, p. 90.

77 Maggie Grant, 'Down with Women's Lib!' *Canadian Magazine*, 1 August 1970. I am grateful to Marijean Suezle for drawing this particularly delightful quotation to my attention.

78 Lockwood, op. cit., 13–16.

79 Hans Gerth and C. Wright Mills, *From Max Weber*, London, Routledge & Kegan Paul, 1948, p. 181.

80 See Rainwater *et al.*, *Workingman's Wife*, New York, Oceana Publications, 1959, in particular ch. 7, 'Not all Americans are Joiners'.

81 De Beauvoir, op. cit., pp. 497–8. Her emphasis.

82 Greer, op. cit., p. 97.

83 Millett, op. cit., p. 33.

84 Ibid., p. 159.

85 See Ch. 4.

86 Juliet Mitchell, *Woman's Estate*, p. 150.

87 A more extended discussion of the future of the family is to be found in the concluding chapter of this book.

88 Rapoport, op. cit., p. 18.

89 Morgan (ed.), op. cit., pp. 385–417. See also William Hinton, *Fanshen*, Harmondsworth, Penguin, 1972, pp. 184–8, 469–73.

90 Ronald Frankenberg, 'Educating the Educators', *China Now*, no. 12, June 1971, p. 2.

91

> China is not our model. Its needs and desires are very different from ours. Women are *told* what they should be and do—that's not the way it could be here. But Mao and the Chinese Communists do show us that society is changing by changing people's daily lives. Working side by side with men partially liberates women. Freedom—however you want it—comes from new ways of living together.

Charlotte Bonny Cohen, 'Experiment in Freedom—China', in Morgan (ed.), op. cit., p. 417.

92 Joseph Downing, 'The Tribal Family and the Society of Awakening', in Otto (ed.), op. cit., p. 123.

93 Ibid., p. 131.

94 Ross V. Speck, *The New Families*, London, Tavistock, 1972. (Ch. 6 is entitled 'Les Girls: Pets on the Periphery'.)

95 Ron E. Roberts, *The New Communes*, Englewood Cliffs, Prentice-Hall, 1971, pp. 86–90.

6 Sex and capitalism

1 For a useful summary of the main characteristics of the Frankfurt School, see David Fernbach, 'Sexual Oppression and Political

Practice', *New Left Rev.*, no. 64, November/December 1970, pp. 87–8.
2 Karl Marx and Frederick Engels, *Manifesto of the Communist Party*, in *Selected Works*, vol. 1, Moscow, Foreign Languages Publishing House, 1958, p. 51.
3 See also Frederick Engels, *The Condition of the Working Class in England*, London, Panther, 1969, pp. 128–9.
4 Ira. L. Reiss, *The Social Context of Premarital Sexual Permissiveness*, New York, Holt, Rinehart & Winston, 1967, p. 19.
5 Holbrook uses the term 'sexual fascism' although never fully brings out the political dimensions of his attack on dehumanized sex. See David Holbrook, *Sex and Dehumanization*, London, Pitman, 1972, p. 25.
6 Herbert Marcuse, *Eros and Civilization*, London, Abacus, 1972, p. 23. The main writings of Freud on this theme are: *Civilization and its Discontents* and *The Future of an Illusion*. Both these works are to be found in the *Complete Works* (ed. J. Strachey), vol. 21, London, Hogarth Press, 1961. See also S. Freud, *Character and Culture* (ed. P. Reiff), New York, Collier, 1963.
7 Marcuse, op. cit., p. 45.
8 Men are 'not spontaneously fond of work'. S. Freud, *The Future of an Illusion*, p. 8.
9 See Ch. 1, pp. 29–35.
10 Quoted in Paul A. Robinson, *The Sexual Radicals*, London, Paladin, 1972, p. 29.
11 W. Reich, *The Mass Psychology of Fascism* (new trans.), New York, Farrar, Straus & Giroux, 1970, p. 28.
12 See R. Reiche, *Sexuality and Class Struggle*, London, New Left Books, 1970, pp. 14–15. See also W. Reich, *The Sexual Revolution*, London, Vision Press, 1951.
13 Marcuse, op. cit., p. 42.
14 Ibid.
15 For a sustained critique of Marcuse see A. McIntyre, *Marcuse*, London, Fontana, 1970.
16 Ira L. Reiss, 'How and Why America's Sex Standards are Changing,' in John H. Gagnon and William Simon, *The Sexual Scene*, Chicago, Transaction Books (Aldine), 1970, p. 57.
17 R. V. Sherwin and G. C. Keller, 'Sex on the Campus', in M. Barash and A. Scourby (eds), *Marriage and the Family*, New York, Random House, 1970, pp. 330–50.
18 H. P. Dreitzel (ed.), *Family, Marriage and the Struggle of the Sexes*, New York, Macmillan, 1972, p. 13.
19 Julian Roebuck and S. Lee Spray, 'The Cocktail Lounge: A Study of Heterosexual Relations in a Public Organization', *Am. Journ. Soc.*, vol. 72, 1967, pp. 388–95. I understand from the reviews that Gilbert Bartell's *Group Sex* (New York, Peter H. Wyden, 1971) also presents a similar picture.
20 Reiche, op. cit., pp. 107–8.
21 Ibid., p. 100.
22 Ibid., p. 98.

23 Gillian Freeman, *The Undergrowth of Literature*, London, Nelson, 1967.
24 Holbrook, op. cit., p. 184.
25 Robinson, op. cit., pp. 50–51. See also W. Reich, *The Sexual Revolution*, pp. 7–8.
26 S. Freud, 'Psychoanalysis' (1922), in *Character and Culture*, p. 249.
27 L. Trilling, *Freud and the Crisis of Our Culture*, Boston, Beacon Press, 1955, p. 42.
28 Marcuse appears to express a certain degree of pessimism on this score, particularly in *One-Dimensional Man* (London, Routledge & Kegan Paul, 1964). Sexual liberation is still possible and must be part of any revolutionary struggle but this struggle will be longer, more difficult and its outcome less certain than would appear from a reading of *Eros and Civilization*.
29 W. Reich, *The Sexual Revolution*, especially p. 181.
30 For an excellent account of the revolution at a local level, see William Hinton, *Fanshen*, Harmondsworth, Penguin, 1972.
31 Philip Slater, 'On Social Regression', *Am. Soc. Rev.*, 28, 1963, pp. 339–58. Reprinted in Norman W. Bell and Ezra F. Vogel (eds), *A Modern Introduction to the Family*, rev. ed., New York, Free Press, 1968, pp. 428–41. 'Libidinal diffusion is the social cement which binds living entities together.The more objects an individual can cathect at once, the larger the number of individuals who can co-operate in a joint endeavour.' (Ibid., p. 429.)
32 Freud, *The Future of an Illusion*, p. 6.
33 Engels, op. cit.
34 N. Dennis, F. Henriques and C. Slaughter, *Coal is Our Life*, London, Eyre & Spottiswoode, 1956, p. 231.
35 Reprinted in William J. Goode (ed.), *Readings on the Family and Society*, Englewood Cliffs, Prentice-Hall, 1964, pp. 104–7.
36 See Reiche, op. cit., pp. 54–60.
37 Reiss, op. cit.
38 Robert F. Winch, 'The Functions of Dating in Middle-Class America'. Summarized in Goode, op. cit., pp. 32–3; W. F. Whyte, 'A Slum Sex Code', reprinted in Peter Worsley (ed.), *Problems of Modern Society*, Harmondsworth, Penguin, pp. 351–6; Gerald R. Leslie, *The Family in Social Context*, New York, Oxford University Press, 1967, pp. 414–15.
For similar patterns in a different culture see M. Frielich and L. A. Coser, 'Structural Imbalances of Gratification: The Case of the Caribbean Mating System', *Brit. Journ. Soc.*, vol. 23, 1972 which discusses the 'sex/fame game' in sections of Caribbean society.
39 It has been suggested to me that the scarcity value of the Pirelli calendars provides a particularly striking example of this association between sex and status.
40 Holbrook, op. cit., p. 25.
41 Ibid., p. 3.
42 It need hardly be said that this is still a contentious area in sociology, but there is not the space here to present the main arguments in any detail. For support of the above paragraph see John H. Goldthorpe,

David Lockwood, Frank Bechhofer and Jennifer Platt, *The Affluent Worker: Industrial Attitudes and Behaviour*, Cambridge University Press, 1968; J. H. Westergaard, 'Sociology: The Myth of Classlessness', in Robin Blackburn (ed.), *Ideology in Social Science*, London, Fontana, 1972, pp. 119–63.

43 See Reiche, op. cit., pp. 60–73.

44 To be fair Reiche does give some recognition of the older working-class patterns of resistance.

45 On the sexual dimension of counter-cultural politics see John O'Neill, 'On Body Politics', in Dreitzel, op. cit., pp. 251–67.

46 See Goldthorpe *et al.*, op. cit.

47 Trilling, op. cit., p. 36.

48 Reich, *The Mass Psychology of Fascism*, p. 30. His emphasis.

49 T. Adorno *et al.*, *The Authoritarian Personality*, New York, Harper & Row, 1964; Erich Fromm, *Fear of Freedom*, London, Routledge & Kegan Paul, 1960; M. Horkheimer, 'Authoritarianism and the Family', in R. N. Anshen (ed.), *The Family: Its Function and Destiny*, rev. ed., New York, Harper & Row, 1959, pp. 381–98. For a useful and critical summary of some of these themes see Roger Brown, *Social Psychology*, New York, Free Press, 1965.

50 In a sense the paper by Horkheimer can be said to provide a link between the specific analysis of a particular family structure conducted by Reich and the later accounts, playing down the role of the family, of Marcuse and Reiche. Horkheimer appears to suggest that the family structure which formed the basis for the willing acceptance of fascism was based on the persistence of an old patriarchal form without the substance (property, land, etc.) which gave meaning to that form. There was a contradiction between this increasingly meaningless structure and the increasing rationality of industry and capitalism (Horkheimer, op. cit.).

51 This is part of the criticism of Fernbach, op. cit., p. 92.

52 Reich, *The Mass Psychology of Fascism*, pp. 105–6.

53 For a useful brief discussion of women in 'consumer society' see J. Israel and R. Eliasson, 'Consumption Society, Sex Roles and Sexual Behaviour', in H. P. Dreitzel, op. cit., pp. 173–97, especially pp. 176–8.

54 See Sartre's definition of the Obscene in *Being and Nothingness*, London, Methuen, 1957, pp. 401–2.

55 See John Berger's discussion of women in western art in J. Berger, *Ways of Seeing*, Harmondsworth, Penguin, 1972.

56 Vance Packard, *The Sexual Wilderness*, Longmans, 1968, p. 18.

57 J. A. C. Brown, *Freud and the Post-Freudians*, Harmondsworth, Penguin, 1961, p. 20.

58 E. P. Thompson, *The Making of the English Working Class*, Harmondsworth, Penguin, 1968, especially pp. 400–11.

59 Freeman, op. cit., pp. 66–7. Freeman also considers the writings of Enid Blyton, which again include a fair number of beatings, as possible candidates.

60 Quoted in Robin Wood, *Hitchcock's Films*, London, Zwemmer, 1969, p. 98.

61 Reich approached this when he argued that 'biological' change tended to take place over a longer stretch of time than social change. W. Reich, *The Sexual Revolution*, p. xxiv.
62 For a further discussion on these lines and particularly of the way in which sex expresses and provides a rhetoric for the non-sexual, see the papers by Gagnon and Simon in John H. Gagnon and William Simon (eds), *The Sexual Scene*, Chicago, Transaction Books, 1970.
63 See the critical comments by McIntyre, op. cit., p. 47.
64 It should be noted that the word 'dehumanized' may have one of two connotations. It might refer to something that falls into the animal side of the animal/human distinction or, alternatively, into the machine (or alienated man) side of the machine/human distinction. Much dehumanized sex would appear to be machine based rather than animal based—consider the wide variety of mechanical images for sexual intercourse and for the penis, images which also derive from the male orientated world of work.
65 I have borrowed the title, although little else, from Frederik L. Polak, *The Image of the Future*, New York, Oceana Publications, 1961.
66 For an account of the way in which 'motives' for sexual offences are derived from the available and changing stock of motives and are deemed more or less legitimate by authorities, see Laurie Taylor, 'The Significance and Interpretation of Replies to Motivational Questions: The Case of Sex Offenders', *Soc.*, vol. 6, no. 1, 1972, pp. 23–39.
67 See, for example, Albert Reiss Jnr, 'The Social Integration of Peers and Queers', in Howard S. Becker (ed.), *The Other Side*, New York, Free Press, 1964, pp. 181–210.
68 Reich, *The Sexual Revolution*, p. 115.
69 De Beauvoir, *Old Age*, especially pp. 320–1.
70 C. Arensberg and S. T. Kimball, *Family and Community in Ireland*, Cambridge, Mass., Harvard University Press, 1948.
71 See the brief but stimulating discussion about relationship between the erotic sphere and religion in Hans Gerth and C. Wright Mills, *From Max Weber*, London, Routledge & Kegan Paul, 1948, pp. 343–350. In these few pages Weber anticipated much of the argument presented by the neo-Freudians discussed here.
72 Gerth and Mills, op. cit., p. 349.
73 Just as some decades ago Parsons pointed to the professionalization of the role of the housewife, so, today, it is almost possible to talk of the professionalization of sexuality. This is not merely a matter of the increasing number of 'experts' who set sexual standards and definitions of good or bad sex but also of the increasing number of different traditions that find their point of convergence in the bedroom from Eastern mysticism and Yoga, to Masters and Johnson and Freudian, neo-Freudian or anti-Freudian psychology.
74 Reiche, op. cit., p. 28.

Conclusion

1 Percy Cohen, *Modern Social Theory*, London, Heinemann, 1968, p. 5.
2 This image does appear in some of Marcuse's later writings.
3 Max Weber, *The Protestant Ethic and the Spirit of Capitalism*, London, Unwin, 1930, p. 182.
4 Carle C. Zimmerman, 'The Future of the Family in America', *Journ. Mar. Fam.*, vol. 34, no. 2, 1972, pp. 323–33. This article contains references to Zimmerman's earlier works. For a useful summary see Gerald R. Leslie, *The Family in Social Context*, New York, Oxford University Press, 1967, pp. 223–30.
5 Cooper, although usually associated with Laing, might be included in this group in that his attack on the family is linked with a consideration of the communal alternative. See David Cooper, *Death of the Family*, Harmondsworth, Penguin, 1972.
6 Peter L. Berger and Hansfried Kellner, 'Marriage and the Construction of Reality: An Exercise in the Microsociology of Knowledge', reprinted in the Open University, School and Society Course Team, *School and Society*, London, Routledge & Kegan Paul, 1971, pp. 23–31.
7 Ibid., p. 23.
8 Peter L. Berger and Thomas Luckmann, *The Social Construction of Reality*, New York, Doubleday Anchor Books, 1967, pp. 129–37.
9 Alice Rossi, 'Naming Children in Middle-Class Families', *Am. Soc. Rev.*, vol. 30, 1965, pp. 499–513.
10 See the use of this as an analytical tool in the cases outlined by Henry and Hess and Handel. Jules Henry, *Pathways to Madness*, London, Jonathan Cape, 1972; R. D. Hess and G. Handel, *Family Worlds*, Chicago University Press, 1950.
11 The title of a book by Bossard and Boll. To date this is one of the few works to examine systematically this qualitative aspect of family living. J. H. S. Bossard and E. S. Boll, *Ritual in Family Living*, Philadelphia, Pennsylvania University Press, 1950.
12 I once observed a family where, periodically, the father would pick up the evening paper and say 'I see old so and so's dead'. The wife would say 'who's that' and he would reply 'I don't know'.
13 J. R. Seeley, R. A. Sim and E. W. Loosley, *Crestwood Heights*, Toronto University Press, 1956. See also Henry, op. cit., for some discussion of the use of space within modern American families. Bollnow has some suggestive remarks to make about the dwelling in O. F. Bollnow, 'Lived-Space', included in N. Lawrence and D. O'Connor (eds), *Readings in Existential Phenomenology*, Englewood Cliffs, Prentice-Hall, 1967, pp. 180–2.
14 See Ch. 1, pp. 53–4.
15 The traditional association of the 'key of the door' with reaching the age of majority may not now fully accord with reality but still serves us as a reminder of this fact.
16 See Ch. 4, pp. 111–13.
17 See the series of articles in the *Sunday Times* on 28 January, 4 February

and 11 February 1973. These articles draw on much current sociological literature, including the work of the Pahls and the Rapoports.

18 Richard Sennett, *Families Against the City*, Cambridge, Mass., Harvard University Press, 1970.

19 J. Ponsioen, 'Qualitative Changes in Family Life in the Netherlands', in C. C. Harris (ed.), *Readings in Kinship in Urban Society*, Oxford, Pergamon, 1970.

20 For a useful examination of some of the themes raised in this section see Donald W. Ball, 'The "Family" as a *Sociological* Problem. Conceptualization of the Taken-for-Granted as Prologue to Social Problems Analysis', *Soc. Prob.*, vol. 19, 1971–2, pp. 295–307.

21 Or to put the same point another way, nowhere is this more obscurely seen than in the context of the family.

22 For a similar line of argument see Warren G. Bennis and Philip E. Slater, *The Temporary Society*, New York, Harper & Row, 1968, ch. 2.

23 Keith Thomas, 'Women and the Civil War Sects', *Past and Present*, 1958, pp. 42–62.

24 See Ch. 1, pp. 54–6 and Ch. 5, p. 135.

25 T. Caplow, *Two Against One*, Englewood Cliffs, Prentice-Hall, 1968, especially chs 6 and 7, pp. 62–113.

26 For a more detailed discussion see Ch. 4, especially pp. 108–11.

27 Wilfrid Desan, *The Marxism of Jean-Paul Sartre*, New York, Doubleday Anchor Books, 1966, p. 66.

28 Similar but not identical, for the Weberian emphasis on interpretive understanding has often been linked with the development of 'ideal types', something alien to the spirit of Sartre's existential approach.

29 Desan, op. cit., p. 57.

30 David Cooper, in R. D. Laing and D. Cooper, *Reason and Violence*, London, Tavistock, 1964, pp. 51–2.

31 Desan, op. cit., p. 269.

32 For a case study on these lines see D. H. J. Morgan, 'The British Association Scandal: The Effects of Publicity on a Research Project', *Soc. Rev.*, vol. 20, no. 2, 1972, pp. 185–206.

33 Seeley *et al.*, op cit.

34 The notion of 'identity' which may be used in conjunction with 'project' involves a dialectic between self-realization and mutual communal realization. It can be seen as a bridge, a sense of continuity, linking what an individual was to what he is about to become. See Rainwater (using Erikson's notion of identity) in G. Handel (ed.), *Psychosocial Interior of the Family*, London, Allen & Unwin, 1968, p. 387.

35 The concept of 'spiralist' was first developed by Watson and outlined in his paper 'Social Mobility and Social Class in Industrial Communities', in Max Gluckman (ed.), *Closed Systems and Open Minds: The Limits of Naivety in Social Anthropology*, Oliver & Boyd, 1964. It has proved to be particularly useful in analysing the interaction between middle-class careers and family life style. See Colin Bell, *Middle Class Families*, London, Routledge & Kegan Paul, 1968;

Stephen Edgell, 'Spiralists: Their Careers and Family Lives,' *Brit. Journ. Soc.*, vol. 21, 1970, pp. 314–23.

36 Seeley *et al.*, op. cit., p. 135. Their emphasis.

37 Ackerman provides a brief but useful account of the multiplicity of meanings a child may have for a father. See Nathan W. Ackerman, *The Psychodynamics of Family Life*, New York, Basic Books, 1958, p. 181.

38 See also D. Aberle and K. Naegele, 'Middle-Class Fathers' Occupational Role and Attitudes towards Children', in Norman W. Bell and Ezra F. Vogel, *A Modern Introduction to the Family*, rev. ed., New York, Free Press, 1968, pp. 188–98.

39 James W. Ramey, 'Communes, Group Marriage and the Upper Middle Class', *Journ. Mar. Fam.*, vol. 34, no. 4, 1972, pp. 647–55.

40 Betty Friedan, *The Feminine Mystique*, Harmondsworth, Penguin, 1965.

41 Mirra Komarovsky, *Blue-Collar Marriage*, New York, Random House, 1962.

42 Robert Dubin, 'Industrial Workers' Worlds: A Study of the "Central Life Interests" of Industrial Workers', in Arnold M. Rose (ed.), *Human Behaviour and Social Processes*, London, Routledge & Kegan Paul, 1962, pp. 247–66.

43 'Aspirations for the future find their fullest expression in parental hopes for children'. (Komarovsky, op. cit., p. 287.) See also J. H. Goldthorpe *et al.*, *The Affluent Worker in the Class Structure*, Cambridge University Press, 1969, pp. 129–34.

44 For example the useful paper by John P. Spiegel, 'The Resolution of Role Conflict in the Family', in Bell and Vogel, op. cit., pp. 391–411.

45 Philippe Ariès, *Centuries of Childhood*, New York, Random House, 1962.

46 Sennett, op. cit., p. 66.

47 Simone de Beauvoir, *Old Age*, London, André Deutsch and Weidenfeld & Nicolson, 1972.

48 Ibid., pp. 204–6.

49 The preceding remarks have, it will be noted, been influenced by some of the newer ethnomethodological approaches to the 'family'. To date there has been little systematic attention paid to this institution by ethnomethodologists; perhaps the most accessible papers are those by Speier. See Matthew Speier, 'Some Conversational Problems for Interactional Analysis', in David Sudnow (ed.), *Studies in Social Interaction*, New York, Collier-Macmillan, 1972, and 'The Everyday World of the Child', in J. Douglas (ed.), *Understanding Everyday* Life, London, Routledge & Kegan Paul, 1971. The differences that I have with the ethnomethodological project will, I hope, become apparent in the next few paragraphs.

50 R. D. Laing, *The Divided Self*, Harmondsworth, Penguin, 1960; R. D. Laing and A. Esterson, *Sanity, Madness and the Family*, Harmondsworth, Penguin, 1970; A. Esterson, *The Leaves of Spring*, Harmondsworth, Penguin, 1972. For a fuller discussion see Ch. 4.

51 Jules Henry, *Culture Against Man*, New York, Random House, 1963, chs 5, 6, 9 and 10; *Pathways to Madness*.
52 Hess and Handel, op. cit.
53 R. Coles, *Children of Crisis*, Boston, Little, Brown, 1964; *Migrants, Sharecroppers, Mountaineers*, Boston, Little, Brown, 1967; *The South Goes North*, Boston, Little, Brown, 1967. O. Lewis, *Five Families*, New York, Mentor, 1959; *The Children of Sanchez*, London, Secker & Warburg, 1962; *La Vida*, New York, Random House, 1965. For a brief methodological statement see O. Lewis, 'An Anthropological Approach to Family Studies', *Am. Journ. Soc.*, vol. 55, 1950, pp. 468–475.
54 O. Lewis, 'An Anthropological Approach . . .'.
55 There is a possible danger here in that poverty may be seen as being a problem of the poor themselves instead of being viewed in terms of the society as a whole.
56 Ariès, op. cit.
57 Sennett, op. cit.; Anderson, *Family Structure*. I have benefited from conversations with Colin Creighton who is at present carrying out investigations into the nineteenth-century working-class family at the University of Hull.
58 See the brief examination of novels with a family inter-generational theme in Viola Klein, *The Feminine Character*, London, Kegan Paul, Trench & Trubner, 1946. Also Millett's examination of the writings of Lawrence, Henry Miller, Mailer and Genet in Kate Millett, *Sexual Politics*, New York, Doubleday, 1970.
59 In this criticism I am including my own contribution to a textbook. See Peter Worsley (ed.), *Introducing Sociology*, Harmondsworth, Penguin, 1970, ch. 3.
60 See Kingsley Davis, 'The Sociology of Parent-Youth Conflict', *Am. Soc. Rev.*, vol. 5, 1940, pp. 523–35. Reprinted in Rose L. Coser (ed.), *The Family: Its Structure and Functions*, New York, St Martin's Press, 1964, pp. 455–71.
61 Alvin W. Gouldner, 'Metaphysical Pathos and the Theory of Bureaucracy', *Am. Pol. Sc. Rev.*, vol. 40, 1955, pp. 496–507. Reprinted in A. Etzioni (ed.), *Complex Organizations*, Holt, Rinehart & Winston, 1961, pp. 71–82.
62 See Huber's editorial to 'Changing Women in a Changing World', a special edition of the *Am. Journ. Soc.*, vol. 78, no. 4, January 1973.
63 For an extensive discussion of ways of handling predictions about the future see Daniel Bell, 'Twelve Modes of Prediction', in J. Gould (ed.), *Penguin Survey of the Social Sciences*, Harmondsworth, Penguin, 1965, pp. 96–127.
64 Frederick H. Stoller, 'The Intimate Network of Families as a New Structure', in Herbert A. Otto (ed.), *The Family in Search of a Future*, New York, Appleton-Century-Crofts, 1970, pp. 145–59.
65 Literature on modern communal experiments, at least within sociology, is still sparse. Interested readers should consult Ron E. Roberts, *The New Communes*, Englewood Cliffs, Prentice-Hall, 1971; R. V. Speck, *The New Families*, London, Tavistock, 1972. Also, J. Downing,

'The Tribal Family and the Society of Awakening', in Otto (ed.), op. cit., pp. 119–35.

66 There are dangers in the reification of the notion of 'commune' just as there are dangers in the reification of the notion of family. The material listed in the last footnote, sparse though it is, draws our attention to the variety of communal experiments and the variety of ideological bases for these experiments, from the radical psychoanalytical approaches of Laing and Cooper to the work of Skinner, from Zen Buddhism to urban guerilla movements.

67 For similar normative assessments see Speck, op. cit., pp. 176–85, and Mitchell, op. cit., pp. 150–1.

Bibliography

ABERLE, DAVID F. and NAEGELE, KASPAR D., 'Middle-Class Fathers' Occupational Role and Attitudes towards Children', in BELL and VOGEL, pp. 188–98.

ACKER, JOAN, 'Women and Social Stratification: A Case of Intellectual Sexism', *Am. Journ. Soc.*, 1973.

ACKERMAN, NATHAN W., *The Psychodynamics of Family Life*, New York, Basic Books, 1958.

ADAMS, B. N., *Kinship in an Urban Setting*, Chicago, Markham, 1968.

ADAMS, R. N., 'An Inquiry into the Nature of the Family', in GOODY, pp. 19–37.

ADORNO, T. W. *et al.*, *The Authoritarian Personality*, New York, Harper & Row, 1950.

ANDERSON, MICHAEL, *Family Structure in Nineteenth Century Lancashire*, Cambridge University Press, 1971.

ANDERSON, MICHAEL (ed.), *Sociology of the Family*, Harmondsworth, Penguin, 1971.

ANSHEN, R. N. (ed.), *The Family: Its Function and Destiny*, rev. ed., New York, Harper, 1959.

ARENSBERG, C. and KIMBALL, S. T., *Family and Community in Ireland*, Cambridge, Mass., Harvard University Press, 1948.

ARIÈS, PHILIPPE, *Centuries of Childhood*, New York, Random House, 1962.

ARON, RAYMOND, *Progress and Disillusion: The Dialectics of Modern Society*, Harmondsworth, Penguin, 1972.

ATKINSON, DICK, *Orthodox Consensus and Radical Alternative*, London, Heinemann, 1971.

BALDWIN, ALFRED L., 'The Parsonian Theory of Personality', in BLACK, pp. 153–90.

BALES, R. F. and SLATER, P. E., 'Role Differentiation in Small Groups', in PARSONS and BALES, pp. 259–306.

BALL, DONALD W., 'The "Family" as a *Sociological* Problem. Conceptualization of the Taken-for-Granted as Prologue to Social Problems Analysis', *Soc. Prob.*, vol. 19, 1971–2, pp. 295–307.

BANTON, MICHAEL (ed.), *The Social Anthropology of Complex Societies*, London, Tavistock, 1966.

BARASH, M. and SCOURBY, A. (eds), *Marriage and the Family*, New York, Random House, 1970.

BARKER, DIANA, 'The Confetti Ritual', *New Soc.*, 22 June 1972, pp. 614–17.

BARNES, J. A., 'Discussion: Physical and Social Kinship', *Phil. of Sc.*, vol. 28, 1961, pp. 296–9.

BARNES, J. A., 'Discussion: Physical and Social Facts in Anthropology', *Phil. of Sc.*, vol. 31, 1964, pp. 294–7.

BARNES, J. A., *Three Styles in the Study of Kinship*, London, Tavistock, 1971.

BARR, JOHN (ed.), *The Environmental Handbook*, London, Pan, 1971.

BARTELL, GILBERT, *Group Sex: A Scientist's Eyewitness Report on the American Way of Swinging*, New York, Peter H. Wyden, 1971.

BATTLE-SISTER, ANN, 'Conjectures of the Female Culture Question', *Journ. Mar. Fam.*, vol. 33, no. 3, August 1971, pp. 411–20.

BAUM, MARTHA, 'Love, Marriage and the Division of Labour', in DREITZEL, pp. 83–106.

BEATTIE, J. H. M., 'Kinship and Social Anthropology', *Man*, vol. 64, 1964, pp. 101–3.

BEBEL, A., *Women: Past, Present and Future*, London, Wm. Reeves, n.d.

BECKER, HOWARD S. (ed.), *The Other Side*, New York, Free Press, 1964.

BELL, COLIN, *Middle-Class Families*, London, Routledge & Kegan Paul, 1968.

BELL, COLIN, 'Social Anthropologists on Kinship' (review article), *Soc.*, vol. 6, no. 3, 1972, pp. 457–61.

BELL, DANIEL, 'Twelve Modes of Prediction', in GOULD, pp. 96–127.

BELL, NORMAN W. and VOGEL, EZRA F. (eds), *A Modern Introduction to the Family*, rev. ed., New York, Free Press, 1968.

BELL, WENDELL, 'Familism and Suburbanisation: One Test of the Social Choice Hypothesis', in EDWARDS, pp. 101–11.

BENNIS, WARREN G. and SLATER, PHILIP E., *The Temporary Society*, New York, Harper & Row, 1968.

BERGER, BENNETT M., HACKETT, BRUCE M. and MILLAR, R. MERVYN, 'Child-Rearing Practices in the Communal Family', in DREITZEL, pp. 271–300.

BERGER, JOHN, *Ways of Seeing*, Harmondsworth, Penguin, 1972.

BERGER, PETER L. and KELLNER, HANSFRIED, 'Marriage and the Construction of Reality: An Exercise in the Microsociology of Knowledge', in OPEN UNIVERSITY (School and Society Unit Team), pp. 23–31.

BERGER, PETER L. and LUCKMANN, THOMAS, *The Social Construction of Reality*, New York, Doubleday Anchor Books, 1967.

BETÉILLE, ANDRÉ (ed.), *Social Inequality*, Harmondsworth, Penguin, 1969.

BIRMINGHAM, STEPHEN, *Our Crowd: The Great Jewish Families of New York*, New York, Dell, 1967.

BLACK, MAX (ed.), *The Social Theories of Talcott Parsons*, Englewood Cliffs, Prentice-Hall, 1961.

BLACKBURN, ROBIN, 'A Brief Guide to Bourgeois Ideology', in COCKBURN and BLACKBURN, pp. 163–213.

BLACKBURN, ROBIN (ed.), *Ideology in Social Science*, London, Fontana, 1972.

BLUMER, HERBERT, *Symbolic Interactionism: Perspective and Method*, Englewood Cliffs, Prentice-Hall, 1969.

BOLLNOW, O. F., 'Lived-Space', in LAWRENCE and O'CONNOR, pp. 178–186.

BOSSARD, JAMES H. S. and BOLL, ELEANOR STOKER, *Ritual in Family Living*, Philadelphia, Pennsylvania University Press, 1950.

BOSSARD, JAMES H. S., and BOLL, ELEANOR STOKER, *The Large Family System*, Philadelphia, Pennsylvania University Press, 1956.

BOSSARD, JAMES H. S. and SANGER, W. P., 'The Large Family System: A Research Report', *Am. Soc. Rev.*, vol. 17, 1952, pp. 3–9.

BOTT, ELIZABETH, *Family and Social Network*, 2nd ed., London, Tavistock, 1971.

BOURDOURIS, JAMES, 'Homicide and the Family,' *Journ. Mar. Fam.*, vol. 33, no. 4, 1971.

BOYERS, R. and ORRILL, R. (eds), *Laing and Anti-Psychiatry*, Harmondsworth, Penguin, 1972.

BRIM, ORVILLE G., JNR, 'Family Structure and Sex-Role Learning by Children', in BELL and VOGEL, pp. 526–40.

BROWN, J. A. C., *Freud and the Post-Freudians*, Harmondsworth, Penguin, 1961.

BROWN, JAMES S., SCHWARTZWELLER, HARRY K. and MANGALAM, JOSEPH J., 'Kentucky Mountain Migration and the Stem Family', in BELL and VOGEL, pp. 150–8.

BROWN, ROGER, *Social Psychology*, New York, Free Press, 1965.

CANADIAN DEPT OF LABOUR: WOMEN'S BUREAU, *Women's Bureau '69*, 1970.

CAPLOW, T., *Two Against One*, Englewood Cliffs, Prentice-Hall, 1968.

CHINOY, ELY, *Society*, 2nd ed., New York, Random House, 1967.

COALE, A. J. (ed.), *Aspects of the Analysis of Family Structure*, Princeton University Press, 1965.

COCKBURN, A. and BLACKBURN, R. (eds), *Student Power*, Harmondsworth, Penguin, 1969.

COHEN, CHARLOTTE BONNY, 'Experiment in Freedom-China', in MORGAN, ROBIN, pp. 385–417.

COHEN, PERCY, *Modern Social Theory*, London, Heinemann, 1968.

COLEMAN, JAMES S., 'Relational Analysis: The Study of Social Organisations with Survey Methods', in ETZIONI, pp. 441–53.

COLES, ROBERT, *Children of Crisis*, Boston, Little, Brown, 1964.

COLES, ROBERT, *Migrants, Sharecroppers, Mountaineers*, Boston, Little, Brown, 1967.

COLES, ROBERT, *The South Goes North*, Boston, Little, Brown, 1967.

COLES, ROBERT, *Uprooted Children*, Pittsburgh University Press, 1970.

COLLINS, RANDALL, 'A Conflict Theory of Sexual Stratification', in DREITZEL, pp. 53–79.

COOPER, DAVID (ed.), *Dialectics of Liberation*, Harmondsworth, Penguin, 1968.

COOPER, DAVID, *The Death of the Family*, Harmondsworth, Penguin, 1972.

COSER, ROSE L. (ed.), *The Family: Its Structure and Functions*, New York, St Martin's Press, 1964.

COULSON, M., 'Role: A Redundant Concept in Sociology?', in JACKSON, pp. 107–28.

CRANSTON, M. (ed.), *The New Left*, London, Bodley Head, 1970.

CUMMING, E. and SCHNEIDER, D. M., 'Sibling Solidarity: A Property of American Kinship', *Am. Anth.*, vol. 63, 1961.

DAHLSTROM, E. (ed.), *The Changing Roles of Men and Women*, London, Duckworth, 1967.

DANZIGER, KURT, *Socialization*, Harmondsworth, Penguin, 1971.

DAVIS, KINGSLEY, 'The Sociology of Parent–Youth Conflict', in COSER, pp. 455–71.

DAWE, ALAN, 'The Two Sociologies', *Brit. Journ. Soc.*, vol. 21, 1970, pp. 207–18.

DAWE, ALAN, 'The Role of Experience in the Construction of Social Theory: An Essay on Reflexive Sociology', *Soc. Rev.*, vol. 21, no. 1, 1973, pp. 25–55.

DE BEAUVOIR, SIMONE, *The Second Sex*, Harmondsworth, Penguin, 1972.

DE BEAUVOIR, SIMONE, *Old Age*, London, André Deutsch and Weidenfeld & Nicolson, 1972.

DENNIS, N., HENRIQUES, F. and SLAUGHTER, C., *Coal is Our Life*, London, Eyre & Spottiswoode, 1956.

DESAN, WILFRID, *The Marxism of Jean-Paul Sartre*, New York, Doubleday Anchor Books, 1966.

DOUGLAS, J. (ed.), *Understanding Everyday Life*, London, Routledge & Kegan Paul, 1971.

DOUGLAS, MARY, *Purity and Danger*, Harmondsworth, Penguin, 1970.

DOWNING, JOSEPH, 'The Tribal Family and the Society of Awakening', in OTTO, pp. 119–35.

DREITZEL, HANS PETER (ed.), *Family, Marriage and the Struggle of the Sexes* (Recent Sociology No. 4), New York, Macmillan, 1972.

DUBIN, ROBERT, 'Industrial Workers' Worlds: A Study of the "Central Life Interests" of Industrial Workers', in ROSE, pp. 247–66.

DURKHEIM, EMILE, 'La Famille conjugale', *Revue Philosophique*, vol. 41, 1921, pp. 1–14.

EDGELL, STEPHEN, 'Spiralists: Their Careers and Family Lives', *Brit. Journ. Soc.*, vol. 21, 1970, pp. 314–23.

EDWARDS, JOHN N. (ed.), *The Family and Change*, New York, Knopf, 1969.

ENGELS, FREDERICK, *The Origins of the Family, Private Property and the State*, Moscow, Foreign Languages Publishing House, 1954.

ENGELS, FREDERICK, *The Condition of the Working Class in England*, London, Panther, 1969.

EPSTEIN, C. F., 'Positive Effects of the Multiple Negative: Explaining the Success of Black Professional Women', *Am. Journ. Soc.*, 1973.

ERIKSON, ERIK H., 'Inner and Outer Space: Reflections on Womanhood', in BELL and VOGEL, pp. 442–63.

ESTERSON, AARON, *The Leaves of Spring*, Harmondsworth, Penguin, 1972.

ETZIONI, A. (ed.), *Complex Organizations*, New York, Holt, Rinehart & Winston, 1961.

ETZKOWITZ, HENRY, 'The Male Sister: Sexual Separation of Labor in Society', *Journ. Mar. Fam.*, vol. 33, no. 3, 1971, pp. 431–4.

EVANS-PRITCHARD, E. E., 'The Comparative Method in Social Anthropology', in *The Position of Women in Primitive Society*, London, Faber & Faber, 1965.

FALLDING, HAROLD, 'Only One Sociology', *Brit. Journ. Soc.*, vol. 23, 1972, pp. 93–101.

FANON, FRANTZ, *A Dying Colonialism*, Harmondsworth, Penguin, 1970.

FARBER, BERNARD, *Kinship and Class*, New York, Basic Books, 1971.

FAVA, SYLVIA FLEIS, 'The Status of Women in Professional Sociology', *Am. Soc. Rev.*, vol. 25, no. 2, 1960, pp. 271–6.

FERNBACH, DAVID, 'Sexual Oppression and Political Practice', *New Left Rev.*, no. 64, November/December 1970, pp. 87–96.

FIRESTONE, SHULAMITH, *The Dialectic of Sex*, London, Paladin, 1972.

FIRESTONE, SHULAMITH and KOEDT, ANNE (eds), *Notes from the Second Year*, New York, Radical Feminism, 1970.

FIRTH, R., *Two Studies of Kinship in London*, London, Athlone Press, 1956.

FIRTH, R., HUBERT, J. and FORGE, A., *Families and their Relatives*, London, Routledge & Kegan Paul, 1969.

FLETCHER, RONALD, *The Family and Marriage in Britain*, rev. ed., Harmondsworth, Penguin, 1966.

FOGARTY, M. P., RAPOPORT, R. and RAPOPORT, R., *Sex, Career and Family*, London, Allen & Unwin, 1971.

FORTES, M., *Kinship and the Social Order*, London, Routledge & Kegan Paul, 1970.

FOX, R., *Kinship and Marriage*, Harmondsworth, Penguin, 1967.

FRANKENBERG, R., *Communities in Britain*, Harmondsworth, Penguin, 1966.

FRANKENBERG, R., 'Educating the Educators', *China Now*, no. 12, June 1971, p. 2.

FREEMAN, GILLIAN, *The Undergrowth of Literature*, London, Nelson, 1967.

FREEMAN, JO, 'The Women's Liberation Movement: Its Origins, Structures and Ideas', in DREITZEL (ed.), pp. 201–16.

FREEMAN, JO, 'The Origins of the Women's Liberation Movement', *Am. Journ. Soc.*, 1973.

FREEMAN, J. D., 'On the Concept of Kindred', *Journ. Royal Anth. Inst.*, 1961, pp. 192–220.

FREUD, S., 'Psychoanalysis' (1922), in *Character and Culture* (ed. P. Reiff), New York, Collier Books, 1963.

FREUD, S., 'The Resistance to Psychoanalysis', in *Character and Culture*, op. cit.

FREUD, S., 'Civilization and its Discontents', in *Complete Works* (ed. James Strachey), London, Hogarth Press, vol. 21, 1961.

FREUD, S., 'The Future of an Illusion', in *Complete Works*, vol. 21, op. cit.

FRIEDAN, BETTY, *The Feminine Mystique*, Harmondsworth, Penguin, 1965.

FRIELICH, M. and COSER, L. A., 'Structural Imbalances of Gratification: The Case of the Caribbean Mating System', *Brit. Journ. Soc.*, vol. 23, 1972, pp. 1–19.

FROMM, ERICH, *Fear of Freedom*, London, Routledge & Kegan Paul, 1960.

GAGNON, JOHN H. and SIMON, WILLIAM (ed.), *The Sexual Scene*, Chicago, Transaction Books (Aldine), 1970.

GARIGUE, PHILIPPE, *La Vie familiale des Canadiens français*, Presses de l'Université de Montréal, 1970.

GEIGER, H. KENT, *The Family in the Soviet Union*, Cambridge, Mass., Harvard University Press, 1968.

GELLNER, E., 'Ideal Language Kinship Structure', *Phil. of Sc.*, vol. 24, 1957, pp. 235–42.

GELLNER, E., 'The Concept of Kinship', *Phil. of Sc.*, vol. 27, 1960, pp. 187–204.

GELLNER, E., 'Nature and Society in Social Anthropology', *Phil. of Sc.*, vol. 30, 1963, pp. 236–51.

GERTH, H. H. and MILLS, C. WRIGHT, *From Max Weber*, London, Routledge & Kegan Paul, 1948.

GIBSON, GEOFFREY, 'Kin Family Networks: Overheralded Structures in Past Conceptualizations of Family Functioning', *Journ. Mar. Fam.*, vol. 34, no. 1, February 1972, pp. 13–23.

GLUCKMAN, MAX, *Custom and Conflict in Africa*, Oxford, Blackwell, 1956.

GLUCKMAN, MAX (ed.), *Closed Systems and Open Minds*, London, Oliver & Boyd, 1964.

GOLDTHORPE, JOHN H., LOCKWOOD, DAVID, BECHHOFER, FRANK and PLATT, JENNIFER, *The Affluent Worker: Industrial Attitudes and Behaviour*, Cambridge University Press, 1968.

GOLDTHORPE, JOHN H., LOCKWOOD, DAVID, BECHHOFER, FRANK and PLATT, JENNIFER, *The Affluent Worker in the Class Structure*, Cambridge University Press, 1969.

GOODE, W. J., 'The Sociology of the Family', in MERTON, BROOM and COTTRELL, vol. 1, pp. 178–96.

GOODE, W. J., 'A Deviant Case: Illegitimacy in the Caribbean', in COSER, pp. 19–35.

GOODE, W. J., *The Family*, Englewood Cliffs, Prentice-Hall, 1964.

GOODE, W. J. (ed.), *Readings on the Family and Society*, Englewood Cliffs, Prentice-Hall, 1964.

GOODE, W. J., *World Revolution and Family Patterns*, New York, Free Press, 1970.

GOODE, W. J., 'Force and Violence in the Family', *Journ. Mar. Fam.*, vol. 33, no. 4, November 1971.

GOODY, J., 'Incest and Adultery', in GOODY, pp. 64–81.

GOODY, J. (ed.), *Kinship*, Harmondsworth, Penguin, 1971.

GOUGH, KATHLEEN, 'The Origins of the Family', *Journ. Mar. Fam.*, vol. 33, no. 4, 1971, pp. 760–71.

GOULD, J. (ed.), *Penguin Survey of the Social Sciences*, Harmondsworth, Penguin, 1965.

GOULDNER, ALVIN W., 'Metaphysical Pathos and the Theory of Bureaucracy', in ETZIONI, pp. 71–82.

GOULDNER, ALVIN W., *The Coming Crisis of Western Sociology*, London, Routledge & Kegan Paul, 1970.

GRANT, MAGGIE, 'Down with Women's Lib!', *Canadian Magazine*, 1 August 1970.

GREEN, ARNOLD W., 'The Middle-Class Male Child and Neurosis', in BELL and VOGEL, pp. 618–27.

GREER, GERMAINE, *The Female Eunuch*, London, Paladin, 1971.

HACKER, ANDREW, 'Sociology and Ideology', in BLACK, pp. 289–310.

HACKER, HELEN M., 'Women as a Minority Group', *Soc. For.*, vol. 30, October 1951, pp. 60–9.

HANDEL, G. (ed.), *Psychosocial Interior of the Family*, London, Allen & Unwin, 1968.

HARDIN, GARRETT, 'The Tragedy of the Commons', in BARR, pp. 47–65.

HARRIS, C. C. (ed.), *Readings in Kinship in Urban Society*, Oxford, Pergamon, 1970.

HARRIS, MARVIN, *The Rise of Anthropological Theory*, London, Routledge & Kegan Paul, 1969.

HENRY, JULES, *Culture Against Man*, New York, Random House, 1963.

HENRY, JULES, *Pathways to Madness*, London, Jonathan Cape, 1972.

HESS, R. D. and HANDEL, G., *Family Worlds*, Chicago University Press, 1950.

HINTON, WILLIAM, *Fanshen*, Harmondsworth, Penguin, 1972.

HOLBROOK, D., 'R. D. Laing and the Death Circuit', *Encounter*, August 1968, pp. 41–2.

HOLBROOK, D., 'Madness to Blame Society?', *Twentieth Century*, 1969, pp. 29–32.

HOLBROOK, D., *Sex and Dehumanization*, London, Pitman, 1972.

HORKHEIMER, M., 'Authoritarianism and the Family', in ANSHEN, pp. 381–398.

HUBER, JOAN (ed.), 'Changing Women in a Changing World', special issue of *Am. Journ. Soc.*, vol. 78, no. 4, January 1973.

ISRAEL, JOACHIM and ELIASSON, ROSEMARI, 'Consumption Society, Sex Roles and Sexual Behaviour', in DREITZEL, pp. 173–97.

JACKSON, J. A. (ed.), *Role* (*Sociological Studies 4*), Cambridge University Press, 1972.

JANEWAY, ELIZABETH, *Man's World, Woman's Place*, New York, Morrow, 1971.

JOFFE, CAROLE, 'Sex Role Socialization and the Nursery School: As the Twig is Bent', *Journ. Mar. Fam.*, vol. 33, no. 3, August 1971, pp. 467–75.

KIRSCHNER, B. F., 'Introducing Students to Women's Place in Society', *Am. Journ. Soc.*, January 1973.

KLEIN, VIOLA, *The Feminine Character*, London, Kegan Paul, Trench & Trubner, 1946.

KNUDSEN, D. D., 'The Declining Status of Women', *Soc. For.*, vol. 48, 1969, pp. 153–93.

KOMAROVSKY, M., *Blue-Collar Marriage*, New York, Random House, 1962.

KUHN, T., *The Structure of Scientific Revolutions*, Chicago University Press, 1962.

LAING, R. D., *The Divided Self*, Harmondsworth, Penguin, 1960.

LAING, R. D., 'Series and Nexus in the Family', *New Left Rev.*, no. 15, 1962, pp. 7–14.

LAING, R. D., *Politics of Experience and the Bird of Paradise*, Harmondsworth, Penguin, 1967.

LAING, R. D., 'Family and Individual Structure', in LOMAS.

LAING, R. D., *The Politics of the Family and Other Essays*, London, Tavistock, 1971.

LAING, R. D. and COOPER, D., *Reason and Violence*, London, Tavistock, 1964.

LAING, R. D. and ESTERSON, A., *Sanity, Madness and the Family*, Harmondsworth, Penguin, 1970.

LAING, R. D., PHILLIPSON, H. and LEE, A. R., *Interpersonal Perception*, London, Tavistock, 1966.

LAWRENCE, N. and O'CONNOR, D. (eds), *Readings in Existential Phenomenology*, Englewood Cliffs, Prentice-Hall, 1967.

LESLIE, GERALD R., *The Family in Social Context*, New York, Oxford University Press, 1967.

LE VINE, ROBERT A., 'Intergenerational Tension in Extended Family Structures in Africa', in SHANAS and STREIB, pp. 188–204.

LÉVI-STRAUSS, C., 'The Principles of Kinship', in GOODY (ed.), pp. 47–63.

LEVY, MARION J., JNR, 'Some Hypotheses about the Family', in DREITZEL, pp. 23–41.

LEWIS, OSCAR, 'An Anthropological Approach to Family Studies', *Am. Journ. Soc.*, vol. 55, 1950.

LEWIS, OSCAR, *Five Families*, New York, Mentor, 1959.

LEWIS, OSCAR, *The Children of Sanchez*, London, Secker & Warburg, 1962.

LEWIS, OSCAR, *La Vida*, New York, Random House, 1965.

LISON-TOLOSANA, C., 'The Family in a Spanish Town', in HARRIS, C. C., pp. 163–78.

LITWAK, EUGENE, 'Extended Kin Relations in an Industrial Democratic Society', in SHANAS and STREIB, pp. 290–323.

LITWAK, E. and SZELENYI, I., 'Primary Group Structures and their Functions: Kin, Neighbours and Friends', in ANDERSON, pp. 149–63.

LOCKWOOD, D., *The Black-Coated Worker*, London, Allen & Unwin, 1958.

LOMAS, PETER, 'Childbirth Ritual', *New Soc.*, 31 December 1964.

LOMAS, PETER (ed.), *The Predicament of the Family*, London, Hogarth Press, 1967.

LUPTON, T. and WILSON, C. SHIRLEY, 'The Kinship Connexions of "Top Decision Makers" ', in WORSLEY (ed.), 1970, pp. 151–64.

LYNES, JUDITH L., LIPETZ, MILTON E. and DAVIS, KEITH E., 'Living Together: An Alternative to Marriage', *Journ. Mar. Fam.*, vol. 34, no. 2, 1972, pp. 305–11.

MCGREGOR, O. R. and ROWNTREE, G., 'The Family', in WELFORD, pp. 405–36.

MCINTYRE, A., *Marcuse*, London, Fontana, 1970.

MAGAS, BRANKA, 'Sex Politics, Class Politics', in DREITZEL, pp. 217–50.

MAO TSE-TUNG, *On Contradiction*, Pekin, Foreign Languages Press, 1958.

MARCUSE, H., *One-Dimensional Man*, London, Routledge & Kegan Paul, 1964.

MARCUSE, H., *Eros and Civilization*, London, Abacus, 1972.

MARCUSE, H., *Studies in Critical Philosophy*, London, New Left Books, 1972.

MARTIN, DAVID, 'R. D. Laing', in CRANSTON, pp. 179–208.

MARX, K. and ENGELS, F., *Manifesto of the Communist Party*, in *Selected Works*, vol. 1, Moscow, Foreign Languages Publishing House, 1958, pp. 21–65.

MARX, K. and ENGELS, F., *The German Ideology*, London, Lawrence & Wishart, 1965.

MEAD, MARGARET, *Male and Female*, Harmondsworth, Penguin, 1962.

MEILLASSOUX, CLAUDE, 'From Reproduction to Production', *Econ. and Soc.*, vol. 1, no. 1, 1972.

MERTON, ROBERT K., *Social Theory and Social Structure*, rev. ed., Chicago, Free Press, 1957.

MERTON, ROBERT K., 'Insiders and Outsiders: A Chapter in the Sociology of Knowledge', *Am. Journ. Soc.*, vol. 78, no. 1, July 1972, pp. 9–47.

MERTON, ROBERT K., BROOM, LEONARD and COTTRELL, LEONARD S., *Sociology Today*, vol. 1, New York, Harper Torchbooks, 1965.

MILLETT, KATE, *Sexual Politics*, New York, Doubleday, 1970.

MILLS, C. WRIGHT, *The Sociological Imagination*, Harmondsworth, Penguin, 1970.

MISHLER, E. G. and WAXLER, N. E. (eds), *Family Process and Schizophrenia*, New York, Science House, 1968.

MITCHELL, J. CLYDE (ed.), *Social Networks in Urban Situations*, Manchester University Press, 1969.

MITCHELL, JULIET, 'Women: The Longest Revolution', *New Left Rev.*, no. 40, 1966, pp. 11–37.

MITCHELL, JULIET, *Woman's Estate*, Harmondsworth, Penguin, 1971.

MITCHELL, W. E., 'Theoretical Problems in the Concept of Kindred', *Am. Anth.*, 1963, pp. 343–54.

MONTAGUE, ASHLEY, *The Natural Superiority of Women*, London, Macmillan, 1968.

MOORE, BARRINGTON, JNR, 'Thoughts on the Future of the Family', in EDWARDS (ed.), pp. 455–67.

MORGAN, D. H. J., 'Theoretical and Conceptual Problems in the Study of Social Relations at Work: An Analysis of Differing Definitions of Women's Roles in a Northern Factory', University of Manchester, unpublished Ph.D. thesis, 1969.

MORGAN, D. H. J., 'The British Association Scandal: The Effects of Publicity on a Research Project', *Soc. Rev.*, vol. 20, no. 2, 1972, pp. 185–206.

MORGAN, ROBIN (ed.), *Sisterhood is Powerful*, New York, Random House, 1970.

MURDOCK, G. P., *Social Structure*, New York, Macmillan, 1949.

MUSIL, JIRI, 'Some Aspects of Social Organization of the Contemporary Czech Family', *Journ. Mar. Fam.*, February 1971, pp. 196–206.

MYRDAL, GUNNAR, *An American Dilemma*, New York, Harper & Row, 1944.

NEEDHAM, R., 'Discussion: Descent Systems and Ideal Language, *Phil. of Sc.*, vol. 27, 1960, pp. 96–101.

NEEDHAM, R. (ed.), *Rethinking Kinship and Marriage*, London, Tavistock, 1971.

OLESEN, VIRGINIA, 'Context and Posture: Notes on Socio-Cultural Aspects of Women's Roles and Family Policy in Contemporary Cuba', *Journ. Mar. Fam.*, August 1971, pp. 548–60.

O'NEILL, JOHN, *Sociology as a Skin Trade*, London, Heinemann, 1972.

O'NEILL, JOHN, 'On Body Politics', in DREITZEL, pp. 251–67.

O'NEILL, JOHN (ed.), *Modes of Individualism and Collectivism*, London, Heinemann, 1973.

OPEN UNIVERSITY, *Socialization* (Units 6–9 of Social Science Foundation Course), Bletchley, Open University Press, 1971.

OPEN UNIVERSITY (School and Society Course Team) (eds), *School and Society*, London, Routledge & Kegan Paul, 1971.

OTTO, H. A. (ed.), *The Family in Search of a Future*, New York, Appleton-Century-Crofts, 1970.

PARSONS, TALCOTT, *Essays in Sociological Theory*, rev. ed., New York, Free Press, 1964.

PARSONS, TALCOTT, *The Social System*, London, Routledge & Kegan Paul, 1964.

PARSONS, TALCOTT, 'Reply to his Critics', in ANDERSON, pp. 120–1.

PARSONS, TALCOTT, 'The Point of View of the Author', in BLACK.

PARSONS, TALCOTT, 'The Incest Taboo in Relation to Social Structure', in COSER, pp. 48–70.

PARSONS, TALCOTT, 'The Super-ego and the Theory of Social System', in COSER, pp. 433–49.

PARSONS, TALCOTT and BALES, R. F., *Family: Socialization and Interaction Process*, London, Routledge & Kegan Paul, 1956.

PARSONS, TALCOTT and FOX, RENEE C., 'Illness, Therapy and the Modern Urban American Family', in BELL and VOGEL, pp. 377–90.

PEARSALL, RONALD, *The Worm in the Bud*, Harmondsworth, Penguin, 1971.

POLAK, FREDERIK, L., *The Image of the Future* (*Enlightening the Past, Orientating the Present, Forecasting the Future*), 2 vols, New York, Oceana Publications, 1961.

PONSIOEN, J., 'Qualitative Changes in Family Life in the Netherlands', in HARRIS, pp. 271–8.

POPITZ, H., 'The Concept of Social Role as an Element of Sociological Theory', in JACKSON, pp. 11–39.

PRATHER, JANE E., 'When the Girls Move In: A Sociological Analysis of the Feminization of the Bank Teller's Job', *Journ. Mar. Fam.*, vol. 33, no. 4, November 1971, pp. 777–82.

RAINWATER *et al.*, *Workingman's Wife*, New York, Oceana Publications, 1959.

RAMEY, JAMES W., 'Communes, Group Marriage and the Upper Middle Class', *Journ. Mar. Fam.*, vol. 34, no. 4, November 1972.

RAPOPORT, R. and RAPOPORT, R., *Dual-Career Families*, Harmondsworth, Penguin, 1971.

REICH, W., *The Sexual Revolution*, London, Vision, 1951.

REICH, W., *The Mass Psychology of Fascism*, New York, Farrar, Straus & Giroux, 1970.

REICHE, REIMUT, *Sexuality and Class Struggle*, London, New Left Books, 1970.

REISS, ALBERT J., JNR, 'The Social Integration of Peers and Queers', in BECKER, pp. 181–210.

REISS, IRA L., *The Social Context of Premarital Sexual Permissiveness*, New York, Holt, Rinehart & Winston, 1967.

REISS, IRA L., 'How and Why America's Sex Standards are Changing', in GAGNON and SIMON, pp. 43–57.

REISS, PAUL J., 'Extended Kinship Relations in American Society', in RODMAN, pp. 204–9.

RIVIÈRE, P. G., 'Marriage: A Reassessment', in NEEDHAM, pp. 57–74.

ROBERTS, RON E., *The New Communes: Coming Together in America*, Englewood Cliffs, Prentice-Hall, 1971.

ROBINSON, PAUL A., *The Sexual Radicals*, London, Paladin, 1972.

RODMAN, HYMAN, 'Talcott Parsons's View of the Changing American Family', in RODMAN, pp. 262–86.

RODMAN, HYMAN (ed.), *Marriage, Family and Society*, New York, Random House, 1967.

ROEBUCK, JULIAN and SPRAY, S. LEE, 'The Cocktail Lounge: A Study of Heterosexual Relations in a Public Organization', *Am. Journ. Soc.*, vol. 72, 1967, pp. 388–95.

ROSE, ARNOLD M. (ed.), *Human Behaviour and Social Processes*, London, Routledge & Kegan Paul, 1962.

ROSSI, ALICE, 'Naming Children in Middle-Class Families', *Am. Soc. Rev.*, vol. 30, 1965, pp. 599–613.

RYCROFT, CHARLES, *Reich*, London, Fontana, 1971.

SAFILIOS-ROTHSCHILD, C. and GEORGIOPOULOS, J., 'A Comparative Study of Parental and Filial Role Definitions', *Journ. Mar. Fam.*, August 1970, pp. 381–9.

SARTRE, JEAN-PAUL, *Being and Nothingness*, London, Methuen, 1957.

SCHNEIDER, D. M., 'The Nature of Kinship', *Man*, vol. 64, 1964.

SCHNEIDER, D. M., *American Kinship: A Cultural Account*, Englewood Cliffs, Prentice-Hall, 1968.

SCHNEIDER, D. M. and HOMANS, G., 'Kinship Terminology and the American Kinship System', *Am. Anth.*, vol. 57, 1955, pp. 1194–208.

SCHORR, ALVIN L., 'Filial Responsibility and the Aged', in RODMAN, pp. 186–97.

SEDGWICK, P., 'Laing's Clangs', *New Soc.*, 15 January 1970, pp. 103–4.

SEELEY, JOHN R., SIM, R. ALEXANDER and LOOSLEY, E. W., *Crestwood Heights*, Toronto University Press, 1956.

SENNETT, RICHARD, *Families Against the City*, Cambridge, Mass., Harvard University Press, 1970.

SHANAS, ETHEL and STREIB, GORDON F., *Social Structure and the Family: Generational Relations*, Englewood Cliffs, Prentice-Hall, 1965.

SHERWIN, R. V. and KELLER, G. C., 'Sex on the Campus', in BARASH and SCOURBY, pp. 330–50.

SLATER, PHILIP, 'On Social Regression', in BELL AND VOGEL, pp. 428–441.

SLATER, PHILIP, 'Parental Role Differentiation', in COSER, pp. 350–70.

SMELSER, N., *Social Change in the Industrial Revolution*, London, Routledge & Kegan Paul, 1959.

SOUTHWOLD, MARTIN, 'Meanings of Kinship', in NEEDHAM, pp. 35–56.

SPECK, ROSS V., *The New Families*, London, Tavistock, 1972.

SPEIER, MATTHEW, 'The Everyday World of the Child', in DOUGLAS, pp. 188–217.

SPEIER, MATTHEW, 'Some Conversational Problems for Interactional Analysis', in SUDNOW, pp. 397–427.

SPIEGEL, JOHN P., 'The Resolution of Role Conflict in the Family', in BELL and VOGEL, pp. 391–411.

STEINEM, G., 'What It Would Be Like if Women Win', *Time*, 31 August 1970, pp. 24–5.

STOLLER, FREDERICK H., 'The Intimate Network of Families as a New Structure', in OTTO, pp. 147–59.

STUCKERT, ROBERT P., 'Occupational Mobility and Family Relationships', in BELL and VOGEL, pp. 160–8.

SUDNOW, DAVID (ed.), *Studies in Social Interaction*, New York, Collier-Macmillan, 1972.

SUSSMAN, MARVIN B., 'Relationships of Adult Children with their Parents in the United States', in SHANAS and STREIB, pp. 62–92.

SUSSMAN, MARVIN B. and BURCHINALL, LEE, 'Kin Family Network: Unheralded Structure in Current Conceptualizations of Family Functioning', in EDWARDS, pp. 133–52.

TAYLOR, LAURIE, 'The Significance and Interpretation of Replies to Motivational Questions: The Case of Sex Offenders', *Soc.*, vol. 6, no. 1, 1972, pp. 23–39.

THOMAS, KEITH, 'Women and the Civil War Sects', *Past and Present*, 1958, pp. 42–62.

THOMPSON, E. P., *The Making of the English Working Class*, Harmondsworth, Penguin, 1968.

THOMPSON, K. and TUNSTALL, J. (eds), *Sociological Perspectives*, Harmondsworth, Penguin, 1971.

TIGER, LIONEL, *Men in Groups*, London, Nelson, 1969.

TOWNSEND, P., *The Family Life of Old People*, rev. ed., Harmondsworth, Penguin, 1963.

TRILLING, LIONEL, *Freud and the Crisis of Our Culture*, Boston, Beacon Press, 1955.

TURNER, RALPH, *Family Interaction*, New York, Wiley, 1970.

VOGEL, EZRA F. and BELL, NORMAN W., 'The Emotionally Disturbed Child as the Family Scapegoat', in BELL and VOGEL, pp. 412–27.

WEBER, MAX, *The Protestant Ethic and the Spirit of Capitalism*, London, Unwin, 1930.

WELFORD, A. T., *et al.*, *Society: Problems and Methods of Study*, rev. ed., London, Routledge & Kegan Paul, 1968.

WESTERGAARD, J. H., 'Sociology: The Myth of Classlessness', in BLACKBURN, pp. 119–63.

WHYTE, W. F., 'A Slum Sex Code', in WORSLEY (ed.), 1972, pp. 351–56.

WILLIAMSON, ROBERT N., *Marriage and Family Relations*, 2nd ed., New York, Wiley, 1972.

WIRTH, LOUIS, 'Urbanism as a Way of Life', *Am. Journ. Soc.*, vol. 44, 1938–9, pp. 1–24.

WOLLHEIM, RICHARD, *Freud*, London, Fontana, 1971.

WOOD, ROBIN, *Hitchcock's Films*, London, Zwemmer, 1969.

WORSLEY, PETER, 'The Origins of the Family Revisited' (unpublished paper).

WORSLEY, PETER *et al.* (ed.), *Modern Sociology*, Harmondsworth, Penguin, 1970.

WORSLEY, PETER *et al.* (ed.), *Introducing Sociology*, Harmondsworth, Penguin, 1970.

WORSLEY, PETER *et al.* (ed.), *Problems of Modern Society*, Harmondsworth, Penguin, 1972.

YOUNG, M. and WILLMOTT, P., *Family and Kinship in East London*, rev. ed., Harmondsworth, Penguin, 1962.

ZELDITCH, MORRIS, JNR, 'Role Differentiation in the Nuclear Family: A Comparative Study', in PARSONS and BALES, pp. 307–51.

ZIMMERMAN, CARLE C., 'The Future of the Family in America', *Journ. Mar. Fam.*, vol. 34, no. 2, 1972, pp. 323–3.

Author index

Subject index

Routledge Social Science Series

Routledge & Kegan Paul London and Boston

68–74 Carter Lane London EC4V 5EL

9 Park Street Boston Mass 02108

Contents

Authors wishing to submit manuscripts for any series in this catalogue should send them to the Social Science Editor, Routledge & Kegan Paul Ltd, 68–74 Carter Lane, London EC4V 5EL

●*Books so marked are available in paperback*
All books are in Metric Demy 8vo format (216×138mm approx.)

International Library of Sociology

General Editor John Rex

GENERAL SOCIOLOGY

Barnsley, J. H. The Social Reality of Ethics. *464 pp.*
Belshaw, Cyril. The Conditions of Social Performance. *An Exploratory Theory. 144 pp.*
Brown, Robert. Explanation in Social Science. *208 pp.*
● Rules and Laws in Sociology. *192 pp.*
Bruford, W. H. Chekhov and His Russia. *A Sociological Study. 244 pp.*
Cain, Maureen E. Society and the Policeman's Role. *326 pp.*
Gibson, Quentin. The Logic of Social Enquiry. *240 pp.*
Glucksmann, M. Structuralist Analysis in Contemporary Social Thought. *212 pp.*
Gurvitch, Georges. Sociology of Law. *Preface by Roscoe Pound. 264 pp.*
Hodge, H. A. Wilhelm Dilthey. *An Introduction. 184 pp.*
Homans, George C. Sentiments and Activities. *336 pp.*
Johnson, Harry M. Sociology: *a Systematic Introduction. Foreword by Robert K. Merton. 710 pp.*
Mannheim, Karl. Essays on Sociology and Social Psychology. *Edited by Paul Keckskemeti. With Editorial Note by Adolph Lowe. 344 pp.*
Systematic Sociology: *An Introduction to the Study of Society. Edited by J. S. Erös and Professor W. A. C. Stewart. 220 pp.*
Martindale, Don. The Nature and Types of Sociological Theory. *292 pp.*
●**Maus, Heinz.** A Short History of Sociology. *234 pp.*
Mey, Harald. Field-Theory. *A Study of its Application in the Social Sciences. 352 pp.*
Myrdal, Gunnar. Value in Social Theory: *A Collection of Essays on Methodology. Edited by Paul Streeten. 332 pp.*
Ogburn, William F., and **Nimkoff, Meyer F.** A Handbook of Sociology. *Preface by Karl Mannheim. 656 pp. 46 figures. 35 tables.*
Parsons, Talcott, and **Smelser, Neil J.** Economy and Society: *A Study in the Integration of Economic and Social Theory. 362 pp.*
●**Rex, John.** Key Problems of Sociological Theory. *220 pp.*
Discovering Sociology. *278 pp.*
Sociology and the Demystification of the Modern World. *282 pp.*
●**Rex, John** (Ed.) Approaches to Sociology. *Contributions by Peter Abell, Frank Bechhofer, Basil Bernstein, Ronald Fletcher, David Frisby, Miriam Glucksmann, Peter Lassman, Herminio Martins, John Rex, Roland Robertson, John Westergaard and Jock Young. 302 pp.*
Rigby, A. Alternative Realities. *352 pp.*
Roche, M. Phenomenology, Language and the Social Sciences. *374 pp.*
Sahay, A. Sociological Analysis. *220 pp.*
Urry, John. Reference Groups and the Theory of Revolution. *244 pp.*
Weinberg, E. Development of Sociology in the Soviet Union. *173 pp.*

FOREIGN CLASSICS OF SOCIOLOGY

●**Durkheim, Emile.** Suicide. *A Study in Sociology. Edited and with an Introduction by George Simpson. 404 pp.*

Professional Ethics and Civic Morals. *Translated by Cornelia Brookfield. 288 pp.*

●**Gerth, H. H.**, and **Mills, C. Wright.** From Max Weber: *Essays in Sociology. 502 pp.*

●**Tönnies, Ferdinand.** Community and Association. (*Gemeinschaft und Gesellschaft.*) *Translated and Supplemented by Charles P. Loomis. Foreword by Pitirim A. Sorokin. 334 pp.*

SOCIAL STRUCTURE

Andreski, Stanislav. Military Organization and Society. *Foreword by Professor A. R. Radcliffe-Brown. 226 pp. 1 folder.*

Coontz, Sydney H. Population Theories and the Economic Interpretation. *202 pp.*

Coser, Lewis. The Functions of Social Conflict. *204 pp.*

Dickie-Clark, H. F. Marginal Situation: *A Sociological Study of a Coloured Group. 240 pp. 11 tables.*

Glaser, Barney, and **Strauss, Anselm L.** Status Passage. *A Formal Theory. 208 pp.*

Glass, D. V. (Ed.) Social Mobility in Britain. *Contributions by J. Berent, T. Bottomore, R. C. Chambers, J. Floud, D. V. Glass, J. R. Hall, H. T. Himmelweit, R. K. Kelsall, F. M. Martin, C. A. Moser, R. Mukherjee, and W. Ziegel. 420 pp.*

Jones, Garth N. Planned Organizational Change: *An Exploratory Study Using an Empirical Approach. 268 pp.*

Kelsall, R. K. Higher Civil Servants in Britain: *From 1870 to the Present Day. 268 pp. 31 tables.*

König, René. The Community. *232 pp. Illustrated.*

●**Lawton, Denis.** Social Class, Language and Education. *192 pp.*

McLeish, John. The Theory of Social Change: *Four Views Considered. 128 pp.*

Marsh, David C. The Changing Social Structure of England and Wales, 1871-1961. *288 pp.*

Mouzelis, Nicos. Organization and Bureaucracy. *An Analysis of Modern Theories. 240 pp.*

Mulkay, M. J. Functionalism, Exchange and Theoretical Strategy. *272 pp.*

Ossowski, Stanislaw. Class Structure in the Social Consciousness. *210 pp.*

Podgórecki, Adam. Law and Society. *About 300 pp.*

SOCIOLOGY AND POLITICS

Acton, T. A. Gypsy Politics and Social Change. *316 pp.*

Hechter, Michael. Internal Colonialism. *The Celtic Fringe in British National Development, 1536–1966. About 350 pp.*

Hertz, Frederick. Nationality in History and Politics: *A Psychology and Sociology of National Sentiment and Nationalism. 432 pp.*

Kornhauser, William. The Politics of Mass Society. *272 pp. 20 tables.*

Laidler, Harry W. History of Socialism. *Social-Economic Movements: An Historical and Comparative Survey of Socialism, Communism, Co-operation, Utopianism; and other Systems of Reform and Reconstruction. 992 pp.*

Lasswell, H. D. Analysis of Political Behaviour. *324 pp.*

Mannheim, Karl. Freedom, Power and Democratic Planning. *Edited by Hans Gerth and Ernest K. Bramstedt. 424 pp.*

Mansur, Fatma. Process of Independence. *Foreword by A. H. Hanson. 208 pp.*

Martin, David A. Pacifism: *an Historical and Sociological Study. 262 pp.*

Myrdal, Gunnar. The Political Element in the Development of Economic Theory. *Translated from the German by Paul Streeten. 282 pp.*

Wootton, Graham. Workers, Unions and the State. *188 pp.*

FOREIGN AFFAIRS: THEIR SOCIAL, POLITICAL AND ECONOMIC FOUNDATIONS

Mayer, J. P. Political Thought in France from the Revolution to the Fifth Republic. *164 pp.*

CRIMINOLOGY

Ancel, Marc. Social Defence: *A Modern Approach to Criminal Problems. Foreword by Leon Radzinowicz. 240 pp.*

Cain, Maureen E. Society and the Policeman's Role. *326 pp.*

Cloward, Richard A., and **Ohlin, Lloyd E.** Delinquency and Opportunity: *A Theory of Delinquent Gangs. 248 pp.*

Downes, David M. The Delinquent Solution. *A Study in Subcultural Theory. 296 pp.*

Dunlop, A. B., and **McCabe, S.** Young Men in Detention Centres. *192 pp.*

Friedlander, Kate. The Psycho-Analytical Approach to Juvenile Delinquency: *Theory, Case Studies, Treatment. 320 pp.*

Glueck, Sheldon, and **Eleanor.** Family Environment and Delinquency. *With the statistical assistance of Rose W. Kneznek. 340 pp.*

Lopez-Rey, Manuel. Crime. *An Analytical Appraisal. 288 pp.*

Mannheim, Hermann. Comparative Criminology: *a Text Book. Two volumes. 442 pp. and 380 pp.*

Morris, Terence. The Criminal Area: *A Study in Social Ecology. Foreword by Hermann Mannheim. 232 pp. 25 tables. 4 maps.*

Rock, Paul. Making People Pay. *338 pp.*

● **Taylor, Ian, Walton, Paul,** and **Young, Jock.** The New Criminology. *For a Social Theory of Deviance. 325 pp.*

SOCIAL PSYCHOLOGY

Bagley, Christopher. The Social Psychology of the Epileptic Child. *320 pp.*

Barbu, Zevedei. Problems of Historical Psychology. *248 pp.*

Blackburn, Julian. Psychology and the Social Pattern. *184 pp.*

●**Brittan, Arthur.** Meanings and Situations. *224 pp.*

Carroll, J. Break-Out from the Crystal Palace. *200 pp.*

●**Fleming, C. M.** Adolescence: Its Social Psychology. *With an Introduction to recent findings from the fields of Anthropology, Physiology, Medicine, Psychometrics and Sociometry. 288 pp.*

● The Social Psychology of Education: *An Introduction and Guide to Its Study. 136 pp.*

Homans, George C. The Human Group. *Foreword by Bernard DeVoto. Introduction by Robert K. Merton. 526 pp.*

● Social Behaviour: *its Elementary Forms. 416 pp.*

●**Klein, Josephine.** The Study of Groups. *226 pp. 31 figures. 5 tables.*

Linton, Ralph. The Cultural Background of Personality. *132 pp.*

●**Mayo, Elton.** The Social Problems of an Industrial Civilization. *With an appendix on the Political Problem. 180 pp.*

Ottaway, A. K. C. Learning Through Group Experience. *176 pp.*

Ridder, J. C. de. The Personality of the Urban African in South Africa. *A Thermatic Apperception Test Study. 196 pp. 12 plates.*

●**Rose, Arnold M.** (Ed.) Human Behaviour and Social Processes: *an Interactionist Approach. Contributions by Arnold M. Rose, Ralph H. Turner, Anselm Strauss, Everett C. Hughes, E. Franklin Frazier, Howard S. Becker, et al. 696 pp.*

Smelser, Neil J. Theory of Collective Behaviour. *448 pp.*

Stephenson, Geoffrey M. The Development of Conscience. *128 pp.*

Young, Kimball. Handbook of Social Psychology. *658 pp. 16 figures. 10 tables.*

SOCIOLOGY OF THE FAMILY

Banks, J. A. Prosperity and Parenthood: *A Study of Family Planning among The Victorian Middle Classes. 262 pp.*

Bell, Colin R. Middle Class Families: *Social and Geographical Mobility. 224 pp.*

Burton, Lindy. Vulnerable Children. *272 pp.*

Gavron, Hannah. The Captive Wife: *Conflicts of Household Mothers. 190 pp.*

George, Victor, and **Wilding, Paul.** Motherless Families. *220 pp.*

Klein, Josephine. Samples from English Cultures.

1. Three Preliminary Studies and Aspects of Adult Life in England. *447 pp.*
2. Child-Rearing Practices and Index. *247 pp.*

Klein, Viola. Britain's Married Women Workers. *180 pp.*

The Feminine Character. *History of an Ideology. 244 pp.*

McWhinnie, Alexina M. Adopted Children. *How They Grow Up. 304 pp.*

● **Myrdal, Alva,** and **Klein, Viola.** Women's Two Roles: *Home and Work. 238 pp. 27 tables.*

Parsons, Talcott, and **Bales, Robert F.** Family: Socialization and Interaction Process. *In collaboration with James Olds, Morris Zelditch and Philip E. Slater. 456 pp. 50 figures and tables.*

SOCIAL SERVICES

Bastide, Roger. The Sociology of Mental Disorder. *Translated from the French by Jean McNeil. 260 pp.*

Carlebach, Julius. Caring For Children in Trouble. *266 pp.*

Forder, R. A. (Ed.) Penelope Hall's Social Services of England and Wales. *352 pp.*

George, Victor. Foster Care. *Theory and Practice. 234 pp.*

Social Security: *Beveridge and After. 258 pp.*

George, V., and **Wilding, P.** Motherless Families. *248 pp.*

●**Goetschius, George W.** Working with Community Groups. *256 pp.*

Goetschius, George W., and **Tash, Joan.** Working with Unattached Youth. *416 pp.*

Hall, M. P., and **Howes, I. V.** The Church in Social Work. *A Study of Moral Welfare Work undertaken by the Church of England. 320 pp.*

Heywood, Jean S. Children in Care: *the Development of the Service for the Deprived Child. 264 pp.*

Hoenig, J., and **Hamilton, Marian W.** The De-Segregation of the Mentally Ill. *284 pp.*

Jones, Kathleen. Mental Health and Social Policy, 1845-1959. *264 pp.*

King, Roy D., Raynes, Norma V., and **Tizard, Jack.** Patterns of Residential Care. *356 pp.*

Leigh, John. Young People and Leisure. *256 pp.*

Morris, Mary. Voluntary Work and the Welfare State. *300 pp.*

Morris, Pauline. Put Away: *A Sociological Study of Institutions for the Mentally Retarded. 364 pp.*

Nokes, P. L. The Professional Task in Welfare Practice. *152 pp.*

Timms, Noel. Psychiatric Social Work in Great Britain (1939-1962). *280 pp.*

● Social Casework: *Principles and Practice. 256 pp.*

Young, A. F. Social Services in British Industry. *272 pp.*

Young, A. F., and **Ashton, E. T.** British Social Work in the Nineteenth Century. *288 pp.*

SOCIOLOGY OF EDUCATION

Banks, Olive. Parity and Prestige in English Secondary Education: a Study in Educational Sociology. *272 pp.*

Bentwich, Joseph. Education in Israel. *224 pp. 8 pp. plates.*

●**Blyth, W. A. L.** English Primary Education. *A Sociological Description.*

1. Schools. *232 pp.*
2. Background. *168 pp.*

Collier, K. G. The Social Purposes of Education: *Personal and Social Values in Education. 268 pp.*

Dale, R. R., and **Griffith, S.** Down Stream: *Failure in the Grammar School. 108 pp.*

Dore, R. P. Education in Tokugawa Japan. *356 pp. 9 pp. plates.*

Evans, K. M. Sociometry and Education. *158 pp.*

● **Ford, Julienne.** Social Class and the Comprehensive School. *192 pp.*

Foster, P. J. Education and Social Change in Ghana. *336 pp. 3 maps.*

Fraser, W. R. Education and Society in Modern France. *150 pp.*

Grace, Gerald R. Role Conflict and the Teacher. *About 200 pp.*

Hans, Nicholas. New Trends in Education in the Eighteenth Century. *278 pp. 19 tables.*

● Comparative Education: *A Study of Educational Factors and Traditions. 360 pp.*

Hargreaves, David. Interpersonal Relations and Education. *432 pp.*

● Social Relations in a Secondary School. *240 pp.*

Holmes, Brian. Problems in Education. *A Comparative Approach. 336 pp.*

King, Ronald. Values and Involvement in a Grammar School. *164 pp.*

School Organization and Pupil Involvement. *A Study of Secondary Schools.*

● **Mannheim, Karl,** and **Stewart, W. A. C.** An Introduction to the Sociology of Education. *206 pp.*

Morris, Raymond N. The Sixth Form and College Entrance. *231 pp.*

● **Musgrove, F.** Youth and the Social Order. *176 pp.*

● **Ottaway, A. K. C.** Education and Society: An Introduction to the Sociology of Education. *With an Introduction by W. O. Lester Smith. 212 pp.*

Peers, Robert. Adult Education: *A Comparative Study. 398 pp.*

Pritchard, D. G. Education and the Handicapped: *1760 to 1960. 258 pp.*

Richardson, Helen. Adolescent Girls in Approved Schools. *308 pp.*

Stratta, Erica. The Education of Borstal Boys. *A Study of their Educational Experiences prior to, and during, Borstal Training. 256 pp.*

Taylor, P. H., Reid, W. A., and **Holley, B. J.** The English Sixth Form. *A Case Study in Curriculum Research. 200 pp.*

SOCIOLOGY OF CULTURE

Eppel, E. M., and **M.** Adolescents and Morality: *A Study of some Moral Values and Dilemmas of Working Adolescents in the Context of a changing Climate of Opinion. Foreword by W. J. H. Sprott. 268 pp. 39 tables.*

● **Fromm, Erich.** The Fear of Freedom. *286 pp.*

● The Sane Society. *400 pp.*

Mannheim, Karl. Essays on the Sociology of Culture. *Edited by Ernst Mannheim in co-operation with Paul Kecskemeti. Editorial Note by Adolph Lowe. 280 pp.*

Weber, Alfred. Farewell to European History: *or The Conquest of Nihilism. Translated from the German by R. F. C. Hull. 224 pp.*

SOCIOLOGY OF RELIGION

Argyle, Michael and **Beit-Hallahmi, Benjamin.** The Social Psychology of Religion. *About 256 pp.*

Nelson, G. K. Spiritualism and Society. *313 pp.*

Stark, Werner. The Sociology of Religion. *A Study of Christendom.*
Volume I. *Established Religion. 248 pp.*
Volume II. *Sectarian Religion. 368 pp.*
Volume III. *The Universal Church. 464 pp.*
Volume IV. *Types of Religious Man. 352 pp.*
Volume V. *Types of Religious Culture. 464 pp.*

Turner, B. S. Weber and Islam. *216 pp.*

Watt, W. Montgomery. Islam and the Integration of Society. *320 pp.*

SOCIOLOGY OF ART AND LITERATURE

Jarvie, Ian C. Towards a Sociology of the Cinema. *A Comparative Essay on the Structure and Functioning of a Major Entertainment Industry. 405 pp.*

Rust, Frances S. Dance in Society. *An Analysis of the Relationships between the Social Dance and Society in England from the Middle Ages to the Present Day. 256 pp. 8 pp. of plates.*

Schücking, L. L. The Sociology of Literary Taste. *112 pp.*

Wolff, Janet. Hermeneutic Philosophy and the Sociology of Art. *About 200 pp.*

SOCIOLOGY OF KNOWLEDGE

Diesing, P. Patterns of Discovery in the Social Sciences. *262 pp.*

● **Douglas, J. D.** (Ed.) Understanding Everyday Life. *370 pp.*

● **Hamilton, P.** Knowledge and Social Structure. *174 pp.*

Jarvie, I. C. Concepts and Society. *232 pp.*

Mannheim, Karl. Essays on the Sociology of Knowledge. *Edited by Paul Kecskemeti. Editorial Note by Adolph Lowe. 353 pp.*

Remmling, Gunter W. (Ed.) Towards the Sociology of Knowledge. *Origin and Development of a Sociological Thought Style. 463 pp.*

Stark, Werner. The Sociology of Knowledge: *An Essay in Aid of a Deeper Understanding of the History of Ideas. 384 pp.*

URBAN SOCIOLOGY

Ashworth, William. The Genesis of Modern British Town Planning: *A Study in Economic and Social History of the Nineteenth and Twentieth Centuries. 288 pp.*

Cullingworth, J. B. Housing Needs and Planning Policy: *A Restatement of the Problems of Housing Need and 'Overspill' in England and Wales. 232 pp. 44 tables. 8 maps.*

Dickinson, Robert E. City and Region: *A Geographical Interpretation 608 pp. 125 figures.*

The West European City: *A Geographical Interpretation. 600 pp. 129 maps. 29 plates.*

● The City Region in Western Europe. *320 pp. Maps.*

Humphreys, Alexander J. New Dubliners: *Urbanization and the Irish Family. Foreword by George C. Homans. 304 pp.*

Jackson, Brian. Working Class Community: *Some General Notions raised by a Series of Studies in Northern England. 192 pp.*

Jennings, Hilda. Societies in the Making: *a Study of Development and Redevelopment within a County Borough. Foreword by D. A. Clark. 286 pp.*

●**Mann, P. H.** An Approach to Urban Sociology. *240 pp.*

Morris, R. N., and **Mogey, J.** The Sociology of Housing. *Studies at Berinsfield. 232 pp. 4 pp. plates.*

Rosser, C., and **Harris, C.** The Family and Social Change. *A Study of Family and Kinship in a South Wales Town. 352 pp. 8 maps.*

RURAL SOCIOLOGY

Chambers, R. J. H. Settlement Schemes in Tropical Africa: *A Selective Study. 268 pp.*

Haswell, M. R. The Economics of Development in Village India. *120 pp.*

Littlejohn, James. Westrigg: *the Sociology of a Cheviot Parish. 172 pp. 5 figures.*

Mayer, Adrian C. Peasants in the Pacific. *A Study of Fiji Indian Rural Society. 248 pp. 20 plates.*

Williams, W. M. The Sociology of an English Village: *Gosforth. 272 pp. 12 figures. 13 tables.*

SOCIOLOGY OF INDUSTRY AND DISTRIBUTION

Anderson, Nels. Work and Leisure. *280 pp.*

●**Blau, Peter M.,** and **Scott, W. Richard.** Formal Organizations: *a Comparative approach. Introduction and Additional Bibliography by J. H. Smith. 326 pp.*

Eldridge, J. E. T. Industrial Disputes. *Essays in the Sociology of Industrial Relations. 288 pp.*

Hetzler, Stanley. Applied Measures for Promoting Technological Growth. *352 pp.*

Technological Growth and Social Change. *Achieving Modernization. 269 pp.*

Hollowell, Peter G. The Lorry Driver. *272 pp.*

Jefferys, Margot, *with the assistance of Winifred Moss.* Mobility in the Labour Market: *Employment Changes in Battersea and Dagenham. Preface by Barbara Wootton. 186 pp. 51 tables.*

Millerson, Geoffrey. The Qualifying Associations: *a Study in Professionalization. 320 pp.*

Smelser, Neil J. Social Change in the Industrial Revolution: *An Application of Theory to the Lancashire Cotton Industry, 1770-1840. 468 pp. 12 figures. 14 tables.*

Williams, Gertrude. Recruitment to Skilled Trades. *240 pp.*

Young, A. F. Industrial Injuries Insurance: *an Examination of British Policy. 192 pp.*

DOCUMENTARY

Schlesinger, Rudolf (Ed.) Changing Attitudes in Soviet Russia.

2. The Nationalities Problem and Soviet Administration. *Selected Readings on the Development of Soviet Nationalities Policies. Introduced by the editor. Translated by W. W. Gottlieb. 324 pp.*

ANTHROPOLOGY

Ammar, Hamed. Growing up in an Egyptian Village: *Silwa, Province of Aswan. 336 pp.*

Brandel-Syrier, Mia. Reeftown Elite. *A Study of Social Mobility in a Modern African Community on the Reef. 376 pp.*

Crook, David, and **Isabel.** Revolution in a Chinese Village: *Ten Mile Inn. 230 pp. 8 plates. 1 map.*

Dickie-Clark, H. F. The Marginal Situation. *A Sociological Study of a Coloured Group. 236 pp.*

Dube, S. C. Indian Village. *Foreword by Morris Edward Opler. 276 pp. 4 plates.*

India's Changing Villages: *Human Factors in Community Development. 260 pp. 8 plates. 1 map.*

Firth, Raymond. Malay Fishermen. *Their Peasant Economy. 420 pp. 17 pp. plates.*

Firth, R., Hubert, J., and **Forge, A.** Families and their Relatives. *Kinship in a Middle-Class Sector of London: An Anthropological Study. 456 pp.*

Gulliver, P. H. Social Control in an African Society: a Study of the Arusha, Agricultural Masai of Northern Tanganyika. *320 pp. 8 plates. 10 figures.*

Family Herds. *288 pp.*

Ishwaran, K. Shivapur. *A South Indian Village. 216 pp.*

Tradition and Economy in Village India: *An Interactionist Approach. Foreword by Conrad Arensburg. 176 pp.*

Jarvie, Ian C. The Revolution in Anthropology. *268 pp.*

Jarvie, Ian C., and **Agassi, Joseph.** Hong Kong. *A Society in Transition. 396 pp. Illustrated with plates and maps.*

Little, Kenneth L. Mende of Sierra Leone. *308 pp. and folder.*

Negroes in Britain. *With a New Introduction and Contemporary Study by Leonard Bloom. 320 pp.*

Lowie, Robert H. Social Organization. *494 pp.*

Mayer, Adrian C. Caste and Kinship in Central India: *A Village and its Region. 328 pp. 16 plates. 15 figures. 16 tables.*

Peasants in the Pacific. *A Study of Fiji Indian Rural Society. 248 pp.*

Smith, Raymond T. The Negro Family in British Guiana: *Family Structure and Social Status in the Villages. With a Foreword by Meyer Fortes. 314 pp. 8 plates. 1 figure. 4 maps.*

SOCIOLOGY AND PHILOSOPHY

Barnsley, John H. The Social Reality of Ethics. *A Comparative Analysis of Moral Codes. 448 pp.*

Diesing, Paul. Patterns of Discovery in the Social Sciences. *362 pp.*

● **Douglas, Jack D.** (Ed.) Understanding Everyday Life. *Toward the Reconstruction of Sociological Knowledge. Contributions by Alan F. Blum. Aaron W. Cicourel, Norman K. Denzin, Jack D. Douglas, John Heeren, Peter McHugh, Peter K. Manning, Melvin Power, Matthew Speier, Roy Turner, D. Lawrence Wieder, Thomas P. Wilson and Don H. Zimmerman. 370 pp.*

Jarvie, Ian C. Concepts and Society. *216 pp.*

Pelz, Werner. The Scope of Understanding in Sociology. *Towards a more radical reorientation in the social humanistic sciences. 283 pp.*

Roche, Maurice. Phenomenology, Language and the Social Sciences. *371 pp.*

Sahay, Arun. Sociological Analysis. *212 pp.*

Sklair, Leslie. The Sociology of Progress. *320 pp.*

International Library of Anthropology

General Editor Adam Kuper

Brown, Paula. The Chimbu. *A Study of Change in the New Guinea Highlands. 151 pp.*

Lloyd, P. C. Power and Independence. *Urban Africans' Perception of Social Inequality. 264 pp.*

Pettigrew, Joyce. Robber Noblemen. *A Study of the Political System of the Sikh Jats. 284 pp.*

Van Den Berghe, Pierre L. Power and Privilege at an African University. *278 pp.*

International Library of Social Policy

General Editor Kathleen Jones

Bayley, M. Mental Handicap and Community Care. *426 pp.*

Butler, J. R. Family Doctors and Public Policy. *208 pp.*

Holman, Robert. Trading in Children. *A Study of Private Fostering. 355 pp.*

Jones, Kathleen. History of the Mental Health Service. *428 pp.*

Thomas, J. E. The English Prison Officer since 1850: *A Study in Conflict. 258 pp.*

Woodward, J. To Do the Sick No Harm. *A Study of the British Voluntary Hospital System to 1875. About 220 pp.*

International Library of Welfare and Philosophy

General Editors Noel Timms and David Watson

● **Plant, Raymond.** Community and Ideology. *104 pp.*

Primary Socialization, Language and Education

General Editor Basil Bernstein

Bernstein, Basil. Class, Codes and Control. *2 volumes.*

1. *Theoretical Studies Towards a Sociology of Language. 254 pp.*
2. *Applied Studies Towards a Sociology of Language. About 400 pp.*

Brandis, W., and **Bernstein, B.** Selection and Control. *176 pp.*

Brandis, Walter, and **Henderson, Dorothy.** Social Class, Language and Communication. *288 pp.*

Cook-Gumperz, Jenny. Social Control and Socialization. *A Study of Class Differences in the Language of Maternal Control. 290 pp.*

● **Gahagan, D. M.,** and **G. A.** Talk Reform. *Exploration in Language for Infant School Children. 160 pp.*

Robinson, W. P., and **Rackstraw, Susan D. A.** A Question of Answers. *2 volumes. 192 pp. and 180 pp.*

Turner, Geoffrey J., and **Mohan, Bernard A.** A Linguistic Description and Computer Programme for Children's Speech. *208 pp.*

Reports of the Institute of Community Studies

Cartwright, Ann. Human Relations and Hospital Care. *272 pp.*

● Parents and Family Planning Services. *306 pp.*

Patients and their Doctors. *A Study of General Practice. 304 pp.*

● **Jackson, Brian.** Streaming: *an Education System in Miniature. 168 pp.*

Jackson, Brian, and **Marsden, Dennis.** Education and the Working Class: *Some General Themes raised by a Study of 88 Working-class Children in a Northern Industrial City. 268 pp. 2 folders.*

Marris, Peter. The Experience of Higher Education. *232 pp. 27 tables.*

Loss and Change. *192 pp.*

Marris, Peter, and **Rein, Martin.** Dilemmas of Social Reform. *Poverty and Community Action in the United States. 256 pp.*

Marris, Peter, and **Somerset, Anthony.** African Businessmen. *A Study of Entrepreneurship and Development in Kenya. 256 pp.*

Mills, Richard. Young Outsiders: *a Study in Alternative Communities. 216 pp.*

Runciman, W. G. Relative Deprivation and Social Justice. *A Study of Attitudes to Social Inequality in Twentieth-Century England. 352 pp.*

Willmott, Peter. Adolescent Boys in East London. *230 pp.*

Willmott, Peter, and **Young, Michael.** Family and Class in a London Suburb. *202 pp. 47 tables.*

Young, Michael. Innovation and Research in Education. *192 pp.*

● **Young, Michael,** and **McGeeney, Patrick.** Learning Begins at Home. *A Study of a Junior School and its Parents. 128 pp.*

Young, Michael, and **Willmott, Peter.** Family and Kinship in East London. *Foreword by Richard M. Titmuss. 252 pp. 39 tables.*

The Symmetrical Family. *410 pp.*

Reports of the Institute for Social Studies in Medical Care

Cartwright, Ann, Hockey, Lisbeth, and **Anderson, John L.** Life Before Death. *310 pp.*

Dunnell, Karen, and **Cartwright, Ann.** Medicine Takers, Prescribers and Hoarders. *190 pp.*

Medicine, Illness and Society

General Editor W. M. Williams

Robinson, David. The Process of Becoming Ill. *142 pp.*

Stacey, Margaret, *et al.* Hospitals, Children and Their Families. *The Report of a Pilot Study. 202 pp.*

Monographs in Social Theory

General Editor Arthur Brittan

● **Barnes, B.** Scientific Knowledge and Sociological Theory. *About 200 pp.*

Bauman, Zygmunt. Culture as Praxis. *204 pp.*

● **Dixon, Keith.** Sociological Theory. *Pretence and Possibility. 142 pp.*

● **Smith, Anthony D.** The Concept of Social Change. *A Critique of the Functionalist Theory of Social Change. 208 pp.*

Routledge Social Science Journals

The British Journal of Sociology. *Edited by Terence P. Morris. Vol. 1, No. 1, March 1950 and Quarterly. Roy. 8vo. Back numbers available. An international journal with articles on all aspects of sociology.*

Economy and Society. *Vol. 1, No. 1. February 1972 and Quarterly. Metric Roy. 8vo. A journal for all social scientists covering sociology, philosophy, anthropology, economics and history. Back numbers available.*

Year Book of Social Policy in Britain, The. *Edited by Kathleen Jones. 1971. Published annually.*

Printed in Great Britain by Unwin Brothers Limited
The Gresham Press Old Woking Surrey
A member of the Staples Printing Group